HIGHER EDUCATION
=== IN ===
AMERICAN SOCIETY

HIGHER
EDUCATION
IN
AMERICAN
SOCIETY

Third Edition

Edited by Philip G. Altbach,
Robert O. Berdahl,
and Patricia J. Gumport

 Prometheus Books

59 John Glenn Drive
Amherst, NewYork 14228-2197

Published 1994 by Prometheus Books

Inquiries should be addressed to
Prometheus Books
59 John Glenn Drive
Amherst, New York 14228–2197
VOICE: 716–691–0133, ext. 207
FAX: 716–564–2711
WWW.PROMETHEUSBOOKS.COM

04 03 02 01 00   6 5 4 3 2

Library of Congress Cataloging-in-Publication Data

Higher education in American society / edited by Philip G. Altbach, Robert O.
    Berdahl, and Patricia J. Gumport — 3rd rev. ed.
        p. cm. — (Frontiers of education)
    Includes bibliographical references and index.
    ISBN 0–87975–905–4 (pbk. : acid-free paper)
    1. Education, Higher—United States. 2. Educational sociology—United
States. I. Altbach, Philip G. II. Berdahl, Robert Oliver. III. Gumport, Patricia J.
IV. Series.

LA228.H5   1994
378.73—dc20
                                                                    94–26224
                                                                        CIP

Printed in the United States of America on acid-free paper

Contents

Acknowledgments   7

Foreword: American Society Turns More Assertive:
A New Century Approaches for Higher Education in the United States
Clark Kerr   9

Introduction: Higher Education in American Society
Patricia J. Gumport, Philip G. Altbach, and Robert O. Berdahl   15

PART ONE: THE SETTING

1. Campus and Commonwealth: A Historical Interpretation
John R. Thelin   21

2. Academic Freedom in Delocalized Academic Institutions
Walter P. Metzger   37

3. Autonomy and Accountability: Some Fundamental Issues
Robert O. Berdahl and T. R. McConnell   55

4. Academic Freedom at the End of the Century:
Professional Labor, Gender, and Professionalism
Sheila Slaughter   73

5. Economics and Financing of Higher Education:
The Tension Between Quality and Equity
W. Lee Hansen and Jacob O. Stampen   101

PART TWO: EXTERNAL FORCES

6. The Federal Government and Higher Education
   *Lawrence E. Gladieux, Arthur M. Hauptman,
   and Laura Greene Knapp*   125

7. The States and Higher Education
   Aims C. McGuinness, Jr.   155

8. The Courts
   Walter C. Hobbs   181

9. Other External Constituencies and Their Impact on Higher Education
   Fred F. Harcleroad   199

PART THREE: THE ACADEMIC COMMUNITY

10. Problems and Possibilities: The American Academic Profession
    Philip G. Altbach   225

11. College Students in Changing Contexts
    Eric L. Dey and Sylvia Hurtado   249

12. Comparative Reflections on Leadership in Higher Education
    Martin Trow   269

13. It's Academic: The Politics of the Curriculum
    Irving J. Spitzberg, Jr.   289

14. Graduate Education: Changing Conduct in Changing Contexts
    Patricia J. Gumport   307

PART FOUR: CONCLUDING PERSPECTIVE

15. Current and Emerging Issues Facing Higher Education
    in the United States
    Ami Zusman   335

16. The Insulated Americans: Five Lessons from Abroad
    Burton R. Clark   365

Contributors   377

Index   381

Acknowledgments

This is the third edition of *Higher Education in American Society*. The first was published in 1981, a time when "crisis" was becoming a common term in higher education and when the fiscal problems that are now so common were not yet so serious. The first edition also drew largely from faculty members who had a connection with the Higher Education Program at the State University of New York at Buffalo. We have tried, over the past decade, to keep this book up to date by revising it regularly to take into account new realities in higher education. Our focus has remained the same—to shed light on the complex set of relationships that link higher education to the broader social and political context in the United States. This revised edition has added a new co-editor, Patricia J. Gumport of Stanford University. The contents of this edition are significantly altered. All but three of the chapters have been significantly updated from the second edition and we have added several entirely new chapters.

Any edited book requires a great deal of cooperation. We are indebted especially to our contributors, many of whom have worked with us since 1981 on the several editions of this book. Manuscript preparation was done at the State University of New York at Buffalo. We appreciate the help of Patricia Glinski at the Center for Learning and Technology. Jason Tan, at the Comparative Education Center, assisted with the editing. Nandini Chowdhury prepared the index. Steven Mitchell, our editor at Prometheus Books, has worked with us on all three editions of this book. His support is appreciated.

We dedicate this book to our colleague Clark Kerr, President Emeritus of the University of California. He helped to shape American higher education—and influenced our thinking.

Philip G. Altbach, Buffalo, N.Y.
Robert O. Berdahl, College Park, Md.
Patricia J. Gumport, Stanford, Calif.

7

Foreword

American Society Turns More Assertive: A New Century Approaches for Higher Education in the United States
Clark Kerr

America now faces, potentially, the most stressful period of interactive relations between higher education and the surrounding society in the more than three-and-one-half centuries since the founding of Harvard in 1636. These sixteen essays that constitute *Higher Education in American Society* set forth, as of 1994, many prospective aspects of this new period—with emphasis on the word "prospective" defined as expected but not yet assured.

In America, colleges and universities have never inhabited the upper stories of that fabled Ivory Tower of the historic myth. They have always been subject to some pressures and constraints from their surrounding societies. And, in turn, they have always been at work influencing the course of their host societies to one degree or another. Customarily, they have lived with more autonomy from constraints and more room to guide their own affairs than most other institutions of society, except for churches—more than government agencies controlled by laws, more than business enterprises constrained by markets, more than trade unions checked and balanced by employers. They have mostly been comparatively privileged entities of tolerant societies exercising great self-restraint toward them. And their principal participants—the faculties—have had more leeway to conduct their lives according to their individual wishes than most other members of the modern labor force—they have not viewed themselves or been viewed by others as "employees." It has been a world of comparative institutional autonomy and comparative individual academic freedom.

However, over the years there has been a secular trend, with many shorter term reversals within it, from a position closer to the first end of that long spectrum of alternatives from autonomy to control to a position closer to, but still far removed from, the other. The trend has been, as one university president in Oklahoma once said to me in the colloquial language of today, for the "corrals to be getting smaller and the barbed wire around them to be getting higher." That is what this volume is about—such a process in the United States in the 1990s and beyond. But the same process is taking place in many other nations of the world, including Great Britain—once the great paragon of autonomy and freedom. The whole world of higher education is changing. The secular change goes sometimes faster and sometimes slower, and now we are in a time when it is going somewhat faster. How much faster and farther?

Society in the western world has mostly been in an active mode toward its colleges and universities beginning with the city-states in Italy, and the Church and royalty in France and England, although sometimes, as with Oxbridge in the 18th century, society has pretty much forgotten about the universities and let them stagnate for a while. Colleges and universities have mostly, in return, been in an active mode toward their societies in retrieving old knowledge (as with the knowledge of Aristotle in late medieval Italy) or originating new knowledge, and in creating an ever larger component of educated people; and even very occasionally in supporting revolutions. But there have been great variations in:

1. the general intensity of the mutual interactions;
2. the primary source (or sources) of the initiatives;
3. the purposes of the initiatives; and
4. whether the initiatives were mutually supportive or caused conflict among the participants.

Let me try to sketch out such variations with reference to certain selected periods in the history of higher education in the United States. I choose from periods of particular historic significance:

1. *The founding of American colleges in the Colonial period.* They were mostly founded jointly by churches and the colonial governments. The general purpose was, as stated for Harvard: "to advance Learning and perpetuate it to Posterity; dreading to leave an illiterate Ministery to the Churches, when our present Ministers shall lie in the Dust."[1] This was a bilateral, mutually supportive endeavor. The endeavor, by common effort, was expanded from the creation of a ministry to encompass the other historic professions of teaching, law and medicine. The relation was intense, bilateral, with a common goal, and thus cooperative.

2. *The founding of American research universities after the War Between the States.* This was another period of enhanced interaction. There were two sources of new initiatives—one external and one internal. The external one was government (initially the federal government and then also the states) with the Land Grant movement. This movement reflected the new economy based on the rise of industry and on the rise of commercial agriculture as a great source of exports. The nation needed better educated farmers, and more and

better educated engineers. The internal initiative originated with articulate academic adherents of the German model of the research university, with its orientation toward scientific investigation and training. The goals of these initiatives were compatible, or became compatible, but were not identical—the first placed more emphasis on applied technology, and the second more on basic research; and some temporary battles ensued, as at Berkeley at the time of President David Coit Gilman in the 1870s. However, a more fundamental and enduring conflict was also inherent between the old religion and the new science, between the competing visions of revelation and reason, between theologians and scientists in the faculties, between ministers and businessmen on boards of trustees—a conflict that, in much more subdued form, still continues in residual forms. American higher education underwent a revolution in the control of its colleges and universities (the state versus the church), in the content of the curriculum (science versus morality), and in many other ways.

3. *The "great transformation" during and after World War II.* This was, once again, a time of heightened intervention and of new initiatives—this time far more complex than the two prior periods. Federal support of scientific research was one new initiative, to win first the hot war and then the cold war. Equality of opportunity was a second initiative, first to reward the returning GIs and then to accommodate the emerging minorities and women. The third initiative came from labor force requirements, particularly centered around the new electronics symbolized by the computer. In each of these initiatives, higher education (mostly) joined in—it also wanted more research, more equality of opportunity, more high-level training of skills. It was a Golden Age.

All of these initiatives were external. Of external origin, also, was the Senator McCarthy period of ideological witch hunts, but, in this instance against the consent of higher education. But one additional initiative was internal and also not so compatible—the cultural revolution (American style) of dissident students and of some faculty members in the 1960s, partly as a backlash to McCarthy. This was an attempt to "reconstitute" American higher education, American society, and the content of American lifestyles—the third, the more successful of the three, as the new morality challenged the old with the campus as a main battlefield.

4. *The "time of troubles"—the 1990s and beyond.* Here society is mostly the initiator, with higher education, for the first time, mostly the defender of the status quo rather than the joint initiator, or at least a cooperative partner, in the new endeavors. Society is the aggressor for powerful reasons.

(a) Society has fewer new resources to spread around. Historically, labor productivity has advanced from the War Between the States to World War II at an average rate of two percent a year, which results in a doubling every 40 years. Then, from 1945 to the middle 1970s, it advanced at three percent, which causes a doubling every 25 years. That rate dropped back to two percent in the 1970s and then fell to one percent (a doubling every 75 years) and in some years to zero percent in the 1980s and early 1990s.

(b) Society has more claimants on its resources. Taxpayers have revolted—no more taxes. Simultaneously, competition for public resources has increased—for health care, for child care, for care of the aged, for care of prisoners, among others; and higher education faces Tidal Wave II of students (1997 to 2012 or later) with about the same number of additional students as Tidal Wave I (1965–1975), but much less money available on a percentage basis. There is intensified warfare going within the welfare state—education confronts head on health care, child care, care of the aged, care of prisoners. In California over the past ten years, state general revenue devoted to prisons has gone from four to eight percent, and for four-year colleges and universities from thirteen to nine percent. In the early 1990s, for the U.S. as a whole, real GNP has risen five percent but state support for higher education, on the same basis, has gone down five percent—25 percent in California. Higher education has been losing the war for funding.

(c) American society demands that higher education, as never before, concentrate on support of the economy, engaged as it is in intensified international economic competition. The Carnegie Commission once identified the five major purposes of higher education as the developmental growth of the individual student, advancing human capability, educational justice, pure learning, and the evaluation of society. Number one priority is now clearly being given to advancing human capability, with educational justice in second place; with lesser places (if any at all) to developmental growth, pure learning, and evaluation (criticism) of society.

For all of these reasons, heavy pressure is ensuing on tuition, on faculty salaries, on faculty teaching loads, on fields of pure learning, and on many other sensitive aspects of current practice. Privatization of support for public institutions will be one path to the future, just as private institutions once became more public with federal research funds and student financial aid. Society can hardly be expected to leave higher education so much to its own devices—not when half of youth now attend colleges, not when around half of all skill-related productivity increases and half of all new knowledge-related productivity increases are based in substantial part on the contributions of our colleges and universities. Higher education is now too important both politically and economically to be ignored.

Society is demanding of higher education both more efficient use of the resources given to it and a reordering of their uses. This confronts higher education with a whole series of conflicts: tuition versus faculty salaries, "core" fields versus those more on the periphery, support of administrative versus more directly educational services, humanities versus vocational and professional fields, maintenance of libraries and of plant and equipment versus continuation of employment positions, among many others; and trustees versus presidents versus faculties; and public control versus institutional self-governance. Never before have so many been engaged in fighting so many and prospectively for so long, nor has there been so much endemic internal guerilla warfare.

Higher education in the 1990s has, thus far at least, been mostly reactive with only one major exception: political correctness. Here elements of higher education, mostly confined to the humanities, are on the aggressive, attacking proponents of the majority and established culture. P.C. aside, however, it has been mostly a street with one-way traffic.

Among the four periods noted, this last one involves a unique combination of (1) intense interaction of higher education with society, (2) dominant initiatives by society, (3) limited overall agreement on goals and methods, and (4) potentially prolonged and rising conflict—a "time of troubles."

Some General Comments on the Essays that Follow

1. I agree with several of the authors (chapters 1 through 4) that, of the two great historic issues between society and higher education, individual academic freedom and institutional autonomy, that the latter is by far the bigger issue in the prospective future, with academic freedom now more an internal than an external issue.

2. I also agree that equity may be mostly winning out over quality (chapter 5).

3. I believe that the states are now much more important, in the area of public higher education, than the federal government—the governors are the new men of power, but so also are the judges (chapters 6 through 9).

4. I think that Philip Altbach in his overarching central-themes essay (chapter 10) may be too pessimistic when he says that "American higher education is in a period of unprecedented decline," but too optimistic when he writes that "it is likely that the medium term future will be somewhat more favorable than the immediate past"; but I agree that "the essential structure of American higher education remains unaltered"—so far, at least. It is a historic time when pessimism, optimism, realism are all in contention. (See also chapter 15—the other most inclusive central-themes essay).

5. Students of today are more conservative politically and more vocationally oriented personally, with dreams of "the revolution" and prospects for the humanities the two great losers (chapter 11).

6. Leadership is under great pressure. The new divide among presidents is between those who are pro-active to the new range of problems and those who are reactive—so far the great majority are on the reactive side of that divide. Will that change? Who, if anyone, will take charge? (chapter 12)

7. Current faculty members, in general, are taking less interest in the welfare of the whole campus and, in particular, in the curriculum, as Irving J. Spitzberg notes (chapter 13). Spitzberg also raises these intriguing questions: What will the "new blood" (recruited 1995 to 2010) be like? This will be a central issue. Will campuses "navigate or be pushed aground"?

8. The campus really is less of a *community* and more a *series of communities* than it has been historically (chapter 14 and elsewhere).

9. One great lesson, around the world, as Burton Clark (chapter 16) writes, is that "central bureaucracy cannot effectively coordinate mass higher education." But who or what can?

10. Institutional self-governance is a threatened species (chapters 1 through 16). Observation: The best way to preserve self-governance is by way of outstanding performance—the price of autonomy is eternal self-discipline.

In Conclusion. These essays explore in depth one of the important issues of our time: the possible futures of higher education. How much our times are changing is well demonstrated by the more status quo tone of the first edition of these essays (1981) as contrasted with the more doomsday ambience of this third edition (1994). In my understanding of the evolving situation, this third edition is the more in contact with reality. This volume is an excellent way to start trying to comprehend what the new reality is and might become.

Clark Kerr
Berkeley, California
December 1993

Note

1. "New England's First Fruits, 1643," in *American Higher Education: A Documentary History,* ed. Richard Hofstadter and Wilson Smith (Chicago: University of Chicago Press, 1961), 1:6.

Introduction

Higher Education in American Society
Patricia J. Gumport, Philip G. Altbach, and Robert O. Berdahl

As in the first two editions of this volume, the third edition of *Higher Education in American Society* seeks to capture several critical dynamics in the higher education/society nexus. Since the second edition, many aspects of the relationship between colleges and universities and their external environments have gained increased visibility—if not outright scrutiny—in the media. The topics have included such heated issues as demands for multiculturalism in the curriculum, scrutiny of racially-based undergraduate admissions quotas, attempts to control violence and hate crimes on campus, graduate student teaching assistants going on strike, increased prominence of university-industry partnerships and technology transfer activities, occasional allegations of scientific misconduct/fraud, the alleged mis-management of indirect cost funds, and most recently dramatic consequences from massive budget cuts brought about by a national economic downturn and often accompanied by explicit "downsizing" mandates from state legislatures.

In a system of higher education that is as large and decentralized as that of the United States, it is difficult to do a comprehensive analysis of the cumulative record of twentieth century strains and transitions, let alone to reassess priorities in order to survive and prosper in the future. However, as a preliminary step in this direction, the third edition of this volume retains and extends what we, as editors, believe to be a major theme: *There is much analytical utility in examining the affairs of colleges and universities within their changing social contexts.* Accordingly, the editors and the authors share a common view of colleges and universities as social institutions that are embedded in the wider society and in various ways subject to its constraining social forces.

Implicit Conceptual Frameworks

While all of the chapters in this volume deal with the relationship between colleges and universities and their social contexts, that relationship is conceptualized differently by each author. Moreover, some of the underlying conceptual frameworks are not made explicit by the authors. To assist the reader in gaining the most from the substantive insights of the chapters, we suggest that the reader consider how each author presumes the higher education/society nexus to work. Specifically, we encourage the reader to consider for each chapter: What are the purposes, functions and characteristics of American higher education? How have these evolved over time? How might we account for these changes?

Scholars of higher education in the United States may draw from a wide range of conceptual frameworks to understand the nature of the relationship between colleges and universities and the wider society.[1] For example, presuming that higher education is structurally determined by external social forces, changes can be examined and explained as resulting from historically specific political-economic circumstances in which higher education functions as an agent of reproduction.[2] Alternatively, at the other end of the continuum, one can view higher education through an internalist perspective, where colleges and universities are characterized as pro-active in nature; the presumption that defines this view is that institutional initiatives may exert powerful affects that shape the wider society.[3]

In this volume, neither conceptual extreme is represented in its pure form; rather, the fifteen authors occupy various scholarly locations along a wider middle ground. In some chapters the authors view colleges and universities as bounded organizations that strive to work effectively by drawing resources from a wider, external environment. A variant of this approach is to conceive of the environment not as a singular whole, but as a multiplicity; in this view, still seen as external, the infinitely complex environments call for adaptive responses as colleges and universities continue to be challenged by the environment's ever-changing constraints and opportunities.[4]

In other chapters the authors view colleges and universities as arenas of conflict and change. Rather than employing "the organization" as the key *a priori* theoretical construct, the conceptual line that demarcates the organization from the "external" environment is questioned.[5] The result is that the affairs of colleges and universities are framed as a more open empirical question, one that views higher education as settings that are simultaneously embedded in and constituted by the wider society. What is unique about this conceptual position is that wider societal forces are seen as interactive and dynamic, rather than unidirectional and external; these forces are characterized as mediated by institutional filters and played out on campuses in a number of crucial processes such as governance, resource allocation, curricular change, and research training, to name only a few.

In considering this range of implicit conceptual frameworks, we invite the reader to participate more actively in the text. Chapter conclusions may be evaluated more thoughtfully in light of authors' beginning assumptions. Furthermore, in understanding where an author is "coming from" conceptually, the reader will be better able to make sense of how imminent changes for higher education in the coming decades might be interpreted in light of alternative interpretations.

Organization of the Third Edition

As this edition goes to press and the twentieth century comes to a close, we are especially concerned with the cumulative record of how colleges and universities have dealt with the array of daunting economic, political and demographic challenges. Our contributors, experts in their respective fields, bring their expertise to examine particular historical and contemporary aspects of these complex social forces.

In Part I we begin with John Thelin's historical chapter. The rationale is that an appreciation of the evolution of higher education helps to develop perspective on contemporary issues, since historical context often reveals that our present problems are not all new ones. We then follow with Walter Metzger's piece on the origin of the American definition of academic freedom. His essay suggests that the original definition was primarily aimed at protecting academic freedom from internal constituencies, that is, trustees and presidents. According to Metzger, the original definition is no longer adequate when institutions have become "delocalized," that is, operate in an environment in which many external forces have come to play important roles in the institution's development.

The Berdahl/McConnell chapter picks up that theme by noting that the definition of academic freedom has been expanded to include protection from external threats as well as from retaliation for having participated in institutional governance processes. The authors examine whether academic freedom is more an individual right than an institutional one, and advocate that "autonomy" is more properly the term to use in discussing the corporate freedom of the university or college. Sheila Slaughter's chapter analyzes the more recent developments concerning academic freedom in its broader definitions. According to Slaughter, it is essential that we examine academic freedom in the context of transformations in professional labor.

We have retained the Hansen and Stampen essay from the second edition in order to address economic issues, specifically the tradeoffs between access and quality. Although some of their specific data have been superseded, the basic analysis of the tension between access and quality remains pertinent.

In Part 2 our authors examine the role of the major external constituencies: the federal government, state governments, the courts and non-governmental groups (e.g., private foundations, accrediting associations and voluntary consortia). While Gladieux et al. focus on the federal level, McGuinness highlights state governments. Both chapters analyze the complex web of relationships and issues that link higher education to government. These chapters are followed by discussions of other key external forces that affect colleges and universities—these include the courts as well as an array of agencies, such as accrediting bodies. For each chapter, we encourage readers to consider the possible impact of each of these external forces on the academic freedom of campus actors as well as on the autonomy and accountability of the institutions.

Part 3 then addresses challenging issues within segments of the academic community. These chapters are united by their analyses of how those working within the higher education system are affected by societal trends, the decisions of the political system, and economic currents in American society. The section opens with Altbach's comprehensive assessment of changes in the academic profession. Dey and Hurtado discuss trends pertaining to undergraduate students. Trow deals with the role of leadership and administration in the context of the higher education-society nexus. Spitzberg focuses on how the undergraduate curriculum has responded to external as well as internal pressures, and reflects the interplay between politics and higher education. Gumport concludes this section by analyzing emergent patterns in graduate education. Trow discusses the role of campus presidents and the broader issues of leadership in a period of rapid change.

Part 4 brings the volume to closure with Ami Zusman's analysis of emerging issues in higher education as well as Burton Clark's piece on the value of comparative perspectives. The editors conclude with a brief summary chapter.

Notes

1. Note that there are potentially far more conceptual frameworks available than have yet been developed by scholars of higher education. A recent study of higher education literature found that 98 percent of journal article publications were located in a functionalist framework: John Milam, "The Presence of Paradigms in the Core Higher Education Journal Literature," *Research in Higher Education* 32, no. 6 (1991): 651–68.

2. See, for example, Samuel Bowles and Herbert Gintis, *Schooling in Capitalist America* (New York: Basic Books, 1976) and more recently grounded in critical theory William Tierney, ed., *Culture and Ideology in Higher Education: Advancing a Critical Agenda* (New York: Praeger, 1991) and Sheila Slaughter, *The Higher Learning and High Technology* (New York: SUNY, 1991).

3. See, for example, Burton Clark, "The Organizational Conception," in *Perspectives on Higher Education: Eight Disciplinary and Comparative Views* (Berkeley: University of California Press, 1984).

4. Burton Clark, "The Problem of Complexity in Modern Higher Education," in *The European and American University Since 1800*, ed. Sheldon Rothblatt and Bjorn Wittrock (Cambridge: Cambridge University Press, 1993).

5. On this point, see the alternative work developed by British organizational theorists: Lucien Karpik, *Organization and Environment* (London and Beverly Hills: Sage, 1978); Michael Reed, *Redirections in Organizational Analysis* (London: Tavistock, 1985.)

PART ONE

THE SETTING

1

Campus and Commonwealth:
A Historical Interpretation
John R. Thelin

In 1982, a study group commissioned by the Carnegie Foundation for the Advancement of Teaching prefaced its report on campus governance with the observation, "There remains in the control of higher education an inherent tension. Colleges and universities are expected to respond to the needs of society of which they are a part—while also being free to carry on, without undue interference, their essential work."[1] To university presidents who at that time faced double pressures of increased government regulations and decreased federal funding for research and student financial aid, this characterization was painfully accurate.

In contrast, historians of higher education found the Carnegie Foundation's statement to be an intriguing hypothesis but a premature conclusion, leading them to ask, "Has this pairing of institutional autonomy and responsibility to 'meet societal needs' always existed? If so, has it always been characterized by tension? Were there periods when it was a source of harmony?" Hence, although the Carnegie Foundation report dealt with institutional governance of the 1980s, its side effect was to raise essential questions about the historical context of higher education in American culture.

The questions surface because historians resist attributing present conditions to the past and do not assume that there must be a fixed, one-to-one correspondence between school and society. As Lawrence Stone argued in his 1971 essay, "The Ninnyversity?," a university might have been in accord with the national culture at one time, while in another decade in conflict with its surrounding political environment.[2] Furthermore, conflicts between university and society have shown markedly different configurations: an intellectually "radical" campus in one era may be reactionary in another. Absence of state involvement in higher education might eliminate a threat of coercion, but equally plausible is that it could indicate government indifference or neglect. To make sense out of the continuity and changes over time in the complex relations between campus and culture constitutes what Alexander Astin has called higher education's "moving target research."[3]

Historical Perspective: The Commonwealth Legacy

A good starting point is one general statement upon which historians agree when discussing higher education and American society, whether in 1693 or 1993: colleges and universities have been—and are—serious business. To found, construct, and oversee these institutions calls for sustained commitment of time and money. And, as suggested by the 1982 Carnegie Foundation report, it does include the official obligations categorized as "government relations." This poses a conceptual problem: the vocabulary of "federal regulation" and "state control" is incomplete because it masks the essential good will that has undergirded the American academic enterprise. Government relations with higher education are best understood as one part of a larger *societal* expression about what higher education ought to be. So the question is not simply, "How have government agencies and other external groups controlled colleges?," but rather, "What are features of American society that have led groups to take the trouble to build and nurture colleges?"

A clue to our heritage comes from the 17th century colonial notion of *commonwealth* because it expresses the close, supportive relations between American society and higher education. And, resurrecting the term *commonwealth* builds in the reminder that if higher education has been serious business, it also has been a labor of love. Despite the laments of campus leaders about constraints government has placed on higher education today, colleges and universities usually have been the favored children in the history of American institutions.

This legacy is found in the language of the charters, letters, and pamphlets from the colonial era. The historic bond of campus and commonwealth extended beyond government relations, as its lifeblood was a tradition of philanthropy which in 1633 prompted a leader of an economically lean Massachusetts Bay colony to argue, "for if we norish not Larning both church & common wealth will sinke. . . ."[4] And, according to an early fund raising prospectus, following the initial college donors, "others after them cast in more, and the publique hand of the State added the rest. . . ."[5]

Raising funds for colleges was an unlikely pursuit, since colonies were intended primarily to serve the Crown as a source of revenue from tobacco or, in some cases, as a convenient sanctuary for England's sundry religious dissenters. The unexpected enthusiasm for colleges showed a mix of optimism and earnest commitment that created a distinctively American combination of individual and state support for higher education.

The American impulse to build colleges was no transient whim, as it continued into the 18th century and spread from New England to the Mid-Atlantic and Southern regions. The colonial colleges' mission of higher education for leadership in public service was tied to the corollary that society had a permanent commitment to the institution. For example, the charter for the College of William and Mary stated that the institution was "To be supported and maintained in all Time coming. . . ."[6] To put this commitment into perspective, today the ten oldest chartered American colonial colleges are still operating while over 80 percent of small businesses fail within a year. Whereas the 1982 Carnegie Study emphasized higher education's concerns about government intrusion, in the colonial period, institutional endurance was only achieved by mutual respect of college and state. Often the government dedicated proceeds of a lottery, a land sale, bridge tolls, or a tobacco tax as a source of regular income for a chartered university.[7] It also meant that a governor was a member of the board of trustees or had authority to appoint board members.

From Medieval to Modern Institutions

What may be termed the distinctive "American way" in higher education was a hybrid form derived in part from the medieval European universities' legal definitions of corporate structure and certification.[8] It was the idea of an institution defined by a charter granted by an external governing body (whether crown, papacy, or emperor). With this right to exist came the power to confer degrees, perhaps the most coveted function of an academic institution. Charters then were accompanied by elaborate statutes and by-laws which spelled out institutional rights and obligations; they also distinguished scholars as a legal group, subject to certain protections in dealings with civil authorities. In return for such rights, university representatives agreed to abide by codes of conduct and to offer instruction and examinations in designated fields. The notion of legal protection from the lay population was the root of what we call the distinction between "Town and Gown." It provided for physical safety of masters and scholars, a warning to local citizens that the university was under the auspices of either royal or ecclesiastic authority.

Apart from these legacies, the new American colonial colleges exhibited some significant departures from the medieval model.[9] Foremost was their conscious decision to vest power in an external board, a feature transplanted from Scottish universities. At the time that the first colonial colleges were established, there was coincidentally a low ebb in academic life of both professors and students at Oxford, whose constituent colleges followed the medieval model of governance by a faculty guild; in the colonies this led to a distrust of unchecked faculty authority and a preference for an external board, usually with administration by a strong president who reported directly to the board. And, as suggested earlier, from the start the American colonial model placed a strong reliance on philanthropy for funding colleges.

To understand the "collegiate way" of living and learning in American higher education, one must look to Oxford and Cambridge of the early modern period for the notions of the landscaped "campus" and the residential "college" and quadrangles, even though such models often proved to be too expensive for the provincial institutions to replicate. The American colleges differed markedly from the medieval university in their allowance for some secular learning; religion remained a strong component, but in the colonies there was diversity of church affiliation, whereas medieval universities were under the auspices of the Catholic Church. Furthermore, after the Middle Ages, Oxford and Cambridge had oaths of allegiance to the Church of England, practices that endured through the late nineteenth century. The trend in America was to fuse higher learning with the Christian faith, but sometimes with measures of religious toleration. The charter of Brown, for example, explicitly prohibited religious tests, emphasizing that "the public teaching shall in general respect the sciences, and that sectarian differences of opinion, and controversies on the peculiarities of principle, shall not make any part of the public and classical instruction. . . ."[10] Furthermore, although church affiliation remained integral, colonial colleges never were "seminaries" primarily committed to education of clergy.

The Problem of "Public" and "Private" Categories

In tracking down continuities between colonial colleges and contemporary universities, the most dangerous fallacy is to attribute our distinction between "public" and "private" institutions to the seventeenth and eighteenth centuries.[11] Such a categorical distinction would have made little sense: a college was a "public" institution because it was integral to the fabric of the colony; its chartering was strictly defined by the civil government. A college was seen as a resource to be both nurtured and protected. It did have some autonomy as spelled out in its charter and statutes, but an academic institution was not "private" in the sense that it was exempt from accountability to its host colony.

One litmus for this "school and society" balance is that there was roughly one college per colony, reflected in the choice of such institutional names as the College of New Jersey; the College of Rhode Island and Providence Plantations; the College of William and Mary in Virginia; and the University of Pennsylvania. Tangible evidence of the importance of college founding was that college buildings were prestigious, often the largest, most impressive structures in their community—and whose construction costs were often paid by tax levies. Ironically, every one of these colonial colleges today is known as a "private institution." "The College of New Jersey" is now known to us as "Princeton," whereas "The College of Rhode Island" has become "Brown University." But, as shall be explained later, this represented a conscious change in definition that did not take place until the mid-nineteenth century.

Regional Rivalries and Competition for Colleges

Chartering and building colleges were undertakings often accompanied by fierce competitions and rivalries, which indicates that in American society, colleges usually have been attractive institutions. A chartered college was a coveted resource for a community and its acquisition usually involved years of effort, whether a royal body was petitioned (as was the case of William and Mary) or the civil authorities in the colony. The high stakes associated with obtaining a chartered college were most evident in episodes where petitions to establish another new college in the same colony were resisted by representatives of an existing institution. A good illustration of this phenomenon came about in 1762 when Harvard officials argued against proposals to found a new college in the western part of Massachusetts.

The basis of the Harvard opposition was that a new college would dilute support from both government and private donors; it would split allegiances within the colony, resulting in two weak institutions left to compete for scarce resources and students. Moreover, "the natural consequence hereof would be, not only the filling too many important civil offices, but a great part of our pulpits, with comparatively unlettered persons, at once to the detriment both of the Commonwealth, and of the churches here established. . . ."[12] Harvard's campaign obviously was self-serving and illustrated the pitfalls of arrogance that could accompany an academic monopoly. Despite its partisan tone, however, the Harvard brief did contain an element of foresight because in the nineteenth century government policies allowing over-building of colleges would become a fundamental weakness in American higher education.

When the governor ruled in favor of Harvard, it brought about yet another example of the real and symbolic importance of colleges as a source of regional pride in American life. Eleazar Wheelock, the founder of Dartmouth, led a campaign among disgruntled farmers and merchants in western Massachusetts who had been denied their petition for a college charter. Wheelock proposed they secede from Massachusetts and join with dissidents from Vermont to form a new colony, with Wheelock himself as governor. The bait was that Wheelock would bring with him the charter of Dartmouth College.[13] Wheelock's political scheme eventually fell apart, but did illustrate the importance of college charters as a prize in community development.

Colleges and the New Nation: State Charters and "Booster Colleges"

After the break from colonial status to the new nationalism of the federal period, the themes of commonwealth and collegiate service to society continued to enjoy support well into the early nineteenth century. This was demonstrated in the address by the President of Bowdoin College in 1802, who said: "It ought always to be remembered that literary institutions are founded and endowed for the common good, and not for the private advantage of those who resort to them for education. . . . [E]very man who has been aided by a public institution to acquire an education and to qualify himself for usefulness, is under peculiar obligations to exert his talents for the public good."[14]

The Bowdoin president's speech also adds documentary substance to the interpretation that Americans had yet to distinguish a "private" college from a "public" one. Elsewhere, the colonial tradition of commitment to advanced education for civic purposes continued with important innovations with Jefferson's new University of Virginia. Invoking the colonial rhetoric of institutional mission, however, was deceptive in that the change from colonies to the United States up-ended colleges' legal and financial environment.

By the late eighteenth century the role of a civil government to authorize and support colleges within its domain underwent a dramatic reversal that fundamentally changed colleges' relations with American society. First, the national government was restricted in its power to create or oversee educational institutions; the individual states were the units that replaced the colonies as the chartering authorities. Second, after 1800 many state governments, especially in the South and West, abandoned the customary restraint colonial governments had shown in granting college charters. State legislatures opened the floodgates for the founding of several hundred new colleges between 1800 and 1850. In contrast, in England there were only four degree granting universities during the same period.

At the same time many state legislatures did not subscribe to the colonies' principle that a civil government had an obligation to support those colleges to which it had granted charters. Charters now were viewed as a relatively easy way to reward special interest constituencies. Building colleges might promote growth and development, all at little risk or expense to the state government. A convenient way for a state to show support was to provide cheap land, as distinguished from an annual appropriation from a tax or lottery. Hence new colleges and universities typically were small, had little endowment, and could not rely on the state for regular funding. A good example of the product of such policies was the University of Georgia, which received its state charter in 1785; it offered no classes, enrolled no students, and conferred no degrees for over fifteen years until it eventually opened with the name "Franklin College."[15]

New trends in state policies transformed the American college from a sponsored institution to a contest enterprise in which a college's survival depended on its ability to attract consumers and donors, usually within the immediate locality. The consequence was that the nineteenth century was the era of the "booster college" in which campus construction was fused with civic pride, church support, community development, and even real estate promotion. In such an environment a college president and board continually had to assess its curriculum and other proposed activities in terms of popularity in a market economy: Would a course of study attract paying students? What activities would generate support of donors and local residents? Would new programs offend regional mores? Failure to heed such questions explained the high rate of closings among American colleges in the nineteenth century. Most of all, without the cushion of civic pride, a college risked losing tax exemptions, property donations, and other benefits crucial to survival.

The corollary of strong state and local presence in higher education was the relative absence of federal involvement. There was, for example, no United States Ministry of Education. Some memorable attempts to establish a national observatory or a national university did not reach fruition. Probably the best example of federal concern with higher education was the founding of the United States Military Academy at West Point and the United States Naval Academy at Annapolis. These institutions, however, were exceptions to the rule of state level initiatives.

Since both West Point and Annapolis were committed to the professional education of military and naval officers and to engineering and applied sciences, their examples raised the question of the curriculum's popular appeal: namely, when and where did "useful" education come to be a part of higher education's attempt to "respond to societal needs?"

From Public Policies to Popular Interest

On balance, the public policies which shaped nineteenth century American higher education reflected a peculiar paradox: Americans' zeal for college building as a part of civic boosterism surpassed public interest in the substance and relevance of the college curriculum. Enrollments declined as a percentage of the population and higher education seemed disengaged from the American economy, as earning a college degree had little if any connection to a young adult's job prospects, even for entrance into learned professions of law and medicine. Many colleges responded to declining enrollments with the self-destructive practice of lowering tuition charges in a futile attempt to lure reluctant students.

One explanation for this chasm between colleges and the popular culture was that American higher education of the early nineteenth century was characterized by what has been called the "old time college": a poorly endowed, denominational institution dependent on donations and tuition payments, and offering the "neo-classic curriculum" whose pedagogy emphasized daily recitations and which held declining appeal to the American public. The allegedly moribund college curriculum is puzzling to social historians because the 19th century higher education marketplace seemed ripe for innovation and experimentation, simply because colleges depended on tuition payments to operate. There was nothing to stop a school from adding engineering, sciences, a medical school, a law school, or a commerce course; in fact, many did.

The peculiar finding is that this was an era in which student choices sometimes defied conventional wisdom of consumerism. Philip Lindsley, articulate and innovative president of the new "University of Nashville", banked his career on the proposition that what the "West" (i.e., area beyond the Appalachian mountains) "needed" was a modern, nonsectarian university as an antidote to the tendency for a proliferation of small, denominational colleges. His unexpected discovery was that in the 1840s there was little popular demand in Tennessee for his modern vision; denominations liked and continued to build their own small colleges for the sons (and later the daughters) of the faithful. Facile expectations about how a curriculum could respond to "societal needs" faced harsh tests because a number of places, including Union College, Columbia, Rensselaer, and Transylvania, tried offering new "tracks" or curricula, often with only modest success.

Federal Presence: The Land Grant Legacy and "Useful Studies"

The obvious temptation is to say that higher education's detachment from useful studies changed in 1862 when the United States congress passed the Morrill Act for establishment of land grant colleges. The conventional view of the Morrill Act is to praise its pioneering work in utilitarian, accessible popular higher education. It also is cited as a turning point both in federal involvement in higher education and in the emergence of the great multi-purpose state ("public") universities. The caveat is that recent research complicates the scope and timing of the "A&M" legacy.

Passage of the Morrill Act did not mean the federal government was establishing public universities; rather, its practice of earmarking land grant sales to be used by designated states for educational programs was an off-shoot of a larger national land policy. Nor did the Morrill Act say much about institutional forms or educational programs. Many states first relied on historic liberal arts colleges as a place to affix the new programs in agriculture or mining. Building new state universities was slow to start; not until lobbying took place in the 1890s led by George Atherton, a political economist at Rutgers and later president of Pennsylvania State College, did the land grant institutions acquire collective strength in Washington, D.C. The real rise of the great state universities and their involvement in large scale applied research took place after World War I, thanks in part to added legislation in the second land grant, the Hatch Act, and the Smith Lever Act, and due to the interest of legislatures in prosperous states of the Midwest and West.[16]

American Culture: College Student Life and Curriculum

Since consumer appeal was the new key to college survival, American college students became an increasingly important constituency. The distinction of "Town and Gown" from universities in the Middle Ages had set a precedent for student cultures as a conspicuous group within community life. In the United States, students were an elite in that they were a relatively small percentage of their age group cohort and often were going to be future influential leaders. College students, however, were not always a wealthy elite; regardless of socio-economic class, they were to be indulged by the public and sometimes fleeced by local landlords and merchants.

The big change in the place of the American college in popular culture started to gain momentum in the 1880s: an unprecedented situation in which a scarce, elite activity attracted vicarious popular fascination. It meant that "going to college" became fashionable and coveted. Clothing fashions, feature articles, and fiction generated a big surge in adulation for the "college man" and "college woman" as American culture heroes. This in turn was followed by a persistent yet gradual expansion of the percentage of Americans between the ages of 18 and 22 who went to college. Consider the popularity of *Frank Merriwell of Yale,* a weekly pulp fiction magazine which enjoyed a circulation of over two million readers for a span of more than 15 years. During the same years colleges were building stadiums for football contests, some with seating capacities for crowds of more than forty thousand. In sum, the collegiate life of undergraduates suddenly became one of the most popular dimensions of American culture—fraught with tensions, of course, but with great public allowance for eighteen- to twenty-two-year-olds to create a world pretty much on their own terms.

One explanation for this rising popularity of colleges was that in the United States between 1880 and 1920 the colleges finally had responded to the society's strong demand for "useful" studies. Indeed, this contention is strengthened by the appeal such "new professions" as engineering, agriculture, business administration, and forestry held for new undergraduates and their pragmatic parents. The complication is that all courses of study, including the once maligned liberal arts, soared in higher education's rising tide after 1890. A more accurate estimate of the popular support for college was that the functions of socialization and certification concerned families most, with relatively little intrusion into classroom and curricular matters.

The single most important feature of the relation between American society and higher education was that "going to college" came to be viewed as a way of "getting ahead." It was a cultural phenomenon that had little, if any, connection with higher education's government relations and public policies. As an undergraduate told historian Henry Adams in 1871, "A degree from Harvard is worth money in Chicago." Whether or not that was always true was less important than the social fact that the American public believed it to be so over the next century.

Philanthropy and Higher Education's Maturation

After 1880 the attractiveness of colleges appealed to new, wealthy donors as well as to an expanding student constituency. This unexpected groundswell of philanthropy revitalized American higher education because the vagaries of state legislatures' appropriations in the nineteenth century, combined with the meager revenues generated by tuition charges at most colleges and universities, had left most institutions financially weak.

Philanthropy took four major paths. First, the idea of education for service in learned professions had traditionally strong support from missionary societies and educational foundations, which were committed to providing tuition scholarships for undergraduates who intended to serve as ministers, teachers, and missionaries. Second, the booster colleges' gains in popularity included the multiplier effect of alumni loyalty, as campus affiliation became a source of lifelong commitment and donations by a growing number of former students. Third, the most dramatic and unexpected change in voluntary giving was in the form of large scale philanthropy to single institutions, often reflected in a college adopting the family name of a generous patron. This trend, illustrated in the early 1800s when the College of Rhode Island became "Brown University," continued and expanded between 1880 and 1920, with such names as Vassar, Vanderbilt, Stanford, Rice, Cornell, Tulane, and Duke providing the large scale support necessary for endowing magnificent modern universities.

Equally interesting was that by 1900 large scale philanthropy acted as a *horizontal* force as well as a *vertical* presence in the form of foundations. This latter strand of voluntary support for higher education provided a strategy whereby a donor could develop a theme that cut across many institutions, instead of concentrating on founding a single campus. A good example of the role of a foundation was concern about improving quality and raising thresholds of academic performance nationally. The concerted effort for "standardization" was best seen as the product of private power for the public good, due in large measure to the role of the Carnegie Foundation for the Advancement of Teaching.[17] Other important examples of large scale philanthropy influencing policies and practices included the Rockefeller General Education Board and the creation of the College Entrance Examination Board and the Educational Testing Service.

Civic and State Pride and the Popularity of Higher Education

By 1920 the American campus was a monument to state and alumni pride. Its architecture, including magnificent bell towers, libraries, and football stadiums, provided visible testimony to generous support and prestige. Reliance on extracurricular activities provided a means by which the campus could generate widespread popularity with alumni, voters, and legislators. Presidents discovered that intercollegiate athletics brought local enthusiasm and even statewide affiliation with higher education to a scope and scale of boosterism beyond imagination of the small town settlers of the midwest and far west of 1870 and 1880. And well into the twentieth century, Americans continued to be preoccupied with the competition for college construction.

Virtually every state and region experienced its own battles about where a new campus was to be built. In California, the flagship state university at Berkeley ended up facing a prolonged, effective campaign by Los Angeles civic groups to build a new, full-fledged campus in the prosperous and populated Los Angeles area. While the state university was going through its civil war, the privately endowed "University of Southern California" took on the mission of serving Los Angeles by emphasizing professional schools and services. A variation on this theme surfaced in Massachusetts where, between 1945 and 1970, a concentration of high powered private universities in the Boston area competed among themselves for constituencies and donors, but showed signs of cooperation in dealing with the legislature to oppose plans to invest in building a high-powered state university in the western part of the state—not unlike Harvard's opposition to plans for a new college in the eighteenth century![18] The net result of such episodes, whether in California, Massachusetts, or elsewhere, was that in the half century between 1920 and 1970 American higher education enjoyed an unprecedented period of support and expansion. In structural terms it meant that public higher education would shift from the model of a single great flagship university, moving increasingly toward an arrangement of multi-campus systems or a consolidated governing board.

A Note on Faculty and Academic Freedom

Although "going to college" enjoyed prestige in twentieth century American life, public confidence in American higher education was unevenly distributed. Faculty, for example, seldom commanded the popular adulation Americans gave to undergraduate activities. This reflected in part a historic mistrust of professors, a societal attitude manifested in the American preference for having colleges governed by an external board, with virtually no legal power accruing to the collective faculty. True, between 1900 and 1970 the faculty would gain in matters of salary, tenure proceedings, grievances, and even pension plans— testimony to their importance as experts. But the legal structure of the American campus clearly left ultimate authority with the board and, secondarily, the administration.

A complete survey of academic freedom is beyond the scope of this essay. Attention here is confined to one pivotal episode in the years after the heroic battles between 1890 and 1920 in which the American Association of University Professors made great gains in academic freedom cases. Despite such gains, following World War II the American professoriate faced a crisis of confidence during the so-called McCarthy Era of the early 1950s. One image of those years is that of a hostile "witch hunt" in which public outrage about alleged radicalism within faculty ranks prompted various federal and state legislators to purge colleges and universities of professors who were sympathetic to, or members of, the Communist Party. Beyond that familiar depiction, the important nuance for this study of relations between society and higher education is to consider the structural protections the university provided (and did not provide) its faculty in dealing with the external social and political environment. As Ellen Schrecker has shown in *No Ivory Tower,* an often overlooked phenomenon was that at several major universities, campus administrators overreacted in their compliance with the inquiries by McCarthy and other legislators who saw themselves as fulfilling a popular demand for faculty loyalty.[19] In other words, university presidents often were found to be more stringent and punitive toward their own faculty than were the critical legislators and the general public! This may have been due to the lack of confidence university presidents felt about their ability to defend academic principles to external groups. At worst, it indicated that some university presidents were not really champions of faculty rights or guardians of academic freedom. The enduring implication was that the good standing of faculty in American society was more likely to be a function of economic conditions (namely, stature as an expert in a prestigious field) rather than a legacy of enduring civil rights or professional protection.

The Perils of Prosperity: Public Policy in the Contemporary Era

Despite the Morrill Act and subsequent agricultural research legislation, one can hardly say that prior to World War II there was a significant, conscious federal "public policy" toward higher education.[20] Even the prodigious G.I. Bill of 1945, which expanded the societal presence of colleges by providing financial aid and college admissions for large numbers of students, had only a secondary connection to higher education; its primary intent was to give tribute to servicemen and to reduce problems of unemployment in a post-war economy. If one wants to find any semblance of a coherent nationwide "policy" involving higher education between 1900 and 1940, one must look not to the federal government, but to the initiatives and programs carried out by the great private philanthropic foundations of Carnegie and Rockefeller.

The coagulation of scattered federal programs into what might be termed a "public policy" emerged after World War II, with concentration in two areas: sponsored research and development projects and need-based student financial aid.[21] The coincidence of these massive federal investments, combined with an affluent national economy, expanded philanthropy, and robust state support meant that American colleges and universities gained international stature for their ability to enroll unprecedented numbers and percentages of students, and at the same time conduct high level research and development in a wide range of fields. By 1965 one could speak of an "academic revolution" in which American society had come to rely on and accept the expertise of colleges and universities, indicative of an "information society" whose foundation was a "knowledge industry." Student enrollments had grown, both in actual numbers and as a proportion of total population, such that higher education had been transformed from elite to mass access.[22]

The paradox—or peril—of success was that the expanded, active roles of American colleges and universities from time to time raised questions as to whether the institutions were adhering to their historic charge and to new definitions of the public trust. This essay started with citations of the college charters from the colonial era, noting that the language of "commonwealth" was their legacy. Since the nineteenth century, however, Americans have relied on consumerism instead of commonwealth as the ethos by which to establish the relations between society and higher education. Dependence on a loose consumerism has been an imperfect resolution, not without its ambiguities. American colleges and universities, in acquiring success, have also inherited the burden of high, rising expectations from a variety of social groups and constituencies. The pertinent question for the late twentieth century is thus: If, indeed, colleges describe themselves and see themselves as a business or commercial activity, will the government and the public in turn treat higher education as a business? For example, to speak the language of a "knowledge industry" may eventually jeopardize the protective moorings of tax exemptions and other privileges Americans have customarily afforded colleges as educational institutions. Whereas in 1910 a college was seen as an enterprise to be protected, by 1980 federal agencies often saw higher education as an industry to be regulated, with increasing attention to issues of gender and race in admissions and employment.[23] If colleges and universities have not heeded government concern with social justice and civil rights, perhaps an explanation is that the various state and federal policies have at the same time prompted colleges and universities to edge toward an entrepreneurial posture in the competition for grants and resources. Universities in turn have bristled at what they consider to be intrusions on their historic institutional autonomy.[24] In either case, higher education in American society at the dawn of the twenty-first century faces once again a re-examination of its structural and cultural compacts no less wrenching than the continuity and changes that colleges faced two centuries ago in the shift from colonies to states.

Notes

1. Carnegie Foundation for the Advancement of Teaching, *Control of the Campus: A Report on the Governance of Higher Education* (Princeton, N.J.: Carnegie Foundation for Advancement of Teaching, 1982), pp. 3–4.

2. Lawrence Stone, "The Ninnyversity?" *New York Review of Books,* January 28, 1971.

3. Alexander W. Astin, "VMI Case Dramatizes Basic Issues in the Use of Educational Research," *Chronicle of Higher Education,* July 24, 1991, p. A24.

4. "A College First Proposed for Massachusetts Bay, 1633." in *American Higher Education: A Documentary History,* ed. Richard Hofstadter and Wilson Smith (Chicago: University of Chicago Press, 1961), vol. 1, pp. 5–6. See also, James Axtell, *A School on a Hill: Education and Society in Colonial New England* (New Haven: Yale University Press, 1974), pp. 201–244.

5. "New England's First Fruits, 1643." Reprinted in Samuel Eliot Morison, *The Founding of Harvard College* (Cambridge, Mass., 1935), pp. 432–33.

6. *The Royal Charter of 1693 of The College of William and Mary in Virginia* (Williamsburg, Va.: Charter Day 1993).

7. Frederick Rudolph, "The Colonial College" and "The Collegiate Way," in *The American College and University: A History* (New York: Alfred A. Knopf, 1962), pp. 3–22, 86–109; Margery Somers Foster, *"Out of Smalle Beginnings . . .": An Economic History of Harvard College in the Puritan Period, 1636 to 1712* (Cambridge, Mass.: Belknap Press of Harvard University Press, 1962).

8. Charles Homer Haskins, *The Rise of the Universities* (New York: Henry Holt, 1923); Helene Wieruszowski, *The Medieval University* (Princeton, N.J.: Van Nostrand, 1966).

9. Clark Kerr, *Another First: The Means of Governance* (Williamsburg, Va.: College of William and Mary, 1986 Charter Day Address), pp. 1–6. See also, W. H. Cowley and Don Williamson, "Germination: 1636 to 1776," in *International and Historical Roots of American Higher Education* (New York and London: Garland Publishing, 1991), pp. 71–96.

10. "Charter of Rhode Island College (Brown University), 1764," in *American Higher Education: A Documentary History,* ed. Hofstadter and Smith (Chicago: University of Chicago Press, 1961), pp. 134–36.

11. John Whitehead, *The Separation of College and State: Columbia, Dartmouth, Harvard, and Yale, 1776-1876* (New Haven and London: Yale University Press, 1973).

12. "Harvard Opposes a New College in the West, 1762," in *American Higher Education: A Documentary History,* ed. Hofstadter and Smith, vol. 1, pp. 131–33.

13. John Whitehead, "Dartmouth: A Small College," in *The Separation of College and State: Columbia, Dartmouth, Harvard, and Yale, 1776-1876,* pp. 53–88.

14. President Joseph McKeen at Bowdoin in 1802, quoted in Frederick Rudolph, *The American College and University: A History,* pp. 58–59.

15. "Charter of the University of Georgia, 1785," in *American Higher Education: A Documentary History,* ed. Hofstadter and Smith, vol. 1, pp. 147–49; see also Thomas G. Dyer, *The University of Georgia: A Bicentennial History, 1785-1985* (Athens: University of Georgia Press, 1985).

16. Roger L. Williams, *The Origins of Federal Support for Higher Education: George W. Atherton and the Land-Grant College Movement* (University Park: Pennsylvania State University Press, 1991). See also Earl F. Cheit, *The Useful Arts and the Liberal Tradition* (New York: Macmillan for the Carnegie Commission on Higher Education, 1975).

17. Ellen Condliffe Lagemann, *Private Power for the Public Good: A History*

of the Carnegie Foundation for the Advancement of Teaching (Middletown, Conn.: Wesleyan University Press, 1983).

18. Richard M. Freeland, *Academia's Golden Age: Universities in Massachusetts, 1945-1970* (New York and Oxford: Oxford University Press, 1992).

19. Ellen Schrecker, *No Ivory Tower: McCarthyism and the Universities* (New York: Oxford University Press, 1985).

20. Francis Keppel, "The Role of Public Policy in Higher Education in the United States: Land Grants to Pell Grants and Beyond," in *The Uneasy Public Policy Triangle in Higher Education: Quality, Diversity, and Budgetary Efficiency,* ed. David H. Finifter, Roger G. Baldwin, and John R. Thelin (New York: Macmillan for the American Council on Education, 1991), pp. 9-17.

21. Chester E. Finn, Jr., *Scholars, Dollars, and Bureaucrats* (Washington, D.C.: The Brookings Institution, 1978).

22. Christopher Jencks and David Riesman, *The Academic Revolution* (Garden City, N.Y.: Doubleday Anchor, 1968); Clark Kerr, *The Uses of the University* (Cambridge, Mass.: Harvard University Press, 1964); Robert M. Rosenzweig with Barbara Turlington, *The Research Universities and Their Patrons* (Berkeley: University of California Press, 1982); Roger Geiger, *To Advance Knowledge: The Growth of American Research Universities* (New York and Oxford: Oxford University Press, 1986).

23. Nathan Glazer, "Regulating Business and the Universities: One Problem or Two?," *The Public Interest* (Summer 1979): 42-65.

24. Derek C. Bok, "The Federal Government and the University," *The Public Interest* (Winter 1980): 80-101.

2

Academic Freedom in Delocalized Academic Institutions

Walter P. Metzger

EDITOR'S NOTE: This essay, written in 1969, provides a relevant historical perspective to many of the issues discussed in this volume. We reprint it because the issues it raises are so relevant to contemporary debates and because it considers how American higher education developed at a crucial historical period.

The gist of the argument that follows is that the theory of academic freedom as it has been articulated in this country has become, in critical respects, outmoded. By this I do not mean to imply that the value of academic freedom has diminished; it is not only relevant to the modern university, but essential to it—the one grace that institution may not lose without losing everything. A theory of academic freedom, however, goes beyond an affirmation of its value to a description of the forces and conditions that place this desired thing in peril, and a prescription of the norms and strategies that may offset those specific threats. It is in this latter sense, as a mode of analysis and advice concerning the realities of social power, that I believe the inherited canon has, to a large degree, outlived its day.

One should not suppose that the American theory of academic freedom owes its staleness to senescence. Though it draws on an ancient legacy of assumptions, it did not become crystalized in this country until as late as 1915, when Arthur O. Lovejoy of The Johns Hopkins University, E. R. A. Seligman and John Dewey of Columbia University, and a number of other academic luminaries wrote the *General Report on Academic Freedom and Academic Tenure* for the newly founded American Association of University Professors.

Reprinted with permission from Walter P. Metzger, et al., *Dimensions of Academic Freedom* (Urbana, Ill.: University of Illinois Press, 1969), pp. 1–33.

To call this report a classic is to comment on its quality, not its venerableness—a document only two generations old hardly qualifies as antique. But a short period in the life span of ideas may constitute a millennium in the time scale of institutions, especially American institutions, which have been known to change at breakneck speeds. What has happened in the half-century since 1915 is that American universities have been remodeled while the ideas once consonant with them have not. The result has been a growing discrepancy between milieu and theory—an ever widening culture lag.

By the lights of 1915, a violation of academic freedom was a crime designed and executed within the confines of the university. Dissident professors were the victims, trustees and administrators were the culprits, the power of dismissal was the weapon, the loss of employment was the wound. Concentrating on this stage and scenario, the authors of the 1915 statement concluded that the key to crime prevention lay in the adoption of regulations that would heighten the security of the office-holder and temper the arbitrariness of the "boss." So persuaded, they persuaded others, and in time these institutional regulations, known as academic tenure and due process, came to be widely adopted if not always faultlessly applied. It should be noted, however, that by defining a violation of academic freedom as something that happens *in* a university, rather than as something that happens *to* a university, these writers ignored a set of issues that had caused their foreign counterparts much concern. Nothing was said in this document about the relations of the academy to state authority. Except for brief allusions to the class obsessions of wealthy donors and the populistic foibles of local legislators, nothing was said about the external enemies of the university, though history made available such impressive candidates as the meddlesome minister of education, the inquisitorial church official, the postal guardian of public morals, the intruding policeman, and the biased judge. Finally, nothing was said about threats to the autonomy of the university that were not, at one and the same time, threats to the livelihood of its members; indeed, it was not even clearly acknowledged that a corporate academic interest, as distinct from an individual academic's interest, existed and had also to be preserved. In short, 1915's criminology (and the criminology operative today—cf. the policing efforts of Committee A of the AAUP) was wise to the ways of the harsh employer, but it lacked a theory and vocabulary for dealing with the outside offender and the nonoccupational offense.

Along with this definition of the crime went a recommended rule of good behavior: a university, the report declared, should never speak as an official body on matters of doctrine or public policy. In the lengthy history of universities this gospel of institutional restraint had not had many preachers or practitioners. Indeed, there were many more examples of commitment: e.g., the adherence of the continental universities after the Reformation to the confessional preferences of the local rulers, the involvement of Oxford and Cambridge in the dynastic struggles of Tudor England, the proselytizing efforts of the church-built colleges in America prior to the Civil War. The authors of the 1915 statement took aim at this tradition by attacking some of its basic premises: that truth is something to be possessed rather than endlessly discovered; that truth-questions yield to the edicts of institutions rather than to the competitive play of minds. Intellectual inquiry, they insisted, had to be ongoing and individual; organizational fiats defeat it because organizations are mightier than individuals and fiats are inevitably premature. In support of their brief for neutrality they likened the true university to an "intellectual experiment station" where new ideas might safely germinate, to an "inviolable refuge" where men of ideas might safely congregate, and—most simply—to a "home for research." By no stretch of analogy was the modern university to be considered a missionary society, a propaganda agency, an arm of a political party: it was a residence, a hothouse, a sanctuary—the figures of speech were adoring, but they left the university with nothing of substance to proclaim.

How was this no-substance rule to be effectuated; what were the means to this lack of ends? Here our near-yet-distant academic forefathers made another enduring contribution. Conceivably they could have argued, taking a cue from the independent newspaper with its balanced display of editorials, that an academic institution achieves neutrality by appointing men of varying opinions to its faculty. Or they could have argued, with an eye on the renunciative code of conduct common in the military and civil service, that an academic institution achieves neutrality by prohibiting its members from speaking out on public issues, especially on those foreign to their specialties. Significantly, the authors of the AAUP report did not accept either of these possibilities, but instead set forth a formula possibly suggested by the economic market: let the university disown responsibility for everything its members say or publish and then let it permit its members to say and publish what they please. This formula, which was to be made more explicit in later decretals, had obvious advantages over the others. Neutrality by disownment was easier to administer than neutrality by selection, harder to abuse than neutrality by proscription. But it also created a peculiar asymmetry: it asserted, in effect, that professors had the right to express opinions but that their colleges and universities did not.

By including the concept of personal freedom under the rubric of academic freedom, these writers made their doctrine even more asymmetrical. Traditionally, academic freedom had merely offered on-the-job protection: freedom of teaching and research. These, it had been supposed, were the main arenas where professors exhibited special competence and where they deserved a special latitude; beyond lay a terrain of utterance which professors, like any other citizens, were presumed to enter at their own risk. The authors of the 1915 report would not accept such zonal ordinances. Academic freedom, they asserted, protects professors in all of their identities—as teachers, scholars, scientists, citizens, experts, consultants—and on every sort of platform. It applies not to a category of speech but to a category of persons.

The first and most important thing to be said about the college or university of 1915 was that it possessed and exercised impressive powers within a demarcated area. This attribute, which I shall call its "localness," derived in part from the clarity of that demarcation. The lands of the college of that period usually made up a contiguous property and were often marked off by fences that kept the students in corral and warned the outsider of the line of trespass. Usually they were located in sequestered regions either on the outskirts of major cities or in the bucolic settings of college towns. Spatially these institutions lived apart, and this apartness contributed to their autonomy.

In addition to acreage and location, style and organization fostered localness. Administratively, with the exception of a shrinking number of ecclesiastically controlled institutions, each unit was entirely discrete, with its own board of regents or trustees, its own executive figure, its own sublieutenancy of deans, its own budget, its own rules and regulations. Legally each was endowed by charter or statute with a vast amount of discretionary authority. Extensive in the management of property, that authority was virtually without limit when it came to the regulation of persons. In 1915 neither outside law nor internal dissonances restrained the exercise of student discipline. It was common in those days for students to live under rules they did not fashion and to be expelled for infractions without a trial. When students asked the courts to intervene they usually were disappointed, the courts generally taking the position that students had, by implied or explicit contract, consigned themselves to the mercies—quasi-parental and therefore tender—of those who had initially let them in. It should not be supposed that students submitted gladly to this regimen. The annals of these institutions disclose too many revels in the springtime, too many rebellions in the fall and winter, to support the view that, uniquely in America, 18 to 22 were the docile years. Yet it is also clear that few in this febrile population challenged the legitimacy of that regimen. Students sought to outfox, not unseat, their elders; they made a game of the rules, but accepted the rules of the game. This kind of popular acquiescence, together with the virtual absence of serious judicial review, gave the academy the appearance of a foreign enclave, ruling indigenous peoples with laws of its own devising, enjoying a kind of extraterritoriality within the larger state.

Of course institutions calling themselves academic came in many different shapes and sizes. The grandest institutions of the period—those that had gathered into their custody the tools of modern scholarship and research— were much more involved with the world around them than colleges that were little more than *écoles*. But the worldliness of the Harvards and Wisconsins did not yet undercut their localness. For one thing, research tools were on the Edison scale of cost: Brookhaven magnitudes were not yet imagined. By means of the usual fund drives and appropriations, these institutions could sustain the cost internally and thus keep control of what their members did and spent. For another thing, the scholars and scientists they assembled were still burdened with heavy academic duties. At this point in time, while there were many teachers who did no research, there were practically no researchers who did not teach—

and teach assiduously and regularly. In a much more than *pro forma* sense, men who worked *in* the university also worked *for* the university and were responsive to its interests and requirements.

Even in their transactions with their patrons the colleges and universities of 1915 had a great deal of decisional independence. It is a convention of academic history to deny this, to conclude from their chronic neediness, their perennial courting of the legislatures, their incessant wooing of potential donors, that they were the most obsequious of creatures. But I suspect that those who assert this take as their implicit model of comparison the English university of the nineteenth century, an institution that owed its aplomb and self-reliance to ancient clerical endowments, enormous property holdings, and the privileges of the class it served. Without that invidious comparison, the American college would seem to have been made of sterner stuff. For one thing, the bulk of collegiate instruction was still going on in private institutions which, despite many resemblances to the public ones, had a narrower constituency to account to, and far more discretion in defining that constituency. Some were dependent on very rich patrons, and not the braver for it; still, very often, behind the captains of industry who invested fortunes in universities, there would be a charismatic president who told them how their money should be spent. In the public sector, the whims of the men who held the purse strings had to be catered to more consistently, and presidents of state institutions were often chosen for that capacity. Yet even here the processes of negotiation that took place between legislators and administrators left considerable discretion in local hands. Members of appropriations committees seldom developed the educational expertise needed to initiate novel policies. Far from being sources of innovation, these committees were political arenas where administrators would bargain with their counterparts for public monies and where the essential educational decisions would concern the division of the take. Nor was there much regulation of the system, either in the public or the private areas. Large-scale private philanthropy, though it had worked important reforms in such limited fields as medical education, was not yet a ubiquitous improver; agencies for self-regulation, like the regional accrediting associations, tended to be self-protective bodies, shielding the run-of-the-mill establishment against its fly-by-night competitor. Far less than in railroads or in banking were the firms in academe made to conform to specific standards. And the reason for this is not hard to find. Serving a small segment of the population, not yet central to the economy, taken more seriously for its fun and frolics than for its earnest devotions, the college or university of 1915 was regarded as a public ornament and curiosity, not yet as a public utility.

Above all—and this is what makes the period seem an age of innocence, our own academic *belle epoque*—the organs of the central state were not intrusive. For years the federal government had given land to universities without conditions, or had laid down conditions (e.g., the furtherance of agriculture and technology) without imposing very strict controls. In 1915 Washington did not even have an apparatus for dealing systematically with academe. The federal interest in education, which was at that time almost negligible, could be contained in a lowly Bureau of Education whose primary task was to get statistics; the federal interest in (nonagricultural) science, which was even at that time quite considerable, could be met by governmental agencies like the Geological Survey and the Naval Observatory, and did not impinge on the universities. Americans tended to attribute this phenomenon—substantial federal assistance without a significant federal presence—to the genius of their Constitution and their history. Doubtless a literal reading of the Tenth Amendment, plus the hold of Jeffersonian prejudices, did erect barriers to state intrusion. Where such barriers did not exist, as in Great Britain in the nineteenth century, universities felt much more statist pressure. Thus, for all their vaunted independence, Oxford and Cambridge were compelled to submit to extensive changes suggested by royal commissions in the 1850s and 1870s and enforced by parliamentary decrees. But there was still another explanation, albeit one less visible to contemporaries, for the special state of American affairs. In large part our federal government was undemanding simply because it had no urgent demands to make. A nation that had just entered world politics but had not yet become a world power, that lived in the Edenic security of a miniscule army and a safe frontier, lacked one of the principal motives for intermeddling— the motive of martial necessity. Let that motive be supplied, as it would in a future far more imminent than most Americans in 1915 could foresee, and the central state would not scruple to lay a levy on the spirit of the university, as well as on its faculties and young men. Full recognition of this came in 1918   when, on behalf of a country mobilized and gladiatorial, the Congress transformed every college male into a soldier, every college dormitory into a barracks, every college lawn into a training ground under the aegis of the Secretary of War. The Student Army Training Corps, like the agencies of propaganda filled with scholars, was decried as a folly and an aberration as soon as World War I closed. But at the outbreak of World War II the academic system was once more militarized, and this time the marriage of Mars and Minerva would not only be solemnized but preserved.

It is not very difficult to see why the authors of the 1915 statement on academic freedom ignored the macrocosm of society and concentrated on the smaller campus world. It was there that significant things could happen. A college or university was then no mere appendage of government, no mere component in a great machine. It was a unit of considerable completeness, an agency possessed of powers that were almost governmental in kind. It suggested a checkerboard view of power and a concept of academic freedom that was equally sectioned and discrete.

So much for the general bias of the theory. To account for its specific arguments one has to note another feature of the system: its capacity to generate within each unit an inordinate amount of status strain. This was the period when the academic profession came of age: when it came to think of itself as specialized, competent, and scientific; when it sought to act as mentor to society on a wide range of social issues; when it demanded the deference and the courtesy that befitted these pretensions and that role. It happened, however, that this was also the period when many academic trustees and administrators adopted a style of management that conceded little to these demands. Derived from the views and manners of prerogative-minded business managers, falling between an older authoritarianism with its familial emphasis and a yet-to-come bureaucratism with its codes and forms, the style struck many professors as both overweening and capricious, and in any case hostile to their status claims.

An example of the irritating potential of this new managerial psychology can be found in one of the earliest academic freedom cases investigated by the AAUP. In 1915 the Board of Trustees of the University of Pennsylvania dismissed the economist Scott Nearing on grounds they refused to disclose. (The evidence is all but conclusive that they took exception to his opinions, which were radical then, but not yet Marxist.) In explaining why he did not have to explain, George Wharton Pepper, a prominent trustee of the university, said: "If I am dissatisfied with my secretary, I suppose I would be within my rights in terminating his employment." Was, then, a professor simply a clerk? an amanuensis? The chancellor of Syracuse was willing to concede that he was more than that, that he dealt in some fashion with ideas. Still, this administrator did not believe that the creative function of the professor gave him leave to oppose the man who signed his check. The dismissal of Nearing, Chancellor Day believed, was entirely proper. "That is what would happen to an editorial writer of *The Tribune* if he were to disregard the things for which the paper stands. . . ." Were, then, the trustees of a university, like the publishers of a newspaper, the formal proprietors of the property? The editors of the New York *Times,* in choosing not to go so far, offered their own enlightening treatise on academic relationships in America. As they saw it, the university belonged to the donors, who were its fount of wisdom and ideology *in saecula saeculorum;* the trustees were the agents of the donors, charged with the execution of that immortal claim. Professors? They were simply spoilsports, ever ready, under the academic freedom cover, to ask for privileges they never bought:

> Men who through toil and ability have got together enough money to endow universities or professors' chairs do not generally have it in mind that their money should be spent for the dissemination of the dogmas of Socialism or in the teaching of ingenuous youth how to live without work. Yet when Trustees conscientiously endeavor to carry out the purposes of the founder by taking proper measures to prevent misuse of the endowment, we always hear a loud howl about academic freedom.
>
> We see no reason why the upholders of academic freedom in this sense should not establish a university of their own. Let them provide the funds, erect the buildings, lay out the campus, and then make a requisition on the padded cells of Bedlam for their teaching staff. Nobody would interfere with

the full freedom of professors; they could teach Socialism and shiftlessness until Doomsday without restraint.

Among the changes wrought by time has been the departure of this kind of liveliness from the editorial pages of the New York *Times*.

Cast in general terms, the report of the AAUP professors did not seem to stoop to rebuttal. Yet these Gothic business doctrines shaped the contours of its major themes. The norm of institutional neutrality was not just an ethicist's abstraction: it was a denial of the proprietary claims of trustees, donors, and their spokesmen. The widening of the zone of academic freedom was not simply a reflex of libertarianism: it was an effort to reduce the sphere in which philistine administrators could take action. And the notion that men were in conflict with their organizations—and that this conflict drew the battle lines of freedom—stemmed only in part from an individualistic ethos: it also expressed the viewpoint of a profession whose institutional existence offered too meager status gains. For all its transcendent qualities, the 1915 report was a tract developed for its times.

The times, I submit, have changed. Not everywhere, not in all respects. A small denominational college may still look as it looked in 1915. A major university may still be living off the precedents set long ago. Here and there a donor may still wish to establish an ideology in the course of establishing a schoolroom, or a trustee may still be tempted to utter the platitude of possession. But at the height where one loses particulars and gains synopsis one can see enormous transformations. Of these, one of the most important has been the flow of decisional power from authorities on the campus to those resident outside. Richer, larger, more complex than ever before, the typical modern institution of higher learning is less self-directive than ever before. It has become, to coin a word, "delocalized," with consequences we are just beginning to perceive.

Delocalization has not been a single process but a congeries of processes, all working in the same direction and achieving a common end. The engulfing of many universities by the central city, with the result that everything that they do in the way of land use becomes imbued with political implications and ensnarled in municipal law, is one delocalizing process. The growth of bureaucratized philanthropy as a principle source of academic innovation, the subordination of the judgment of admissions officers to legislative judgments concerning civil rights, the involvement of universities in social welfare and thus with clients it can serve but not control, may be considered others. And so too may the integration of public higher education, the assault on the principle of extraterritoriality, and the enlargement of federal influence due to federal sponsorship of research. These latter processes are so important, both in affecting the character of academic institutions and the viability of the academic freedom theory, that I should like to examine each in some detail.

In 1915 only two states attempted to coordinate the activities of their tax-supported institutions of higher learning. By 1965 only nine states let their state university, land-grant colleges, technical institutes, and teachers' colleges go their separate ways. The trend, moreover, has not only been toward greater coordination but also toward higher degrees of integration. By 1965 as many as fifteen states had given superordinate public bodies the power to alter and create new schools by plan. SUNY, the gigantic State University of New York, was established in 1949 to take charge of forty-six existing public institutions and to set up as many new ones as its over-all blueprint would prescribe. By current reckoning the California Master Plan brings seventy-six junior colleges, eighteen state colleges, and a nine-campus university under the sway of dovetailing central bodies. In the coordinated systems the power of central bodies may be limited to reviewing budgets and programs initiated by the institutions themselves. In the more integrated systems the off-campus boards of control may make decisions on capital investment and tuition levels, architectural design and new site locations, entrance requirements and degree capacities, while the on-campus boards and administrations may make decisions on how those decisions will be carried out. These vertical and horizontal combinations of plants in similar and diverse lines, these unequal allocations of power between the central office and the local branch, this division of territorial markets state by state, make the integrated academic organization and the modern business corporation seem very much alike, if not of kin. And these resemblances are not lost on the faculties they appoint. If we are employed by the educational duplicate of General Motors or United States Steel, some of them seem to be saying, let us be responsive to that reality: let us elect a single bargaining agent to match the collective strength of management; let us fight for our economic interests without the constraints of a service ethos; let us, if need be, strike. Localized institutions tended to generate professional resentment, but delocalized institutions seem to eviscerate professional élan.

The rationalization of public higher education proceeds from three demands that are made upon it: (1) that it accommodate vast enrollments; (2) that it stimulate economic enterprise; (3) that it accomplish both objectives at something less than crushing public cost. These very demands speak eloquently of the new importance that has come to be attached to this activity. So high is the putative correlation between income earned and degree awarded that a college education has become compulsory, not by the edict of law but by the mandate of ambition. So close is the symbiosis of productive industry on the knowledge industry, so glaring is the cheek-by-jowl abutment of technological parks and college greens, that the advertised presence of a campus has become, next to tax abatements, a primary lure to new investment. Private higher education has grown as a consequence of these connections, but public higher education has grown much faster, so that today it enrolls almost two-thirds of all academic students, and is much more heavily subsidized, receiving one hundred dollars in tax money for every thirty-five dollars its private competitors receive in gifts. With the change in the public-private balance, the old popular affection for the small-scale venturer has given way to a quest for tax economies, and the alleged efficiencies of central planning is urged successfully even in staid legislative halls. What had once been regarded as a mere propaedeutic enterprise has thus become, in the course of time, a key to the life chances of everyone, an object of urgent public policy, and a stimulant to the GNP. New layers of relevance have been added; but in the process the old attribute of localness has been stripped away.

The assault on extraterritoriality—the second delocalizing process—engages another set of forces, at work both in the private and public sectors, both on the campuses and beyond. On the campuses the assault is being mounted by a new generation of student radicals: white revolutionaries and Negro militants, advocates of more effective student power, persons lonely in their alienations or drawn into dissentient subcultures—the varied student cadres that distinguish the convulsive present from the prankish and catatonic past. Each group has its own visions and motivations, as can be seen from the instability of their alliances; and none is yet numerically dominant in any student body in the land. But they are increasingly becoming a powerful, pace-setting minority and they share, amid all their differences, a common animus against the discipline which their predecessors did not oppose. Different groups issue different challenges to that discipline. Advocates of student power dispute the validity of rules that are made for but not by the student client; theirs is a constitutional challenge aimed, as are all the challenges of emergent classes, at the habit and principle of exclusion. Partisans of the New Left break the rules to change the policies these rules facilitate; theirs is a tactical challenge aimed, as are all radical challenges, at the going morality of ends and means. At times these challenges overreach their mark. The breaking of certain rules may mean the disruption of the operations of the university, which may require the intercession of police forces and the use of violence on a massive scale. The end of this chain of consequences is a greater loss of internal authority than any may have anticipated or approved. The surrender of the administration to the harsh protectorship of policemen is often more costly to its authority than the precipitating student offense. On the other hand, only the most Sorelian of student radicals could delight in all aspects of this denouement: the substitution of military for civilian options, the traumatization of students by police attack, the devolution of a community based on shared assumptions into a community nakedly based on force. Of late, the politics of confrontation has found another way to exceed its immediate object. Students engaged in coercive protest have come to insist that amnesty be granted before they will agree to relent. For those who reject the legitimacy of the guardians and who wish to stay to do battle yet another day, this demand serves practical and symbolic purposes. But amnesty wrested from the institution may not always bring total forgiveness: violations involving trespass or vandalism may result in criminal arrests. Where the institution is the sole complainant, it may influence the disposition of these cases; but it may find it hard to convince the courts to dismiss the charges when it has surrendered the means to protect itself. The natural effect of amnesty, granted under duress, is thus to displace the disciplinary power from the universities to the civil courts. Whether courts or universities act more justly is a question one need not resolve. It is clear, however, that they do act differently, the one being more interested in behaviors, the other in underlying intentions; the one just beginning to grant academic freedom legal status, the other having long made this the value it cherishes above all. But the thrust of modern student politics is to give the temporal rather than the spiritual authority a legitimate judicial role.

Meanwhile, forces outside the university have been working to constrain academic discipline when it *is* applied. Starting in 1961, the federal courts have been deciding that the disciplinary actions of officials in publicly supported colleges and universities must adhere to the due process standards of the Fourteenth Amendment of the Constitution. Whether the officials of private institutions must adjust their conduct to these standards is not, at the moment, certain; but it is highly probable that they will one day be made to do so or suffer reversal in the courts. One may note that the cases setting the legal precedent involved the interests of Negro students who had been punished for participating in sit-ins by administrators of Negro colleges yielding to the pressures of Southern whites. Clearly the judicial concern for student rights was inspired by a judicial concern for civil rights and not by purely academic considerations. Here again, the college, in acquiring new social significance, has lost a measure of its old autonomy. But here one may be permitted the conclusion that, on balance, justice gained.

I come finally to the last delocalizing tendency: the growing involvement of the federal government with the affairs and fortunes of academe. This is perhaps not the order or the language that the most passionate critics of that involvement would prefer. But the virtue in saving it till last is that we may then perceive it not as something *sui generis* but as part of a broader development; and the virtue in using the word "delocalizing" when a more accusative vocabulary is at hand is that we can avoid the dubious imputation of Pentagon plotting, power elitism, establishment cooption, and the like. Nevertheless, after this dispassionate preface, I hasten to admit that I believe the issue now before us is of burning importance. The advent of a formidable central state—harnessed almost without limit for a world struggle apparently without end, richer than any other benefactor by virtue of the federal income tax resource, able to seek solutions to any social problem, if need be, by purchasing compliance with the cure—is a momentous event in the life of our universities. Such a behemoth, as it draws close, cannot help but siphon authority from other agencies. In part, but only in part, the speed and volume of the drain from the universities can be measured by the increase in its assistance. In 1964 federal contributions to higher learning totaled $1.5 billion. Though this came to only one-tenth of the total funds received, it constituted, because of its distribution, a large percentage of the incomes of the major places—83 percent of Cal Tech's, 81 percent of MIT's, 75 percent of Princeton's. For home reference, it may be noted that Columbia, third among recipients, got $51,000,000, an intake that amounted to almost half of that year's operating budget, while the University of Illinois, then sixth in order, got $44,000,000, a smaller part of its total budget but a not inconsiderable sum. By 1966 the federal contribution had doubled and the federal share of total contributions had risen to approximately one-fifth. In that year the largesse was a little more evenly distributed, but the major institutions were even more glaringly beholden to the generosity of the central state.

It is in the "how" as well as in the "how much" that we locate the delocalizing pressure. During and after World War II, academic scientists high in government and governmental and military officials high on science hit on two devices for channeling federal funds to universities. One was the project grant or contract, which a faculty member negotiates with the granting agency with minimal involvement by his university; the other was the specialized research center, which the university operates for the agency, sometimes without the participation of any faculty member. These devices are supposed to confer a variety of social and scientific benefits. It is claimed that the distant granting agency, with its advisory panels of distinguished scientists, is more likely to rate applicants on their merits than are members of a department when they judge their own. It is claimed that the separation of federal subsidy from federal employment helps preserve individual research initiative, since an academic scientist is free, as a governmental scientist is not, to pursue the project of his own desire. And it is claimed that the funds allocated under these formulas make possible the purchase of scientific apparatus which would otherwise be lost to the academy in the expensive space and atomic age. It is tempting to investigate these claims, to ask whether personal, institutional, or regional loyalties never tincture the judgments of reviewing panels, whether certain kinds of extravagantly priced equipment— like accelerators with ever increasing BEVs—deserve the national priority they have been given, whether freedom of choice is not subtly constrained by the workings of the well-known principle that a man need not marry for money, he may simply seek out the company of wealthy women and marry one of them for love. But these are not the questions before us: what is pertinent is that these devices rob the university of autonomy, the one by making it a bystander in the fostering and reward of its members' talents, the other by making it a kind of subcontractor, dispensing someone else's cash to attain someone else's objectives. Here one might add a quantitative footnote: today, from two-thirds to three-quarters of all money expended on academic research comes from the federal giver through these circumventive routes.

"Washington," notes Clark Kerr, in his study of the "multiversity," the delocalized institution unsurpassed, "did not waste its money on the second-rate." Did it make what was first-rate even better? Looking at the institutional breeding places of the greatest scientific advances of the last two decades,

Kerr concludes that the federal research effort did give existing excellences an added gloss. But on the evidence he himself musters, a more pessimistic conclusion might be formed. Taking what is given without question and doing what is asked for by the gift, the front-rank university tends to find itself rich but troubled, powerful in its impact on the nation but weak in the control of its own affairs. It falls prey to what Kerr refers to as "imbalances": the dominance of science over the humanities, the dominance of research over teaching, the dominance of graduate interests over undergraduate concerns. It takes on an ever increasing number of those whom Kerr refers to as "unfaculty": scholars who are added to the staff to assist externally aided projects. Set to the sponsored task but performing no other service to the institution, never eligible for tenure no matter how often contracts are renewed, this new academic breed lives at the periphery of the profession. Fifty years ago only a relatively small group of graduate students, serving as assistants to their senior faculty, was in as marginal a position. Since then, the ranks of this subaltern force have grown, to take care of the burden of instruction that the increased number of students has created and that a research-minded faculty will not assume. In the leading universities these two anomalous groups—the teacher who is still a student and the researcher who is not a teacher—make up a very large part of the total academic work force. With enrichment, then, has come a new diminishment: an increase in the number of appointees who are in but not of the university, sharing in its tasks but not its perquisites, existing under the predestinarian doctrine (so alien to professional doctrine) that good works can never assure election.

A full estimate of the losses incident to gains must include the acceptance of secrecy and deceit, not as adventitious vices but as part of the academic way of life. Federal support for military research must bear a part of the responsibility for the institutionalizing of shady tactics. The aim of military research is to secure time advantages against the enemy; often, to secure these time advantages, it is necessary to prevent premature disclosures; frequently, to prevent disclosures, it is necessary to test the loyalty of participants, limit access to facilities, guard the research records, or control what appears in print. With the Pentagon no less interested in quality than the National Science Foundation or the National Institutes of Health, it was inevitable that funds for the necrophilic sciences, as well as funds for the healing and heuristic arts, would flow to the better universities. But federal support for military research does not account for all the slyness and covertness that afflict modern academic life. Only a small part of federal support is avowedly military (in 1966, of the total sum applied by the granting agencies, only 10 percent went to academia from the Department of Defense). If the secretiveness of warrior organizations accounts for something, the enfeeblement of academic organizations accounts for more. A high susceptiveness to deception was built into the very flabbiness of the grant arrangement. Almost any agency out to promote an unpleasant mission can find a pretext for lodging it in the university, to acquire guilt by association. Federal undercover agents find it easier to carry on their impostures amid the para-academic members of a research project than amid the faculties at large. Above all, universities involved in the project system developed a trained incapacity to look suspiciously at their gift horses, if indeed they looked at all. Thus it happened at Michigan State University that a program for training policemen for Vietnam, set up by a mission-minded agency without close monitorship by the university, was infiltrated by agents of the CIA. The structure, if it did not require hugger-muggery, was certainly not well made to prevent it. And thus it happened that the same surreptitious body gave secret subsidies to a variety of academic enterprises, ranging from area study institutes to international conferences; once inserted, trickery by government became routine.

This is not to say that trickery by government does not exist on the campus in other forms. Modes of underhandedness have long been associated with law enforcement: viz., the policeman posing as a student, the student doubling as a policeman, the government employer asking teachers to snitch on their students and peers. Especially prominent in "Red scare" periods, these forms of deception are not uncommon in the current period, when drugs take precedence over dogmas as items on the list of search. But these tricks have the capacity to outrage professors in almost all institutions where they are practiced. The secret subsidies of the CIA, by contrast, seem to be a good deal less inflaming. For a decade or so they went undetected, though not without the collaboration of a good many professors and administrators in the know. When some of these were uncovered (largely by left-wing student muckrakers), they did cause a stir in certain faculties. Still, it is almost certain that the taint has not been removed from certain projects and that administrative and professional winking goes on. As late as 1964 Clark Kerr could maintain that the federal grant procedure was "fully within academic traditions." Since the CIA revelations, the academic mood has probably not been so complaisant. Yet it is doubtful that many members of the profession would think it wise to change the title of their book from *The Uses of the University* to *How the University Has Been Used.*

How to account for the differences in responses? Simply to say that one form of police penetration serves to enrich professors while the other may serve to chastise them puts the matter of self-interest much too crudely. It would be, I think, both more subtle and more accurate to say that no process of delocalization, unless it threatens the well-being of professors, is presumed to violate academic freedom; and that without a violation of academic freedom, no insult to the university causes broad alarm. In fact, by the tests which the inherited creed imposes, some of the trends I have spoken of seem to have strengthened academic freedom. Ideological dismissals have become rare to the point of being oddities in the larger delocalized institutions. This is all the more impressive because outspoken opposition to war in wartime, which had always been subject to academic penalties, has been allowed to flourish in these places. Furthermore, with very few verified exceptions, the governmental granting agencies have not discriminated against opponents of governmental policies. Not only in crimes, but also in crime prevention, the current period seems to improve upon the past. Tenure (for those eligible to receive it) is at least as safe in integrated public systems as in any other. Academic due process has, if anything, become more rigorous and more codified as the scattered *gemeinschafts* of before merge into centralized *gesellschafts*. Federal-grant universities, with their congeries of projects, are less likely to get domineering presidents (they are lucky to get presidents able and alert enough to keep track of all that is going on). Less privileged colleges and universities, hoping for federal assistance, are less likely to prescribe religious or other doctrines (this is one reason why certain Catholic institutions are moving toward lay boards of control and even toward the norm of neutrality). For renowned professors the new order is particularly comfortable and protective. If they have greater leverage in bargaining with their institutions, they may thank the federal grantor for adding to their other marketable assets the value of a movable money prize. The flow of perquisites from Washington dissolves their reliance on the local paymaster, while the tenure granted by alma mater prevents their subservience to the outside source. Status satisfactions only dreamed of may now in actuality be possessed. The autonomy and integrity of universities? These heavenly things on earth are not contained in this philosophy.

This is hardly the place to write an academic freedom theory that would meet this day's demands. All I can do is sketch out certain areas where changes in the reigning wisdom would do us good. I ask you to take this as a prolegomenon; a theoretical and practical formulation of the academic ethics we require must await another Lovejoy or Dewey, distilling salient ideas from new institutional experiences.

At the top of the list of credos ripe for change I would put the view that a crime against academic freedom is a crime against an academic person's rights. In relevant doctrine it may still be that; but it may also be an attack on academic integrity, sustained by the university as a whole. It should be the name we give to the intrusion of lock-and-key research into an ostensibly open enterprise.

Next I would part with the notion that curbs on administrative power answer all of academic freedom's needs. They answer only part of its needs; the other and equally essential instrument is effective academic government. It was well understood by the makers of our Constitution that freedom could be jeopardized by the weakness, as well as the tyranny, of officials.

In the quest for relevant doctrine, I would also take issue with the notion that the only respectable university is a politically neutral university. It may not be easy to reconceive this notion. The norm of institutional neutrality has rolled through our synapses so often we hardly ever challenge it with thought. Therein lies the problem: applied unthinkingly to every issue, it loses its value as a norm and becomes a recipe for paralysis. One illustration may make this clear. The Selective Service Administration recently decreed that college students would be deferred if they achieved a certain grade-ranking or passed a certain standardized test. In other words, instead of classifying by status (all college students), it classified by status and performance (only *good* college students), and fixed the criterion of judgment. To grasp the implications of this procedure one need only ask what the consequences would have been if the draft authorities had decided to defer not all women but only *good* women, not all husbands but only *good* husbands, not all workers in essential industries but only *good* workers in essential industries. In academic no less than in conjugal and economic matters, privacy and autonomy are threatened when virtue is not its own but the state's reward. The academy, however, took little corporate action to defend its corporate rights. Proposals for institutional reliance (say by not ranking students or sending in the grades) were usually defeated by the argument that such acts would be politically unneutral, signifying institutional opposition to the draft or the war in Vietnam. This ritualistic application of the neutrality principle resulted from a failure to distinguish between essentially political questions and essentially educational questions having political implications. A theory adequate for our times would have to emphasize that distinction. It would have to serve the norm of institutional neutrality for questions of the former sort and for them alone. For questions of the latter sort, and I believe the class-rank issue falls squarely within this category, it would formulate a different norm—a norm of institutional regulation, under which things central to the academy could be dealt with by the academy and not passed to other powers by default. Some questions would fall on or near the borderlines and raise jurisdictional dilemmas. But many more would fall to one side or another once the theoretical line was drawn. Thus, whether the state should built an arsenal of secret weapons would plainly be a political question; on this, for reasons that were given long ago and have never lost their validity, the university should be mute. But whether classified research, under state support, should be permitted on the campus would plainly be an academic question; on this, for different reasons, the university should be heard. To assert a normative choice is to reject the radical view that the university must always be political or consent to the evils of society, and the traditionalist view that the university must always be neutral or succumb to the divisiveness of society. Neither argues potently that the university must be independent, and act or not act as its needs demand.

Even if theories were remade, many pressures to delocalize would continue. To ask that the academy come to grips with these is to ask it to formulate counter-policies in apparent conflict with its needs. Delocalization is in part a product of the growing importance of the university: no one could realistically suggest that it retreat to its older insignificance. Delocalization is in part an answer to the financial exigencies of the university: it would be difficult to demand an autonomy that required enormous dollar sacrifices. Moreover, certain delocalizing forces serve as a counter to the overreach of others: large universities in consolidated public systems may squeeze a measure of autonomy from the fact that they can draw on federal subsidies as well as on state appropriations. Nevertheless, some measure of localness can be restored in ways neither retreatist nor impoverishing. The breaking up of large public configurations into smaller subregional complexes might be a step in this direction. The use of collaborative techniques like the sharing of faculties among independent colleges might be another. The diversion of federal aid into student loans, on a scale large enough to let client fees bear the major burden of client costs; the increase in federal aid in the form of institutional lump-sum payments; the decrease in federal aid for big science under academic auspices (other auspices might handle it as well)—all might reinvigorate local power. The localist need not be contemptuous of the rationalizer or believe that he is living in a cost-free system. He need only insist that rationalizations be really rational and that, in the building and rebuilding of systems, costs of every kind be assayed.

3

Autonomy and Accountability: Some Fundamental Issues
Robert O. Berdahl and T. R. McConnell*

In this chapter we wish to build on the preceding essay by agreeing with Metzger that the definition of academic freedom must be expanded from its earlier focus on threats from *within* the Academy to recognize that, in modern "delocalized" institutions (to use his term), outside forces may also play a threatening role. The good news is, as he observed in 1969, that such threats are appearing less and less often since their heyday in the Cold War period of McCarthyism. Sheila Slaughter in the following essay examines the several different facets of academic freedom in recent decades, including its protection of the rights of faculty to participate in institutional governance without punishment for having uttered critical thoughts deemed excessive by the campus administration and/or governing board.

However, we want to take slight issue with Metzger's other plea: that the definition of academic freedom also be expanded to include external threats to the intellectual freedom of the Academy, as well as those to *individuals* within it. There are two reasons for our reluctance to follow his suggestion: first, constitutional scholarship since his essay has failed to reveal any case law which explicitly recognizes and defines corporate academic freedom; second, by far the larger number of issues emerging between universities and colleges and their external environments fall into areas where academic freedom concerns are not at play. For example, if a state government in the form of its statewide coordinating board denies a university request for a new medical school, that would be, by our perspective, an autonomy issue rather than one of academic freedom. Tying the two points together is a quote from David Leslie:

---

*This chapter is a revision of one in a previous edition by T. R. McConnell who has since died. It is dedicated to his memory.

If such autonomy exists, and if such autonomy has been tested vis-à-vis individual rights—as it has many times—then the argument for expanding and protecting university autonomy under a newer theory of corporate freedom needs to account for whatever inadequacies may exist under the traditional theories. Such an accounting does not seem to have been offered in the key decisions on this new corporate freedom.[1]

According to this schema, while any threat to academic freedom is to be stoutly resisted, there are no *a priori* grounds for judging the rightness or wrongness of external interventions which impact on autonomy. The issues must be examined one by one. The remainder of this chapter will elaborate on the interplay between academic freedom and autonomy issues on the one hand, and accountability to the public interest on the other.

Autonomy and Academic Freedom

If a college or university is effectively to define its goals and select or invent the means of attaining them, it must have a high degree of substantive autonomy. Bowen has observed that the "production process" in higher education is far more intricate and complicated than that in any industrial enterprise.[2] Turning resources into human values defies standardization. Students vary enormously in academic aptitude, in interests, in intellectual dispositions, in social and cultural characteristics, in educational and vocational objectives, and in many other ways. Furthermore, the disciplines and professions with which institutions of higher learning are concerned require different methods of investigation, diverse intellectual structures, different means of relating methods of inquiry and ideas to personal and social values, and variable processes of relating knowledge to human experience. Learning, consequently, is a subtle process, the nature of which may vary from student to student, from institution to institution, from discipline to discipline, from one scholar and/or teacher to another, and from one level of student development to another. The intricacy and unpredictability of both learning and investigation are factors that require a high degree of freedom from intellectually limiting external intervention and control if an institution of higher education is to perform effectively.

On first thought one might identify academic freedom with autonomy. Certainly a high degree of intellectual independence is necessary for faculty and students in choosing the subjects of study and investigation, searching for the truth without unreasonable or arbitrary restrictions, and expressing their scholarly conclusions without censorship. Some forms of external control or even some kinds of subtle efforts to influence teaching, learning, or research may endanger intellectual freedom. However, academic freedom and university autonomy, though related, are not synonymous. Academic freedom as a concept is universal and absolute, whereas autonomy is of necessity parochial and relative.

Presumably statewide boards of higher education designating the missions of sectors or particular institutions after appropriate studies and consultation would not be an unwarranted invasion of autonomy. Specifying the academic programs, academic organization, curriculum, and methods of teaching for the attainment of designated missions is likely to be considered an unjustified form of intervention. A coordinating or governing board might phase out a doctoral program at a particular campus (after appropriate study and consultation) without unwarranted invasion of institutional autonomy or violation of academic freedom. The federal government might impose anti-discrimination procedures in admitting students, or appointing and promoting faculty members, without interfering unjustifiably in academic affairs provided the means do not make unreasonable demands on the institutions or violate necessary confidentiality of records. If appropriate safeguards are followed, no invasion of academic freedom need be suffered.

Requirements for accountability may impose onerous procedures on an institution, e.g., accounting for the use of research grants (as noted later in this chapter), but even these restraints may not endanger academic freedom. Whether restrictions on DNA research, referred to below, put an undesirable limit on choice of problems for investigation remains to be seen. In this case public protection may justify what seems to be an infringement on academic freedom.

In any event, Dressel, in an analysis of the autonomy of public institutions, came to the following conclusion: "Academic freedom is not ensured by institutional autonomy, and recent restrictions of institutional autonomy have had relatively little effect on academic freedom."[3]

One may agree that the absence of external controls does not guarantee academic freedom, and that certain elements of external control do not endanger intellectual independence. But an institution's right to mobilize its intellectual resources—and, within reasonable limits, even its financial resources—toward the attainment of its agreed-upon purposes is at least strongly fortified by a relatively high degree of autonomy.

Nature of Accountability

Intellectual freedom in colleges and universities is not under special threat, but autonomy is being steadily eroded. Financial austerity causes legislatures, statewide coordinating boards, and even consolidated governing boards to look more critically at institutional roles, at the availability and distribution of functions and programs, at effectiveness, and at educational and operational costs. As the federal government extends support for higher education, it prohibits discrimination in the admission of students, and in the appointment and promotion of faculty members. This is an example of the fact that the public at large is becoming more conscious of its institutions of higher education.

States and localities are more demanding of education and service, more critical of what they perceive institutions to be doing, more vocal in expressing their criticisms and desires. Public institutions, always answerable to the general interest, will no longer be excused from defending what they do or don't do. No longer can a university shunt public criticism aside as a mere expression of intellectual shallowness. It will increasingly have to explain itself, defend its essential character, and demonstrate that its service is worth the cost. It will become increasingly answerable, i.e., accountable, to its numerous constituencies for the range of its services and the effectiveness of its performance. "The extension of substantive autonomy to an individual, organization, or group implies responsibility and accountability," Dressel wrote recently.[4] He went on to outline the elements of accountability as follows:

> Responsible performance, then, involves using allocated resources legally and wisely to attain those purposes for which they were made available. Responsible performance requires continuing accumulation of evidence of the extent to which purposes are achieved; reviewing the evaluation evidence to clarify the avowed goals and their interpretation; consideration of the relevance, effectiveness, and costs of the processes used to achieve the goals; and continuing effort directed at improving the educational processes used or finding more effective processes.[5]

Relationships between the federal government and research universities have recently become strained as the former has attempted to impose techniques of accountability for federal research grants that the institutions have considered unreasonable, onerous, and unnecessarily expensive. In 1978 the National Commission on Research was organized for the purpose of proposing means of resolving the differences between the two parties. The Commission recognized three forms of accountability: financial and administrative, involving evidence of financial propriety and compliance with administrative regulations; scientific, concerned with achievement of results and progress toward scientific objectives; and social, referring to the extent to which specific social goals have been fulfilled. The Commission concluded that "When well designed, the system of accountability involves an appropriate balance between independence and control, between incentives and constraints, and between the costs and benefits of the various procedures and requirements used."[6]

Accountability and Intervention

Accountability is not confined to an institution's external relationships. Internally, a college or university is a complex of mutual responsibilities and reciprocal pressures for accountability. Important as these bases of accountability are, this chapter will be devoted to a discussion of accountability to external agencies.

External accountability often emanates from external intervention, but intervention often goes well beyond reasonable requirements for accountability. In any event, intervention and accountability should be discussed together. The first subject is higher education's accountability to the public interest.

Accountability to the Public

Ultimately, public institutions of higher education are broadly answerable to the people who support them. After California voters had failed to approve a state bond issue providing large sums for the construction of medical school facilities and had given other evidences of disaffection, the president of the University of California recognized the ultimate public accountability of the University when he said to the Assembly of the Academic Senate:

> Make no mistake, the university is a public institution, supported by the people through the actions of their elected representatives and executives. They will not allow it to be operated in ways which are excessively at variance with the general public will. By various pressures and devices the university will be forced to yield and to conform if it gets too far away from what the public expects and wants.[7]

At one time the people were relatively remote from their public institutions, but citizens now find their future economic, social, and cultural life increasingly influenced, in some cases virtually determined, by their colleges and universities. Consequently, the public university has had to become responsive to a wider range of economic interests and to a more diverse pattern of ethnic and cultural backgrounds and aspirations. Minority groups are pressing for financial assistance, for remedial programs when necessary for admission or attainment of academic standards, and for academic programs that will meet their interests and perceived needs. As special interest groups have pressed the university to provide the services they believe they need, students have organized to promote their interests. With the prospect of declining enrollments, many colleges and universities have responded to that student market by establishing new vocational and professional programs of study, and most institutions are struggling to redistribute faculty, equipment, and resources as students shift from liberal arts courses to vocational and professional curricula. This trend has been especially observable in the community colleges, and the effect will change the pattern of enrollment in four-year institutions to which community college graduates have transferred in large numbers in the past.

Serving the public interest has become a complicated process; not all institutions will undertake the same missions or serve common purposes. Accountability is still further complicated by a question of what special interests should be served and what should be put aside. Only when an institution's goals are defined, the groups to be served are identified, and the relevant programs of teaching, research, and public service are determined can an institution's effectiveness be estimated. Thus, accountability is both general—to the broad public interest—and particular—to more limited constituencies.

Accountability to the public is mediated by the operation of several layers of representation between it and the institutions in question. Colleges and universities are answerable immediately to their governing boards. Most boards have statutory status. They were created by legislatures and are in nearly all respects under legislative control. Seven or eight states have given constitutional status to their public universities. This unusual situation has been characterized as follows:

> The idea was to remove questions of management, control, and the supervision of the universities from the reach of politicians in state legislatures and governors' offices. The universities were to be a fourth branch of government, functioning co-authoritatively with the legislature, the judiciary, and the executive.[8]

The purpose in creating their constitutional position was to give the universities a much greater degree of autonomy and self-direction than statutory status would provide. Their autonomy, however, has been materially eroded over the years. A study of statutory and constitutional boards showed that the supposedly constitutionally autonomous university "is losing a good deal of its ability to exercise final judgment on the use not only of its state funds but also of those derived from other sources. It now undergoes intensive reviews of budgets and programs by several different state agencies, by special commissions, and by legislative committees, all of which look for ways to control."[9]

Government Interference

STATE GOVERNMENT INTERVENTION

Whether an institution has statutory or constitutional status, or even whether it is public or private, it is moving into the governmental orbit. As Clark put it: "In the changing relation between higher education and government, higher education . . . moves inside government, becomes a constituent part of government, a bureau within public administration."[10]

Most students of university governance believe that government officials should not serve on governing boards, since this identifies the institution too closely with political and governmental agencies. In California the governor, the lieutenant governor, the superintendent of public instruction, the president of the state board of agriculture, and the speaker of the legislative assembly are among the ex officio voting members of the Board of Regents of the University of California. A governor may also use his/her appointive power in attempting to influence governing boards, although most boards have staggered terms which prevent governors from appointing a majority of members until they have served several years in office.

However, sometimes a governor can accomplish through other means what he/she lacks the power to do through direct appointment of trustees/regents. For example, when Ronald Reagan was Governor of California, he heartily disapproved of the way that President Clark Kerr was handling the mid-1960s' student uprisings. There was already a minority of University Regents who agreed with Governor Reagan; to them he added a few appointments which had fallen vacant. He still lacked a majority, however, until he emphatically noted that the University's budget did not have constitutional autonomy, and that he would not look kindly at continued resistance to his point of view. Consequently, Clark Kerr later noted that he had left the University as he had come to it: "fired with enthusiasm!" For enough additional Regents had been intimidated by the Governor's statements to swing to his side.

Although he/she may thus influence institutions via their governing boards, it is ". . . through the executive budget process that the governor makes his/her impact and gives significant leadership on major issues of higher education policy."[11] The state finance or budget officer, who is ordinarily responsible to the governor, may also exercise an important element of authority by controlling shifts or changes in line-item budgets. Some state finance departments conduct pre-audits of expenditures that not only pass on the legality of the use of itemized funds, but give the state officer the opportunity to rule on the substance or purpose of the expenditures. In recent times the long arms of state finance officers have reached into academic affairs by conducting program audits or even program evaluations.[12]

Important as the understanding and support of executive officers of state government may be, public colleges and universities are even more directly answerable to the legislature. The institutions are dependent on legislative understanding of their broad missions and programs, the legislature's financial support, and the lawmakers' judgment of the institutions' educational effectiveness.

As noted above, even a constitutionally autonomous public university is ultimately accountable to the legislature for the ways in which it uses its state-appropriated funds and for the effectiveness of its educational services. Legislators have become increasingly restless in the face of what some regard as the continuing neglect of undergraduate teaching and the over-emphasis on research. Studies of faculty workload are becoming more common, with some legislatures considering mandated faculty teaching loads.

PROGRAM AUDITING

State agencies including legislatures have also begun to move into program evaluation. Dressel has outlined what is involved in program auditing:

Issues raised in program evaluation include the consistency of the program with the assigned institutional role and function; the adequacy of planning in regard to the objectives, program structure, processes, implementation, and evaluation of outcomes; the adherence of program operation to the objectives, structural features, processes, sequence, and outcome appraisal originally specified or the presentation of a sound rationale for any deviations from the original prescription; an evaluation of planning and operation and use of feedback for alteration and improvement, and provision for cost benefit analyses.[13]

After investigating legislatively mandated program evaluations in Wisconsin and Virginia, one of us found that academic programs, quality considerations, course content, and faculty evaluation had always been considered too close to the heart of academe to be subjected to normal state accountability measures.[14] If institutions, systems, or statewide coordinating boards, in company with colleges and universities under their surveillance, do not keep their academic programs under periodic appraisal, external agencies will take over this function.

ACCOUNTABILITY TO STATE COORDINATING BOARDS

Financial austerity, the need to diversify opportunities for higher education, governmental demands for accountability, and other influences have pushed decision making upward in the authority structure both internally and externally. In the course of this development, statewide governing and coordinating boards have come to play an influential, often critical, role in the evolution of higher education.

Three broad kinds of agencies have been organized for statewide or system-wide planning and coordination. These are (1) the advisory coordinating board, (2) the regulatory coordinating board, and (3) the consolidated governing board. There are ten advisory boards, eighteen regulatory boards, twenty consolidated governing boards, and two states with executive planning agencies only.[15]

Consolidated governing boards are by definition powerful bodies, because they literally govern the institutions which they also plan and coordinate. Their identification as advocates for the institutions is pretty clear in most states with consolidated boards.

In contrast, regulatory coordinating boards, with which we are mainly concerned here, have a more ambivalent status, poised as they are between the institutional governing boards and the state offices. Recently they have also become influential agencies. Where does the coordinating board fall between institutions or systems and the state government? Millett, who once served as chancellor of the Ohio Board of Regents, a statewide coordinating board, believes that such an agency is a part of state government and as such "will inevitably be identified primarily with state government officials and processes," while the consolidated governing board is identified with state institutions of higher education.[16]

Another view of the status and function of statewide coordinating boards is that they should not be "identified primarily with state government officials and processes," as Millett asserts,[17] but that they should be "suspended at a strategic—and extremely sensitive—point between the institutions and sectors, on the one hand, and the public and its political representatives, on the other." The function of coordinating boards as intermediaries has been expressed as follows:

Coordinating agencies have the responsibility for helping protect institutions (and sectors) from ill-advised influences and incursions by the legislative and executive branches of government and from unwise public pressures, and the responsibility of leading the system of higher education to serve demonstrable and appropriate public needs—all the while retaining the confidence of both sides.[18]

This view brings the nature of the coordinating board more nearly to that of the consolidated governing board, although the latter will in most cases be more intimately identified with the institutions. The primary function of coordinating boards is to plan the development of higher education in their states in cooperation with institutions of postsecondary education and their basic constituencies. Then, according to Glenny, the board should provide a thorough analysis and evaluation of system-wide or statewide academic programs in relation to long-range strategy. Proposed budgets should be appraised in relation to educational priorities, differential institutional functions, and relevant allocation of financial resources.[19] Thus the boards may exert their influence and authority by holding institutions or systems accountable for the effective performance of the functions for which they have accepted responsibility. Dressel has declared that coordination is here to stay, and that it will continue to confront institutions of higher education with issues of autonomy and sometimes debatable requirements for accountability.[20]

FEDERAL INTERVENTION

With increasing federal financial support and numerous federal laws and regulations governing use of the funds, both public and private educational institutions find themselves increasingly accountable to agencies of the federal government. Total federal support in fiscal 1992 reached about 29 billion dollars, awarded and controlled by a variety of governmental bureaus. It was both inevitable and appropriate that higher institutions should be held accountable for the way in which they expend these funds. However, tension between universities and federal granting agencies has steadily increased as the institutions have been subjected to regulations and accounting procedures they consider unnecessarily extensive, expensive, and often inappropriate.

One of the major causes of strain between the federal government and the universities is the failure of government agencies to recognize, in the words of the report of the National Commission on Research, that "[u]niversities carry out teaching, research, and service as an integrated whole, not as separate functions." The Commission went on to say that since teaching, research, and perhaps public service are closely related, accurate costs cannot be assessed to each of the related outcomes.[21] Nevertheless, the Commission recognized the necessity for accountability. What is needed, said the Commission, is a joint effort between research universities and government bureaus to devise methods of accountability that recognize the peculiar characteristics of the academic enterprise.

An example of the federal government's demand for accountability is its regulation of DNA research. After an international group of 150 scientists met to discuss how DNA research should be conducted, the National Institutes of Health appointed a committee that promulgated regulations governing the safety of recombinant DNA research done with NIH funds. It was not long until a university faculty member experienced first hand the new strictures of DNA investigation. A bio-safety committee of the University of California at San Diego forbade a faculty member in biology to conduct any more cloning experiments after it was charged that he copied genetic material from a virus then banned from use in such investigations. The University's bio-safety committee reported its action to the National Institutes of Health and the NIH said that it would form a committee to study the University's report and consider what action it might take against the University or the professor. The NIH Committee found the faculty member guilty of violating the federal guidelines.

It would be an exaggeration to say that research universities have become departments of federal and state governments, but it is not too much to say that they have become more directly accountable to government agencies in manifold ways, and that it has become difficult to distinguish governmental *intervention* in university affairs from *reasonable* governmental requirements for accountability. It is clear, however, that recent issues and events have accelerated invasions of university autonomy. Senator Moynihan has gone so far as to say that "universities must now expect a long, for practical purposes permanent, regimen of pressure from the federal government to pursue this or that national purpose, purposes often at variance with the interests or inclinations of the universities themselves."[22]

GOVERNMENTAL ACCOUNTABILITY OF PRIVATE INSTITUTIONS

Although governmental intervention, regulation, and incipient control of certain activities may threaten public more than private institutions of higher education, the latter are increasingly held accountable by governmental agencies. Private research universities, as are publicly supported ones, are accountable for the way in which they use federal grants. Furthermore, private institutions are required to comply with other federal regulations, such as those prohibiting discrimination in employment.[23] The Carnegie Council on Policy Studies in

Higher Education recommended that "[f]inancial aid to students should be the primary (though not necessarily the exclusive) vehicle for the channeling of state funds to private institutions."[24] Some state governments, however, do make direct grants to private colleges and universities. An Illinois commission recommended that as a means of avoiding government intervention in private higher institutions, direct state grants should be channeled to them in the form of contracts administered by the statewide coordinating board.[25]

Judicial Intervention

RECOURSE TO THE COURTS

Increasingly intimate relationships between government and higher education mean that colleges and universities are in and of the world, not removed and protected from it. Toward the end of the period of student disruption on college campuses one of us observed:

> Judicial decisions and the presence on campus of the community police, the highway patrol, and the National Guard symbolize the fact that colleges and universities have increasingly lost the privilege of self-regulation to the external authority of the police and the courts. . . . It is apparent that colleges and universities have become increasingly accountable to the judicial system of the community, the state, and the national government.[26]

Kaplin's book on higher education and the law summarizes legal conditions bearing on higher institutions, and gives numerous examples of court decisions involving trustees, administrators, faculty members, and students, as well as cases involving relationships between institutions and both state and federal governments. Recourse to the courts to settle disputes has increased greatly during the past decade. Faculty members may sue over dismissal, appointment, tenure, and accessibility to personnel records. Students may sue to secure access to their records, over discrimination in admissions (e.g., the DeFunis case at the University of Washington and the Bakke case at the University of California in Davis), and over failure by an institution to deliver what it promised from the classroom and other academic resources. Institutions may take governments to court for the purpose of protecting their constitutional status and, as we have illustrated above, in contention over the enforcement of federal regulations.

The traditional aloofness of the campus has been shattered. Kaplin has pointed out that "higher education was often viewed as a unique enterprise which could regulate itself through reliance on tradition and consensual agreement. It operated best by operating autonomously, and it thrived on the privacy which autonomy afforded."[27] The college or university sanctuary was once considered to be a necessary means of protecting the institution and its constituencies from repressive external control and from invasions of intellectual freedom. Now other means must be devised to protect an institution's essential spirit while it bows to the world of law and tribunal.

Accountability to Other Agencies

ACCOUNTABILITY TO ACCREDITING AGENCIES

Accreditation is a process for holding postsecondary institutions accountable to voluntary agencies for meeting certain minimum educational standards. Recently, however, both federal and state governments have entered this arena too.

Institutional and program accreditation are the two types usually noted. Six regional agencies are responsible for accrediting entire institutions with their schools, departments, academic programs, and related activities. Program accreditation, extended by professional societies or other groups of specialists or vocational associations, is extended to a specific school, department, or academic program in such fields as medicine, law, social work, chemistry, engineering, or business administration. A variation is an agency for accrediting single-purpose institutions, such as trade and technical schools. These kinds of accrediting bodies are independent, voluntary agencies.

Two of the principal factors that have brought accreditation to the fore in discussions of accountability are the consumer movement and the allocation of state and federal aid to postsecondary education. Certain federal laws require the Secretary of Education to publish a list of nationally recognized agencies considered to be "reliable" evaluators of academic quality as a basis for distributing federal aid. An account of the federal government's attitude toward voluntary accrediting bodies noted that the head of the Division of Eligibility and Agency Evaluation of the U.S. Department of Education had urged that federal oversight of accreditation should be strengthened. "Stressing the need for greater public accountability," said the report, "he and his supporters say it is more important than ever for the government to know how its money is being spent, especially in light of some institutions' widely reported abuses in handling student-aid funds."[28] The recent self-closure of the Council on Postsecondary Accreditation leaves a vacuum, which a Task Force of the American Council on Education is trying to make recommendations to fill.

In the meantime, state governments have become parties to the debate as they determine eligibility for state aid to both public and private post-secondary institutions. Most states charter and license degree-granting institutions, but some observers believe that in most instances the standards specified are insufficient to assure quality. The Education Commission of the States has urged that the states should establish minimum quality standards for all postsecondary institutions.

Accountability for Student Development:
A Complicated Process

It is apparent that educational institutions are increasingly to be held answerable for the attainment of their professed goals in the form of demonstrable changes in students. Bowen had declared that "the idea of accountability in higher education is quite simple. It means that colleges and universities are responsible for conducting their affairs so that the outcomes are worth the cost."[29] This view may be simple in conception, but it is also extremely difficult in implementation. First of all, it is difficult but essential to translate goals into relevant outcomes. An even more complicated task is to devise means of determining the extent to which students have attained these outcomes. The first question to be asked is, how has the student changed at a given point in relation to this characteristic at entrance? This requires information on how students vary at the starting point, not only in previous academic achievement, but in general and special academic aptitude; intellectual dispositions, such as a theoretical or pragmatic orientation; and interests, attitudes, values, and motivations, to mention only some of the dimensions of personality that are relevant to the educational process. These attributes not only establish base lines for estimating the amount of change over stated periods, but some of them are indicative of students' educability.

Studies of the influence of institutions on student development also require means of measuring or describing college characteristics, "the prevailing atmosphere, the social and intellectual climate, the style of a campus," as well as "educational treatments."[30] One of the complications involved in describing college environments is that student characteristics and institutional qualities are by no means unrelated. Furthermore, most institutions are not all of a piece and the "total environment" may have less influence on particular students than the suborganizations or subcultures of which they are members.

It is even more difficult to determine the impact of the environment on students. We have mentioned some of the difficulties elsewhere:

First, environmental variables probably do not act singly, but in combination. Second, changes which occur in students may not be attributable to the effect of the college environment itself. Developmental processes established early in the individual's experience may continue through the college years; some of these processes take place normally within a wide range of environmental conditions, and in order to alter the course and extent of development, it would be necessary to introduce fairly great changes in environmental stimulation. Third, changes which occur during the college years may be less the effect of college experience as such than of the general social environment in which the college exists and the students live.[31]

For these and many other reasons it is extremely difficult to relate changes in behavior to specific characteristics of the college or to particular patterns of educational activity. Studies of change in students' characteristics have revealed wide differences from person to person and detectable differences from institution to institution.

Bowen has summarized the evidence on changes in students in both cognitive and noncognitive outcomes, and also differences in the effects of different institutions. "On the whole," he wrote, "the evidence supports the hypothesis that the differences in impact are relatively small—when impact is defined as value added in the form of change in students during the college years."[32] Nevertheless, institutions are accountable for stimulating the development of students in ways which give evidence that colleges and universities have attained their professed goals in reasonable measure.

To date, the research on changes in students has been done mainly in undergraduate education. Fundamental studies on the attainment of outcomes also need to be made in professional and graduate education, as well as in research and public service. Bowen has discussed at some length the social benefits that flow from professional training and the social outcomes from research and public service. He also has emphasized the interaction of liberal and professional studies, and the contribution of research and public service to education of various kinds and levels. Learning is an integrated process which may involve scholarship, investigation, and the relationship of knowledge to personal enrichment and social welfare.[33] Although the definition and measurement of outcomes are especially difficult at higher educational levels and the environmental forces involved are hard to determine, studies of student development in such fields as professional training, graduate education, and research should be pursued.

State Assessment Programs

Notwithstanding the complexity of the processes described above, a considerable number of states have established policies seeking to assess student learning in one form or another. The early pathbreakers were Florida, Virginia, New Jersey and Ohio, followed by about ten other states in differing forms of programs. In a very few states mandated state testing of undergraduates was required, sometimes serving as a gateway process to upper division study. But in most states the key policy makers were persuaded to place the responsibility for developing the assessment program at the door of each public institution, allowing them to develop programs appropriate to their particular role and mission. While it is sometimes considered a drawback of this route that the results of the varying assessment programs cannot be compared across the institutions, with judgments about "winners and losers", the conventional wisdom response is that only by allowing for such diversity is it likely that the institutions will gain a sense of ownership in the process and be encouraged to use the results for self-improvement. In its 1986 report, *Time for Results,* the Task

Force on College Quality of the National Governors' Association revealed an awareness of this problem, but also made forceful recommendations about moving the process along more quickly.[34]

Educational Costs

After summarizing the available evidence on the outcomes of higher education, Bowen observed that "a tidy dollar comparison of costs and benefits is conspicuously absent." However, he summarized the financial value of higher education as follows:

First, the monetary returns from higher education alone are probably sufficient to offset all the costs. Second, the nonmonetary returns are several times as valuable as the monetary returns. And third, the total returns from higher education in all its aspects exceed the cost by several times.[35]

It is usually said that institutions should be accountable for both effectiveness and efficiency, the latter having to do with the cost of the outcomes attained. But costs are extremely difficult to compute in analyzing differences in student change both within and among institutions. And, as pointed out above, it is extremely difficult to relate changes to significant features of educational environments. Nevertheless, as enrollments in postsecondary education level off or decline, institutions will be increasingly held accountable for the attainment of goals inherent in their assigned or professed missions. "Accountability accentuates results," wrote Mortimer; "it aims squarely at what comes out of an educational system rather than what goes into it."[36] Perhaps it would be more telling to say that accountability aims squarely at what comes out of an educational system in relation to what goes into it. The outcomes to be attained must be more explicitly defined and the means of determining accomplishment must be more expertly devised. Then resources must be distributed among institutions and among academic services in accordance with chosen educational values and defensible costs of their attainment. Bowen has made a significant contribution to the analysis of institutional costs including expenditures per student, cost differences among institutions, and the implications of cost data for administrative policies and decisions.[37] But we have a long way to go before sound means of determining cost-effectiveness are developed.

Conclusion

Although autonomy cannot be absolute, only a high degree of independence will permit colleges and universities to devise and choose effective academic means of realizing their professed goals. First of all, institutions must assure academic freedom to faculty and students. Autonomy does not guarantee intellectual independence, but some forms of external intervention, overt or covert, may undermine such freedom.

While intellectual fetters must be decisively opposed, institutions may legitimately be expected to be held accountable to their constituencies for the integrity, and as far as possible, for the efficiency of their operations. Colleges and universities are answerable to the general public, which supports them and needs their services. Responding to the public interest, federal and state governments are increasingly intervening in institutional affairs. At times government pressure may induce an institution to offer appropriate services; at other times government agencies may attempt to turn an institution, or even a system, in inappropriate directions. Only constructive consultation, and requirements for accountability that recognize the fundamental characteristics of academe will effectively serve the public interest and give vitality to the educational enterprise.

Most institutions, including those supported by legislatures, are not immediately controlled by the general public. Public accountability is mediated by several layers of representation. Institutions are directly answerable to their governing boards. They may be responsible to a consolidated governing board. They may be first responsible to institutional or systemwide governing boards, and these in turn may be in certain regards under surveillance of statewide coordinating boards. Institutions thus may be controlled by a hierarchy of agencies, an arrangement that may complicate their procedures for accountability, but that may provide a measure of protection from unwise or unnecessary external intervention.

Colleges and universities are moving into a period when they will be expected to provide, not only data on the attainment of defined outcomes, including changes in students during undergraduate, graduate, and professional education, but evidence that results have been gained at "reasonable" cost. Institutions of higher education will have to specify their aims, stand ready to justify activities by demonstrating their contribution to objectives, and defend the cost of the enterprise.

Notes

1. David Leslie, "Academic Freedom for Universities," *The Review of Higher Education* 9 (1986): 135–57.

2. Howard R. Bowen, *Investment in Learning* (San Francisco: Jossey-Bass, 1977), p. 12.

3. Paul L. Dressel, ed., *The Autonomy of Public Colleges* (San Francisco: Jossey-Bass, 1980), p. 13.

4. Ibid., p. 5.

5. Ibid., p. 96.

6. National Commission on Research, *Accountability: Restoring the Quality of*

the Partnership (Washington, D.C., 1980), p. 17.

7. C. J. Hitch, "Remarks of the President" (Address delivered to the Assembly of the California Academic Senate, Berkeley, Calif., June 15, 1970).

8. Lyman A. Glenny and Thomas K. Dalglish, *Public Universities, State Agencies, and the Law: Constitutional Autonomy in Decline* (Berkeley, Calif.: University of California, Center for Research and Development in Higher Education, 1973), p. 42.

9. Ibid., p. 143.

10. Burton R. Clark, "The Insulated Americans: Five Lessons from Abroad," *Change* 10 (November 1978).

11. John W. Lederle, "Governors and Higher Education," in *State Politics and Higher Education,* ed. Leonard E. Goodall (Dearborn, Mich.: University of Michigan, 1976), pp. 43–50.

12. Paul L. Dressel, *Autonomy of Public Colleges,* p. 40.

13. Ibid., p. 43.

14. Robert O. Berdahl, "Legislative Program Evaluation," in *Increasing the Public Accountability of Higher Education,* ed. John K. Folger (San Francisco: Jossey-Bass, 1977), pp. 35–65.

15. See chapter 7 in this volume.

16. John D. Millett, "Statewide Coordinating Boards and Statewide Governing Boards," in *Evaluating Statewide Boards,* ed. Robert O. Berdahl (San Francisco: Jossey-Bass, 1975), pp. 61–70.

17. Ibid., p. 70.

18. Kenneth P. Mortimer and T. R. McConnell, *Sharing Authority Effectively* (San Francisco: Jossey-Bass, 1978), p. 225.

19. Lyman A. Glenny, *State Budgeting for Higher Education: Interagency Conflict and Consensus* (Berkeley, Calif.: Center for Research and Development in Higher Education, University of California, 1976), pp. 148–50.

20. Paul L. Dressel, ed., *The Autonomy of Public Colleges,* pp. 99–100.

21. National Commission on Research, *Accountability,* p. 3.

22. Daniel Patrick Moynihan, "State vs. Academe," *Harpers* 261 (December 1980): 31–40.

23. Robert O. Berdahl, "The Politics of State Aid," in *Public Policy and Private Higher Education,* ed. David W. Breneman and Chester E. Finn, Jr. (Washington, D.C.: Brookings Institution, 1978), pp. 321–52.

24. Carnegie Council on Policy Studies in Higher Education, *The States and Private Higher Education* (San Francisco: Jossey-Bass, 1977), p. 63.

25. Commission to Study Nonpublic Higher Education in Illinois, *Strengthening Private Higher Education in Illinois: A Report on the State's Role* (Springfield, Ill.: Board of Higher Education, 1969).

26. T. R. McConnell, "Accountability and Autonomy," *Journal of Higher Education* 42 (June 1971): 446–63.

27. William A. Kaplin, *The Law of Higher Education* (San Francisco: Jossey-Bass, 1983), p. 4.

28. *Chronicle of Higher Education* 20 (June 16, 1980).

29. Howard R. Bowen, "The Products of Higher Education," in *Evaluating Institutions for Accountability,* ed. Howard R. Bowen (San Francisco: Jossey-Bass, 1974), pp. 1–26.

30. C. R. Pace, "When Students Judge Their College," *College Board Review* 58 (Spring 1960): 26–28.

31. T. R. McConnell, "Accountability and Autonomy."

32. Howard R. Bowen, *Investment in Learning,* p. 257. Other evidence on changes in students over the college years is presented in Alexander W. Astin, *Four Critical Years* (San Francisco: Jossey Bass, 1977).

33. Ibid.

34. National Governors' Association Task Force on College Quality, *Time for Results* (Washington, D.C.: National Governors' Association, 1986).

35. Howard R. Bowen, *Investment in Learning,* pp. 447–48.

36. Kenneth P. Mortimer, *Accountability in Higher Education* (Washington, D.C.: American Association for Higher Education, 1972), p. 6.

37. Howard R. Bowen, *The Cost of Higher Education* (San Francisco: Jossey-Bass, 1980).

4

Academic Freedom at the End of the Century: Professional Labor, Gender, and Professionalization

Sheila Slaughter

In this chapter I review the academic freedom cases investigated by the Association of American University Professors (AAUP) between 1980 and 1990, and compare them to my 1983 article on academic freedom cases for the decade 1970–1980.[1] Given that challenges to academic freedom shift as historical conditions change, I thought that a comparison between the two decades would be useful, allowing us to see how closely we need to guard established danger zones, and to see if there are new terrains in need of protection.[2] I use a broad construction of academic freedom, similar to that used by the American Association of University Professors.[3] I see academic freedom as encompassing faculty rights to free inquiry under all circumstances and to free communication in the classroom; faculty rights to hire, fire and promote colleagues; and collective faculty rights to self-governance. Generally, I assume that faculty are the heart of the university, and understand that all faculty rights have corresponding responsibilities related to sustaining the common good of the professoriate's teaching, research and service endeavors.

Very generally, there were a number of changes in academic freedom cases during the past two decades. Financial exigency or retrenchment cases accounted for the largest numbers of dismissals of tenured faculty in both decades.[4] In the 1970s, retrenchment was usually preceded by declarations of financial exigency, and was an unexpected, cataclysmic event. In the 1980s, retrenchment initiated a general restructuring of postsecondary education. In the 1970s, gender did not figure in the academic freedom cases; in the 1980s, sex discrimination emerged as a category. In the 1970s, cases related to the student movement and faculty opposition to the war in Vietnam were numerous; in the 1980s, there were fewer cases that turned on the faculty's ideological deviance. Administrative abuse cases, in which administrators arbitrarily and capriciously abrogated faculty rights, occurred in both decades, increasing somewhat in the 1980s.

My analysis of the academic freedom cases concentrates on the cases of the 1980s. I use the cases of the 1970s primarily to illuminate the changes that have occurred. In addition to analysis of specific cases of the 1980s, I try to contextualize these cases in broad social and political economic perspectives that have implications for academic freedom. The perspectives to which I give most attention are: (1) challenges to academic freedom that result from concentration of decision-making powers in university management; (2) threats to academic freedom that arise from a broad restructuring of professional labor; (3) problems that stem from contested gender ideologies; (4) difficulties created by the failure of faculty professionalization to curb or counter administrative exercise of power, especially at small, non-elite institutions.

Data and Method

The data for this article are all of the cases reported in the Committee A "Academic Freedom and Tenure" section of Academe between January 1980 and December 1990. The AAUP is probably the best central, national data source for academic freedom cases. However, the AAUP has several weaknesses as a data source: it is not comprehensive, and it is not the only source. Many violations of academic freedom are probably not reported at all. Although the AAUP investigates complaints regardless of whether or not faculty members who brings them are members of the association, the timorous, deviant or cynical may never contact the Association. Faculty who choose to pursue violations of academic freedom have a number of alternatives to the AAUP. They can resort to institutional grievance procedures. They can litigate. They can turn to unions or other academic organizations, such as associations of learned or professional societies. They can approach the press. Faculty who take these routes usually do not involve the AAUP, and their cases are not captured in this sample.

The cases reported in Academe present another problem as a data source; they are not necessarily representative of the complaints received by the AAUP.[5] Academe publishes only a fraction of the complaints the AAUP receives. The cases finally reported in Academe are the most serious, the ones that the AAUP staff thought were worth pursuing, the ones that could not be settled by informal mediation, the ones that call for a formal investigation by a committee of AAUP members, or the ones that result in censure. However, the process by which the AAUP staff chooses cases for Academe probably compensates for their unrepresentativeness and serves well my concern with understanding threats to academic freedom. The AAUP staff selects cases for *Academe* because they illuminate pressing problems facing the academic community.

As I read each of the forty-seven cases from the 1980s, I developed categories based on substantive topics. The development of categories was informed but not dictated by the categories that emerged from my previous study of the 1970s, which, in turn, was guided but not definitively shaped by the historical and sociological literature treating academic freedom cases.[6] The categories for the 1980s cases were retrenchment and program restructuring, administrative abuse, civil liberties, and sex discrimination. The cases were analyzed in terms of years they occurred, the issues involved, the characteristics of the faculty—race, gender, area of specialization—and what they said about power relations within the academy, and then treated in terms of the broader perspectives outlined above.

In the interests of brevity, at the beginning of each section and subsection of this article, I outline what I take to be the important trends in the several cases that constitute a category or sub-category. I select cases to illustrate the points I am making, but do not speak to each case nor to any case in great depth. Those interested in fuller presentation of data can look at the cases themselves, or, for retrenchment or program restructuring cases, at my article, "Retrenchment Cases in the 1980s: The Politics of Prestige and Gender."[7]

The document that constitutes a case—the report appearing in Academe— was prepared by an investigating committee with the aid of the AAUP staff. An investigating committee usually consists of two or three persons selected by AAUP staff and Committee A members. Their reports are based on examination of available documents and on-campus interviews with the faculty and administrators who are willing to talk to them. In interpreting these reports, I may make judgments and reach conclusions with which the investigating committees, Committee A and the AAUP may disagree.

Retrenchment and Program Restructuring Cases

In the 1970s, financial exigency cases accounted for approximately 10 percent of the AAUP cases, and 85 percent of the firings reported in *Academe*. In the 1980s, financial exigency cases represented 36 percent of such cases, and 81.5 percent of dismissals (see Table 1). In the 1970s, economic justification for dismissals usually involved a declaration of a financial exigency, or a statement that the institution as a whole was in serious financial straits. Substantial numbers of faculty were fired, as was the case with the City University of New York (CUNY), from which roughly one thousand faculty were fired.[8] Usually there was some concern with seniority and tenure, as in the CUNY case, in which nearly all the fired faculty were untenured. If more selective cuts were employed, administrators usually felt compelled to cut an entire unit or program rather than a single individual, and to dismiss the most senior faculty last.[9]

Table 1
Number of Cases and Number of Faculty Fired
in AAUP Academic Freedom Cases, 1980–1990

Category	Retrenchment/Program Restructuring	Administrative Abuse	Religious	Civil Liberties	Sex Discrimination	Misc.	TOTAL
Number of Cases*	17 (36%)	16 (34%)	5 (10%)	2 (4.5%)	2 (4.5%)	5 (10%)	47
Year	Number of Faculty						
1980	04	3	0	1	0	1	9
1981	22	0	0	0	0	2	24
1982	21	2	0	0	0	0	23
1983	30	2	0	1	0	0	33
1984	41	0	0	0	0	0	41
1985	35	7	1	0	0	0	43
1986	10	5	1	0	0	2	18
1987	27	1	1	0	0	1	30
1988	0	2	0	1	1	0	4
1989	0	1	3	0	0	0	4
1990	0	3	0	1	0	0	4
TOTALS	191** (82%)	26 (11%)	6 (2.5%)	2 (11%)	2 (11%)	6 (2.5%)	233

Source: Academic Freedom cases reported in *Academe*, 1980–1990

*Number of cases are different from number of faculty because each case may include many faculty

**The number of faculty retrenched in Table 1 differs somewhat from the number in Table 2 because Table 2 records all faculty who received dismissal notices, some of whom were later reinstated. Table 1 reports only those faculty who were clearly dismissed.

In the 1980s, retrenchment was not conceived of as an isolated event unlikely to occur again in the near future. "Retrenchment," as a concept, gave way to "restructuring." Academic managers—presidents, chancellors, provosts and other high level campus or system administrators—no longer declared states of financial exigency prior to terminating faculty. Instead, projected economic difficulties were used to justify firing faculty who were unproductive, a criterion that was variously defined. Academic administrators who engaged in restructuring never utilized across-the-board cuts and were rarely concerned with seniority and tenure. They no longer cut whole programs, but cut selectively within programs. Almost all faculty were vulnerable to consideration for dismissal during restructuring.

The 17 cases of financial exigency involved 190 faculty, 81.5 percent of all faculty fired between 1980–1990. Cases were almost evenly divided between public (9) and private (8) institutions. The number of faculty fired in the public higher education sector was much greater than the private, undoubtedly because of the larger size of public institutions. Four of the 17 institutions, all public, were organized to bargain collectively.[10]

PROGRAM RESTRUCTURING AND ACADEMIC FREEDOM

The most obvious opportunity that program restructuring offered for violation of academic freedom was dismissal under cover of retrenchment of professors whose speech was for some reason offensive to the administration. Although the investigating committees had difficulty proving selective firing under the guise of financial exigency, administrators occasionally were so flagrant in their pursuit of their faculty critics that their intentions were fairly obvious. Sonoma State College provided an example of an administrator who used financial difficulties as a pretext for firing faculty who disagreed with him.

In early 1982, in response to declining enrollments, the president at Sonoma State announced that he was restructuring existing programs to deal with students' shift in interests. To inform the faculty of the dimension of the restructuring proposed, he issued a "jeopardy list" that named fifty-three faculty as candidates for termination.[11] The professors at risk were on the list because their Teaching Services Area (TSA) faced "lack of funds or lack of work."[12] Although the president claimed to honor seniority in dismissals, the flexibility of the unit of retrenchment made determination of seniority difficult. A professor's TSA was determined by the administration, either in individual negotiations with faculty or unilaterally. TSAs were not co-terminous with departments. For example, in biology, the administration could define a TSA in molecular biology and a TSA in conventional biology, keep the former and eliminate the latter. The TSA was essentially a mechanism that allowed the president to consider each faculty member individually.

Professor William Crowley, chair of geography, publicly disagreed with the president about issues pertinent to the football program. Crowley was fourth in seniority in his TSA, and the President decided to keep only three tenured faculty. Crowley was terminated, even though one of his junior colleagues escaped dismissal because the untenured professor was able to transfer his TSA from geography to the "safe area" of computer science. Using the TSA as the unit of retrenchment, the administration was able to rid itself of a senior member of the department who acted as a critic, and keep a junior professor deemed more valuable.

STRATEGIC PLANNING AND ACADEMIC FREEDOM

Eight (47 percent) of the seventeen financial exigency cases explicitly used the planning process to identify faculty for dismissal. Administrators faced with declining enrollments or a marked shift in enrollment patterns used strategic planning to reshape programs by identifying faculty they termed non-productive. Although faculty participated in the planning process, administrators usually had the last word.

Goucher College provided an example of how strategic planning was used. Goucher had wrestled with declining enrollments and a precarious financial situation in the 1970s and had survived by aggressively building endowment and recruiting students.[13] By the early 1980s, Goucher had turned itself around: it substantially increased its enrollment, created a budget surplus and built up a healthy endowment. However, institutional projections for the 1980s indicated that the future was perilous. The president interpreted this data to mean that Goucher could survive the 1980s only by getting rid of classrooms in low enrollment fields and by building new programs more attractive to students. The president shared her data with the faculty, who interpreted them differently, objecting to making courses' popularity with students the basis of curricular decisions, and questioning the economic necessity for retrenchment. Despite faculty requests for reconsideration of the projections, the president fired five faculty, three of whom were tenured.

Temple University provided an example parallel to Goucher, but at a large, doctoral-granting public institution.[14] The president at Temple, like Goucher's president, saw himself as addressing the future with his plans for faculty terminations. He thought he would preempt future crises by firing faculty in fields with declining enrollments, better preparing the institution for the future. The faculty in the college most deeply affected by the president's strategic planning developed an alternative plan, but it did not satisfy the administration, and thirty-four faculty were dismissed.

Temple was unionized; the AAUP was the collective bargaining agent. The Chapter brought two grievances aimed at halting the dismissals. One alleged lack of faculty participation in the terminations, the other argued that the faculty could have been reassigned to areas related to their expertise. Both grievances went to outside arbitration and both lost, in part because the AAUP had negotiated a relatively weak retrenchment protection clause for the period during which the firings took place.[15]

Through strategic planning, college and university administrations asserted their right to make long range decisions about the curriculum. The authority to make such decisions was often formally vested in the administration through state administrative codes, as was the case at Sonoma State. In private institutions, as was the case at Goucher College, Boards of Trustees often specifically delegated power to retrench to administrators, excluding faculty from financial deliberations. Although administrators had formal authority for institutional decision making, they were also often bound by faculty by-laws and personnel policies that called for faculty participation in shared governance. The faculty devoted a great deal of effort to these processes. At Yeshiva, Goucher, Metropolitan Community Colleges (Missouri), Temple, and Morgan State, the faculty, through either the Senate or a collective bargaining agency, opposed administrative efforts, offered alternative analyses of institutional fiscal health, and developed strategies for institutional savings that preserved tenured faculty positions.[16] This activity drew on a deep reservoir of creative energy and institutional commitment on the part of faculty. The alternative strategies for retrenchment devised by the faculty were politely received by the various administrations, and largely ignored.

Administrators saw their plans as embodying broad concern for institutional health and for the institution as a whole. In other words, they saw themselves as concerned with student enrollments, work load patterns, the development of new and marketable areas of study, and the preservation of a core of basics. Administrators portrayed faculty as primarily concerned with saving their jobs and promoting their specialties. In the words of the Temple university attorney:

> The AAUP [chapter] seems to be ideologically unable to grasp the notion that it might be eminently reasonable for a university to spend its limited money strengthening academic departments in which student enrollments are stable and rising rather than subsidizing the salaries of faculty members who have no students to teach.[17]

Administrators took the moral high ground and were successfully able to preempt claims to represent the public interest or common good of the institution, while faculty, resting their authority on academic freedom, tenure, and expertise, were represented as a special interest.

Strategic planning posed problems to academic freedom because the process often undercut faculty authority with regard to curricular decisions and faculty review. In effect, administrators took over long range curricular decision making when they, not faculty, made decisions to expand some programs and cut others. Administrators also reviewed all faculty, tenured or not, when decisions to cut were made, effectively substituting their judgments about hiring and firing for peer review committees' judgments on promotion and tenure.

PART-TIME LABOR AND ACADEMIC FREEDOM

In the 1970s, there were no cases involving the use of part time labor; in the 1980s, there were three. Faculty salaries were the largest fixed cost of an institution. The use of part-time labor allowed institutions to reduce faculty costs significantly. Part-time professionals were paid a fraction of full-time faculty costs, received few or no benefits, and could be laid on or off to meet fluctuating institutional requirements. Part-time professional workers usually performed what were regarded as the most onerous institutional tasks—teaching and grading of undergraduate students.

At Eastern Oregon State College, program restructuring raised the possibility of the institution's rehiring fired full-time faculty on a part-time basis. Professor Carol E. Rathe, Music Education, was one of four faculty who were terminated in program reduction. Initially, she was kept on as a part-time tenured faculty. In other words, she was paid for a fraction of her tenured appointment. She was then reduced to a "teach only" basis.[18] This new status meant that she was re-hired to teach part of her former load, but on a per course basis rather than at a fraction of her former salary. The per course cost was much lower than a fraction of a tenured professor's salary. The rationale for the very low "teach only" salary was that she was not engaged in student advising, curriculum planning, supervising, and research. Finally, she was let go altogether.

The case caused a great deal of furor in the college and the system. Faculty passed a vote of no confidence on the president. A state system investigating committee was appointed. The state system committee eventually found that program reduction needed to be more clearly defined, but thought that the specific decision to fire Rathe was justified in order "to maintain strong programs and a sound budget." The faculty at Eastern Oregon State College took a position against tenuring faculty whose load was less than 1.0 FTE, on the grounds that the possibility of part-time tenure for faculty would be an invitation to reduce institutional costs by changing full-time faculty to part-time status. At Temple University the part-time labor issue was quite different than at Eastern Oregon State. At Temple, the issue was not change in the status of tenured faculty from full- to part-time, but reassignment of tenured faculty from one area to another.[19] A number of faculty slated for retrenchment at Temple claimed that they were able to teach in general education or in remedial programs, areas in which the university was currently hiring. Indeed, several of the faculty were already regularly teaching courses in these areas. However, the administration did not want to assign (relatively) highly paid, full-time faculty to low cost slots. The administration had a policy that kept the ratio of part to full-time faculty high in order to reduce costs through the use of graduate students and full-time non-tenured staff. At the Metropolitan Community Colleges (Missouri) the administration tried to increase faculty productivity by "speed-ups"—eliminating faculty, increasing the teaching load of the remaining faculty, and increasing the number of part-time faculty. Faced with a projected budget shortfall, the administration used strategic planning in an attempt to change the Master Plan ratios of full- to part-time faculty. The trustees and administrators changed the institution staffing parameters so that full-time faculty, who taught 80 percent of the credit hours, would teach 65 percent, thereby creating an excess 21 full-time faculty, who were slated for retrenchment. During a protracted struggle with the administration, lay-off notices were issued to 21 full-time faculty. Several of those faculty, in an attempt to protect their jobs, began working part-time on a substantially lower salary scale. A number of new part-timers were hired, and "overloads were assigned in most of the disciplines from which tenured faculty members had either been placed on layoff or, while continuing to teach, had been removed from tenured status."[20] Ultimately, the board and the administration compromised on the ratio of full- to part-time faculty, and only eight faculty were fired. In the part-time labor cases faculty were able to contain administrators' attempts to convert numerous full-time faculty members into part-time faculty, but they were not able to halt administrators' increased use of part-timers. The increased use of part-timers often meant speed-ups for full time faculty. Because part-time faculty were usually hired on a per-course basis, that meant full-time faculty had to give more time to advising students, commitee work, planning the curriculum, and supervising part-timers. Every time ratios of part- to full-time faculty increased, full-time faculty workload increased. The increased use of part-time faculty probabaly heightened the antagonism between part- and full time faculty, increasing the distaince between the two groups, with full-time faculty attempting to codify their rights and privileges in relation to part-time faculty. Indeed, these cases suggested the development of a two tier labor force, one full-time, the other part-time. The full-time tier had benefits and a degree of job security, and was at one and the same time supported and threatened by part-timers, who made full-timers workload possible even as they increased that workload and constituted a reserve labor pool, implicitly challenging the continued security of full-time jobs.

A two tier work force posed many problems for academic freedom. A two tier work force often resulted in a divided academy, marked by internal inequities and unequal rights. Faculty in the second tier were generally not incorporated into the system of rights and responsibilities that had evolved for faculty. Increased reliance on second tier faculty for cheap labor meant that fewer faculty generally had access to tenure and to the academic freedom that accompanies tenure.

Patterns of Preference

When administrators provided rationales for retrenchment and reallocation, they usually talked about productive and non-productive faculty, programs or departments. Generally, they presented cut-backs as a rational response to student choice, which had shifted from the arts and sciences to professional schools and programs. However, none of the administrators advocated making cuts solely on the basis of numbers of students served. Administrators usually took the position that they were able to assess intangible factors, such as quality or centrality, that influenced patterns of reallocation and retrenchment.[21]

In practice, what patterns of preference emerged in the cuts made in the 1980s? Which programs and departments were privileged, which were cut, and why? At first glance, the AAUP sample (see Table 2) suggests that those programs *least* likely to be cut were those best able to position themselves close to the upper end of the market. For example, the physical sciences, medical schools, business schools and law schools were unlikely to be cut. Those programs *most* likely to be cut were those associated not with the market, but with the social welfare functions of the state, as was the case with education and home economics. Fields with an indeterminate and unclear relationship to the market, for example, the liberal arts and social sciences, were also quite vulnerable to cuts.

Although administrators invoked the market as if an invisible hand were making the choices as to which programs would be cut, the workings of the academic market were far from free. Department of Defense spending shaped the demand for scientists and engineers much more strongly than private sector labor force needs.[22] Similarly, the demand for physicians remained high because the supply of doctors was artificially contained by professional limits set on the number of medical students and schools.[23] Fields such as business and law were directly concerned with commerce, but demand for graduates was irregular and uneven. The sometimes considerable distance of these fields from the market was masked by the high salaries and broad privileges that some, but certainly not all, graduates from these fields were able to attain. Moreover, professors within these fields actively attempted to position themselves close to the market, often associating growth and discovery in science with productivity and general prosperity.[24]

The field that was more deeply cut than any other in the 1980s was education. Of the faculty fired in the AAUP sample, 36.7 percent were educators (see Table 2). Like faculty in the sciences and engineering, law, business and medicine, educators often tried to position themselves close to the market, arguing that their services were essential for human capital development and ultimately for increased productivity. However, education was strongly associated with the social welfare function of the state. Indeed, education was singled out by the Reagan and Bush administrations as a signifier of state agency incompetence. Although educators tried to position themselves close to the market, their claims were not taken seriously, even though there was continued strong demand for teachers. Perhaps not coincidentally, teachers were members of the largest and strongest labor unions in the country.

Liberal arts faculty in the AAUP sample, including social scientists,

Table 2
Fields Retrenched*

Field	Number of Faculty Cut	Percentage
Allied Health	1	0.5
Journalism, Communication	2	1
Pharmacy	2	1
Mathematics	4	2
Science Life 4 (2%) Physical 1 (.5%)	5	2.5
Social science	21	10.7
Agriculture & Industrial Technology	39	19.9
Liberal Arts**	50	25.5
Education	72	36.7
	196+	99.8

*Data were compiled from the dismissals listed by Committee A, "Academic Freedom and Tenure," in *Academe* 1980–1990.

**Includes humanities & fine arts

The data include all instances in which colleges or universities issued termination notices, regardless of whether or not faculty were finally terminated. The total number of faculty who received notice was 221. The discipline or filed of the faculty was unknown in 25 cases (11.3%) of the total. Table 1 reports only those faculty where field was known.

SOURCE: Sheila Slaughter, "Retrenchment in the 1980s: the Politics of Prestige and Gender," *Journal of Higher Education* 64 (May–June 1993): 250–82.

accounted for 36.2 percent of those fired. Faculty in the liberal arts and social sciences generally did not try to position themselves close to the market. Faculty in those fields easily could have made a case for their contribution to productivity, but they usually did not. Instead, new fields, such as communications and media arts, used a vocation rhetoric and the techniques and methods of the humanities, fine arts, and the social sciences, and grew rapidly in the early 1980s. In other words, faculty in some fields, for whatever reasons, chose not to try to position themselves close to the market. These fields were often cut.

The faculty in heavily restructured fields were predominantly male, as were the faculty fired. However, there tended to be more women faculty in the restructured fields than in the unrestructured ones.[25] Education, liberal arts, and home economics and social sciences, all fields that draw many women, both as faculty and students, accounted for approximately 82.9 percent of fired faculty.[26] In terms of students, the heavily restructured fields, with the exception of social sciences, currently at 43.8 percent women, had majority female student populations.[27]

In sum, those fields best able to represent themselves as close to the market were generally least likely to be cut, even though the strength of these markets often called for a good deal of state maintenance. These were usually the same fields that were best able to provide external resources, resources above and beyond fixed formula allotments, whether through grants or gifts. The fields that were cut were often seen as part of the social welfare function of the state, did not hold out the promise of external resources for their institutions, and tended to have majority female student bodies. The patterns of preference expressed in the AAUP sample suggests that full academic citizenship does not extend to fields with heavily female student populations, that faculty in these fields are somehow different, that they do not have the same rights and freedoms of faculty in other fields, given that their tenure is fairly easily abrogated.

Sex Discrimination, Ideologies, and Beliefs

As gender was an underlying element in financial exigency cases, so gender escaped the boundaries of sex discrimination and spilled over into cases concerned with ideologies and beliefs. Gender issues were not limited to equal representation in the academic labor force; they were also at the heart of the majority of cases in which faculty were fired for their ideologies, beliefs and practices. Male and female faculty were dismissed because they explored nontraditional gender issues and questions in public forums, in their classrooms and in their life-styles. In the 1970s, Committee A did not investigate any sex discrimination cases. In the 1980s, it investigated two (see Table 1). In the 1970s, only eleven women, 5 percent of the faculty in the cases where gender was known, were involved in academic freedom cases. In the 1980s, twenty-one women (33 percent) of the cases where gender was known, were involved in academic freedom cases. In part, the increase in numbers of women in the 1980s is explained by the greater number of women who joined the academic labor force. However, the pervasiveness of gender issues in the 1980s academic freedom cases—whether these were financial exigency cases, as discussed in the previous section, or cases related to ideologies and beliefs—suggests that gender issues go far beyond questions of work force equity and raise questions about the nature of power and authority in the academy.

SEX DISCRIMINATION AND ACADEMIC FREEDOM

Auburn University provided the only clear cut finding of sex discrimination by the AAUP.[28] The Auburn case brought together some of the issues faced by the first wave of women to enter the academy: problems associated with child rearing, paternalistic treatment, unclear career lines, spousal roles. The AAUP's interest in Lida Mayfield's complaint led to a broad investigation of the status of women at Auburn.

Lida Mayfield was hired by a long time family friend, the chair of the Music department, where her father had worked as an adjunct instructor. She alleged that when she was hired she was told she did not have to get a master's degree. The Dean and the department chair indicated that they had not wanted to pressure Mayfield about the MA degree because she had two small children. Although Mayfield always worked full-time, even while her children were young, the administrators initially classified her appointment as temporary, without informing Mayfield. Over time, the character of the department changed, and the majority came to hold advanced degrees. Mayfield was told she had to acquire one or face termination. She quickly attained an MA and was put up for tenure after having served as a full-time faculty member for 12 years. Her department was very hostile to her, perhaps in part because she had received special treatment from an earlier administration, perhaps in part because Mayfield's husband, an administrator in the School of Education, sat on a committee dealing with the relation between the Music Department and the School of Education and that committee made a decision regarded by the Music Department as detrimental. To Mayfield's surprise, she was not given tenure. The portion of the faculty review available to Mayfield characterized her as a "very difficult person to work with," "lacking in restraint and professional demeanor," "highly opinionated and quite self-serving," as "severe and even abusive" in her criticisms, and as having a "generally uncooperative and un-compromising attitudinal stance."[29]

Mayfield's case illustrated the difficulties faced by women in an institution which defined the normative employee as male. Although she did not stop-out for child rearing, the senior administrators in her department put her on a "mommy track" without consulting or informing her. This treatment, at once patriarchal and preferential, delayed her tenure clock and probably heightened her colleagues' antagonism toward her. Her spouse held a position in which he could and did exercise indirect and negative authority over his wife's colleagues, all without violating any nepotism rules.

Mayfield was probably not a feminist, nor even concerned with women's issues. She may well have filed a sex discrimination charge because such a complaint provided her only hope of redress. Mayfield initially benefitted, perhaps even exploited her statuses as daughter, wife and mother to gain the support of the administration, and in so doing turned the faculty against her.

However, Mayfield's intentions are largely unimportant. What is important is that she had to deal constantly with her gender status, facing issues that men rarely had to deal with at all.

Mayfield was not the only woman to encounter problems at Auburn. The university had over 30 faculty who had served more than seven years who were working full time at the rank of instructor, 25 of whom were women. Shortly before the AAUP investigation of the Mayfield case, each of these instructors had received a letter from the administration, asking them to sign an acknowledgement that as instructors they were untenurable and would never seek tenure at Auburn. A number of the instructors said they thought that if they had not signed the letters, they would have been fired immediately. Although Auburn probably did not treat all women faculty as it did these instructors, a disproportionate number of persons in the instructor category— a category marked by lack of full-time benefits, full-range salary scales and the protection of tenure—were women.

The irregularities in women's faculty positions—indeterminate probationary periods, unclear status with regard to the tenure track, permeable boundaries between work and home—posed problems for academic freedom. As the threatening letter from the Auburn administration suggested, faculty were vulnerable to pressure because of job insecurity. Lack of tenure made those in the instructor category unwilling to speak out.

In the case of Marcia Falk at the University of Judaism, it was difficult to discern what occupied the foreground: sex discrimination or faculty hostility to Falk's religious beliefs, which were intertwined with her feminism. I was uncertain about whether I should put this case in the category of ideological deviance or sex discrimination. I finally opted for sex discrimination, largely because the AAUP investigating committee thought, but could not prove, that sex discrimination was a major factor.[30]

Marcia Falk was a poet, a translator from Hebrew to English, and a feminist. Her scholarship involved re-writing traditional Jewish prayers to include women. The University of Judaism was associated with the conservative wing of the Jewish religion. When Falk joined the faculty, only men, most of whom were rabbis, held tenure. Falk was the only women ever evaluated for tenure at the University of Judaism.

The committee at the University of Judaism that reviewed Falk was completely anonymous; it never reported to the faculty as a whole, or to a faculty body to whom Falk could appeal. The committee's report on Falk was very negative. The Committee claimed its report was based on Falk's external letters of reference. On the basis of the faculty committee review, Falk was denied tenure.

Unbeknownst to the anonymous faculty review committee at the University of Judaism, four of Falk's referees sent her copies of their letters, as did the remaining two after they discovered she did not receive tenure. Falk read the letters as overwhelmingly positive, as did the AAUP investigating committee. The AAUP investigating committee compared the anonymous faculty review committee's treatment of the external letters with the letters themselves. As an Association staff letter to the President of the University of Judaism put it, one "did not overstate the case in asserting that 'one has difficulty recognizing the letter and the report are discussing the same publications and the same person.' "[31] In other words, the faculty review committee at the University of Judaism had so distorted the external referees' evaluation of Falk that very positive recommendations became negative.

The Falk case suggested the limits of academic freedom as defined by the AAUP. The AAUP rested its case against the University of Judaism on procedure. The AAUP took the position that the faculty review committee should not have been anonymous, that Falk had a right to know the committee membership and to appeal to them. However, Falk's knowledge of the names of the faculty review committee would not have helped her. Only her knowledge of the content of the external reviewers' letters allowed her to challenge the decisions. In the normal course of events, she would have known the names of the faculty review committee, but not the content of the external letters.

She would have appealed to the faculty review committee, and have been turned down. The substance of the case—the deep disparity in judgement between the faculty review committee and the external letters—would never have become public. The Falk case points to the problems in the AAUP's heavily procedural approach to academic freedom, an approach that assumes that the collective conscience of the senior faculty exercising judgement over their junior colleagues is fair, just and wise, especially when junior faculty members differ from senior with regard to gender, beliefs and ideology.

RELIGIOUS CASES AND ACADEMIC FREEDOM

Marcia Falk's case bore a disturbing resemblance to a number of other cases involving religion and gender. In all but one of the religious cases, conservative groups in church administrations precipitated the firing of faculty, or the cancellation of the speaking engagements of faculty who spoke out on gender issues or engaged in practices contrary to religious norms on gender. It was tempting to dismiss these cases as anachronistic, vestiges of a time when higher education was more strongly informed by religious than scientific beliefs. However, the hierarchies or officialdom of the churches in these cases had all at one point expressed a commitment to secular standards of academic freedom, and then pulled back. The faculty in the cases were caught in conflicts engendered by changing standards of belief. These cases seemed to reflect the resurgence of conservative and evangelical forces within conventional churches. The churches involved were those to which the large majority of believers in the U.S. belong—Jewish (Falk, discussed above), Catholic, Lutheran and Baptist.

A comparison between the cases of the 1970s and the 1980s pointed to a greater conservatism and a stronger focus on gender. In the 1970s, there were two religious freedom cases; in the 1980s there were five cases (see Table 1). In the 1970s, the central issue in the two religious cases turned on student and faculty concern over issues related to social justice and the student movement. In one of the 1970s cases, forty faculty supported a dismissed colleague by declaring a moratorium on classes, eventually establishing a university in exile. In the 1980s, the main issue was gender, and faculty apparently did not collectively protest the dismissals of their colleagues. In the 1980s cases, church hierarchies or officialdom reasserted traditional positions on gender issues, resulting in the firing of six faculty.

The Maguire case turned on women's procreative rights. During the Reagan-Mondale campaign, Professor Daniel Maguire worked with Vice-Presidential candidate Geraldine Ferraro in an organization called Catholics for Free Choice to let voters know that there was more than one position on abortion in the church. Archbishop O'Connor publicly denied the legitimacy of Maguire's position, saying: "There is no variance and no flexibility—there is no leeway as far as the Catholic Church is concerned . . . Pope John Paul II has said that the task of the church is to reaffirm that abortion is death."[32] The head of the Vatican's Sacred Congregation for Religious and Secular Studies demanded a public retraction on the part of the priests and nuns involved with Catholics for Free Choice. The priests made a pro-forma retraction; the nuns refused. Maguire, a former priest, refused to retract. Following his refusal to retract, his scheduled appearances at four Catholic institutions were canceled. Although Maguire threatened legal action for breach of contract, all but one of the institutions, Boston College, were steadfast in their refusal to allow him to speak.

At the Catholic University of Puerto Rico, the issue was not belief but practice.[33] Professor Jeannette Quilichini Paz, a tenured professor in English and Foreign language, was divorced. The administration informally advised her that if she remarried in a civil ceremony, she would be fired. She did and was, even though the issue of the sacramental status of marriage was never broached in her classroom or writings. On investigation, the AAUP committee discovered that up to the point of the Quilichini Paz case, the administration at Catholic University had not consistently enforced the informal rule on civil marriages. The Quilichini Paz case represented a reassertion of the Church's traditional position on the sanctity of Catholic marriage, which, like many other religions, made an analogy between the church and the family, likening the head of the church to Christ, and the head of the family to the husband, affirming male leadership. Moreover, Catholic University of Puerto Rico expanded its arena of authority from the university to faculty's private life.

At Southeastern Baptist Seminary, conservatives made a clean sweep in Board of Trustee elections and made a number of changes at the institution, including the non-reappointment of adjunct professors M. Mahan Siler, Jr., and Janice Siler.[34] Both Mahans' connections with the school were severed because Mahan Siler, Jr., was not firmly against homosexuality. His wife, Janice, had taken no public position on homosexuality, but she was treated as her husband's adjunct and not reappointed as well. In its position against homosexuality, the Trustees at Southeastern Baptist were concerned with maintaining traditional gender roles, focusing in this instance on the male rather than the female role.

At Concordia Theological Seminary (Indiana), Dr. Alvin A. Schmidt, a tenured and widely published sociologist, was fired because he taught "false doctrine."[35] He "(a) consistently advocated the view that there are no valid theological or biblical grounds for excluding women from the Office of the Public Ministry of Word and Sacrament, and . . . (b) applied hermeneutical principles and procedures to Holy Scripture which, in the absence of further constraints, would have the effect of substituting cultural relativism for all moral absolutes."[36] At issue was not only gender, but cultural relativism. The seminary was against cultural relativism in general, and against cultural relativism that diminished scripturally sanctioned male dominance of clerical offices, in particular.

Taken together, the sex discrimination cases and religious cases that turned on gender issues revealed the tension feminism and gay liberation have caused in the academy by challenging established gender roles. In religious institutions, where it was still possible to invoke traditional hierarchies, changing gender roles were viewed as threatening established doctrine in which power relations were embedded. The gender of the speaker did not matter. The men who spoke for women's right to choose, for women's right to priestly office, for men's freedom with regard to sexual preference were all punished, with sanctions ranging from abrogation of speaking contracts to dismissal. The ability of men and women to address gender issues in religious schools was sharply constrained, in clear violation of their secular claims to academic freedom.[37]

The 1940 statement of academic freedom exempted religious institutions, acknowledging the centrality of particular doctrines to church schools.[38] However, in the 1960s, many religious institutions, among them Catholic and Lutheran ones, voluntarily accepted the AAUP statement of principles in an effort to broaden their scope and approach.[39] In the 1980s, the hierarchies of some of these churches, and the boards of some institutions, moved away from their accommodation to secular codes central to faculty norms. The denominations in the AAUP samples that experienced power struggles between liberal and conservative factions were not isolated occurrences in the 1980s, but part of the broad struggles for dominance between contending groups in these churches. In other words, the question of the sanctity of academic freedom at church-sponsored colleges and universities has been re-opened, and the AAUP may once again have to caution prospective faculty that alternative norms prevail at these institutions.

Politics, Ideologies, and Beliefs

In the 1970s, fifty-five faculty (4 percent of faculty in AAUP reported academic freedom cases) were involved in twenty-two civil liberties or political ideology cases. In the 1980s, two faculty (1 percent of all cases) were involved in two cases (see Table 1). In the 1970s, the cases generally involved faculty participation in the civil rights movement, the student movement, protest against the war in Vietnam, and the black power movement. Faculty who were fired engaged in behavior that ranged from public criticism of political figures and university administrators to flag burning, draft card burning, illegal teach-ins and sit-ins. Among the more famous and notorious cases were the Angela Davis case at UCLA and the Morris Starsky case at Arizona State University. In the 1980s, faculty were apparently less active in social movements and outspoken protest, at least within the university. However, the cases in the 1980s, like many of the cases in the 1970s, reflected the major foreign policy issues of the decade. In the 1980s, these were Central America, South Africa and the Middle East.

Barbara Foley was an assistant professor of English at Northwestern University.[40] She was an ardent supporter of the Sandinista regime in Nicaragua. She thought that allowing Contra leader Adolpho Calero to speak at Northwestern would be countenancing a Fascist rally. She believed that campus events such as the Calero rally were no different from political events held off campus. She thought that heckling and other forms of disruptive audience behavior were acceptable. In other words, she took the position that Calero's right to be heard by the university community did not take precedence over her right to disruptive protest against him. Before Calero's arrival, Foley stood up on the stage and spoke in favor of preventing the rally. When Calero appeared, she participated in the chanting that made it impossible for him to speak. Someone other than Foley threw red liquid at Calero, and the rally was canceled.

Foley faced the Northwestern faculty disciplinary machinery as a result of her actions. The disciplinary committee was disturbed when Foley showed no remorse for her action, but were somewhat mollified when she agreed not to engage in similar behavior again. The punishment the faculty committee arrived at was an official reprimand, to be placed permanently in her file.

At the same time that Foley went before the disciplinary committee, she began the promotion and tenure process. As her case went up the elaborate system, the faculty tried to keep her disciplinary hearing and her promotion and tenure evaluation separate, apparently taking the position that her political behavior should not effect their judgement of her as a scholar. Although the votes on her promotion and tenure were sometimes split at the various levels of the process, there was always a clear majority in her favor. However, the provost turned her down, arguing that he could not separate her "citizenship" from her ability as a scholar.

The faculty was very upset with this decision, and 77 signed a letter expressing their anger. They were convinced that President Weber had made a mockery of the lengthy promotion and tenure deliberations because he had irrevocably made up his mind to fire Foley shortly after the precipitating incident occurred. They thought their deliberations had been spurned.

In fighting against the President's judgement, Foley claimed sex discrimination, arguing that if she had been a man, her behavior would have been evaluated differently. The EEOC gave her the right to sue, probably because Northwestern had a bad statistical record with regard to promoting women. The AAUP investigating committee did not take up the charge of sex discrimination, and did not censure Northwestern, even though the faculty will with regard to the Foley case had been overturned. The cases of the 1970s suggest that Foley was probably not on solid ground when she claimed that had she been a man her actions against Calero would have been evaluated differently, although comparisons are difficult because of the very different numbers of women in the academy in the two decades. Had she been an African-American woman, she might have had a stronger case. In the 1970s, four women faculty, all African-Americans, were involved in cases where they spoke out forcefully or protested against political events. The remaining 51 faculty fired for similar behavior were men.

Northwestern's President Weber probably considered Foley's case particularly egregious because she prevented a speaker from being heard, violating norms with regard to freedom of speech, which are closely related to norms regarding academic freedom.[41] The faculty too were very upset by Foley's behavior, particularly by her lack of remorse. Like President Weber, most faculty were committed to the concept of free speech, regardless of how reprehensible or offensive the words of the speaker. Although the faculty did not condone Foley's actions, they did not take such a harsh view of her citizenship as the president, and defended her right to tenure.

As with the Northwestern case, the SUNY-Stony Brook case involved the administration turning down the advice of faculty on a promotion and tenure decision.[42] Professor Ernest D. Dube was a native of South Africa and an African National Congress member. He was imprisoned on Robben Island for political activity, and released on the condition that he leave South Africa. He did graduate work in cognitive psychology at Cornell University, and then took a job at SUNY Stony Brook, a joint appointment in African Studies and Psychology. On the basis of a student complaint, a visiting Israeli professor accused Dube of linking Zionism with Nazism as a form of racism, of being an anti-Semite and engaging in "gross perversion and blasphemy."[43] The executive committee of the Faculty Senate investigated Dube and found that he had not exceeded the bounds of academic freedom. After deliberating on the executive committee's report, the faculty senate as a whole endorsed the committee's resolution and decision not to pursue the matter further. The New York Jewish community was unhappy with the faculty committee's decision and brought tremendous pressure to bear on Stony Brook's administration to repudiate Dube's position on Zionism. Jewish alumni threatened not to give; legislators threatened to cut SUNY-Stony Brook's budget; Governor Cuomo condemned Dube; the Jewish Defense League disrupted Dube's classes, vandalized his home, and made harassing phone calls.

During this campaign against him, Dube, who had a weak publication record, came up for tenure. By and large, the numerous faculty committees constituted to make and review this decision voted for tenure, on the basis of Dube's citizenship, but against promotion, on the basis of his scholarship. The President turned him down for promotion and tenure, as did the SUNY system Chancellor, Clifton Wharton.

The two political cases raise questions of citizenship and faculty authority. Citizenship is a code word for the intangible factors that go into promotion and tenure decisions. In the two cases, faculty and administration construed citizenship differently. In the Northwestern case, the faculty thought that Foley had not offended the norms of academic citizenship so much as to warrant dismissal; the provost thought she had. In the SUNY-Stony Brook case, the faculty thought Dube merited tenure on the basis of citizenship; the president and chancellor claimed he did not. These cases indicated the limits of faculty power. The faculty had decision-making authority with regard to promotion and tenure delegated to them until the administration disagreed with the decisions that faculty made. At that point, the administration overrode the faculty, and had the bureaucratic and legal authority to do so. Like retrenchment decisions, the administrations' decision in the Foley and Dube cases suggested that faculty were not part of the university management if circumstances departed from the normal. If this is the case, academic freedom is precarious indeed.

Anti-Administration Cases

In the 1970s, thirty-eight faculty (3 percent of those fired) were dismissed for challenging or criticizing the administration on matters relating to management of the institution. In the 1980s, twenty-six faculty (11 percent) were dismissed in sixteen anti-administration cases (see Table 1). Like the 1970s, the 1980s cases centered on faculty efforts to assert or obtain a voice in decision making: faculty wanted a modicum of professional autonomy. As in the 1970s, the cases in the 1980s were at mid-sized state colleges, small private colleges, and optometry or osteopathic colleges. Again like the 1970s, in the 1980s, when gender was known, men (80 percent) tended to figure in this cases to a greater degree than women (19 percent).

The degree of conflict in a typical anti-administration case was intense and all-consuming, permeating the professional lives of the participants. Conflict was usually prolonged, sometimes continuing for years. In a number of cases, faculty throughout the institutions were drawn into the conflict. The issues were almost always the same. Faculty critical of the administration's management of the institution sought a degree of self-governance. They were fired for their criticism, and for their efforts to inaugurate or renovate forms such as faculty senates and councils.

Illinois College of Optometry was illustrative.[44] Professors Alexander and Shansky, who held Ph.D.s in psychology from University of Washington and Syracuse, respectively, had served the college well over seven years, but were still on term contracts, as were all faculty. They attempted to establish a faculty senate and adopt AAUP guidelines as institutional personnel policy.

Alexander was chair of the Faculty Organizing Committee. Alexander and Shansky regularly confronted the administrator who simultaneously held the position of dean and chair of the division in which they worked. They dealt with him in his capacity as dean on issues of governance, and in his capacity as division chair on issues of curriculum. Given that the administrator did not have a degree in an area related to the division specialization, he was somewhat uncertain of his authority. At a meeting with the dean/chair dealing with curriculum, Alexander and Shansky walked out in protest over the time-frame in which the issue was being handled. The dean/chair and the president warned the faculty members that their behavior was unacceptable, and immediately rescheduled the meeting for the afternoon of the same day of the walkout. Alexander and Shansky claimed prior commitments, did not attend, and were fired.

The charges brought against Alexander and Shansky were "irresponsibility, insubordination, and evidence of an unwillingness to cooperate in furthering the purposes of the College."[45] They were summarily dismissed: "The professors were escorted from the College by uniformed campus security police and were subsequently allowed to retrieve their effects only in the presence of the police and the College legal counsel."[46] The professors filed charges with the National Labor Relations Board, to no avail. They instituted a civil suit, but failed to win a preliminary injunction to forestall dismissal.

A number of the anti-administration cases (5, or 38 percent) were at historically African-American institutions. Like faculty at other institutions, faculty at these colleges were attempting to professionalize, and in the process confronted autocratic administrators. In the years after 1965, the demand for African-American faculty at predominantly white institutions grew, creating many more options than were previously available for them. Faculty with greater market options probably felt more able to challenge administrators.

Talladega College illustrated the problems encountered by faculty at traditionally African American institutions. Howard Rogers chaired the social science division, which sent a memo to the board of trustees, voicing:

> their concern with . . . the general academic environment at the college and
> a perceived absence of administrative commitment to open dialogue and
> communication with the faculty, an absence of administrative concern for

the integrity of the academic program . . . , and an absence of any administrative vision for the future of this college beyond mere survival.[47]

The faculty doubted "the capacity of this administration to address these concerns."[48]

The president charged the faculty with attempting to "preempt [his] office" and "circumvent established lines of communication."[49] Faculty complaints about the administration were taken up by the Faculty Concerns Committee, which eventually charged the administration with trying to pack the committee with college personnel who did not have voting status in order to secure outcomes sought by the administration. The Faculty Concerns Committee brought these and other charges to the board of trustees, the members of whom heard out the faculty and then gave full academic support to the president, delegating to him virtually complete discretion for management of the institution. Shortly thereafter, the president terminated the services of Rogers and several other professors who had engaged in criticism of his administration. Two of the professors were locked out of their offices and escorted from the campus by security police. The faculty appealed unsuccessfully to the trustees, and then turned to the courts. The county court judge dismissed their suits, and the case went to appeal.

Whether at predominantly white or at historically African-American institutions, these sixteen cases polarized relations between faculty and administration over issues of faculty autonomy. In many of the cases, the administrations made few concessions to faculty claims to professional status. The administrators treated faculty like "mere employees" rather than like professionals. They charged faculty with "insubordination," "trouble-making," even "sedition." As the AAUP investigating committee remarked in one case, the reasons given by the administration for the dismissals were "more appropriate to a military organization or an industrial enterprise than to an institution of higher learning."[50] The treatment of faculty in these cases seemed designed to illustrate their powerlessness. Boards of trustees emphasized their legal authority over the institutions, the administrations demonstrated their power by using the campus police to supervise faculty as they physically left the insitutions, the courts generally refused to recognize professorial claims to some degree of participation in government. These administrations, then, defined themselves as management and treated faculty like workers.

In eight of the sixteen cases, the faculty as a whole engaged in some sort of collective action designed to support their fired colleagues. Support ranged from writing letters protesting treatment of the dismissed faculty to administrators or trustees to participating in the organization of an informal caucus or even AAUP chapters. In most cases, the administration was able to use its superior bureaucratic and legal powers to defeat the opposition. In a number of these cases, administrative victories may have been pyrrhic, given that the faculty seemed to divide into relatively stable pro- and anti-administration factions, ensuring a high degree of continuing conflict.

Generally, professors have assumed that if faculty obtain the proper credentials and engage in scholarship and expert service, then administrators will give them a participatory institutional voice. In other words, faculty believe that administrators will eventually acknowledge that faculty expertise commands authority, especially in terms of the curriculum, hiring and firing, and academic governance. This benign view of the professionalization process is based largely on the study of elite institutions in periods not marred by social conflict, and does not do justice to the struggle for professional authority in which many professors were and are forced to engage.[51] This view of professionalization minimizes the history of complex negotiations and compromises which faculty at elite institutions have made with administrations in an effort to maintain autonomy.[52] Generally, the array of faculty power bases at elite institutions— positions in associations of learned disciplines, access to external sources of power and status, such as national and international prizes and honors, access to federal and foundation grants, to consulting opportunities—are not figured into conceptions of maintenance of faculty governance and academic freedom. Because of this general lack of attention to the high levels of conflict surrounding efforts at professionalization, central to which is self-governance, faculty, especially those with degrees from research universities who find positions at non-elite institutions, are often unprepared for the viciousness and intensity of struggles over self-governance. By diminishing the degree to which connections with powerful external organizations and agencies, organizational skills and ability to engage in conflict contribute to professional authority, current views of professionalization do faculty a disservice by leaving them unprepared for the conflicts that many will face. And unless faculty are able to achieve a degree of self-governance, they are unlikely to be able to protect their academic freedom.

Conclusion

The seventeen financial exigency cases point to changes that have occurred over the past several decades with regard to faculty rights and privileges, such as tenure and participation in faculty governance. In the mid 1960s, faculty tenure was widely recognized by colleges and universities and in the courts, usually on the basis of personnel policies and Fourteenth Amendment claims. Once granted, tenure was viewed as inviolable, other than for cause or moral turpitude, the first of which was difficult to prove, the second of which was increasingly difficult to define. In the 1970s, tenure as an institution was weakened when financial exigency became grounds for dismissal. However, tenure and seniority remained key criteria for making cuts in the 1970s. In the 1980s, financial exigency cases became reorganization and reallocation cases, seriously undermining tenure. Tenure and seniority did not guide the way in which decisions to fire faculty were made in reorganization and retrenchment cases.

The undermining of tenure that occurred in the 1980s was due in part to university administrators' increased sophistication with regard to tactics and strategies for managing professional labor. In the private sector, the Yeshiva decision, perhaps contrary to its intent, made collective action on the part of faculty almost impossible, clearing the way for university administrators to become primary decision makers. In the public sector, university managers were able to use bureaucratic rules, often embodied in state personnel policies, which vested institutional authority for making decisions about reorganization and reallocation in administrators rather than faculty. Tenure ceased to give faculty meaningful protection because administrators were able to substitute their judgement for collective faculty judgement about personnel and curricula. During reorganization and reallocation crises, administrators reviewed all faculty on criteria that were usually ill-defined and vague, and fired those who were found wanting on the basis of unclear guidelines.

In the 1980s, university managers were engaged in restructuring the professional labor force, using many of the same tactics and strategies that corporate CEOs had used against blue collar labor in the 1970s. In the 1970s, corporate CEOs pushed the blue collar labor force into job loss, speed-ups, give-backs and fragmented labor as a collectivity through increased use of part timers, all of which resulted in the creation of a two tier labor force.[53] In the 1980s, academic administrators pressured faculty into loss of academic lines, heavier teaching loads, reduction of benefits, and the fragmentation of faculty as a collectivity through the increased use of part-timers, all of which resulted in the creation of a two tier labor force. The general political climate during the Reagan and Bush years favored encroachment on the rights of professional labor. Union-busting in the public sector, exemplified by the PATCO strike, was supported, and Reagan and Bush appointees on the courts and on the NLRB generally favored management.

Reorganization and retrenchment cases revealed a pattern of preference in firing that reinforced commitment to a conservative status quo. Professors were most frequently cut in fields that had as students the greatest number of new entrants to higher education—women and minorities. Those fields were also often the same fields from which a critique of the status quo had been developed in the 1960s and 1970s—the social sciences and the liberal and fine arts.

Gender ran like a thread through all the academic freedom cases other than the anti-administration category, testifying to the difficulties that the academy has had in incorporating women. In the reorganization and reallocation cases, the fields in which women were most likely to concentrate as students were usually the fields that experienced the heaviest cuts. Sex discrimination cases emerged as an AAUP category of academic freedom cases for the first time in the 1980s. These cases pointed to women's place in academe—in the bottom tier of a two tier labor force, usually in part time positions with few, if any, benefits. In the ideological deviance cases, faculty who challenged conventional gender ideology were even more likely to be fired than faculty who challenged prevailing political ideologies.

Finally, many faculty at small, undistinguished state colleges and private liberal arts colleges were unable to secure a modicum of professional autonomy. Their lives continued to be dominated by administrators. Efforts that these faculty made to achieve a role in governance, in hiring, firing and promotion, were interpreted by university officials as insubordination and resulted in faculty dismissals. Although anti-administration cases were a factor in the 1970s, they increased in the 1980s, suggesting that the political climate of the 1980s provided less sustenance for professional labor than the climate of the 1970s.

Overall, the academic freedom cases of the 1980s point to the ways in which threats to academic freedom shift as historical conditions change. The financial exigency and retrenchment cases of the 1970s were replaced by reorganization and reallocation, and a deepening threat to tenure. Challenges to political orthodoxy that characterized the 1970s became challenges to gender ideology in the 1980s. Only the struggle on the part of faculty to gain professional autonomy remained fairly constant, although this struggle may have become more difficult.

Notes

1. Sheila Slaughter, "Academic Freedom in the Modern University," in *Higher Education in American Society,* rev. ed., ed. Philip G. Altbach and Robert O. Berdahl (Buffalo, N.Y.: Prometheus Books, 1987), pp. 77–105.

2. Sheila Slaughter, "The Danger Zone: Academic Freedom and Civil Liberties," *Annals of the American Academy of Political and Social Science* 448 (March 1980): 781–819.

3. American Association of University Professors, *American Association of University Professors: Policy Documents and Reports* (Washington, D.C.: AAUP, 1990).

4. The basis of comparison between the 1970s and the 1980s is between my 1983 article (rev. ed. 1987) cited in note 1, and the data presented in this article.

5. A complaint is the registration by a professor of a suspected violation of academic freedom. A complaint becomes a case when the AAUP staff finds it merits further investigation. Forty-three percent of the 2,135 complaints (1975-1979) received were handled by AAUP staff without ever achieving "case" status. Although 1,312 (57 percent) became cases calling for further probing, only 23 cases (2 percent) were subject to full-dress investigation and public report by Committee A. Even if the 366 cases (27 percent) said to be successfully closed are omitted on the grounds that positive resolution does not result in publication, approximately 70 percent of the cases are unaccounted for. "Report of Committee A, 1978–1979," *AAUP Bulletin* 65 (September 1979): 296. For an explanation of the processing of complaints received by the AAUP see "Report of the Special Committee on Procedures for the Disposition of Complaints under the Principles of Academic Freedom and Tenure," *AAUP Bulletin* (May 1965): 210–24.

6. See, for example, Richard Hofstadter and Walter P. Metzger, *The Development of Academic Freedom in the U.S.* (New York: Columbia University Press, 1957); Robert McIver, *Academic Freedom in Our Time* (New York: Columbia University Press, 1955); Walter P. Metzger, "Academic Tenure in America: A Historical Essay," in *Academic Tenure: A Report of the Commission* (San Francisco: Jossey-Bass, 1973), pp. 93–105; Sheila Slaughter, "The Danger Zone: Academic Freedom and Civil Liberties," *Annals of the American Academy of Political and Social Science* 448 (March 1980): 46–61; Ellen W. Schrecker, *No Ivory Towers: McCarthyism and the Universities* (New York: Oxford University Press, 1986); Lionel S. Lewis, *Cold War on the Campus: A Study of the Politics of Organizational Control* (New Brunswick, N.J.: Transaction Books, 1988); William W. Van Alstyne, "Freedom and Tenure in the Academy: The Fiftieth Anniversary of the 1940 Statement of Principles," *Law and Contemporary Problems Special Issue* 52 (Summer 1990).

7. Sheila Slaughter, in "Retrenchment in the 1980s: The Politics of Prestige and Gender," *Journal of Higher Education* 64 (May/June 1993): 250–82, also provides a theoretical explanation of the phenomenon of retrenchment.

8. Committee A, "Academic Freedom and Tenure: City University of New York: Mass Dismissals Under Financial Exigency," *AAUP Bulletin* 63 (1977): 60–81.

9. Committee A, "Academic Freedom and Tenure: The State University of New York," *AAUP Bulletin* 63 (August 1977): 237–60.

10. J. M. Douglas with B. G. Or, *Directory of Faculty Contracts and Bargaining Agents in Institutions of Higher Education* (New York: National Center for the Study of Collective Bargaining in Higher Education and the Professions, Baruch College, City University of New York, 1990), vol. 16.

11. Committee A, "Academic Freedom and Tenure: Sonoma State University (California)," *Academe* 69 (May-June 1983): 4.

12. Ibid.

13. Committee A, "Academic Freedom and Tenure: Goucher College," *Academe* 69 (May-June 1983): 13–23.

14. Committee A, "Academic Freedom and Tenure: Temple University," *Academe* 71 (May-June 1985): 16–27. Goucher had been involved in the termination of four tenured faculty during efforts to stave off budgetary difficulties in 1974–75.

15. Committee A did not condone the work of the AAUP chapter engaged in collective bargaining at Temple, and castigated the chapter for weakening tenure safeguards.

16. Committee A, "Academic Freedom and Tenure: Yeshiva University," *Academe* 67 (August 1981): 187–95; Committee A, "Academic Freedom and Tenure: Goucher College," *Academe* 69 (May-June 1983): 12–23; Committee A, "Academic Freedom and Tenure: The Metropolitan Community Colleges (Missouri)," *Academe* 70 (March–April 1984): 23a–32a; Committee A, "Academic Freedom and Tenure: Temple University," *Academe* 71 (May–June 1985): 16–27; Committee A, "Academic Freedom and Tenure: Morgan State University (Maryland)," *Academe* 73 (May–June 1987): 23–32.

17. Committee A, "Academic Freedom and Tenure: Temple University," *Academe* 71 (May–June 1985): 21.

18. Committee A, "Academic Freedom and Tenure: Eastern Oregon State College," *Academe* 68 (May–June 1982): 2a.

19. Committee A, "Academic Freedom and Tenure: Temple University."

20. Committee A, "Academic Freedom and Tenure: The Metropolitan Community Colleges (Missouri)," *Academe* 70 (March–April 1984): 28a.

21. For a detailed treatment of administrators' positions on retrenchment see Sheila Slaughter, "Retrenchment in the 1980s: The Politics of Prestige and Gender," *Journal of Higher Education* 64 (May–June 1983).

22. L. L. Leslie and R. L. Oaxaca, "Scientist and Engineer Supply and Demand," in *Higher Education: A Handbook of Theory and Research,* ed. John Smart (Bronx, N.Y.: Agathon, 1993).

23. Paul Starr, *The Social Transformation of American Medicine* (New York: Basic, 1983).

24. Gary Rhoades and Sheila Slaughter, "Professors, Administrators and Patents: The Negotiation of Technology Transfer," *Sociology of Education* 64 (April 1991): 65–77; Gary Rhoades and Sheila Slaughter, "The Public Interest and Professional Labor: Research Universities," in *Culture and Ideology in Higher Education: Advancing A Critical Agenda,* ed. W. G. Tierney. (New York: Praeger, 1991), pp. 187–211.

25. A. M. T. Lomperis, "Are Women Changing the Nature of the Academic Profession?" *Journal of Higher Education* 61 (November–December 1990): 643–77.

26. Agriculture and industrial technology accounted for thirty-nine firings, or 19.9 percent of all firings. Agriculture is usually where home economics is housed. I assumed that half of the firings in agriculture and industrial technology were in home economics to come up with the figure 82.9 percent.

27. National Center for Educational Statistics, *The Condition of Education 1990. Vol. 2: Postsecondary Education* (Washington, D.C.: USGPO, 1990); National Center for Educational Statistics, *Digest of Education Statistics 1990* (Washington, D.C.: USGPO, 1991).

28. Committee A, "Academic Freedom and Tenure: Auburn University," *Academe* 69 (May–June 1983): 24–32.

29. Ibid., 27.

30. Committee A, "Academic Freedom and Tenure: University of Judaism (California)," *Academe* 74 (May–June 1988): 29–40.

31. Ibid., 38.

32. "Academic Freedom and the Abortion Issue: Four Incidents at Catholic Institutions, Report of a Special Committee," *Academe* 72 (July–August 1986): 2a.

33. Committee A, "Academic Freedom and Tenure: The Catholic University of Puerto Rico," *Academe* 73 (May–June 1987): 33–38.

34. Committee A, "Academic Freedom and Tenure," *Academe* 75 (May–June 1989): 35–45.

35. Committee A, "Academic Freedom and Tenure: Concordia Theological Seminary (Indiana)," *Academe* 75 (May–June 1989): 62.

36. Ibid., 59.

37. One of the religious cases did not involve gender ideology. Professor Volenski, a Roman Catholic priest, left the priesthood, and in so doing, lost his job at Seton Hall. Committee A, "Academic Freedom and Tenure: Seton Hall University (New Jersey)," *Academe* 71 (May–June 1985): 28–36.

38. AAUP, *American Association of University Professors: Policy Documents and Reports* (Washington, D.C.: AAUP, 1990).

39. "Academic Freedom and the Abortion Issue: Four Incidents at Catholic

100   PART ONE: THE SETTING

Institutions, Report of a Special Committee," *Academe* 72 (July–August 1986): 1a–13a.

40. Committee A, "Academic Freedom and Tenure: Northwestern University: A Case of Denial of Tenure," *Academe* 74 (May–June 1988): 55–70.

41. E. T. Silva and Sheila Slaughter, *Serving Power: The Making of the American Social Science Expert, 1880–1920* (Westport, Conn.: Greenwood, 1984), chapter 2, "Defense of the Expert Role: Social Science Leaders in the AAUP," pp. 273–95.

42. Committee A, "Academic Freedom and Tenure: State University of New York at Stony Brook," *Academe* 76 (January–February 1990): 55–66.

43. Ibid., 55.

44. Committee A, "Academic Freedom and Tenure: Illinois College of Optometry," *Academe* 68 (November–December 1982): 17a–23a.

45. Ibid., 20a.

46. Ibid.

47. Committee A, "Academic Freedom and Tenure: Talladega College (Alabama)," *Academe* 72 (May–June 1986): 7a.

48. Ibid.

49. Ibid.

50. Committee A, "Academic Freedom and Tenure: Illinois College of Optometry," *Academe* 68 (November–December 1982): 22a.

51. See for example, Burton R. Clark, *The Academic Life: Small Worlds* (Princeton, N.J.: Carnegie Foundation for the Advancement of Teaching, 1987).

52. E. T. Silva and Sheila Slaughter, *Serving Power: The Making of the American Social Science Expert,* chapter 2, "Defense of the Expert Role: Social Science Leaders in the AAUP."

53. B. Bluestone and B. Harrison, *The Deindustrialization of America* (New York: Basic Books, 1982); Barry Bluestone and Bennett Harrison, *Plant Closings, Community Abandonment and the Dismantling of Basic Industry* (New York: Basic, 1982). For the way in which movement of capital in deindustrialization affected faculty, see Sheila Slaughter and E. T. Silva, "Toward a Political Economy of Retrenchment: American Public Research Universities," *Review of Higher Education* 8 (Summer 1985): 38–69.

5

Economics and Financing of Higher Education: The Tension Between Quality and Equity

W. Lee Hansen and Jacob O. Stampen

Introduction

This chapter examines the social and economic changes since World War II that affect the allocation and distribution of resources to higher education. The massive expansion of enrollments and the broadened missions of higher education institutions that began in the late 1950s not only required but also stimulated a substantial increase in resources allocated to higher education. However, the past two decades have been markedly different. Relatively less abundant available resources and scaled-back aspirations have been put into place even though demands on institutions of higher education continue to increase. How higher education will respond in the face of such belt-tightening measures remains unclear. To provide some insight into this conflict, we examine how and why the level and allocation of resources has shifted over a forty-year period.

One apparent explanation for the shift is the significant changes in the goals of higher education that have taken place over the past two decades. Substantially increased attention toward promoting wider access resulted in less attention to developing high-quality educational programs. These changes stem from an ongoing concern with social justice, a concern that has always received strong support from higher education. As a result, the character of higher education by the end of the 1970s seemed to have been substantially and permanently altered, with its focus on access, choice, and persistence.

It now appears that this conclusion was premature. Since 1981 we have experienced another dramatic change, evidenced by renewed public concern over quality and related calls for standards that differ markedly from those of the preceding decade. As a result higher education is making a strong bid to raise academic standards so as to improve educational programs, to use its resources more effectively, and to respond judiciously to a widening array of social demands. Partly as a result of these developments institutions of higher education have recently embarked on a major effort, particularly at the state and local levels, to increase available resources.

The path of progress for the higher education sector has not been a smooth one. The pace of change has been erratic at times; the direction has been meandering; and many outside forces have shaped its evolution over the past four decades.

The structure for our analysis is based on a series of questions concerning expenditures in higher education, which reflects society's investment in this area. We then develop criteria that can be used to relate various mandates for change in higher education with social and economic changes. The central focus of the analysis is to identify distinct time periods that can highlight the major forces affecting postsecondary education since World War II. Based on this framework, we proceed to examine the changing investment patterns in higher education, shifts in the allocation of expenditures, and what all of this means for those who pay the costs.

The principal questions that guide our discussion are:

1. How did the various social-political mandates from the past forty years influence societal spending, or investment, in higher education?

2. What were the key events affecting investment in higher education during these forty years?

3. What were the trends in overall expenditures for instruction, tuition and fee changes, and student financial aid?

4. How did these changes affect the sharing of the costs of higher education and the ability of students and their families to finance college attendance?

The data available to address these questions are less than ideal. Routinely gathered federal statistics on higher education have been frequently redefined, thereby making it difficult to document consistently financial trends and changes in higher education activities. Public opinion polls that might capture prevailing views about higher education are sporadic and usually rather vague in the information they elicit. Existing studies and research reports pursue a variety of questions that do not necessarily bear on our topic. For these reasons the variables selected for observation are necessarily broad, and represent a synthesis not entirely free of our own judgments. Nonetheless, the general patterns that emerge seem to offer explanations of changes in higher education that are both plausible and meaningful.

Dating the Periods of Analysis

In reviewing the past four decades in the history of higher education it is evident that this sector was successively buffeted by a variety of unprecedented forces. Perhaps the most noticeable force was demography. The enrollment surge after World War II that resulted from the GI Bill was followed by a relatively stable enrollment until the late 1950s. After a gradual enrollment increase into the early 1960s, an explosion of enrollments occurred as the baby-boom population reached maturity. This enrollment surge continued but at a somewhat slower pace through the 1970s. Since 1980 overall enrollment growth slowed considerably.

Another key factor has been the efforts of the higher education sector to chart its own course, as reflected in a long series of reports that articulate the goals and aspirations of the higher education community. Still another force has been that of economists and other social scientists who periodically introduce new concepts, provide fresh insights, and offer novel proposals that stir the air and stimulate thinking about the economics and financing of higher education. Last but not least, political forces always loom large and are revealed most immediately in governmental actions; ultimately, however, these actions reflect an even more powerful force, namely, the changing priorities of the citizenry who ultimately determine the focus of political action and the availability of resources for higher education.

To facilitate our analysis we define four distinct time periods. The first embraces the years from 1947 to 1958, a period of readjustment following World War II, which began with the GI Bill and concluded with the emergence of higher education as a major factor in the development of American society. The second period, 1958 to 1968, reflects the enormous expansion of the higher education sector and its emphasis on the elusive dimension of quality, spurred by concern that American technology was falling behind that of the Soviets. The next period, 1968 to 1981, represents a sharp change of focus. The first part of the period reflects the search for ways to broaden opportunities for students to attend college, initiated by the federal student loan programs in 1965. This search culminates with the federal decision in 1972 to establish a national need-based student aid system that credited the Pell grants (earlier called Basic Educational Opportunity Grants). The latter part of the period, from 1972-73 onward, can best be described as a time for consolidating the system and resolving equity problems; this experience revealed the great difficulties of dealing effectively with these issues. As most readers are aware, the period 1980-81 to the present represents a sharp swing in the opposite direction, with concerns about quality, efficient use of resources, and broadened missions rising to the forefront once again.

These forces and their changing direction over the past four decades reflect the well-known pendulum effect in social and political affairs.[1] It begins with special concerns about equity that led to the GI Bill, followed by concern for quality in the late 1950s and early 1960s. This is followed by the ascendancy of interest in equity and opportunity in the late 1960s and 1970s. By the early 1980s these forces had run their course and we see our apparent reversion to concerns about quality and effectiveness.

We begin by outlining the major forces operating in each of the four periods.

1947 TO 1958

This period can best be described as one of readjustment after the Great Depression and World War II. It began with the rapid increase in enrollments occasioned by returning veterans who resumed or began their college training with the help of the GI Bill. Despite the declining size of the college-age population in the early 1950s, as a result of falling birth rates in the 1930s, enrollments held up reasonably well with the flow of Korean War veterans into college, also under the GI Bill.

Aside from changes on college campuses brought about by the returning veterans, this period was rather uneventful. The social and economic pressures on higher education were minimal. The resources provided, while not substantial by current standards, matched public expectations that access to higher education should be limited to a modest percentage of high school graduates. The one noteworthy report of the period came from the 1947 Truman Commission on Higher Education (otherwise known as the Zook Commission),[2] which suggested that after the veterans completed their schooling larger proportions of the civilian population should be educated. The commission estimated that half of all high school graduates could benefit from higher education. It called for removing the financial barriers to college attendance by providing loans, grants, and work-study opportunities based on financial need.[3]

The period marked the ascendance of higher education to a new level of prominence in American society. Colleges and universities had been instrumental in easing the transition from a wartime to a peacetime economy, many young people who might not have had a chance to attend college did, and institutions of higher education were able to expand and develop. Knowledge of the important contributions of academe during World War II led to society's increased reliance on it, and people came to believe that colleges and universities could be instrumental in resolving other national problems. Meanwhile, many higher education leaders proved to be persuasive spokesmen for education and exercised positions of leadership on national policy issues that had broad social implications.

1957 TO 1968

This period can be described as one of enormous expansion and a strong emphasis on quality. The most important element was demographic, with the number of young people reaching eighteen years of age rising from 2.3 million in the fall of 1957 to 2.8 million in the same period of 1964 and then jumping to 3.8 million in 1965.[4] By the early 1960s colleges and universities were scrambling to construct facilities and to recruit new faculty members to deal with this unprecedented growth. The emphasis on quality had come earlier and unexpectedly as a result of the Soviet launching of the Sputnik satellite in 1957. This event dramatized the need for augmenting the nation's human resource base and for focusing particular attention on developing the most talented youth; it led to passage of the National Defense Education Act, which provided limited loans and scholarships.

Meanwhile, economists were developing the concept of human capital, which blossomed in the early 1960s and demonstrated the powerful effects of human "investment" in higher education on economic growth and on individual well-being.[5] Simultaneously, social scientists were identifying the "talent loss" resulting from many highly qualified high school graduates who could profit from college neither attending nor planning to attend college. These developments combined to justify the enormous expansion of resources invested in the instructional programs and the facilities of colleges and universities. They were also instrumental in expanding the amount of organized research activity financed largely by the federal government.

Several national reports proved to be influential in focusing the debate and defining paths for subsequent action. A 1957 report by the President's Committee on Education Beyond High School recommended that planning begin for the projected expansion of higher education and that faculty salaries, which had lagged seriously behind those of other comparable groups, be doubled in real terms by 1970 so as to assure an adequate base for the coming expansion of the college population. Equally important was President Eisenhower's Commission on National Goals, which presented its findings in a 1960 report titled *Goals for Americans*.[6] Among the report's twenty-five educational goals was a call for establishing more community colleges, expanding the number of Ph.D.s, state planning of higher education, low interest loans for college construction, fellowships for graduate students, as well as more student loan funds and higher loan amounts.[7] Though not expressed in so many words, the proposed creation of a vast new network of community colleges as well as an expanded and upgraded system of four-year colleges suggested simultaneous pursuit of the goals of improved quality and wider access.

Some progress was achieved during the first half of the 1960s in reducing the financial barriers to college attendance. Several states developed their own financial aid programs, which later became models for federal programs.[8] President Johnson's War on Poverty legislation in 1964 led to the creation of the Work Study Program and to special grants to help minority students attend college. Additional impetus came with passage in 1965 of the Higher Education Act, which provided subsidized loans for college and university students through the commercial banking system. Despite these advances, the total resources devoted to student aid remained quite small.

The period closes with Lecht's 1966 report that articulated a set of national goals and translated them to quantitative terms for 1970 and 1975.[9] The goals included not only an increase to a 100 percent high school graduation rate, but also an increase to 50 percent in high school graduates going to college; these goals were based on the assumption that state financial resources would be available to permit this expansion. At the same time, colleges were expected to double their loans and scholarships, private firms were expected to subsidize the schooling of more of their employees, and federal resources for loans and work-study programs were expected to increase substantially. While the implications of these goals were clear, the problems likely to arise from trying to attain them were not discussed.

1967 TO 1981

The Lecht report marked the end of an era that reflected an almost unbounded optimism about the prospects for higher education. Meanwhile, new forces pushing for greater equality of opportunity moved to the forefront, concern mounted over the "talent loss" resulting from financial barriers to attending college, people became increasingly conscious about poverty and its growth, and the pressures growing out of the civil rights movement focused new attention on equity issues. Taken together, these forces soon pushed concerns about quality into the background.

The opportunities inherent in these developments were quickly recognized by Clark Kerr who was then organizing the Carnegie Commission on Higher Education: he crystallized them in an influential chapter in the 1968 Brookings Institution volume titled *Agenda for a Nation*.[10] Kerr outlined six major issues facing higher education in the 1970s. These included the quest for greater equality of educational opportunity, the problems of financing higher education in view of rising costs, the likelihood of extensive use of new "technology" in learning, the continuing shortages of Ph.D.s and M.D.s, the need for metropolitan universities to develop an urban focus, and the special financial difficulties of black, liberal arts, and state colleges.

To deal with these problems, Kerr pushed for federal solutions through federal funding. This approach no doubt reflected the successes of higher education over the previous decade in garnering federal support for research, college buildings, and special equipment. Yet it also marked a significant departure from the traditional combination of financial supporttuition from students and their parents, state and local tax revenues for public institutions, and voluntary support for private institutions. Rather than push only for institutional support, Kerr called for an expanded program of student financial aid that would increase to fifteen billion dollars annually by 1976. About one-third of this total would go for the continuing support of research, another third would underwrite a system of need-based student financial aid grants, and the remainder would go for construction, institutional support, special programs, and medical education.

This report was followed within a year by two more detailed sets of proposals. One was issued by Kerr's Carnegie Commission on Higher Education[11] and the other emanated from an Advisory Task Force created by the Department of Health, Education, and Welfare under the direction of Alice Rivlin, then Assistant Secretary for Education.[12] These reports proved to be surprisingly similar in their recommendations, calling for a federally-financed system of need-based student financial aid grants, direct institutional grants tied to the number of students receiving support, and various related proposals to deal with special needs. Both reports spent considerable effort to justify their particular recommendations, to estimate their costs, and to assess their likely effects. It is clear that these recommendations constituted a package, with student aid as the centerpiece of an integrated set of proposals. The obvious objective was to promote greater equality of educational opportunity.

Meanwhile, economists were turning their attention to issues of poverty and income distribution as well as their effects on public programs. These studies showed that prevailing policies had the effect of directing the bulk of higher education subsidies to help youths from higher- and middle-income families rather than lower-income families, thereby disputing the conventional wisdom.[13] These findings accentuated the desirability of need-based student financial aid programs to help offset financial barriers to college attendance.

A federal student financial aid system emerged in 1972 with passage of the Basic Education Opportunity Grant (BEOG) program, which provided grants to students based on their financial need.[14] The program was phased in over a four-year period, and thus covered all undergraduates by the 1976-77 academic year. This completed the erection of a federal aid system relying on a combination of grants, loans, and work-study programs to help youths from lower income families overcome the financial barriers to college attendance.

Creation of the national need-based student grant system in 1972 meant the realization of a goal that had first been proposed by the Truman Commission almost a quarter century earlier. Expectations for the new program were high for many reasons. But, with the less buoyant economy of the 1970speriodic episodes of sharp inflation, continuing increases in postsecondary enrollments, and the ascendancy of other social prioritiesthe financial support for academic programs began to erode, and efforts to improve equity became more diffused at the institutional level. This produced increased stress within higher education, and between it and its outside constituencies. For example, middle-income families finding that their children could not qualify for Pell (formerly BEOG) grants pressured Congress to give them access to student loans. The result was passage of the "Middle Income Student Assistance Act of 1978"[15] which eliminated the requirement that students demonstrate financial need when applying for aid from the subsidized Guaranteed Student Loan program. Borrowing expanded rapidly and soon loans displaced grants as the most common form of student aid.

The large-scale movement of middle-income students into the ranks of aid recipients also became a focus of controversy. Examples of middle-income students buying cars or purchasing certificates of deposit with the proceeds of their heavily subsidized student loans rather than using the money to pay for education became commonplace. On a broader scale there were rumblings about whether America had caught the "British Disease," which conjured up the image of public programs exhausting their ability to assist genuinely needy people but becoming increasingly inefficient by including virtually everyone. At the same time there was a developing sense that government regulation of higher education had become overly burdensome and inefficient.

In terms of student aid, however, the latter part of this period, between 1972 and 1980, reflected efforts to consolidate the gains already made and to work out the inevitable difficulties associated with new public programs. It culminated with the reauthorization in fall 1980 of student aid programs that called for a sizeable expansion of grants and loans well into the 1980s.

Meanwhile, many institutions experienced difficulty maintaining support for instruction. Constant dollar declines in support for students occurred in many states even though per-student appropriations on a national basis actually increased. In part, this was explained by public expectations that higher education should maintain programs aimed at solving a wide array of social programs including health, poverty, and the environment, and by increases in the numbers of administrators needed to assure accountability. In addition, the financial squeeze on many state budgets slowed the flow of resources to higher education even though enrollments were steadily rising.

Throughout this period colleges and universities continued to grapple with a myriad of problems associated with student unrest that began in the late 1960s: calls for educational reform, pressures of increased enrollments, growing proportions of women and minority students, and changing preferences among students in their major fields of study. The trickle of literature on these and related developments swelled into a vast torrent, fed in part by the Carnegie Commission's recruitment of legions of scholars to examine every facet of higher education.

1980 TO THE PRESENT

The national elections of 1980, which brought the Reagan administration and a Republican majority to the U.S. Senate, marked an abrupt shift from an almost exclusive focus on equity concerns to one emphasizing economic and political reform. The election campaign and its aftermath drew attention to double-digit inflation, the need to cut federal spending and taxes, deregulation, and the need to enhance America's competitiveness. It also drew attention to declining SAT scores, increased drug problems in the schools, and growing illiteracy. More importantly, it downplayed the role of federal policy in attempting to solve these problems. These changes are documented by Whitt, Clark, and Astuto,[16] who find in the years after 1980 a sudden shift of policy focus from concerns about equity to related issues such as academic performance and institutional improvement; they also find a public consensus in support of this shift.

Student financial aid, the major avenue of federal support for higher education, came under sharp attack early in the ninety-seventh Congress (1981), with Senate-led efforts to reduce substantially appropriations for grant programs. Two important changes were enacted: the re-establishment of income requirements in the Guaranteed Student Loan programs and the elimination of Social Security education benefits. Thereafter, a bipartisan consensus in the Congress prevented further cuts.[17]

A Reagan administration initiative, aimed at improving the quality of education, began to gain bipartisan support at the same time that cuts in student aid were halted. An agenda took shape in a series of national reports focusing on elementary and secondary education.[18] The best known of the reports, *A Nation at Risk,*[19] renounced pre-existing policies as leading to economic, political, and social decline, exhorting educators and the general public to develop new performance standards in the schools aimed at improving the nation's competitive position. Other similar reports were less dramatic but generally supported the need to raise educational standards, even though none were very specific about how this might be accomplished.[20]

Shortly thereafter a similar series of reports began to appear that focused on higher education.[21] These reports called for renewed emphasis on quality, a sharpened focus on institutional missions, and greater attention to student learning. Since then pressures to monitor quality in higher education have continued to mount, just as they did earlier for elementary-secondary education.

It is too soon to tell whether efforts to enhance the quality of education will be effective. However, it is clear that recent calls for improvement have yet to result in new infusions of resources similar to those occurring in previous eras (e.g., the Truman GI Bill, the Sputnik period, the rapid enrollment expansion of the 1960s, and the significant expansion of need-based financial aid in the 1970s). As in previous periods, several recent national reports call for new resources. As yet, the federal and the state governments have shown little inclination to respond. Instead, attention has been focused on new demands for accountability in using existing resources.

The Analysis

Having now established the time periods for this analysis, we turn to the data in the hope of learning whether the changing political-social-economic conditions and the accompanying mandates embodied in commission reports had any lasting effect on higher education. We begin by describing the changing dimensions of the nation's investment in institutions of higher education. Expenditures are then examined in an effort to highlight major trends and to reveal the interplay between external and internal forces affecting the allocation of resources within the higher education sector. This paves the way for measuring the burden of costs and how they are shared among students and parents, state and local taxpayers, private donors, and federal taxpayers through the provision of student financial aid.

In large measure official data from the Department of Education and its predecessor, the U.S. Office of Education, are relied upon. Because of changes in our data collection systems as well as periodic alterations in the definitions of expenditures and revenues, the detailed data are not completely comparable over the forty-year period under study. Nonetheless, the broad categories employed here are consistent. Readers are cautioned that this overall analysis hides differences between public- and private-sector institutions as well as among universities on the one hand, and those between four-year and two-year institutions on the other.[22]

STUDENTS

Enrollment growth is described by two different sets of data: total enrollment, for which the data are readily available, and full-time equivalent (FTE) enrollment, which must be estimated.[23] As shown in columns 1 and 2 of Table 1, full-time equivalent enrollment declined as a percentage of total enrollment. The decline results from the steady increase in the proportion of part-time students (column 3), which is attributable to several developments, the most important being the substantial increase of older students (those age twenty-five and over who typically cannot attend full-time).

The overall growth figures for enrollment reflect the tidal wave-like effect of the baby boom as well as the increasing desire of adults either to begin or to return to college. Enrollments edged up only slightly from the late 1940s to the late 1950s, nearly doubled by the late 1960s, almost doubled again by 1981, and continued increasing but at a much slower pace in the early 1980s. The enrollment increase in the 1980s is at odds with many projections from the 1970s, which had anticipated enrollment declines for the early 1980s.[24]

An appreciation for the implications of enrollment growth is provided by examining the percentages of students enrolled in higher education relative to the college-age population (those 18–24: column 4) and to the adult population (18 and above: column 5). The percentage enrolled among those age 18–24 rose steadily from 16 percent in 1947–48 to 43 percent in 1983–84.[25] The percentage enrolled among those age 18 and over rose from 2.6 percent in 1947–48 to 7.3 percent in 1983–84. For both series the big gains occurred from the late 1950s to late 1960s and from then until 1980.

As these data reveal, a substantial expansion in demand for higher education occurred, but its uneven rate of growth was heavily influenced by demographic forces.

Table 1
Enrollment in Higher Education Institutes

Year	Total Head Count Enrollment (in thousands)	FTE Enrollment (in thousands)	Part Time Enrollment as a Percent of Head Count Enrollment	Head Count Enrollment as a Percent of 18-24-Year-Olds	Head Count Enrollment as a Percent of Total Population
	(col. 1)	(col. 2)	(col. 3)	(col. 4)	(col. 5)
1947–48	2,616	2,222	22%	16%	2.6%
1957–58	3,068	2,395	33%	20%	2.5%
1967–68	6,912	4,591	31%	29%	5.4%
1980–81	12,097	8,819	41%	41%	7.4%
1983–84	12,465	9,166	42%	43%	7.3%

SOURCES:
Column 1: *Historical Statistics Of the United States, Colonial Times to 1957* (Series H 316-326), p. 210. *Statistical Abstract of the United States* (1970), Table 185, p. 132; 1981, Table 266, p. 158; 1985, Table 252, p 150.
Column 2: *Fact Book, 1984–5* (American Council on Education, Macmillan Publishing Company, 1984).
Column 3: Calculated using part-time enrollment data. Pre-1980–81 estimated from data in June O'Neill, *Resource Use in Higher Education* (Carnegie commission on Higher Education, 1971). 1980–81 on from *Digest of Educational Statistics, 1985-86*, p. 101.
Column 4: Calculated using age 18–24 population from U.S. Bureau of the Census.
Column 5: Calculated using Total Population from U.S. Bureau of the Census.

TOTAL RESOURCES FOR HIGHER EDUCATION

Providing for these ever-growing numbers of students meant raising substantial amounts of new revenue from taxpayers, donors, students, supporters of research, and those who purchased services sold by higher education institutions. The major sources of current fund revenue are shown in Table 2 for 1983–84; for comparison, the table also shows the distribution of current fund expenditures.

The growth of revenues for higher education is substantial. Because of economic growth and inflation the linkage between the growth of revenue and increased enrollment is unlikely to be close over any extended period. More interesting for our purposes is the relationship between higher education's revenue growth and the economy's capacity to support higher education. This is illustrated in Table 3, which shows revenues for higher education as a percentage of gross national product (GNP); revenues averaged about 1.0 percent of GNP in the 1940s and 1950s, rose to a little over 2.0 percent in the late 1960s,

Table 2
Major Categories of Current Fund Revenues and Expenditures
for Higher Education Institutions, 1983–84 (Millions of Dollars)

Total Current Fund Revenue	$84,417

Tuition and Fees	19,715
Federal Government	10,406
State Government	24,707
Local Government	2,192
Private gifts, grants, and contracts	4,415
Endowment income	1,874
Sales and service	18,468
Other services	2,640
Total Current Fund Expenditures	$81,993

Education and general	63,741
Instruction	26,436
Research and public service	19,223
Scholarships and fellowships	3,302
Auxiliary enterprises and hospitals	16,630

SOURCES: "Higher Education Finance Trends, 1970–71 to 1983–84," *OERI Bulletin* (U.S. Department of Education, Center for Education Statistics, December 1986, CS 87-303b): 6–10.

and then stabilized at about 2.5 percent of GNP in the 1980s. These results demonstrate the close connection that persists between enrollment levels and the proportion of the nation's total resources required to support higher education. This relationship prevails largely because, at least in the public sector, the funding formulas give considerable if not exclusive weight to enrollments.

The sources of current-fund revenue for institutions of higher education changed in only minor ways as shown in Table 4. The major source is state government, followed closely by tuition and fees, with all three types of funding growing at roughly the same rate. Federal contributions have for the most part been stable, constituting less than a quarter of total revenues.

HIGHER EDUCATION EXPENDITURES

Higher education current-fund expenditures by institutions, as shown in Table 5, represent the other side of the ledger, one that is conditioned by the amount of revenues available. As Howard R. Bowen[26] so aptly explains, higher education is comprised of essentially nonprofit organizations which, while forced to live

Table 3
Total Current Fund Revenues and Expenditures for Higher Education Institutes
and Gross National Product (GNP) and Annual Percentage Rates of Increase

	Total Current Fund Revenues (in millions)	Gross National Product (in billions)	Total Current Funds Revenues as a Percent of GNP (in percent)	Total Current Fund Expenditures (in millions)
	(1)	(2)	(3)	(4)
1947–48	$2,027	$235	0.9%	$1,883
% Annual Change	9%	7%		9%
1957–58	4,676	451	1.0%	$4,509
% Annual Change	14%	6%		14%
1967–68	16,910	816	2.1%	16,556
% Annual Change	11%	10%		10%
1980–81	65,585	2,732	2.4%	64,053
% Annual Change	9%	8%		9%
1983–84	84,417	3,402	2.5%	81,993

NOTE: GNP data are for calendar year in which academic year begins.
SOURCES:
Column 1: *Biennial Survey of Education, Financial Statistics of Higher Education.*
Column 2: *Economic Report of the President, 1986.*
Column 3: Calculated as indicated.
Column 4: Same as Column 1.

within their available resources, seek constantly to increase their revenues in order to better serve their students and society.[27] These current-fund expenditures increase at about the same rate as do current-fund revenues (see Table 2, columns 1 and 3). This similarity is quite understandable in light of the organizational form of higher education institutions. More interesting than the changing level of overall expenditures is how major components of these expenditures grew from period to period.

We see in column I of Table 5 that total current-fund expenditures increased from $1,883 million in 1947–48 to $81,993 million in 1983–84, an increase of almost ten-fold. The rate of increase for the 1947–48 to 1957–58 period proved to be substantial, with total expenditures increasing about two and one-half times over the decade and quadrupling over the next two periods:

Table 4
Sources of Current Fund Revenues for Higher Education Institutions
(Millions of Dollars)

	1947–48	1957–58	1967–68	1980–81	1983–84
Total Income	$2,027	$4,641	$16,825	$65,585	$84,417
Tuition and Fees[a]	305	934	3,380	13,773	19,714
Federal Government	526	707	3,348	8,479	10,406
State Government	352	1,138	4,181	20,106	24,706
Local Government	48	129	504	1,790	2,192
Private Gifts, Grants, and Contracts	91	324	848	3,176	4,415
Endowments	87	182	364	1,364	1,874
Auxiliary Enterprises	465	839	2,482	7,288	9,456
Other Income (includes student aid)[b]	24	70	498	8,173	2,640

NOTES:
a. 1947 to 1967 includes "Student Fees" only.
b. 1947 to 1980 includes student aid with other income; 1983 includes only "other income."

SOURCES:
For 1947–48 see *Historical Statistics. Colonial Times to 1970* (Series H 716-727), p. 384.
For 1957–58 see ibid.
For 1967–58 see ibid.
For 1980–81 see *Digest of Educational Statistics, 1985–86,* Table 137, p. 154.
For 1983–84 see "Higher Education Finance Trends," *OERI Bulletin* (U.S. Department Of Education, Center for Education Statistics, December 1986, CS 87-303b): 6.

the increase was less than a third in the final but appreciably shorter period from 1980–81 to 1983–84.

The data on total current-fund expenditures are not highly illuminating in understanding the impact on higher education of the developments discussed in the first part of this paper. The reason is that total expenditures include funds allocated to carry out activities less central to the educational function of higher education and are in any case often self-financed. To the extent that expenditures for these functions grew more rapidly than total expenditures, this indicates that the residual, which is largely instruction-related expenditures, grew more slowly than the total.

How do we construct estimates of what we have just referred to as instructional or instruction-related expenditures? Several types of expenditures need to be excluded from total current-fund expenditures to arrive at instruction-related expenditures. The first category includes activities that are self-financing,

Table 5
Major Components of Current Fund Expenditures for Higher Education Institutions
and Annual Percentage Rates of Increase

Year	Total Current Fund Expenditures (in millions)	Auxiliary Enterprises, Hospitals (in millions)	Student Financial Aid (in millions)	Organized Research and Public Service (in millions)	Instruction-related Expenses (in millions)
	(1)	(2)	(3)	(4)	(5)
1947–48	$1,883	$492	$40 (est.)	$230	$1,162
% Annual Change	9%	5%	11%	15%	9%
1957–58	$4,509	$775	$113 (est.)	$903	$2,701
% Annual Change	14%	11%	22%	14%	14%
1967–68	$16,566	$2,307	$830 (est.)	$3,312	$10,234
% Annual Change	14%	14%	9%	8%	11%
1980–81	$64,053	$12,721	$2,505	$8,973	$39,854
% Annual Change	9%	12%	9%	.1%	9%
1983–84	$81,993	$18,252	$3,302	$9,222	$51,217

NOTES:
Column 2 includes Auxiliary Enterprises and Hospitals
Column 3 includes Student Financial Aid. Scholarships. and Fellowships
Column 4 includes Organized Research, Public Service, and Expansion
Column 5 includes column 1 less the sum of columns 2–4

SOURCE: *Biennial Survey of Education, Financial Statistics of Higher Education.*

such as auxiliary enterprises (dormitories and the like), hospitals, and related activities. Spending on these activities (column 2) grew at a slightly faster pace than did total expenditures.

A second category includes research expenditures that are heavily financed by outside sources, and also public service expenditures. While research is an integral element in the missions of research institutions, it is not directly related to instruction, especially at the undergraduate level. Research activity builds new knowledge, which is subsequently disseminated through classroom instruction and published journal articles. Research expenditures prove to be a substantial component of total expenditures and, in the 1950s and 1960s spending in this area grew rapidly, with most of this coming because of the growth of research support. By the 1970s, federal interest in research spending waned, having been displaced by spending on new social programs.

A third category of spending to be excluded from total current-fund expenditures is student financial aid, which in recent years has been classified as a part of education and general expenditures; this money is not central to the instructional mission of institutions even though it may be important to the attainment of other objectives. By way of illustration, student financial aid expenditures from institutional sources largely affect the mix of students at individual institutions; they are presumed to exert some effect on overall enrollment levels in the higher education system. Beyond that, they are unrelated to instruction.

Student financial aid expenditures made by and through institutions of higher education increased substantially. They grew from two percent of the total in the 1940s to about four percent in the 1980s. Of course, a more significant amount of financial aidthat provided largely through federal programsdoes not flow through institutions but rather is distributed directly to students through Pell grants and various student loan programs.

If we now exclude each of these categories of expenditures by subtracting columns 2-4 from column 1 in Table 5, we arrive at something that can be identified as costs related to instruction, hereafter called "instruction-related" costs or expenditures. These costs represent about 60 percent of total current-fund expenditures.

INSTRUCTION-RELATED COSTS, TUITION AND FEES, AND STUDENT AID

We now focus on the relationship between instructional costs, what students pay in the form of tuition and fees, and the amounts of financial aid received by students. We interpret student financial aid as an effort to promote equity, and we take changes in student financial aid relative to instruction-related costs as an indicator of the trade-off between quality and equity. Tuition and fees help to highlight the dimensions of this trade-off.

The data needed for this analysis are shown in Table 6, which highlights the growth of student financial aid funding by showing noninstitutional aid as well as total student aid. Built into the table are estimates of financial aid provided through veteran's programs (the GI Bill) for 1947–48 and 1957–58 so as to make the data as comparable as possible over time. It is clear that veterans' educational benefits were enormous, being equal to from 74 to more than 100 percent of all instruction-related costs in 1947–48 and from 18 to 24 percent of those costs in 1957–58.

The evolution of student financial aid resources is clear: a dramatic fall took place from the late 1940s to the late 1950s, followed by a moderate increase to 1967–68, an enormous increase to 1980–81, and a slight decline from 1980–81 to 1983–84. Equally striking is the fact that total student aid funds exceeded total tuition and fee payments in 1947–48 and again in 1980–81. By contrast,

Table 6
Instruction-related Expenditures, Tuition and Fees,
Receipts and Student Financial Aid Funding (Millions of Dollars)

Year	Total Instruction-related Expenditures	Tuition and Fees	Institution-ally Provided Student Financial Aid	Other Student Financial Aid	Total Financial Aid
	(1)	(2)	(3)	(4)	(5)
1947–48	$1,162	670[a]	40	$824–1,249[b]	$864–1,289[b]
% Annual Change	9%	3%	11%	–4%–5%	–4%
1957–58	2,701	934	113	381–520[b]	494–633[b]
% Annual Change	14%	14%	22%	8%–5%	13%–10%
1967–68	10,234	3,380	830	821	1,651
% Annual Change	11%	11%	7%	25%	18%
1980–81	39,854	13,773	2,138	15,209	17,347
% Annual Change	9%	12%	5%	-10%	-2%
1983–84	51,217	19,714	2,502	13,593	16,095

NOTES:
a. Includes tuition and fees paid for veterans under the GI Bill. This $365 million figure may overstate the "tuition" component because of a surcharge paid directly to institutions to help pay the costs of expanding capacity to accommodate the enrollment of veterans.
b. The range reflects our inability to develop a precise estimate of student financial aid provided by the federal government.

SOURCES:
Columns 1 and 3 from Table 5.
Column 2 from Table 4 except for 1947-48 figure. See note.
Column 4 1947-48 and 1957-58 estimated from information in 1948 and 1958 *Annual Reports of the Veteran's Administration* (U.S. Government Printing Office). 1967-68 estimated from data in papers by W. Lee Hansen and Joseph Boyd in *Trends in Postsecondary Education* (Office of Education, 1972). Data for 1980-81 and 1983-84 represent the difference between columns 3 and 5.
Column 5 is the sum of columns 3 and 4 except for 1980-81 and 1983-84. Those data are from Donald A. Gillespie and Nancy Carlson, *Trends in Student Financial Aid* (The College Board, 1985).

Table 7
Sharing the Costs of Higher Education
"Share" as a Percentage of Total Instruction-related Expenditures (costs)

Year	Total	Non-Student[a]	Student	Student Share Net of Instructional Aid	Student Share Net of all Aid
	(1)	(2)	(3)	(4)	(5)
1947–48	100.0	42.3	57.7	54.2	-16.7 to -53.3
1957–58	100.0	65.4	34.6	30.4	16.2 to 11.1
1967–68	100.0	67.0	33.0	24.9	16.9
1980–81	100.0	65.4	34.6	29.2	-9.0
1983–84	100.0	61.5	38.5	33.6	7.6

NOTES:
a. Defined as state and local taxpayers and private donors.

SOURCES:
Column 1: Column 1 of Table 6 set equal to 100.0.
Column 2: Column 1 minus Column 2 of Table 6 set as a percent of Column 1.
Column 3: Column 2 of Table 6 as a percent of Column 1.
Column 4: Column 2 less Column 3 divided by Column 1.
Column 5: Column 2 minus Column 5 divided by Column 1.

student aid funds were only about half of all tuition and fees paid in 1967–68, just when new need-based student aid programs were being launched.

SHARING THE COSTS OF HIGHER EDUCATION

We now take the last step in the analysis, which is to show how the costs of higher education are shared. This is accomplished in Table 7 by rearranging the data from Table 6. Total instructional costs are shared between students who pay tuition/fees and state and local taxpayers and private donors who make up the difference (see columns 1 and 2).

The nonstudent share rose considerably from 1947–48 and then stabilized in the 61 to 67 percent range. The student share of these costs, the exact opposite of the nonstudent share, proved to be surprisingly constant from 1957–58 through 1980–81. By 1983–84 there had been a slight increase because of the rise of tuition levels. The 1947–48 figure shows that students paid an appreciably larger proportion of the costs, by our estimate 58 percent (see note to Table 6).[28]

The student share shown in column 3 of Table 7 is reduced in two ways.

The first is through institutionally provided student financial aid, which has had relatively little impact on the student share (see column 4). The second and more important way is through other types of student aid that, with institutional aid, produce dramatic changes in the student share (see column 5). We find the net student share to be negative in 1947–48 because of the large infusion of student aid provided by the GI Bill. Total student aid reduced the student share by about one-half in 1957–58 and continued to do so through 1967–68. In other words, student aid was equivalent to roughly half of all tuition and fee payments by students.

It needs to be pointed out that student financial aid is designed to do more than simply defray the costs of tuition; it also goes to meet the costs of attendance. Nonetheless, the magnitude of financial aid resources is highlighted by this comparison.

The dramatic effect of the actions taken in the late 1960s and 1970s appears in the data for 1980–81. Total student financial aid grew so rapidly that it exceeded tuition and fee payments by students. With the slower growth of student aid in the early 1980s and continued increases in tuition and fee levels, the student share rose but remained well below the level of the 1950s and 1960s.

The results for 1980–81 do not entirely reflect the equity effects of student aid. At that time Guaranteed Student Loans were awarded without regard to financial need, and hence many middle-income students took advantage of the favorable borrowing opportunities. Were we able to adjust for this, the net student share would probably not have dipped below zero.

The results for 1983–84, which show a rise in the net student share, reflect in considerable part efforts by institutions to offset the slower growth of resources available to higher education institutions from traditional sources (i.e., state tax support and private funds). This led to tuition increases that were required to raise substantially faculty salaries that had been declining in real terms, to increase expenditures for maintenance and modernization of facilities that had earlier been deferred, and for allocation of funds to new technology, such as computers.

We conclude that federal student financial aid represented a powerful injection of new resources into the higher education system. By 1980–81 this amount was enough to more than eliminate tuition and fee assessments against all students. Of course, financial aid funds could not have been used in this way because they are directed largely to students who demonstrated financial need. And by 1983–84 student aid still acted as an important offset for student costs of higher education.

Conclusion

In summing up this analysis, it is clear that the substantial rise in college enrollments led to the need for increased funds to provide instruction and related services. Meanwhile, current-fund income for institutions of higher education rose relative to GNP, but we know this reflects at least in part enrollment increases. It is expenditures rather than income, however, that determine what happens in higher education, and particularly instruction-related expenditures. We find that these expenditures increased at about the same pace as revenues but their level was somewhat lower because of the need to exclude several categories of expenditures that were not (or were less) directly related to student instruction.

Instruction-related expenditures, tuition/fees, and student financial aid rose substantially overall from the late 1940s to the 1980s. Yet the burden on students through their tuition and fees has remained relatively constant in the 38 to 39 percent range since the late 1950s. Once we take into account student financial aid funds, we find that the student share has been substantially reduced by the infusion of federal funds for student financial aid; great progress was made from 1967–68 to 1980–81, with some backsliding since then. However, it needs to be pointed out that a large proportion of the 1980–81 financial aid was not targeted to low-income students as it was in 1983–84. This raises the possibility that the changes from 1967–68 to 1980–81 and 1980–81 to 1983–84 were exaggerated in their impact on overcoming financial barriers to college attendance.

The usefulness of the periods employed in this analysis derives from their ability to differentiate among the social goals. These goals for the most part reflected efforts to resolve problems outside higher education. The goals carried with them only two demands: to improve quality and to improve equity. We do discern the pendulum effect mentioned earlier. The student share diminishes as equity concerns dominate and increases again when greater attention is given to quality.

What progress has been made in pursuing these goals? On equity it is clear that the cost of college attendance for students with incomes low enough to qualify for student aid declined sharply over the past forty years, and this by itself stands as a major accomplishment. The evidence concerning quality is less clear. It is encouraging that no matter of how one looks at higher education institutions and their programs, levels of investment have been maintained.

What do we conclude and what is the issue for the future? Earlier progress toward improving the quality of higher education in the 1950s and 1960s has been eroded by efforts to improve equity in the 1970s. The gains achieved in pushing equity at the expense of quality lead us to expect eroding support for equity. If these funds are reallocated to promote quality, they will do so in a much more restricted fashion, benefiting those students who are most able to pay.

The sentiment favoring increased investment in higher education is mounting. Recent debate in Congress and the results of public opinion polls indicate a sharp rise in the perceived importance of higher education.[29] Calls for the involvement of higher education in stimulating economic development and restoring American competitiveness continue to grow. Increased concern is also voiced about improving quality in higher education by raising academic standards. Despite this, most recent discussions about how to improve quality neglect to point out the need for new investment of resources. Without additional resources the only alternative will be to curtail equity.

Notes

The authors acknowledge the research assistance of Marilyn H. Rhodes as well as the financial support of the National Center for Postsecondary Governance and Finance and the Wisconsin Center for Education Research.

1. David C. McClelland, *The Achieving Society* (New York: Irvington Publishing, 1976).

2. President's Commission on Higher Education, *Higher Education for American Democracy* (Washington, D.C.: U.S. Goverment Printing Office, 1947).

3. Janet Kerr-Turner, *From Truman to Johnson: Ad Hoc Policy Formulation in Higher Education* (Ph.D. dissertation, University of Virginia, 1986).

4. The population of eighteen-year-olds subsequently hovered in the 4.2-4.3 million range from 1975-79 but in l984 had dropped to 3.7 million.

5. See T. W. Schultz, *Journal of Political Economy 46* (October 1962); Edward F. Denison, *The Sources of Economic Growth and the Alternative Before Us* (New York: Committee for Economic Development, 1962).

6. The Report of the President's Commission on National Goals, *Goals for Americans* (Englewood Cliffs, N.J.: Prentice Hall, 1960).

7. Janet Kerr-Turner, *From Truman to Johnson.*

8. Lois Rice, ed., *Student Loans: Problems and Policy Alternatives* (New York: College Entrance Examination Board, 1977).

9. Leonard A. Lecht, *Goals, Priorities, and Dollars: The Next Decade* (New York: The Free Press, 1966).

10. Clark Kerr, *Agenda for a Nation,* ed. Kermit Gordon (Washington, D.C.: The Brookings Institute, 1968).

11. Carnegie Commission on Higher Education, *Quality and Equity: New Levels of Federal Responsibility for Higher Education* (New York: McGraw Hill, 1968).

12. Alice Rivlin, *Toward a Long Range Plan for Federal Financial Support for Higher Education* (Washington, D.C.: Department of Health, Education, and Welfare, January 1969).

13. W. Lee Hansen and Burton A. Weisbrod, *Benefits, Costs, and Finance of Public Higher Education* (Chicago: Markham Publishing Company, 1969).

14. Lawrence Gladieux and Thomas R. Wolanin, *Congress and the Colleges* (Lexington, Mass: Lexington Books, 1976).

15. 1978 Amendments to the Higher Education Act of 1965.

16. E. Whitt, D. Clark, and T. Astuto, *An Analysis of Public Support for Educational Policy Preferences of the Reagan Administration* (Policy Studies Center of the University Council for Educational Administration, December, 1986), Occasional Paper No. 3.

17. Jacob O. Stampen and Roxanne W. Reeves, "Coalitions in the Senates of the 96th and 97th Congresses," in *Congress and the Presidency: A Journal of Capital Studies,* vol. 13, no. 2.

18. E. L. Boyer, *High School: A Report on Secondary Education in America* (New York: Harper and Row, 1983); Business Higher Education Forum, *America's Challenge: The Need for a National Response* (Washington, D.C.: Author, 1983); National Commission on Excellence in Education, *A Nation at Risk: The Imperative for Educational Reform* (Washington, D.C.: Government Printing Office, 1983); National Task Force on Education for Economic Growth, *Action for Excellence* (Denver Education Commission on the States, 1983); D. Ravitch, *The Troubled Crusade: American Education 1945–1980* (New York: Basic Books, 1984); T. R. Sizer, *Horace's Compromise: The Dilemma of the American High School* (Boston: Houghton-Mifflin, 1984); The Twentieth-Century Fund Task Force on Federal Elementary and Secondary Education Policy, *Making the Grade* (New York: Author, 1983).

19. National Commission on Excellence in Education, *A Nation at Risk: The Imperative for Educational Reform* (Washington, D.C.: Government Printing Office, 1983).

20. M. S. Smith, *Educational Improvements Which Make a Difference: Thoughts About the Recent National Reports on Education* (Washington, D.C., 1984a). Paper presented to the Federation of Behavior, Psychological and Cognitive Sciences.

21. *A Nation at Risk;* F. Newman, *Integrity in The College Curriculum: A Report to the Academic Community* (Washington, D.C.: Association of American Colleges, 1984); Ernest L. Boyer, *College: The Undergraduate Experience in America* (Princeton: Carnegie Foundation for the Advancement of Teaching, 1987).

22. We begin with 1947–48 because data for 1946–47 are incomplete.

23. We plan to examine differences between public and private institutions in a subsequent paper.

24. Carol Frances, *The Short Run Economic Outlook for Higher Education* (Washington, D.C.: American Council on Education, 1980).

25. To the extent that the percentage of students age twenty-five and above increased, the rise in the college-going rate is somewhat overstated.

26. Howard Bowen, *The Costs of Higher Education* (San Francisco: Jossey-Bass, 1980).

27. For other recent studies of expenditures, see Joseph Froomkin, "The Impact of Changing Levels of Financial Resources on the Structure of College and Universities"; Paul T. Brinkman and Dennis P. Jones, "Colleges and Universities Adjustment to Changing Financial Enrollment and Structure Implementations of Institutional Adjustment Strategies," presented by the National Science Foundation Conference, July 29, 1986; and Durward Long, "Financing Public Universities and Colleges in the Year 2000," in *The Future State of Universities: Issues in Teaching, Research, and Public Service,* ed. Leslie W. Koepplin and David Wilson (New Brunswick, N.J.: Rutgers University Press, 1985).

28. A considerable fraction of the student share was offset because for veterans the federal government paid tuition/fees directly under the provisions of the GI Bill.

29. Gallup Poll (October 17, 1985).

PART TWO

EXTERNAL FORCES

6

The Federal Government and Higher Education

Lawrence E. Gladieux, Arthur M. Hauptman, and Laura Greene Knapp

Introduction

The framers of the U.S. Constitution lodged no specific responsibility for education with the national government, yet the federal influence on American colleges and universities has been enduring and pervasive. From sponsorship of land-grant colleges in the nineteenth century to the underwriting of student loans and university-based research and development in the twentieth century, the federal government has actively and extensively supported higher education to serve a variety of national purposes.

Today the federal government provides less than 15 percent of all college and university revenues. But in two types of spending, direct aid to students and funds for R&D, federal outlays far exceed those of the states, industry, and other donors. Higher education is also affected by federal tax policies, both in the financing of institutions and in family and student financing of the costs of attendance. Moreover, as a condition of federal spending and tax support, Congress and executive agencies of the government impose a variety of rules and mandates on postsecondary institutions and students.

The federal impact on campuses and on students is substantial, diverse, and constantly changing. It is the product of deeply rooted traditions but also short-term decisions. This chapter analyzes the federal government's relationship to higher education, beginning with the historical underpinnings and current means and dimensions of support. It then discusses issues in student aid, research support, tax policy, and regulation, and concludes with thoughts on federal policy directions for the balance of the 1990s.

The Responsibility for Higher Education in the American System

That the states have the basic responsibility for education at all levels is an American tradition. The Tenth Amendment, reserving powers not delegated to the central government to the states, coupled with the fact that "education" is nowhere mentioned in the Constitution, pointed toward a secondary role for the federal government in this field. While some of the founding fathers urged a national system of education run by the federal government, the majority favored state, local, and private control, perhaps with a national university to cap the system. All proposals to establish such a university in the capital city failed, despite the fervent support of George Washington and several of his successors in the presidency. To this day the federal government does not directly sponsor institutions of higher learning apart from the military academies and a few institutions serving special populations. Still, early federal policy was crucial in promoting higher education as an adjunct of western migration and public land development in the late eighteenth and nineteenth centuries. The Morrill Land-Grant College Act of 1862, for example, fostered the creation and development of what are now some of the nation's great public and private universities.[1]

Federal investment in university-based R&D and in student aid via the GI Bill soared following World War II. Beginning with the Soviet challenge of Sputnik, Congress created a variety of aid-to-education programs in the late 1950s and 1960s, and by the 1970s the federal government became the largest source of direct assistance to individual students for financing their college expenses. Fundamentally, however, federal expenditures have remained supplementary to state subsidies and private support of higher learning. Terry Sanford, former governor of North Carolina, U.S. Senator, and president of Duke University, once put it this way:

> The money for the extras came from the national funds. . . . This is the glamour money. . . . It is needed, it has improved the quality. . . . It is proper to remember, however, for all the advantages brought by the extras, the train was put on the track in the first place by the states, and continues to be moved by state fuel and engineers.[2]

Over the past two centuries, the states have moved with varying speed to create and expand public systems of higher education and, more recently, to assist private colleges and universities or to purchase educational services from them. Today the major public support for postsecondary institutions continues to come from the states. Figure 1, which shows the sources of funding for higher education in 1990, demonstrates the continuing hegemony of the states in this regard.

The traditional division of responsibilities between the federal and state

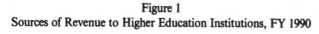

Figure 1
Sources of Revenue to Higher Education Institutions, FY 1990

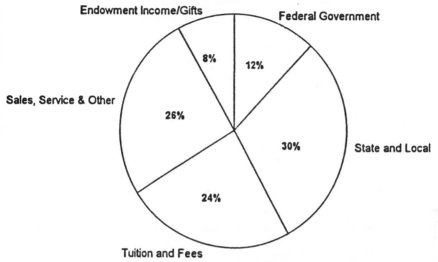

Source: Arthur M. Hauptman, *Higher Education Finance Issues in the Early 1990s* (New Brunswick, N.J.: Consortium for Policy Research in Education, Rutgers University, 1993).

governments was reaffirmed in the early 1970s when Congress debated and ultimately rejected proposals for general-purpose federal institutional aid. In passing the 1972 amendments to the Higher Education Act:

> Congress pulled up short of a plan that amounted to federal revenue sharing with institutions of higher education—across-the-board general operating support distributed on the basis of enrollments. It was unwilling to underwrite the entire system without reference to any national objective other than preserving and strengthening educational institutions. . . . The responsibility for general support of institutions, it was decided, should continue to rest with the states.[3]

This is not to say that the federal government has been unconcerned about the health and capacity of institutions. Certain types of institutions have received special federal attention because of their particular contributions to the national interest. Major research and graduate-oriented universities, particularly their medical schools, are one such category. They are supported by grants and contracts from multiple federal agencies. The historically black colleges are also beneficiaries of federal institution-based support, primarily through programs authorized under Title III of the Higher Education Act.

In addition, a few federal programs address institutional capacity for research. These include the National Institutes of Health's Biomedical Research

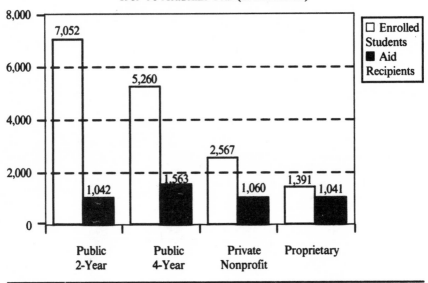

Figure 2
Enrolled Students and Federal Aid Recipients,
1989–90 Academic Year (in Thousands)

	Public 2-Year	Public 4-Year	Private Nonprofit	Proprietary	All Institutions
Number of Students	7,052,280	5,260,484	2,567,051	1,391,453	16,271,268
Number of Federal Aid Recipients	1,041,748	1,562,530	1,060,275	1,040,602	4,743,841
Percent of Federal Aid Recipients	15.0	29.7	41.3	74.8	29.2
Average Cost of Attendance	$3,324	$4,979	$12,057	NA	$6,207
Average of Federal Award per Aid Recipient	$286	$891	$1,535	$2,722	$887

Source: 1990 National Postsecondary Student Aid Study. Cost of attendance (tuition, fees, room and board) data from: *Digest of Education Statistics: 1990* (U.S. Department of Education) and *The College Cost Book 1989–90* (The College Board, 1989).

Support Grants and the National Science Foundation's Institutional Development Program. Other federal funding goes to support the arts and humanities, occupational and vocational education, international exchanges and studies, the provision of military training, and other purposes. Although the amounts are relatively small, they are significant for some institutions and certain parts of the education community.

Student aid also represents an indirect subsidy that affects nearly every institution in the country.[4] As shown in Figure 2, about a third of the 16 million-plus students who attend postsecondary education each year are estimated to receive some federal aid, in the form of grants, loans, or work-study. The aid programs benefit all sectors of postsecondary education, but the rate of student participation is by far the highest in proprietary schools (75 percent), followed by private non-profit colleges (41 percent), public four-year institutions (30 percent), and public two-year institutions (15 percent). The vigorous politics surrounding congressional reauthorization and revision of the student aid programs in 1980, 1986, and 1992 attests to the high stakes involved for postsecondary institutions. Representatives of the various sectors—two-year, four-year, public, private, proprietary—struggled over scores of amendments that determined who got what under Title IV of the Higher Education Act.

In sum, while federal education monies are much sought after, the historical limitations on the federal role continue to prevail in the 1990s. The states retain the fundamental responsibility for higher education, primarily through provision of operating support for public systems of colleges and universities. The federal role is to provide particular kinds of support to meet perceived national objectives, generally without distinguishing between public and nonpublic recipients. The federal government:

- purchases services and supports research capacity of universities;

- fills some gaps (e.g., in college library support, foreign language and area studies, and health professions development); and

- directs the bulk of its aid to students rather than to institutions, with the aim of removing barriers facing individuals who aspire to higher education.

Overview: Mechanisms and Dimensions of Federal Support

In the nineteenth century, states served as intermediaries in federal patronage of higher education. Proceeds from the sale of public lands provided endowments that helped the states establish and finance the early land-grant institutions, agricultural extension programs, and other forerunners of today's comprehensive colleges and universities. The federal grants to the states were broad and carried few restrictions.

Toward the beginning of the twentieth century, however, the pattern began to change. Federal support became piecemeal and started going directly to institutions themselves, bypassing state governments. In recent decades, nearly all federal monies have been channeled to institutions (or to departments, schools, and faculty members within institutions) or to individual students.

For this reason, a federal-state "partnership" in supporting higher education is meaningful only in a general sense. In fact, there is virtually no conscious meshing of funding purposes and patterns between the two levels of government. By and large the federal activity proceeds independently. One observer has concluded:

> With a few modest exceptions, federal postsecondary spending arrangements make no attempt to stimulate state spending, to compensate for differences in state wealth or effort, or to give state governments money to allot as they see fit.[5]

Nor, it might be added, would it be easy to implement a program or funding formula that would effectively achieve any combination of such objectives.

The federal government's activities affecting higher education are so decentralized and so intermixed with other policy objectives that simply trying to enumerate the programs and tally the total investment is problematic. Creation of the U.S. Department of Education in 1979 consolidated only about a fourth of the more than 400 programs that existed then, and less than a third of total federal expenditures for higher education—not substantially more than were encompassed by the old Office of Education in the U.S. Department of Health, Education, and Welfare. The remaining programs and funds are still scattered across a number of federal agencies, from the Departments of Defense, Energy, Agriculture, Transportation, and Health and Human Services to the Veterans Administration, Environmental Protection Agency, National Aeronautics and Space Administration, and Smithsonian Institution. This diffuse pattern within the executive branch is mirrored in Congress, where committee responsibilities tend to follow agency structures. Thus the fragmentary nature of federal influence and support for higher education seems likely to persist.

Table 1 provides an overview of federal support for higher education. In fiscal year 1992, federal spending totaled $29 billion, with 43 percent of this amount going for the cost of student aid, 50 percent for university-based R&D, and the balance for assorted categorical assistance and payments to colleges and universities. The more than $12 billion spent on the student aid programs is considerably less than the amount of aid actually made available to students (see Table 2), because the federal government guarantees and subsidizes private loans and requires non-federal matching in certain other programs.

Table 1
Estimated Federal Financial Assistance to Higher Education by Type and Source
Fiscal Year 1992 (dollars in millions)

Source	Amount	Percentage
Student Aid		
Department of Education	$10,124	
Department of Veterans Affairs	810	
ROTC scholarships and other military assistance	537	
Health professions scholarships/fellowships and training programs	839	
Programs for Native Americans	78	
Other Scholarship/Fellowship Programs	12	
Subtotal	12,400	42.7%
Research and Development	14,652	50.4
Other Institutional Support		
Department of Education	687	
Special Institutions	345	
Military academies	193	
National Science Foundation	310	
International Education/Cultural Exchange	223	
Other	255	
Subtotal	2,013	6.9
Total Federal Aid	$29,065	100.0%

Source: National Center for Education Statistics, *Digest of Education Statistics: 1992,* Washington, D.C.: U.S. Department of Education, 1992, Table 347.

Note: Some figures differ from those in Tables 2 and 5. Student aid here includes federal program costs only for FY 1992; Table 2 gives total aid available to students for academic year 1991-92, including the volume of borrowing generated by federal loan guarantees and subsidies, as well as amounts contributed by states and institutions. Military training assistance is included here but not in Table 2. Research and development figures include federal obligations for research and development centers administered by colleges and universities, unlike comparable figures in Table 5.

Student Aid

LEGISLATIVE HISTORY

From the land-grant college movement to the GI-Bill experience following World War II, public policy has progressively extended educational opportunity to new groups in society. In recent decades a major current in this policy stream has been federal aid to students. In 1963, the federal government invested around $200 million in student aid through the then-fledgling National Defense Student Loan program and a handful of graduate fellowships. Thirty years later, in the academic year 1992-93, the federal government generated an estimated $25 billion for students in postsecondary education, through either direct appropriations or loan guarantees and subsidies. After adjusting for inflation, that is almost a 25-fold increase. During the same period, enrollments also increased, but only about three-fold.

The growth of student assistance over the past quarter century is especially remarkable in light of the controversy surrounding the issue of federal student aid during the 1950s and 1960s. Congress had approved college benefits for military veterans under the GI Bill, but balked at general scholarships to undergraduates, whether based on financial need or on academic merit. Resistance to giving students a "free ride" doomed one such proposal after another in Congress during the Eisenhower and Kennedy years.

The breakthrough came in the mid-1960s. As part of the "Great Society" under President Johnson, the Higher Education Act of 1965 embodied, for the first time, an explicit federal commitment to equalizing college opportunities for needy students. Programs were designed to identify the college-eligible poor and to facilitate their access with grants, replacing contributions their families could not afford to make. Colleges and universities that wanted to participate in the new grant program were required to make "vigorous" efforts to identify and recruit students with "exceptional financial need."

With the 1965 legislation, a new dynamic began to shape the federal role in higher education. Earlier federal support had been prompted by specific national concerns: fostering a democratic citizenry, sponsoring research in the national interest, meeting perceived personnel shortages in the economy, compensating those who had served the country in wartime, and promoting international understanding. In the same vein, scientific and military preparedness was the spark for the National Defense Education Act of 1958. The 1960s did not change the national-interest focus of federal aid to education, but did put the spotlight on a broader moral imperative: removing inequitable barriers to individual opportunity. Also in 1965, Congress added a new benefit to the Social Security program that allowed children of deceased, disabled, or retired parents eligible for Social Security to receive benefits as dependents while they attended college.

Appropriations for student aid grew in the late 1960s, while other forms of federal support, such as construction of academic facilities, gradually faded in importance. In 1972, Congress and the Nixon administration converged with separate proposals for elaborating and greatly expanding the federal commitment to student assistance. Amendments to the Higher Education Act created Basic Educational Opportunity Grants as a floor of direct support for all needy students. Now called Pell Grants, this program in 1992–93 provided over $6 billion to more than 4 million students enrolled in postsecondary education and training.

The 1972 legislation also created the State Student Incentive Grant (SSIG) program to provide federal matching funds for need-based state scholarship programs. Twenty-eight states had already inaugurated scholarships to students, but the federal stimulus of SSIG helped prompt the rest of the states to launch need-based aid programs of their own. Likewise during the 1970s, an increasing number of states responded to federal incentives to help generate credit financing for students through federally guaranteed loans. Pell and SSIG rounded out the federal commitment to student aid, which during the 1960s had already come to include College Work-Study, Supplemental Educational Opportunity Grants (SEOG), National Defense Loans (now called Perkins Loans), and Guaranteed Student Loans (now called Stafford Loans). Assistance was generally targeted at low- and moderate-income students. But in the late 1970s pressure mounted for broadening the base of eligibility for student aid. Proposals for college tuition tax credits built a head of steam in Congress and, to ward them off, the Carter administration went along with a legislative package that resulted in the Middle Income Student Assistance Act (MISAA) of 1978. MISAA liberalized eligibility for Pell grants and opened subsidized loans to students regardless of income or need. Shortly thereafter, Congress let the special allowance to banks participating in the guaranteed-loan program float with Treasury-bill rates, assuring a favorable return for lenders in the program.

The legislative expansion continued through the Education Amendments of 1980, which further liberalized need analysis for student aid, shielded the guaranteed-loan program from cost controls, and established two additional loan programs called Parent Loans for Undergraduate Students (PLUS) and Supplemental Loans for Students (SLS).Then came the 1980 elections and a new administration determined to shrink domestic social spending. While public and congressional reaction blocked wholesale cutbacks in student aid, the growth era in student assistance was clearly over. Many provisions of the Higher Education Act as amended in 1980 were repealed or delayed, guaranteed-loan eligibility was tightened, Social Security benefits for students were phased out, appropriations levelled off, and the purchasing power of federal student aid declined.

RECENT TRENDS AND ISSUES

Table 2 shows the amounts of aid available to students by source in 1992-93 compared to 1980-81. Notwithstanding the retrenchment of the early Reagan years, the federal government continues to supply the lion's share of assistance. As illustrated in Figure 3, the constant-dollar value of federal assistance gradually rebounded toward the end of the 1980s and was slightly higher in 1992-93 than in 1980-81. Several factors at work over the past decade, however, have diluted the impact of federal support in making college affordable.

- Tuition and other costs of attendance in higher education have risen faster than federal aid. At the same time, as shown in Table 3, tuition in both public and private colleges has out-paced per capita disposable personal income and median family income.

- The available aid has been spread over a larger student population, including a substantially increased number of students enrolled in short-term training offered by proprietary schools. Today students in proprietary schools account for about 20 percent of Pell Grants and Stafford Loans.[6]

- The emphasis in federal aid has shifted from grants to loans. Loans accounted for 20 percent of federal aid in 1975–76 and 64 percent in 1992–93, while grant aid has dropped from 76 percent to 33 percent over the same period. The shift in the grant-loan balance has been the result of several factors: the winding down of Vietnam-era veterans educational benefits, the phasing out of Social Security student benefits, the substantial growth of federally guaranteed student borrowing beginning in the late 1970s, and erosion of the Pell Grants' real value over time.[7]

By contrast, in the 1970s the growth in federal aid outstripped growth in tuition and growth in the eligible student population; grant aid was more common than borrowing, especially for low-income students; and family income levels generally rose faster than tuition. All these trends adversely affected college affordability in the 1980s and into the 1990s.

THE GRANT-LOAN ISSUE

The growing predominance of loan financing, a factor frequently cited in relation to the decline of minority and low-income college enrollees, has turned the federal policy commitment to equal opportunity 180 degrees from its origins. The Higher Education Act of 1965 sought to help the disadvantaged through need-based grants, while helping middle-class families through government-guaranteed but minimally subsidized private bank loans. Today, guaranteed

Table 2
Aid Awarded to Postsecondary Students by Program, 1980–81 and 1992–93
(dollars in millions)

Program	Academic Year 1980–81	1992–93	Percentage Change (in constant dollars)
Federally Supported Programs			
Generally Available Aid			
Pell Grants	2,387	6,162	56.9
SEOG	368	630	4.0
SSIG	72	70	–41.0
CWS	660	760	–30.0
Perkins Loans (NDSL)	694	897	–21.4
ICL	0	5	N/A
Stafford and PLUS/SLS	6,202	14,998	46.9
Subtotal	10,383	23,522	37.7
Specially Directed Aid			
Social Security	1,883	0	–100.0
Veterans	1,714	971	–65.6
Military	201	384	16.6
Other Grants	122	160	–19.8
Other Loans	62	418	307.9
Subtotal	3,982	1,934	–70.5
Total Federal Aid	14,365	25,456	7.7
Nonfederal Aid			
State Grant Programs	801	2,126	61.3
Institutional and Other Aid	1,625	6,971	160.8
Total Federal, State, and Institutional Aid	16,791	34,554	25.1

Source: Washington Office of the College Board, *Trends in Student Aid: 1983 to 1993* (Washington, D.C.: Washington Office of the College Board, 1993).

loans are far and away the largest source of aid, even for the lowest-income students. Guaranteed loans provide almost $15 billion in aid annually—two and a half times the size of the Pell Grant program that was meant to be the system's foundation.

When Congress reauthorized the student aid programs in both 1986 and 1992, a major focus of concern was the grant-loan imbalance. Yet the policy drift toward a loan-centered financial aid system remains unchecked. A key proposal in the 1992 reauthorization was to turn the Pell Grant into an entitlement

Table 3
Tuition Fees and Income, 1980–81 to 1991–92

	Public Four-Year	Public Two-Year	Private Four-Year	Private Two-Year	Personal (Per Capita)	Median Family
1980–81	804	391	3,617	2,413	8,424	21,023
1981–82	909	434	4,113	2,605	9,240	22,388
1982–83	1,031	473	4,639	3,008	9,721	23,433
1983–84	1,148	528	5,093	3,099	10,350	24,674
1984–85	1,228	584	5,556	3,485	11,257	26,433
1985–86	1,318	641	6,121	3,672	11,863	27,735
1986–87	1,414	660	6,658	3,684	12,474	29,458
1987–88	1,537	706	7,116	4,161	13,081	30,970
1988–89	1,646	730	7,722	4,817	14,109	32,191
1989–90	1,780	756	8,396	5,196	14,973	34,213
1990–91	1,888	824	9,083	5,570	15,898	35,353
1991–92	2,134	962	9,841	5,784	16,318	35,939
Pct. Chg. from 1980–81 to 1991–92	165%	146%	172%	140%	94%	71%

Source: Washington Office of the College Board, *Trends in Student Aid 1983 to 1993* (Washington, D.C.: Washington Office of the College Board, 1993).

Note: Income data are for the calendar year in which the academic year begins.

or mandated spending program with automatic increases for inflation. But the Bush administration opposed such a change, arguing there were already too many federal entitlements, one reason the federal budget had become so hard to control. Republicans in Congress backed the administration on the issue, as did Budget Committee leaders from both parties in both the House and Senate. So the Pell entitlement provision was withdrawn from the legislation before final passage.

After the Pell entitlement failed, Congress followed a path of less resistance in boosting the dollar ceilings in the existing loan programs. Since loans, unlike Pell Grants, already operate as an entitlement, all eligible students are assured access to funds up to authorized levels. The legislation does raise the authorized maximum Pell Grant, but without the entitlement provision, actual funding levels will depend on annual appropriations. And there has been a widening gap between the authorized and actual Pell maximum in recent years.

The reauthorization bill also establishes an unsubsidized loan option not restricted by need. This is intended to make loans available to those in the middle-

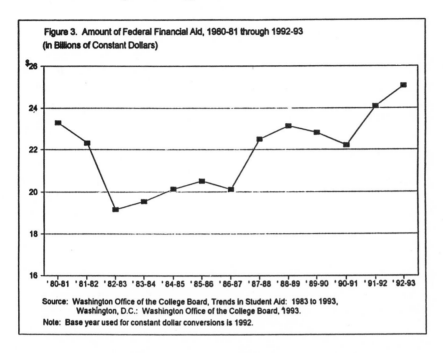

Figure 3. Amount of Federal Financial Aid, 1980-81 through 1992-93 (In Billions of Constant Dollars)

Source: Washington Office of the College Board, Trends in Student Aid: 1983 to 1993, Washington, D.C.: Washington Office of the College Board, 1993.

Note: Base year used for constant dollar conversions is 1992.

income range who have been squeezed out of eligibility for the regular guaranteed loan. The new loans will be less of a drain on the federal budget in that the government will not pay the interest costs while the borrower is in school.

All told, the principal impact of the 1992 legislation is clear: far from correcting the grant-loan imbalance, it will expand borrowing capacity for students and parents at all income levels in the years ahead.

PROVIDING FLEXIBILITY IN LOAN REPAYMENT

While the shift to loans continues, policy makers hope to mitigate the potentially adverse effects on students' career choices and on equity of access to higher education by providing greater flexibility in repayment. The 1992 legislation offers graduated and extended repayment terms to some categories of borrowers, and the Clinton administration is committed to pursuing a policy of allowing students to repay loans as a percentage of their future income through the Internal Revenue Service. The majority of borrowers will probably continue to repay without difficulty on the standard ten-year amortized basis. But for those students who know in advance that they want to pursue relatively low-paying service occupations, as well as those who later fall on hard times, alternative repayment schemes will probably become increasingly important in the 1990s.

LINKING STUDENT AID AND SERVICE

The Clinton administration is also committed to expanding opportunities for students to pay for their education through performance of service to the nation or community. While falling well short of the ambitious program the President had initially proposed, legislation passed in 1993 aims to enable up to 100,000 individuals to earn postsecondary education or training benefits by serving in areas of public need for up to two years. The benefits could be used either to pay post-service educational expenses or to repay educational debts already incurred.

The Clinton service initiative has many historical antecedents, including the Civilian Conservation Corps of the 1930s, the Peace Corps, VISTA, the National Health Service Corps, and a number of loan forgiveness and deferment provisions written into student aid legislation over the past 30 years. The new program seeks to strengthen the linkage between service and college aid—and even in its modified form, would do so on a much larger scale than previously attempted. Critics charge that the program will mainly benefit middle-class students, and that appropriations for it will inevitably cut into the base of funding for Pell Grants and other need-based aid focussed on the disadvantaged.

REFORMING THE STUDENT LOAN PROCESS

One way the Clinton administration intends to pay for the national service program is to capture savings from student loan reform. The Clinton plan, as modified and approved by Congress in the deficit-reduction package of 1993, calls for creation of a system of direct federal lending through postsecondary institutions, replacing at least in part the current program which relies on private banks and other financial intermediaries for loan capital. The aim is to squeeze excess subsidies out of the existing student loan structure, ultimately reducing federal costs by at least an estimated $1 billion a year while at the same time lowering interest expense to students and parents. The Student Loan Reform Act became law as part of the Clinton deficit-reduction package of 1993. The question is whether the federal government can make a successful conversion to direct lending; an under-staffed Department of Education faces a major challenge in launching the new program, and doing so without disruption and increased complexity for students.

WIDENING ELIGIBILITY FOR STUDENT AID

As in the late 1970s, Congress in the early 1990s wanted to extend federal assistance to more of the middle class. So the 1992 reauthorization law incorporates new federal standards for determining family and student ability to pay, and these standards are being used not only to award federal need-based grants and subsidized loans, but a substantial portion of state and institutional aid as well. The new federal standards expand calculated need by several billion dollars. But while the new law promises much on paper, there is little prospect of a corresponding increase in available funds from the federal government, states or institutions. The likely effect will be to shift scarce dollars up the economic ladder, at the expense of disadvantaged, truly needy students and families.

HELPING NONTRADITIONAL STUDENTS

At the same time, many policy makers and analysts worry that the existing aid system, designed primarily for families whose dependent children attend college full-time, is not sensitive to the wide-ranging needs and circumstances of nontraditional students. Increasing numbers of adults beyond traditional college age are returning to higher education for a second chance, retraining, and mid-career change. They often attend less than full-time and have continuing family and work responsibilities while in school.

Whether and how to support these students will be an ongoing policy concern in the 1990s. It may be that conventional aid programs are not the best way to reach nontraditional students. Expanding eligibility of independent adult students for aid will reduce the dollars available to dependent students from low-income families. And need-based grants and loans may not fit with the needs of many nontraditional students attending on a sporadic basis. Policy makers may need to consider new mechanisms outside the traditional forms of student assistance, including incentives to employers for facilitating and supporting employee training and retraining.

GRADUATE STUDENT ASSISTANCE[8]

The bulk of federal student aid goes to undergraduates, and the policy debates in Washington focus largely on issues of educational access and choice at the undergraduate level. Yet a portion of the aid available through the loan and work-study programs goes to graduate and professional students. Federal support for graduate students also comes in the form of research assistantships, fellowships, and traineeships, and much of this support is built into the funding of R&D administered by institutions. Table 4 compares estimated amounts of financial aid for undergraduate and graduate students in 1989–90 by source— federal, state, institutional, and private.

Overall, fellowship and other grant money for graduate students has declined since the 1960s, and universities have looked to alternative sources. The federal work-study program, for example, requires only 20 percent matching and has been increasingly used to fund teaching assistants. But the most common recourse for filling the gap has been student borrowing. Federally guaranteed loans have become an integral part of financing graduate and professional education, and many privately sponsored supplemental loan programs have been created

Table 4
Estimated Financial Assistance for Undergraduate and Graduate Students
1989–90 Academic Year (current dollars in millions)

	Undergraduate Students		Graduate Students	
	Amount	Percent	Amount	Percent
Federal Sources				
Title IV Grants	$ 5,392	21.2%	$ 2	0.0%
College Work Study	607	2.4	56	0.7
Federal Loans	7,710	30.4	3,178	38.1
Other Federal Grants	22	0.1	42	0.5
Other Types of Federal Aid	286	1.1	43	0.5
Subtotal	14,015	55.2	3,321	39.8
State Sources				
Grants	2,153	8.5	104	1.2
Loans	268	1.1	15	0.2
Work Study	42	0.2	4	0.1
Other	342	1.3	32	0.4
Subtotal	2,805	11.0	155	1.9
Institutional Sources				
Grants	4,389	17.3	1,057	12.7
Loans	150	0.6	13	0.2
Work Study	371	1.5	20	0.2
Assistantships	0	0.0	1,564	18.7
Other	397	1.6	1,174	14.1
Subtotal	5,306	20.9	3,829	45.9
Private Sources				
Employer Provided Aid	535	2.1	441	5.3
Grants/Scholarships	1,350	5.3	182	2.2
Loans	428	1.7	262	3.1
Other	961	3.8	153	1.8
Subtotal	3,273	12.9	1,038	12.4
Total Assistance	$25,400	100.0%	$8,350	100.0%

Source: Data are from the *National Postsecondary Student Aid Study* (National Center for Education Statistics, and U.S. Department of Education). Special analyses were conducted by the Washington Office of the College Board.

Note: Graduate research assistantships funded through federal research grants to institutions may appear under Institutional Sources rather than Federal Sources because of the way the data were collected by the National Postsecondary Student Aid Study. Thus, federal graduate assistantships are understated and institutional graduate assistantships are overstated in this table.

to serve students in high-cost fields such as the health professions. It is at this level that concerns about mounting student indebtedness become most acute, especially among students who have already accumulated substantial loan obligations as undergraduates.

Traditionally, graduate institutions and departments have awarded aid primarily on the basis of academic merit. But recent financing trends have created a dual system. Research assistantships and what remains of fellowship support from federal and private sources continue to be awarded on competitive academic criteria, whereas the great proportion of subsidized work, loan, and other aid to graduate and professional students is directed to students according to their financial need.

In general, graduate students are experiencing increased difficulty financing their education when financial rewards accruing to an advanced degree, especially in traditional academic disciplines, are uncertain at best. Many observers worry about the quality and numbers of students pursuing graduate work, and about the adequacy of federal policies to meet national needs for highly trained personnel in the 1990s and beyond.

BEYOND FINANCIAL AID

Whatever the federal policy and commitment to helping students meet postsecondary costs, policy makers increasingly recognize that student aid dollars alone are not sufficient to ensure greater access to higher education by underrepresented groups. Too many variables other than finance—quality of prior schooling, family attitudes, motivation, awareness of opportunities—help to determine college participation. Earlier, larger, and sustained interventions in the education pipeline are necessary.

This need is addressed at the federal level through the so-called TRIO programs of counseling, outreach, and special support services for the disadvantaged, created as a complement to the student aid programs in the original Higher Education Act. Congressional appropriations for the TRIO programs grew even during the most difficult fiscal years of the 1980s, but funding of these efforts still falls far short of the need. Also in this vein, the 1992 reauthorization of the law calls for additional initiatives inspired by Eugene Lang's "I Have a Dream" movement in cities around the country, which seeks to mentor disadvantaged junior high students, widen their horizons, and see them through to high school graduation and postsecondary opportunities.

ACCESS TO WHAT?

For most of the past quarter century, federal policy under Title IV of the Higher Education Act has consistently emphasized access. The ideal that was forged in the mid-1960s—equalizing postsecondary opportunities by removing financial barriers for needy individuals—remains paramount. But high default rates on guaranteed student loans and widely publicized problems of program abuse have raised nagging questions. Are dollars being directed effectively to those who really need help and have a reasonable chance of benefitting from the education and training that is being subsidized? What assurances does the federal government have regarding the quality and utility of such education and training? Is it provided at reasonable cost? Do federal aid recipients complete their programs in a reasonable period of time? Do they secure jobs in the fields for which they have prepared? In short, are students and taxpayers receiving their money's worth? With these questions heard more and more frequently, student aid policy debates in the 1990s are likely to focus as much on academic quality and cost effectiveness as on access.

A principal though not exclusive object of concern regarding quality and standards has been the proprietary trade schools. As noted earlier, a substantial share of the government's student aid commitment now goes to finance training offered by proprietary schools. And much of that financing has focused on very low-income students who lack basic academic skills and enroll in short-term job training programs that may result (at best) in minimum-wage employment. The default rate on student loans in the proprietary sector has averaged over 40 percent—four times that of four-year collegiate institutions.

What kinds of education and training should be fostered through the mechanism of student aid? In the 1970s Congress substituted the term "postsecondary" for "higher" in the student aid statutes, and eligibility was broadened to include short-term vocational training provided by for-profit schools, as well as the traditional programs of public and non-profit private institutions. Congress embraced a marketplace philosophy: students would "vote with their feet," taking their federal aid to institutions that met their needs. But the marketplace rationale begged important questions of institutional effectiveness and accountability. Few foresaw the burgeoning of the trade school industry that would be stimulated by the new federal incentives. Many for-profit programs came to be subsidized almost entirely by tax dollars, basing their prices on the aid package available to students from the federal government.

The federal student aid programs have traditionally relied on a so-called triad of institutional accreditation, state review, and federal oversight to ensure quality control. The federal responsibility, as carried out by the Department of Education, has included certifying accreditation agencies as well as ultimately approving institutions to participate in the federal aid programs. Over time, however, the triad arrangement has proven increasingly inadequate to the task. Federal certification of accrediting agencies and final approval of institutions have been largely pro forma. In many states, the state role has been weakened because a number of state agencies are responsible for reviewing different groups of institutions, with the result that the overall impact of state review is often uncoordinated and diluted. In addition, many states view proprietary schools as small businesses and therefore minimize regulation of them. But the weakest link of the triad has been the accrediting agencies themselves. Concentrating as they should on the academic attributes of institutions, these agencies are typically ill-equipped to make critical judgments about the financial soundness and suitability of institutions to participate in federal programs. Moreover, the fact that the institutions themselves provide the bulk of revenues of the accrediting agencies may create a less than arms-length relationship.

Restoring "integrity" to the student aid process was a principal theme of the 1992 reauthorization of the Higher Education Act. Congressional sponsors recognized that these issues had to be addressed if the programs under Title IV of the Act are to be viable in the intense competition for federal appropriations in the years ahead. The principal new thrust in the 1992 legislation is to place more reliance on state agencies as gatekeepers to help determine which postsecondary institutions should be eligible to participate in the federal Title IV programs. But how effective such an approach will be remains to be seen. The states' responsibility is activated only to the extent that federal funds are provided to support states in carrying out this function. Moreover, states may be reluctant partners in such an endeavor; state officials responsible for licensing and reviewing postsecondary programs have long complained they should not bear the brunt of regulatory problems that the federal government itself created by subsidizing the proprietary sector so substantially.

Meanwhile, the Department of Education has sought to tighten the system by prohibiting institutions with excessively high default rates from continuing to participate in the programs, and these efforts *have* had some impact in reducing the overall level of defaults and eliminating schools that were clearly abusing the system. But establishing the default rate cutoffs is arbitrary and problematic in many respects, and institutions have great incentives to manipulate their numbers to stay below the cutoff level. In addition, the due process entailed in withdrawing federal approval has proved to be so cumbersome that many institutions manage to participate for many years after being targeted as problem schools. In summary, the fundamental issues of institutional eligibility and quality control in the federal aid programs remain to be effectively addressed in the 1990s. The Clinton administration is considering fresh approaches in this area, including new performance and compliance standards that would condition institutional eligibility to participate in the aid programs.

ISSUES OF AFFORDABILITY: QUALITY AT WHAT PRICE?

Concerns about quality ultimately are linked to concerns about cost. The rapid rise in tuition and other costs of attendance over the past decade has stimulated worries about whether college will continue to be affordable for a broad range of Americans and whether it will be worth the price. A number of important works on higher education finance in recent years have echoed this theme of affordability. Michael McPherson and Morton Schapiro wrote a book for the Brookings Institution entitled *Keeping College Affordable*,[9] and the bi-partisan National Commission on Responsibilities for Financing Postsecondary

Education received widespread publicity over its report, *Making College Afford-able Again.*[10] Both studies call for an increased national commitment to need-based student aid to pay rising tuitions. The principal recommendation by the national commission is to make the level of federal aid more predictable and understandable for students and families by establishing a total amount of federal assistance for which any full-time undergraduate might be eligible each year.

Missing in these discussions, however, has been attention to the other side of the affordability equation, namely, how to reduce growth in the costs of a college education. In the final analysis, making college affordable again will depend on controlling the tuition spiral, and policy makers in the 1990s will be looking for ways to promote cost containment in higher education. An overall federal aid maximum, such as proposed by the national commission cited above, might eliminate possible incentives for some institutions to raise tuitions. Increases in the costs of attendance above the maximum would play no role in determining a student's eligibility for federal aid.

A more comprehensive approach to cost containment would be for the Secretary of Education to issue a schedule of "reasonable costs" for different types of postsecondary education and training—perhaps one standard for four-year academic training, one standard for two-year academic programs, and a variety of standards for different kinds of vocational training (based on what it should reasonably cost to provide training in automobile mechanics, cosmetology, computer programming, etc.). In some ways, such reasonable cost standards would be similar to the cost containment provisions in Medicare and Medicaid in which fees for a wide variety of services are prescribed in federal law or regulation. But in one important respect, higher education cost standards as sketched above would differ from those governing health care: namely, institutions would not be required to charge the standard amounts. They could charge students whatever they wanted, but would be reimbursed (through federal student aid) only up to the federal standard.

Research Support

Federal spending on R&D and other aspects of science at colleges and universities antedates the federal commitment to student aid, going back to an 1883 law to support agricultural experiment stations. But the investment in academic science was fairly small until the needs of World War II caused federal spending for campus-based research to skyrocket. The boom in federally-sponsored research continued through the 1950s and early 1960s. Though such support has not continued to grow at anything like the rates of the early postwar decades, the federal government remains the largest source of financing for campus-based research, supplying roughly $10 billion in 1991. R&D expenditures at colleges and universities are summarized in Table 5. In constant dollars, the federal contribution increased by more than 40 percent in the 1980s. Contributions from industry and all other sources grew much more. Overall, the 1980s was a very healthy decade for investment in university-based science. One observer has said, "If the 1960s were the golden age of research, then the 1980s were the gilded age."[11]

Unlike student aid, federal research funding is highly concentrated on a relatively small number of institutions, most of them major research universities. According to the National Science Foundation (NSF), the top 100 doctorate-granting institutions receive more than 80 percent of all federal R&D obligations to academia, a proportion that has remained quite stable over the years.[12] This support flows from multiple federal agencies and policy objectives. When NSF was created in 1950, Vannevar Bush envisioned an agency having broad purview over federal funding of research in the physical sciences, medicine, and defense, with a separate science advisory board to evaluate and integrate technical research sponsored by other government departments.[13] This vision is far from today's diffuse reality, with more than a dozen mission-oriented agencies separately deploying federal R&D resources to academic institutions for a variety of purposes.

While the nation's investment in science during the past half century has been repaid many times over in the form of thousands of pathbreaking discoveries and practical applications, political controversy and skepticism beset the academic research enterprise in the late 1980s and early 1990s. Ethical issues such as the protocols used in animal research have led to shrill campus protests. Publicized cases of research fraud have cast doubts about the conduct of scientific research that could threaten levels of financial support in the future.

Another sensitive issue is the growing practice of congressional earmarks to fund construction of research facilities on particular campuses around the country. More than $700 million was provided to colleges and universities in the form of earmarked appropriations in fiscal year 1992, and nearly $2.5 billion has been provided since 1980 when annual earmarks were roughly $10 million. Traditionally, federal campus-based research funds have been distributed on the basis of a peer review system in which individuals who are familiar with a field of research are asked to grade proposals for funding in that field. These peer reviews, along with considerations of cost effectiveness, largely determine which proposals receive funding. Proponents of peer review argue it ensures that the best research is supported. Opponents argue it is a vintage old boys network that precludes many worthwhile projects because the researchers are not tied into the network.

In part, the earmark phenomenon is a reaction to the heavy concentration of federal R&D spending on a relatively few institutions. Institutions outside this group go to their elected representatives and plead their case, often hiring expensive lobbyists in the process. Earmarking is also a response to a long-term problem affecting virtually all research universities—the deterioration and obsolescence of scientific equipment and facilities. Despite the substantial and

Table 5
R&D Expenditures at Universities and Colleges by Source of Funds
Fiscal Years 1981 and 1991 (dollars in millions)

Source	Fiscal Years		Percentage Increase (in constant dollars)
	1981	1991	
Federal government	4,565	9,650	43.1
State and local governments	546	1,553	92.5
Industry	291	1,250	191.0
Institutional funds	1,008	3,397	128.0
All other sources	436	1,350	109.6
Total	6,846	17,200	70.1

Source: National Science Board, *Science and Engineering Indicators—1991* (Washington, D.C.: National Science Board, 1991).

Note: Federal government dollars do not include amounts for federal funded research and development centers (FFRDCs).

growing federal investment in campus-based research over time, the inadequacy of the research infrastructure has been the subject of many studies and reports over the past decade. Only a small proportion of federal funds for research have been invested in facilities construction, maintenance, and renovation. In the 1950s and 1960s, separate appropriations were made for facilities, but in recent decades the bulk of funds for infrastructure has come through indirect cost recovery, an inefficient way of financing a crucial aspect of the research enterprise.

Indirect cost recovery itself has created the darkest cloud on the horizon for federal support of research. Stanford University was the catalyst for the emergence of this issue when it was revealed that expenses for a number of questionable items, including fancy provisions for the President's home and a donated yacht, had been submitted to the government over the years as part of Stanford's indirect costs on research grants and contracts. Adverse publicity and congressional hearings led to investigations of other research universities. Several institutions were required to return millions of dollars in questionable billings, and some institutions renegotiated their indirect cost recovery rates.

The issues underlying the system of indirect cost recovery, however, stretch far beyond the practices of Stanford and the other institutions that have been investigated. The existing system, which dates back over 30 years to the development of Office of Management and Budget (OMB) Circular A-21, is based on the principle that an institution's indirect cost recovery should be tied to the share of research-related costs in its total budget. But such a system gives institutions great incentive to categorize spending items as part of their pool of research-related costs. While Stanford was one of the most aggressive institutions in seeking indirect cost recovery, it and other universities correctly point out that they were playing according to the rules as they understood them. What complicated matters was the fact that the federal government was never very clear about what those rules were. Untangling this issue, therefore, will require reexamining the fundamental principles of the system itself.[14]

All of these issues take on particular significance in light of the dependence of universities on federal research dollars. While federal grants and contracts constitute less than 10 percent of total revenues of all colleges and universities, at some major research institutions federal dollars represent one-quarter or more of total revenues, and indirect cost reimbursements sometimes exceed 10 percent of a university's budget. Such federal dependence could become highly problematic under various future scenarios, including any radical change in the method of indirect cost recovery or drastic deficit-reduction initiatives such as a balanced budget amendment. Also, the end of the Cold War and the resulting decline in defense spending will likely have a disproportionate impact on institutions that are especially dependent on defense research dollars. The Clinton administration has announced its intention to equalize spending on defense and civilian R&D by 1998. The Clinton plan for R&D investment also assigns high priority to projects with clear potential for commercial applications, job creation, and economic competitiveness. And it calls for a series of multi-agency, inter-disciplinary initiatives emphasizing applied research as well as science, math, engineering, and technology education.

In sum, the tight federal budgetary outlook and questions about past practices will stir continued debate on the federal responsibility for research in the 1990s and beyond. What should be the role of university research in the post-Cold War world? Are universities still the best vehicle for federal investment in research, or should the emphasis shift to a more commercial, industrially-based strategy? Should federal research dollars be focused on the best researchers at a small set of universities, or would spreading the funds more widely produce better results? Whatever the answer to these questions, it is clear that universities will be challenged to do more with less, to identify their comparative advantages, to consolidate efforts with other research institutions, and to articulate more clearly to the public how research contributes to societal goals.

Tax Policies

In addition to direct funding of students and institutions, the government indirectly assists higher education through a variety of tax policies. A number of exclusions, exemptions, and deductions in the federal tax code over the years have benefited education at all levels. Some of these provisions—for example, the personal exemptions parents may claim for students age 19 and over, and the recent tax break on proceeds from U.S. savings bonds that are used for higher education—affect individuals and families in their ability to save for and pay college costs. Other provisions affect the revenue and financing arrangements of colleges and universities; for example, their not-for-profit status allows them to receive tax-deductible contributions.The monetary benefits to institutions and students of these tax provisions, so-called tax expenditures in federal budgetary parlance, are measured by the estimated amount of federal revenue that would be collected in the absence of such provisions. Prior to the passage of the Tax Reform Act of 1986, estimated annual "tax expenditures" for higher education totalled over $4 billion.

Corporate investment in university-based research was promoted by the tax legislation of 1981, which gave tax credits to industry for investment in cooperative, applied research projects with universities and permitted enhanced deductions for gifts of research and research training equipment. The 1986 tax bill amended these provisions to balance the tax incentives for corporate investment in basic and applied research. But overall the reform legislation of 1986, a watershed in federal tax policy, had adverse implications for higher education. For colleges and universities, particularly private non-profit institutions, the principal setback came in the form of limitations on charitable giving. The legislation both tightened tax deductions for gifts of stock, land, works of art, and other appreciated property and terminated the deductibility of gifts by non-itemizing taxpayers. Since these changes went into effect, their impact has not been conclusively demonstrated, but many colleges have reported a drop in donations. Another factor that may have reduced the level of giving is that high-income taxpayers have less incentive to give as a result of lower marginal tax rates on income that were instituted as part of the 1986 reform. The 1986 law also changed the rules for tax-exempt bond financing, thus placing particular constraints on large private universities.

Other changes legislated in 1986 have affected students and parents:

- The elimination of tax-deductible Clifford Trusts designed for very high-income families and changes in taxation of unearned income of children under the age of 14 have reduced the advantage of transferring income from parent to child as a means of saving for educational purposes. For the great majority of families, however, a transfer of income remains a viable college savings technique with a tax benefit.

- An individual may not take a personal exemption on his or her own tax return if he or she is eligible to be claimed as a dependent on another's return. Thus students under the age of 23 who up to 1986 were allowed to benefit from such an exemption are no longer able to claim it.

- The deduction for consumer interest, including interest on education loans to students and parents, was phased out. However, home mortgage interest remains deductible, and taxpayers are able to deduct interest payments on home equity loans used to meet educational expenses.

- Scholarships, fellowships, and federal grants to graduate and under-graduate students are counted as taxable income to the extent these awards, either individually or together, exceed the cost of tuition and related expenses. For most students, the increase in the standard deduction has mitigated the impact of this change, producing little or no tax liability. Those potentially affected are married students with spouses earning income, athletes receiving full scholarships, and, paradoxically, some of the neediest students (those with large grants).

Almost as soon as the Tax Reform Act of 1986 was signed into law, bills were introduced in Congress to restore the exclusion of scholarships and fellowships from taxable income, the deductibility of interest on student loans, the full deduction for gifts of appreciated property, and other provisions that had just been repealed or scaled back. But recovery of losses in the 1986 law has not come easily for higher education or any other constituency. Other than correcting technical errors, the congressional tax-writing committees in the late 1980s were determined to let the new law take effect, holding the line on the 1986 reform.

Moreover, higher education experienced something of a political backlash in the tax reform debate, with a perception in some quarters that well-endowed institutions had abused their tax-exempt status through creative financing schemes that took advantage of tax loopholes. At one point in the late 1980s the House Ways and Means Committee floated a proposal for a five percent tax on endowment income of colleges and universities. Also under scrutiny has been the question of taxing the unrelated business income of non-profit organizations, money gained from activities not directly tied to the organizations' purpose. Small businesses have complained that tax-exempt status gives non-profits an unfair competitive edge, and have singled out college and university travel services, bookstores, and research programs as examples.

With the relentless pressure for deficit reduction, the outlook for higher education in the tax policy arena has not substantially improved in the early 1990s. In 1993, however, higher education did win at least one significant concession as part of the five-year Clinton budget package. As passed by Congress, the legislation restores the full tax deductibility of gifts of appreciated property. The 1993 legislation also retroactively restores two tax provisions that had expired in 1992: the tax break for corporate spending on university research mentioned above, and the exemption from personal income tax of employer-provided educational benefits to employees.

Apart from the recent tax reform movement, higher education continues to absorb the impact of long-term growth in Social Security taxes and unemployment insurance contributions required by employers. Because college and university budgets are made up disproportionately of personnel costs, higher education is more heavily affected by the rapid rise in payroll taxes than are some other sectors.

Federal Regulation and Its Impact

Concern about the impact of federal regulation on the internal affairs of universities was one of the most controversial issues in government-university relations in the late 1970s. One analyst wrote in dramatic tones:

> Not only legislatures and federal agencies but the courts as well are willing to scrutinize every exercise of discretion on the basis of a complaint. This is the twilight of autonomy and authority. The prevailing tides of opinion currently are egalitarian and legalistic and they are joined to a simplistic view of society and the likelihood of its improvement.[15]

Federal regulation of higher education derives from two principal sources: the requirements of accountability that accompany the receipt of federal funds; and the dictates of social legislation, as well as executive orders and judicial decisions stemming from such legislation.[16] To the degree that government officials insist on accountability for the proper expenditure of funds, and congressional mandates addressing a range of social problems remain in force, there will be complexity and strain in the relationship of government and higher education. Tensions are inherent, given the traditions of academic autonomy, the mandates of Congress, the missions of federal agencies, and the responsibilities of those agencies for the stewardship of taxpayer dollars.

The federal government influences higher education through scores of statutes and regulations administered by diverse federal agencies. Some mandates, such as the Americans With Disabilities Act, or regulations of the Environmental Protection Agency and the Occupational Safety and Health Administration, affect all types of organizations equally. Others, such as the Buckley Amendment on privacy rights of students and Title IX of the Education Amendments of 1972 barring sex bias, are specific to educational institutions. Colleges have long argued that such regulatory burdens contribute to their spiralling costs. But there is no documentation of the extent to which higher education is disproportionately affected by federal requirements, thereby justifying the more rapid increases in college charges during the past decade relative to prices of other goods and services in the economy.

The academic community has long been wary of entanglement with government, but only a few, mainly independent, religiously affiliated institutions, have consistently refused funds from Washington. The great majority of colleges have accepted federal patronage, even though it exacts a price in the expenses of compliance and in the distraction and intrusion of external controls. During the 1980s higher education's concerns on this front receded to some degree. The Reagan administration's widely publicized support for regulatory relief altered the climate of regulation. Enforcement eased in some areas, and over the years colleges learned to accommodate to the bureaucratic requirements of the government, tempering previous conflicts. Some institutions actually bargained with the federal government to lessen their regulatory burden. Prior to the highly publicized controversy over indirect costs in the early 1990s, for example, Yale and Stanford had accepted lowered indirect cost reimbursement on research contracts in exchange for reduced federal reporting requirements.But in many respects regulatory burdens have mounted not only for colleges but for all sectors of society in recent years. Higher education, along with other constituencies, has complained about the proliferation of "unfunded mandates" from Washington—legislative and regulatory requirements imposed by the federal government without federal funding to help pay the costs of compliance.

The balance of the 1990s will no doubt be replete with regulatory challenges for higher education. The indirect cost issue remains highly charged and problematic for the research universities. IRS scrutiny of colleges appears to be intensifying as tax regulations and compliance procedures grow more complex for all non-profit institutions. An arena of ongoing debate and litigation will be civil rights enforcement and the desegregation of public systems of higher education.[17] While the Supreme Court's 1954 decision in *Brown* v. *Board of Education* applied to collegiate as well as to elementary and secondary education, it was not until 1992 that the Court handed down a decision providing guidance for ending patterns of racial segregation in state postsecondary systems. In *U.S.* v. *Fordice,* the Supreme Court ordered a lower court to review all policies that "contribute to the racial identifiability" of Mississippi's public colleges and universities, and to eliminate those policies that cannot be justified. Interpreting and applying *Fordice* will take years, both in the federal courts and in the enforcement activities of the Office of Civil Rights of the U.S. Department of Education. A great deal is at stake not only for Mississippi, but for as many as 15 other states that have faced legal challenges to their higher education systems on grounds of alleged discrimination. Finally, a major challenge of the Clinton years will be in the student aid arena where, as suggested earlier in this chapter, the continuing high loan default rates and concerns about program abuse will demand policy solutions for the sake of both taxpayer and consumer protection.

The unique regulatory dilemma in student aid is the sheer number and diversity of schools and kinds of training supported by programs under Title IV of the Higher Education Act. Applying the same rules and simultaneously regulating the use of student aid subsidies by some 5,000 proprietary schools and 3,000 collegiate institutions simply does not work. So far Congress has been unwilling to consider disaggregating federal student aid policy and differentiating delivery mechanisms by postsecondary sector or length and nature of training. But the Clinton administration appears ready to take another look at this issue. Under consideration are proposals to split off vocational training from current student aid programs, possibly transferring responsibility for such training to the Labor Department where it would be supported through federal contract authority.

For collegiate institutions such a shift would have the effect of lifting some of the current burden of default prevention and related measures that are designed primarily to address trade school problems but must be applied across the board. But the colleges would not necessarily be let off the regulatory hook under the Clinton scenario. Traditional institutions of higher education have become increasingly vocational in their offerings, and many, especially two-year colleges, enroll large numbers of students who lack basic skills and enter college requiring remedial training that now is often supported by federal aid programs. If federal policy makers decide to treat postsecondary vocational training separately, many distinctions are going to have to be sorted out as to what constitutes "vocational" as well as "postsecondary."

Moreover, new federal cost and performance standards may be aimed at all types of schools. Clinton administration officials note that K-12 education policy debates are now centered on developing national standards, raising expectations of students and schools, systemic reform, and outcomes-based performance. They hope to spark a similar focus and movement in the postsecondary policy arena. Specific plans have yet to unfold, but lively debate on such proposals can be expected both in Washington and in the postsecondary community during the mid-1990s.

Prospects for the Federal Role in Higher Education

To recap, among key issues that will shape the federal role in higher education in the 1990s and beyond are the following:

- Student aid reforms will continue to focus on improving the delivery of federal dollars to intended beneficiaries. Debates will focus on whether to establish an overall federal aid maximum per student, target Pell Grants to allow for increases in award levels, and strengthen cost and academic standards conditioning institutional eligibility for federal student aid. There may also be consideration of whether student aid is the most appropriate mechanism for funding all postsecondary activities, including short-term vocational training and remediation for students unprepared to do college-level work.

- A principal question looming over the future federal role in research is whether federal funding will continue to increase in real terms given persistent concerns about existing research practices in academia and unrelenting pressure to reduce federal budget deficits. Specific issues will include finding means to upgrade the physical infrastructure of scientific research and reforming the indirect cost recovery process.

- Tax policy debates affecting higher education will center on continued efforts to restore or make permanent provisions that were deleted or made temporary by the 1986 and subsequent tax laws. These issues, however, will be considered in the much broader context of tax policy changes intended to stimulate economic growth and reduce the federal budget deficit.

- The chief regulatory issue for higher education in the 1990s is whether the trend toward unfunded mandates continues under the Clinton administration's campaign to reinvent government. Colleges should also be prepared for regulatory efforts specific to postsecondary student aid, including federal initiatives to promote both cost containment and greater quality control in higher education.

The federal government will undoubtedly continue to make important contributions to enhancing the academic enterprise and equalizing educational opportunities in America. As in the past, federal support will supplement the basic funding provided from state and private sources, and it will spring from objectives such as economic competitiveness rather than from an interest in education for its own sake. And funds, along with regulations, will continue to flow from a variety of agencies in Washington. Such support is untidy, piecemeal, and not without headaches for institutions, students, and states. But the pattern serves a variety of national purposes and, in fact, ultimately may better serve to protect institutional diversity, students' freedom of choice, and independent thought in American education than would an overarching federal policy.

Notes

1. For the historical development of the federal role in higher education, see George N. Rainsford, *Congress and Higher Education in the Nineteenth Century* (Knoxville, Tenn.: University of Tennessee Press, 1972). The two private universities benefitting from the Morrill Land-Grant College Act are MIT (established in 1861) and Cornell University (1865).

2. Terry Sanford, *Storm Over the States* (New York: McGraw Hill, 1967), p. 63.

3. Lawrence E. Gladieux and Thomas R. Wolanin, *Congress and the Colleges: The National Politics of Higher Education* (Lexington, Mass.: Lexington Books, 1976), p. 226.

4. An approach to assessing the indirect effects of student aid has been outlined

by Michael S. McPherson in "Silver Linings: Student Aid's Unintended Good Deeds," paper presented at the Annual Meeting of the American Educational Research Association, April 1987.

5. Chester E. Finn, Jr., "A Federal Policy for Higher Education?" *Alternative,* May 1975, 18–19.

6. Washington Office of the College Board, *Trends in Student Aid: 1983 to 1993* (Washington D.C.: College Entrance Examination Board, 1993).

7. Ibid.

8. For greater depth analysis on graduate student assistance, see Council of Graduate Schools, *Graduate Student Financial Support: A Handbook for Graduate Deans, Faculty, and Administrators* (Washington, D.C.: Council of Graduate Schools, 1990).

9. Michael S. McPherson and Morton Owen Schapiro, *Keeping College Affordable: Government and Educational Opportunity* (Washington D.C.: The Brookings Institution, 1991).

10. National Commission on Responsibilities for Financing Postsecondary Education, *Making College Affordable Again* (Washington D.C.: National Commission on Responsibilities for Financing Postsecondary Education, 1993).

11. Representative Rick Boucher, chairman of the Subcommittee on Science of the U.S. House of Representatives Committee on Science, Space, and Technology, "Science Policy for the 21st Century," *Chronicle of Higher Education,* September 1, 1993.

12. National Science Foundation, Division of Science Resources Studies, *Early Release of Summary Statistics on Academic Science/Engineering Resources* (Washington D.C.: National Science Foundation, 1986).

13. Deborah H. Shapley and Roy Rustum, *Lost at the Frontier* (Philadelphia: Institute for Scientific Information Press, 1985), p. 39.

14. Robert Rosenzweig, "The Debate Over Indirect Costs Raises Fundamental Policy Issues," *The Chronicle of Higher Education,* March 6, 1991; and U.S. General Accounting Office, *Federal Research: System for Reimbursing Universities' Indirect Costs Should Be Reevaluated* (Washington D.C., August 1992).

15. Robert A. Scott, "More Than Greenbacks and Red Tape: The Hidden Costs of Government Regulations," *Change,* April 1978, 16.

16. John T. Wilson, *Academic Science, Higher Education, and the Federal Government: 1950–1983* (Chicago: University of Chicago Press, 1983), pp. 104–106.

17. For more on the impact of civil rights enforcement and other litigation on colleges and universities, see the subsequent chapter in this volume by Walter C. Hobbs on the involvement of the courts in higher education.

7

The States and Higher Education
Aims C. McGuinness, Jr.

The period of the remaining years of the 1990s and well into the next decade is likely to be one of the most troubling in the history of the nation's higher education enterprise. Relations between state government and higher education are likely to be especially strained because of five broad trends:[1]

- *Escalating demands.* These are driven not only by numbers but also by higher expectations for what an increasingly diverse student population should know and be able to do as the result of a college education. The demands extend to virtually every dimension of higher education, including research and service.

- *Severe economic constraints.* Even with gradual economic recovery, it is unlikely that higher education will see significant improvements in funding, at least on a per-student basis, within the next decade. The federal deficit, competing priorities for public funds, public anger about rising student costs, and severe competition for limited corporate and philanthropic funds, will all contribute to the continuing financial constraints.

- *The academy's inherent resistance to change.* As demands increase and resources dwindle, institutions are slowly recognizing that, if they continue to do business as usual, their ability to educate students and continue their research and service missions will be seriously compromised. But translating this slow awareness into changes at the institutional core— in curriculum, in modes of teaching and learning, and in faculty governance—will be a long-term, incremental process. The resulting public frustration with the academy's inability to respond to major societal needs only intensifies the danger of blunt governmental intervention.

155

- *Negative climate of public opinion.* Ironically, the negative public view appears not to be driven by a feeling that higher education lacks value to the individual and society. On the contrary, the problem seems to be that the public values higher education greatly. But they see it being directed by a largely internal agenda disconnected from major societal priorities, and mismanaged in ways that will make it increasingly inaccessible (especially in terms of cost).

- *Instability of state political leadership.* The trend toward term limitations and the demands of political office are contributing to major changes in the state leadership. This is especially pronounced in state legislatures. In 1993 it was common across the nation to have new members comprising a third of one or both of the houses of a state legislature. The relative stability provided by the memory about state higher education policies of long-term legislative leaders is being lost. Other issues are dominating the agendas. The twenty-year trend toward larger and more dominant legislative staffs is accelerating.

These conditions are certain to exacerbate already frayed state relationships with higher education. Constructive resolution of these conflicts is essential both to the continued strength of American higher education and to its capacity to respond to major societal priorities. The purpose of this chapter is to present a framework and basic information about the state role as a beginning point for further reading and study.[2]

Assumptions about State and Higher Education Relationships

Two underlying assumptions are basic to the understanding of state-higher education relations: the essential and legitimate role of the state, and the great variations among states in size, culture, policies and structure.

For some within higher education even the mention of state government conjures up negative images. There continues to be a widespread sense within the academy that virtually any state involvement, other than providing funding with no strings attached, is an infringement on legitimate institutional autonomy. The relationships are viewed along a continuum: at one end, complete institutional autonomy is good; at the other end, state involvement is seen as bad. Frank Newman suggests a different, more constructive view. The point is that both institutional autonomy and state involvement are important. Governments have a legitimate interest in the responsiveness of the academy to major societal needs. At the same time, it is important both for society and for the academy that higher education be able to pursue values and purposes that are different from, and that in some cases may conflict with, the prevailing values and priorities of the state. "What becomes clear," Newman states, "is that the real need is not simply for more autonomy but for a relationship between the university and the state that is constructive for both, built up over a long period of time by careful attention on the part of all parties."[3]

Robert Berdahl makes a similar distinction between the concept of academic freedom, which is universal and absolute, and autonomy, which is "of necessity parochial and relative." He continues by emphasizing that ". . . the real issue with respect to autonomy . . . is not whether there will be interference by the state but whether the inevitable interference will be confined to the proper topics and expressed through a suitably sensitive mechanism."[4]

The key is for the higher education community to recognize that it has a stake, if not responsibility, to engage actively with state political leaders in defining the nature of the relationship. This includes defining the major societal ends toward which the academy should direct its energies, and shaping the policies and other "suitably sensitive" mechanisms that will govern the relationships.

A second point in understanding state-higher education relations is that, despite the appearance of similarity in institutional missions and state structures, states vary significantly in history, culture, and political and economic dynamics. Colleges and universities, as social institutions, reflect, if not amplify, these important, yet often subtle differences. In reports on state policy, one often sees state-by-state listings or figures that convey the false impression that these evolve in a vacuum disconnected from unique state circumstances. In a time when multivariate analysis is greatly eased by computers, researchers should be cautioned that the most important variables may not be easily quantified. Variations on tuition policy and student policy illustrate this point:

- States with comparatively high public tuitions and strong commitments to need-based student aid tend to be those with historically strong private higher education sectors, reinforced by a pattern across all governmental dimensions to rely upon private entities and forces to meet public needs. These states have a history of recognizing the role of the independent sector in serving public purposes. Public colleges and universities evolved as major forces only since the 1960s and the states have only recently, and sometimes hesitantly, developed a commitment to the public sector. More often than not, the state's posture on tuition has evolved not through conscious policy choice but through the interaction of culture and politics over many decades.

- States with comparatively low public tuitions and modest student aid programs, in contrast, are often those whose higher education systems evolved from a more populist tradition and where the private sector played a limited role in meeting public needs in the states' early history.

A particularly informative, yet controversial, way of thinking about state variations is presented by the political science literature on state political "cultures." Daniel Elazar, for example, sets forth a theory of political subcultures and classifies states according to whether they are moralistic, individualistic, traditionalistic, their culture and ethnicity, and whether their "ethos" is "public-regarding" or "private-regarding."[5]

The former Washington State Council on Postsecondary Education made a similar but more limited effort to classify state postures toward higher education, ranging from those with a tradition of treating state institutions likes state-owned and regulating agencies, to those that treated public colleges much like state-assisted private corporations largely exempt from state procedural controls.[6]

The "State Period" in American Higher Education

State governments now play a central, if not dominant role, in American higher education. Historically, states have always provided the legal framework within which both public and private institutions operated. But with the dramatic expansion of the public sector since the 1950s and 1960s, this has also become the case in terms of enrollments and financing. From the 1950s to the end of the 1980s, the share of total enrollments in public institutions (including many community colleges partially funded from local revenue) increased from about 60 percent to 80 percent.[7] The private sector continued to grow but this was outstripped by increases of one-and-a-half times in public four-year enrollments and five times in public two-year institutional enrollments.[8] The proportion of institutions in the private sector dropped from 65 percent to 45 percent.[9]

From a comparative perspective, American higher education remains perhaps the most diverse, decentralized, private, market-driven system (if it can even be called a "system") in the world. Yet state governments have gradually come to play a more central role than is often conveyed in international comparisons. In fact, there appears to be a world-wide convergence toward the kind of mixed public-private system that has evolved in the U.S. While other nations are increasing the private elements in their systems, the U.S. has been moving for several decades toward a more public system.[10]

In the early 1990s, state and local governments provided approximately 32 percent of the overall financial support for higher education, both public and private. This compared with 16 percent from the federal government, 31 percent from tuition and fees, and 21 percent from other sources (including endowments, private philanthropy and corporations).[11]

As Clark Kerr observed in 1985, the decade of the mid-1980s to mid-1990s (and perhaps beyond) would be a decade of state and private leadership in higher education. He pointed out that this has been the dominant pattern in U.S. history. Periods of federal leadership have been relatively brief: 1860-

1890 and 1955-1985. He further observed that as the impact of higher education on the states' economies has become more politically important, the state governors have emerged as the most important political figu es.[12]ᴛ

The late 1980s and early 1990s have underscored Kerr's observations. In fact, states substantially increased support for higher education in the mid-1980s in all but a few cases. Some increases were as high as 90 percent over the ten-year period ending in 1991-92, even when adjusted for inflation.[13] The state and local share of overall funding increased over the same period from 30 to 32 percent, while the federal share decreased from 20 to 16 percent.[14]

While the state share of funding increased in the 1980s, this should not overshadow the reality that the most dramatic increases in higher education revenue came from students and their parents and from other private sources. This relatively affluent period for colleges and universities was made possible both by substantial increases in state appropriations *and* by substantial tuition increases, primarily in the private sector. In the first years of the 1990s, higher education experienced an abrupt down-turn in revenues. For the first time in the 33-year history of collection of data on state appropriations by Illinois State University, an actual decline was recorded.[15] Early indications suggest that some states are experiencing a slight economic turn-around. This will result in a reversal of the decline with state appropriations increasing about 3 percent from 1992–93 to 1993–94.[16]

Despite these positive signs, higher education will likely continue to receive a steadily declining share of state revenues. Even though, in absolute terms, state higher education appropriations increased significantly in the 1980s, the actual percentage of state revenues declined. In other words, the strength of state economies off-set the decline in higher education's share. Now the economy is growing more slowly, and states are faced with largely mandatory increases in funding for health care, prisons and the public schools. In these conditions, states will find it difficult to provide the increases for higher education for the remaining years of the 1990s that are necessary to keep up with increased student demands and inflation.

Dramatic increases in public tuition were a consequence of the fiscal crisis of the early 1990s. In the 1980s, double-digit increases were primarily phenomena of the private sector. In 1991–92, tuition increased 13 to 15 percent on the average but some states such as California increased fees by 40 percent or more. The tradition of low tuition in the public sector is going by the wayside in many states, not as a matter of public choice, but of economic necessity.

In some states, but certainly not all, tuition increases were moderated by increases in state funding for student aid. While appropriations for operations actually declined in 1991–92, as indicated above, the actual amount of state-supported aid to students actually increased. Grants of need- and non-need-based aid increased 14.5 percent from 1990 to 1992, and the change from 1991 to 1992 was 8.2 percent. These increases mask significant decreases in several states, but with few exceptions, these were restored in a subsequent year. For example, Massachusetts reported a 48.5 percent decrease for 1990–91 to 1991–92, but a 94.1 percent increase for 1991–1992 to 1992–1993. In the same periods, New Jersey reported a 13.1 percent decrease in the first year but an 18.6 percent increase in the second year.[17]

As these trends suggest, state higher education financing is undergoing fundamental changes. The resulting tensions will make financing one of the central issues for the next decade. This is reflected in state surveys, as is reported later in this chapter.

Even more important than providing financing support, the states have been, and continue to be, the national leaders in education reform. The governors have spearheaded this movement, using the Education Commission of the States (ECS) and the National Governors' Association (NGA) as primary vehicles. It was the governors who took the initiative in organizing the 1989 Education Summit with President George Bush in Charlottesville, Virginia, and in advocating for the first time in the country's history a series of National Goals. And the governors continue to lead in the pursuit and monitoring of progress toward these goals through the National Goals Panel.

During the 1980s, the states led a fundamental change in the definition of accountability. Up to that point, states had focused primarily on issues of resource allocation and utilization and rarely became involved in basic questions about the outcomes of a college or university education. By the end of the 1980s, questions about outcomes—especially student outcomes—dominated states' agendas. More than any other force, it was state policies requiring institutions to assess student learning and to provide information to the states and the public that stimulated higher education's attention to these issues. As reported in *Campus Trends*, many colleges and universities now report that they have active efforts to assess student learning. While state mandates initially stimulated this attention, it is now being sustained by voluntary accreditation and other forces.[18]

The states also led during the 1980s in developing new funding systems, such as competitive, incentive and performance funding. Use of funding "on the margin" to support centers of excellence in research and technology and to stimulate improvement in undergraduate education was widespread.[19] Relating this to the earlier discussion of autonomy, since the early 1980s, states had been much more willing to enter into the area Berdahl defines as "substantive autonomy."

There are signs that the "state period" in American higher education is fading into a new period in which all levels of government and both public and private sectors will be active participants in shaping nationwide policy.

State Coordination and Governance[20]

Rising expectations for performance and accountability, coupled with serious budget problems, inevitably lead governors and legislators to issues of governance. From 1985 through 1993, about thirty-three states had special studies or blue-ribbon commissions on higher education. In all of these, changes in state structure were an issue. Several other states either enacted or seriously debated reorganization proposals. Changes of some consequence were actually enacted in sixteen states in the period.[21]

Description of State Structures

State structures can be understood from two perspectives: first, in terms of *public institution governance* or how the state governs public institutions; and second, in terms of *coordination* or how the state provides, if at all, for coordination of the overall higher education system, including both public and private institutions.

PUBLIC INSTITUTION GOVERNANCE

All states assign responsibility for the operation of public colleges and universities to governing boards. The names of these boards vary, but "board of trustees" and "board of regents" are the most common. The responsibility of these boards is much the same as that of a board of directors for any nonprofit corporation. They appoint the campus chief executive (and in systems, the system chief executive), establish policies, and approve actions related to faculty and other personnel; ensure institutional fiscal integrity; and perform other policy and management functions. Clark Kerr and Marian Gade categorize public governing boards as follows:[22]

- *Consolidated governance systems.* One board covers all two-year and four-year public campuses or one board covers all four-year campuses, including research universities and other four-year institutions, with separate arrangements for two-year institutions.

- *Segmental systems.* Separate boards cover separate types of campuses, such as research universities, comprehensive colleges and universities, and community colleges.

- *Campus-level boards.* These are "autonomous," have full authority over a single campus, and are not covered by a consolidated governing board or multi-campus system. In four systems, campuses have their own boards. In North Carolina and Utah, the boards have authority delegated by the central board and can make some decisions on their own. In the

State University of New York and the University of Maryland System, the boards are largely advisory.

Governing boards of public institutions were modeled after the lay boards of private nonprofit colleges and universities which, in most instances, govern single institutions. Perhaps for this reason, many retain an impression that the single board—single institution pattern is dominant. The reality is that 75 percent of the students in American public higher education are on campuses that are parts of multi-campus or consolidated systems of multiple campuses all under a single governing board.

Because of the importance of these systems to so much of the nation's higher education enterprise, their performance is under increasing scrutiny.[23] Kerr and Gade made the following comment:

> The drift in the public sector of higher education, especially during the past 40 years, . . . [is] toward consolidation and toward control. . . . We note that this tendency toward consolidation and control runs counter to the development in American national economic policy toward more competition and autonomy. This economic trend is present in most countries—even in the Soviet Union and China. The general government tendency in the United States has also been toward decentralization to the states and localities.[24]

STATEWIDE COORDINATION

"Coordination" is the term used most often to describe the formal and informal approaches taken by states to handle the interconnections between the state and the higher education enterprise. It has become common for "coordination" to refer primarily to the actions of agencies formed explicitly for this purpose. In a broader sense, however, coordination occurs through a wide array of mechanisms, from governors' and legislators' actions to the informal networks and associations about institutions, their administrative staffs, faculties and students.[25, 26]

EIGHT COORDINATING FUNCTIONS

Either states assign the following eight statewide coordinating functions to a single board, or the functions are distributed among two or more boards.

Planning. Most states carry out some form of long-range or master planning. This examines the long-range state needs, establishes state goals and objectives, considers the resources of all institutions (often both public and private) and recommends public policy priorities. In some states, the process focuses on a "master" or "strategic" plan. In others, a conscious decision has been made not to produce a master plan but instead to carry out special studies resulting in a series of reports rather than a single document.

Policy analysis and problem resolution. In addition to the analysis carried out in the formal planning process, states undertake special studies on issues that transcend the concerns of any single institution. These may relate to long-term issues (such as the feasibility of authorizing graduate programs at a rural campus or location). Or, they may concern specific inter-sector or inter-institutional issues such as minority participation and achievement, student transfer and articulation, alternative financing policies, or tuition policy. Often these studies are performed at the request of the governor or legislature.

Mission definition. As an outgrowth of the planning process, a number of states define the missions of each public college and university in terms of degrees to be awarded, the programs to be offered, and clientele to be served. These are used for both institutional and state-level decision-making on new degree and program proposals, budget and financing formula development and other coordinating functions.[27]

Academic Program Review. Most states examine proposals from institutions for new academic programs. Since the late 1970s, many states as well as multi-campus systems have instituted periodic reviews of existing programs. Now, in serious economic conditions, program review is being used as a key element of strategies to identify programs for termination and areas for quality and productivity improvements.[28, 29]

Budget development, funding formulas and resource allocation. All states have processes for reviewing and approving institutional operating and capital budgets, moving these budgets through the decision-making process, allocating funds to systems or institutions, and ensuring accountability. The extent of a higher education agency's role depends largely on the governor's and legislature's roles. In some states, these bodies delegate authority to an agency, whereas in others they maintain direct control of most of the steps in the budget process.[30]

Program administration. States assign administrative responsibilities for state and federal programs to one or more agencies. The most common administrative responsibilities relate to state student grant and loan programs.

Information, assessment and accountability systems. Statewide data systems are among the most common, core capabilities of coordinating boards. In the past decade, the emphasis of these systems has shifted decidedly from resources and inputs toward outcomes or indicators of performance. Several states require institutions to prepare "report cards" to the state and the public on their performance in relation to their missions. Most states now have requirements that institutions establish programs to assess student learning. The focus of these, however, is primarily on use for improvement within the institutions. Requirements tend to be that the institutions demonstrate that they have an assessment program and that they are using the results for their internal renewal purposes. Only a few states actually require institutions to reports the results of their assessments to the government. More recently, states have developed performance indicator systems that provide for reporting to the state (and sometimes the general public).[31]

Institutional licensure and authorization. All states have statutes requiring institutions to be licensed or "authorized" to operate within the state. The standards applied by these entities vary greatly. As a result of a 1992 amendment to the federal Higher Education Act of 1965 creating a new Part H, states are now required to designate a State Postsecondary Review Entity ("SPRE") to be responsible for reviewing postsecondary education institutions for eligibility for federal student aid. Initially, the focus will be on institutions with significant loan default rates. In all but a few cases, the principal state higher education agency is designated as the SPRE.

Classifications of State Structures

A number of classification systems have been developed since the 1960s to describe the variations in state structures. None is entirely satisfactory in reflecting the subtle differences among boards and agencies.[32,33] Most make a basic distinction among three kinds of state structures:

CONSOLIDATED GOVERNING BOARD STATES
(TWENTY-TWO STATES AND PUERTO RICO)

These states assign responsibility for coordinating most, if not all, higher education to a board whose primary responsibilities relate to governing the institutions under its jurisdiction. Most of these boards would be in the category of consolidated governing board as defined by Kerr and Gade, although in several states the responsibility is shared between two segmental boards, one for four-year institutions and the other for community colleges or technical institutions. A consolidated governing board:

- Usually heads a single corporate entity which encompasses all institutions within the system.

- Carries out coordinating responsibilities in addition to its responsibilities for governing institutions under its jurisdiction.

- Has authority both to develop and to implement policy.

- Advocates for the needs of the institutions to the legislature and governor.

- Appoints, sets compensation for, and evaluates system and institutional chief executives.

- Sets faculty personnel policies and usually approves tenure.

- Has authority to allocate and reallocate resources between and among the institutions within its jurisdiction.

COORDINATING BOARD STATES
(TWENTY-FIVE STATES AND THE DISTRICT OF COLUMBIA)

These states choose to govern their institutions through single boards, segmental boards, or some combination of these. Governance, as opposed to coordination, is relatively decentralized. Coordination is assigned to a single board *other than* one of the governing boards. Six of these states and the District of Columbia have coordinating entities that, except for their formal statutory status, have authority not significantly broader than those in the state planning agency states. A coordinating board:

- Does not govern institutions, in the sense that this is defined above (e.g., appoint institutional chief executives or set faculty personnel policies).

- Usually does not have corporate status independent of state government.

- Focuses more on state and system needs and priorities than on advocating the interests of the higher education community. As Berdahl describes the function, these boards serve as "suitably sensitive mechanisms" providing for a continuing transmission of the state's interests to higher education and higher education's needs to the state.[34]

- Plans primarily for the system as a whole. In most states with coordinating boards, this planning includes all institutions, both public and private.

- Appoints, sets compensation for and evaluates only the agency executive officer and staff but not the institutional chief executives. In several states, the governor is the final appointing authority but usually with recommendations coming from the coordinating board.

- May or may not review and make recommendations on budgets. A few coordinating agencies recommend consolidated budgets for the whole public system. Others simply make recommendations to the governor or legislature on individual institutional or segmental budgets.

- May or may not review or approve proposals for new academic programs, and may or may not have authority to require institutions to review existing programs.

PLANNING AGENCY STATES (THREE STATES)

These are states with essentially no statutory entity with much coordinating authority beyond a voluntary planning and convening role and ensuring good communications among institutions and sectors. As indicated, about three coordinating board states and the District of Columbia have agencies with authority not significantly broader than these planning agencies.

Beyond these formal categories, subtle differences tend to make each state unique, despite what may appear to be a structure that is similar to those in other states. The differences in state history and culture mentioned earlier in this chapter are especially important. In addition, these points should be considered:

ROLES OF THE LEGISLATIVE AND EXECUTIVE BRANCHES

In some states the power is in the legislature and the governor has only limited authority. In others it is the governor who wields most of the power.

SIZES OF SYSTEMS

States that have consolidated governing boards usually have systems that are comparatively less complex and with smaller enrollments (less than 100,000, and in some cases less than 25,000). Georgia, North Carolina, and Wisconsin are three major exceptions. Most of the coordinating board states have large enrollments (a third with enrollments over 200,000) and complex systems of multi-campus, segmental and individual governing board arrangements.

TRADITION AND QUALITY OF LEADERSHIP

While traditions may endure, the leadership qualities of board members, state agency chief executives and staffs, and institutional leaders change. A board that is recognized as strong and effective at one point may been seen as weak and ineffective at another. The quality of leadership of the governor and key legislators can also make a profound difference. More than formal authority, those variables that tend to define the strength and effectiveness of a higher education board include:

- Prestige and credibility of board members.

- The board's performance as a cohesive, policy-making group as opposed to a collection of individual interests.

- The reputation of the board and staff for objectivity, fairness, sound judgment and constructive conflict resolution.

- The ability of the board to focus its agenda on major policy issues confronting the state and the higher education system. This means that the board has found ways to organize its work, to delegate and to manage its time effectively.

Changes in State Structures

The basic patterns of state-level organization across the nation today were in place in the early 1970s. The year 1972 marked the culmination of more than a decade of development of state higher education agencies formed to coordinate the massive expansion in the late 1950s and 1960s. By that year, 47 states had established either consolidated governing boards responsible for all senior institutions (and, in some cases, community colleges also) or coordinating boards responsible for statewide planning and coordination of two or more governing boards. Three small states with a limited number of institutions did not form a special statutory agency but continued to handle statewide higher education issues through existing governing boards, informal coordination, and direct involvement of the governor and state legislature.

PERENNIAL ISSUES

Throughout the past twenty years, several issues have consistently spurred governors and legislators to make higher education reorganization proposals. These tend to be long-standing irritants whose urgency increases as the public expectations rise or economic conditions worsen.

Actual or potential duplication of high-cost graduate and professional programs. Most states are confronted with intractable political and economic stresses as growing urban centers compete with rural areas and older economic centers. These stresses are amplified and played out in conflicts within the states' higher education systems. The most common pattern is for a growing urban area to press for accessible graduate and professional programs. In the first stage, the interest usually is simply to have these offered in the area, but this soon leads to demands that a new university be formed either from an existing institution or as a wholly new entity. The issue then becomes further complicated when the prestige of "university status" and graduate programs becomes mixed with issues of community pride and economic development. The likelihood that the new initiatives would duplicate or threaten support for similar programs at the state's major research university becomes a major issue. That many of the major public universities are located away from urban centers complicates the issue. The same scenario is also played out when isolated rural areas struggle to gain access to programs for place-bound adults. What usually sparks governance controversies are "end-runs" to the governor or legislature to get special attention. The ensuing political struggles inevitably lead to major restructuring proposals. Short-term victories gained through "end-running" the established coordinating structures usually lead in the long-run to greater centralization.

Visible conflict between the aspirations of two institutions (often under separate governing boards) located in the same geographic area. Again, conflicts tend to be over which institution should offer high-cost graduate and professional programs. Major reorganization proposals (merger or consolidation) usually occur after years of less dramatic efforts to achieve improved cooperation and coordination.

Legislative reaction to intense institutional lobbying. As governors and legislators face politically difficult and unattractive choices focused on curtailing rather than expanding programs, intense lobbying by narrow, competing institutional interests can spark demands for restructuring. Political leaders seek ways to push such battles away from the immediate political process by increasing the authority of a state board in the hope that it will have the power to resolve the conflicts before they get to the legislature. The reverse situation also frequently occurs. A state board will act to curtail an institutional "end-run" and be faced with a legislative proposal (frequently stimulated by the offending institution) to abolish the board.

Frustrations with barriers to student transfer and articulation. Evidence (usually in the form of constituent appeals to influential legislators) that institutions are making it difficult for students to transfer or are limiting credit transfer, often leads to legislative intervention and, in extreme cases, to reorganization proposals.

Proposals (and related opposition) to close, merge or change institutional missions. At issue may be small, isolated rural institutions or institutions with similar missions that are in close proximity. What sparks the reorganization proposal is the sense that the existing system is unable to address these kinds of problems. Or, once someone makes a proposal and a political firestorm breaks out, reorganization may be proposed because of a sense that the existing state board handled the issue poorly.

Lack of coordination among institutions offering one- and two-year vocational, technical and occupational and transfer programs. Many states have regions or communities where two or more public institutions, each responsible to a different state board or agency, are competing to offer similar one- and two-year programs. In the worst situations, this may involve a postsecondary technical institute, a community college, and a two-year lower-division university. Because of sincere and intense differences among the institutions in their educational missions and philosophies, they may resist program coordination and make it difficult for students to transfer. In a larger scale version of the same issue, many states face escalating demands in their two-year sectors that threaten to take resources from the university sectors. When these battles are fought on the floor of the state legislature rather than being resolved within higher education, they inevitably lead to proposals for restructuring.

Concerns about the effectiveness of the state board. Major reorganization proposals are often made because of a sense that the existing board (or its staff) is providing ineffective leadership or lacks the political influence or judgment to address critical issues facing the state.

Not surprisingly, the "critical issues" may be long-standing irritants such as those mentioned above. Or, the sense may be that an existing board is focused more on detailed administrative, regulatory or internal management issues than on policy leadership. Ironically, where such criticisms of state boards are made it is often a previous legislature that has assigned these management or regulatory functions to the board. Reorganization is frequently proposed not because an agency lacks the formal authority but because of a desire to change the leadership or personalities involved in the process.

"Super board" proposals. Almost without exception in governance debates, the option of consolidating all public institutions under a single, consolidated governing board (frequently called a "super board" in the ensuing media debate) is raised. Because of the inevitable opposition these proposals generate (primarily from institutions who fear that their independence will be threatened), few have actually been enacted in the past twenty years. But this does not deter others from advancing the idea. In lieu of total consolidation, states often consolidate institutional clusters to form segmental systems, comprised of all institutions with similar missions.[35] As an alternative to forming a single statewide governing board, several states have greatly strengthened the existing state coordinating board to the point that its regulatory powers border on authority to govern institutions.

DEBATES FOR AND AGAINST CONSOLIDATION

Kerr and Gade cite two underlying reasons for the trend toward consolidation and control in U.S. higher education:

> The government does have a clear interest in centralizing and controlling some decisions, specifically over missions and over budgets, in order to make effective use of resources and to be sure that all important missions are actually and fairly served. ("Missions" include general admissions policies for students). Government also has an interest in effective review of performance.
>
> State authorities, specifically governors and legislative committees, find it helpful to hold one board and one chief executive officer accountable. They prefer to have to place or receive only one phone call rather than to have to deal with several or many competitive and combative institutions, their representatives, and supporters. This can be time consuming and exasperating. Some infighting, often highly counterproductive, can be kept out of the state capitol.[36]

Despite intense debates for and against consolidated systems, conclusive evidence on either side of the argument is difficult to find. Examples can be found of systems that are working well in terms of providing leadership for the system while ensuring highly diverse missions, decentralized governance and creative use of the benefits of a system to meet the state's educational needs.[37]

At the same time, one can find examples of both coordinating and consolidated governing boards that are giving insufficient time to policy leadership, have lost credibility with the state's political and higher education leadership, are excessively focused on administrative, regulatory and internal management issues, fail to promote mission differentiation, and give insufficient attention to the major policy challenges facing the state.

The greatest danger is that states will adopt one alternative or another without first making clear the ends to be achieved, and without making a serious assessment of whether the alternative is the best means to those ends. The pressure simply to copy another state's structure is often overwhelming. The state's underlying political culture is one of the most important considerations.

When economic times worsen, governance proposals seem to increase. Given the prospects for the 1990s, reorganization will clearly be on the agenda. Many of these will be framed in terms of the "perennial issues" and many of the alternatives will be simply copied from other states. As emphasized later in this chapter, it may be time for states to examine the appropriateness of structures formed for the mid-1900s for the conditions of the next century. It is a time for new, creative thinking about old categories and solutions.

What Issues Are on State Agendas?

In early 1992, the State Higher Education Executive Officers (SHEEO) conducted a survey of state higher education agencies and system governing boards to determine the perceptions of these entities about the most important issues and priorities facing higher education. Responses included a cross-section of the nation's coordinating boards and governing boards for four-year and community college systems.[38] SHEEO undertook the survey initially to ascertain state and system perspectives on faculty workload issues. It became immediately apparent that this narrow issue could not be understood without being placed in a broader perspective. The following is a list of the issues ranked as "very important" in order of the frequency of their mention by the respondents. Those issues that received roughly the same percentage of "very important" responses are clustered:

1. Adequacy of overall state financial support
2. Quality of undergraduate education
3. Minority student access and achievement; effectiveness and accountability
4. Teacher education and preparation; tuition rates and overall costs
5. Faculty workload and productivity; workforce training and education
6. Review of institutional roles and missions
7. Linkages between secondary and postsecondary education; amounts and types of student financial aid; adequacy and maintenance of physical facilities
8. Support for research, graduate education and economic development
9. State roles in addressing faculty needs and issues

Underlying several of these issues is a concern about the severe economic conditions facing the respondents. For this reason, they were asked to sort out the financial from the non-financial issues. When asked to list the most important financial issues in the 1990s, the following issues were mentioned most frequently. It is important to recognize that all these were identified as important by at least some of the respondents.

1. Inadequacy or decline in level of state support; retrenchment; need to downsize
2. Shifting balance between state support and tuition revenues; concern about high tuition and student access
3. General uncertainty; concern about level of state support
4. Need for capital investment and improvements; need to fund for enrollment growth/expansion
5. Concern about cost effectiveness, productivity and accountability; need to fund quality improvement
6. Need to offer competitive faculty salaries or to increase faculty salaries

Then, when asked to identify the most important nonfinancial issues, the boards most frequently responded as follows:

1. Public perceptions; accountability; effectiveness; efficiency; and productivity
2. Quality of undergraduate education; access issues
3. Faculty issues—workload, commitment to teaching
4. Developing/implementing differentiated institutional missions
5. General planning and coordination issues; governance; collaboration among education sectors; articulation and transfer issues
6. Minority issues
7. Admissions standards or related issues; workforce issues

These responses illustrate how much issues of quality and equity are linked. They also show the extent to which financing issues can no longer be considered in isolation. The higher education debate has shifted decidedly from an emphasis on means (quantity and adequacy of resources) toward basic questions of ends (what should students know and be able to do and what public purposes are to be served by the enterprise).

Looking to the Future[39]

Faced with the realities stressed at the beginning of this chapter—expectations, economic constraints, resistance to change, negative public opinion, and instability of state political leadership—American higher education will be forced to undergo a restructuring as fundamental as any attempted in the past fifty years. Higher education faces four basic choices:[40]

- *To do more with less.* If this approach is not accompanied by dramatic changes in the core work of the faculty and changes in the modes of teaching, research and service, it will mean a decade-long decline in quality and a significant lowering of standards at a time when the public demands just the opposite.

- To do less with less. This will mean that thousands of students will be denied access and the nation's worldwide standing in research and graduate education will decline.

- *To take resources from other basic public priorities.* This will include elementary and secondary education, health, public safety, and the environment.

- *Raise additional revenue from other sources.* Most of these are already highly taxed and, even according to the most optimistic view, could not replace losses in other revenue sources.

As institutions face these choices, so also must government—especially state government—assess whether its policies provide a constructive environment for institutional change to take place. This will require challenges to some of the most basic assumptions that have guided state policy during the past twenty years. The following are issues that are likely to be on the state agendas in the next decade:

1. *How can the nation achieve a closer relationship between high participation rates and high educational achievement rates?* After several years of intense debate about the quality of American public schools, the focus has shifted to higher education. As suggested earlier, in the mid-1980s the debate about higher education accountability shifted sharply from resources to outcomes, and the rapid spread of assessment, stimulated in part by state mandates, was the result. But the debate is now taking a new turn. These questions are being asked:

- Are too many students simply being "processed" through higher education with no clear sense of what they should know and be able to do upon graduation?

- Aside from a few, usually highly selective institutions, are the expectations for student learning for many of the students enrolled in higher education not much higher than those for students in secondary education?[41]

- Should the U.S. shift its focus from higher education to education for the "non-college" bound student, and to vocational/technical and apprenticeship training?[42]

- Why is it taking students longer and longer (now averaging six years) to complete a baccalaureate degree? Could the time to complete a degree be significantly shortened?[43]

- Should the states or even the nation set standards or expectations about what students should know and be able to do upon completing a baccalaureate degree (or perhaps at the level of two years of postsecondary education or training)?[44]

- Should the basic structure of postsecondary education in the U.S. be altered? The basic structure of institutions and degrees that has characterized American higher education since World War II may be on the verge of change. This may include changing the roles of secondary schools, open-access comprehensive community colleges, and four-year colleges and universities, both public and private.

2. *How should institutional forms, methods of program delivery, and governance be changed to create a more responsive, cost-effective, and flexible system?* Serious questions are being raised about the traditional structure and management practices of the nation's major public and private research universities. A series of reports by the Pew Higher Education Research Program at the University of Pennsylvania has played a leading role in shaping the debate about the need for the fundamental restructuring of higher education, especially the research university.[45] Questions are being raised that the higher education community would not have dared to consider just a few years ago:

- Should some sectors of public higher education be shifted to largely private non-profit status, with less public funding and more dependence on student and other non-governmental revenue?

- Should some large public multi-campus systems be broken up into smaller units or radically decentralized to give greater independence to individual units under a smaller central staff?

- Could a higher proportion of the undergraduate population be served off-campus through the use of technology at home or on the job, thus avoiding the need to build new facilities (or even allowing institutions to be scaled down or closed)?

3. *Should both sources and methods of financing for students and institutions be changed in fundamental ways?* As suggested earlier, the prospects for increased revenue from *any* major source are dim—especially when matched

with the realities of increased demand and inevitable cost increases. The survey responses from the states and systems underscore that financing issues cut across all other concerns and are intertwined with issues of quality and access. There is a growing sense that the traditional debates about who benefits and who pays that characterized the mid-1970s simply do not fit the conditions of the 1990s. A basic question now on the agenda is whether methods of student and institutional finance could be tied to incentives for both students and institutions to speed up the time-to-degree. New questions are being raised about consolidating funding now provided separately for secondary schools, multiple training options, and the first two years of college to create new, more flexible and powerful approaches to raising the skills and knowledge levels of the population.

4. *How must state government policy change to support the transformation of the higher education system?* Given the likely political instability and economic pressures facing governors and state legislators, the 1990s could witness one of the most pronounced periods of bureaucratic centralization in recent U.S. history.

- Return to more detailed, line-item budget controls.

- Extending state agency authority over higher education purchasing, personnel and pensions, managing facilities and equipment.

- Eliminating state subsidy for private nonprofit colleges and universities (for students or programs).

- Centralizing and consolidating governance.

- Eliminating state coordination and planning agencies and shifting oversight functions directly to the governor's office and the state legislature.

- Restricting use of state resources for out-of-state (and especially international) purposes, thereby limiting the movement of both students and higher education faculty and staff.

In other words, while most major private corporations and nations in the European Community and elsewhere in the world seem to be finding ways to reduce bureaucracy and increase flexibility, many American state governments could be moving in the opposite direction. Because of this danger, the Education Commission of the States, in collaboration with the State Higher Education Executive Officers and the National Center for Higher Education Management Systems, has been at work designing ways for states to assess the impact of their policies on the capacity of their universities and colleges to respond to the new realities.[46] The aim is to assist states to shape a new generation of policies, many of which will reflect the themes of change in other sectors of the economy and other nations:

- Decentralizing institutional governance.

- Reconceiving and reorienting central state functions to emphasize setting and monitoring expectations and standards; providing incentives for change, productivity improvement and partnerships; and encouraging a high degree of differentiation in institutional missions and functions.

- Providing the public with better information about performance of students, institutions and the higher education system as a whole.

- Establishing independent, non-governmental "third-party" entities whose mission it is to monitor and report to the public on progress of the enterprise in addressing basic societal needs and priorities.

An example of new thinking is the California Higher Education Policy Center, an independent non-profit entity committed to raising fundamental policy questions about the future of higher education in that state, questions that the current policy and education leadership cannot or will not raise. The aim is to engage the public in the debate in the hope that future directions will be set by conscious policy choice, not policy drift.

As suggested earlier, it is time for new and creative thinking about the "suitably sensitive mechanisms" necessary to bridge the growing gap between the public and the academy on the societal purposes of the enterprise. New thinking is needed about the policies most likely to stimulate and sustain lasting restructuring of the system to ensure its capacity to serve these ends.

5. *Is the nation reaching the end of the "state period" to which Clark Kerr referred in the mid-1980s?* Countering the tendency for states to turn inward in difficult economic times, the U.S. is experiencing a greater interest in nationwide education leadership than at any time in its history. This is most strikingly illustrated by the National Education Goals and the emerging debate about national standards. The need for a renewed discussion about the role of the federal government and "federalism" goes far beyond education. As one example, the largest single factor in the decline of state support for higher education is the transfer of unfunded federal mandates to the states in non-education areas such as health care.[47]

6. *Are today's concepts of policy for nation-states and regional economic blocs inconsistent with, or even barriers to, the internationalization of knowledge and worldwide movement of students and scholars?* Clark Kerr recently addressed this issue from the perspective of nation-states, and concluded that the record is mixed but generally positive: nation-states have been and continue

to be major forces in the advancement of higher education but at times have certainly not been.[48] In the case of the U.S., it is remarkable how international networks have exploded in recent years largely without, or even in spite of, government action. In addition to the thousands of foreign students and researchers who come every year to major U.S. research universities, the international contacts are reflected in a myriad of informal links among scholars and researchers, cooperative agreements among colleges and universities, and rapidly expanding telecommunications contacts.[49]

Have the states outlived their usefulness as "communities of solution" for higher education policy in a global economy? In a subtle way, this question is already on the nation's agenda. Rather than shift back to a "federal period," the emphasis will increasingly be on *nationwide* policy. Using the benefits of modern technology and telecommunications, alternatives will be shaped with all stakeholders. Local entities, institutions, states, the federal government, the private sector, and more than ever the general public will be actively engaged in the debate.

Notes

1. Aims C. McGuinness, Jr., "Lessons from European Integration for U.S. Higher Education," paper prepared for the Eleventh General Conference of Member Institutions, Programme on Institutional Management in Higher Education, Organisation for Economic Development and Co-operation, Paris, France, September 2–4, 1992.

2. See Edward R. Hines, *Higher Education and State Governments: Renewed Partnership, Cooperation, or Competition?* ASHE-ERIC Higher Education Reports No. 5 (Washington, D.C.: Association for Study of Higher Education, 1988) for a useful overview of the issue. Also, Richard Novak, *State Issues in Higher Education— A Bibliography*, 9th edition (Washington, D.C.: American Association of State Colleges and Universities, 1992).

3. Frank Newman, *Choosing Quality* (Denver: Education Commission of the States, 1987), p. 9.

4. Robert O. Berdahl, *Statewide Coordination of Higher Education* (Washington, D.C.: American Council on Education, 1971), p. 9.

5. Daniel Elazar, *American Federalism: A View from the States* (New York: Thomas Y. Crowell, 1966), chapter 4.

6. Washington Council for Postsecondary Education, *Higher Education in Washington: The Next Six Years* (Olympia: The Washington Council for Postsecondary Education, 1983), pp. 4–7.

7. National Center for Education Statistics, *Digest of Education Statistics, 1989* (Washington, D.C.: U.S. Department of Education, 1989), Table 148, p. 167.

8. Ibid., Table 149, p. 168.

9. Ibid., Table 196, p. 217.

10. Clark Kerr, "The American Mixture of Higher Education in Perspective: Four Dimensions," *Higher Education* 19 (1990).

11. Robert Atwell, "Financial Prospects for Higher Education," *Policy Perspectives,*

The Pew Higher Education Research Program, Philadelphia (September 1992).

12. Clark Kerr, "The States and Higher Education: Changes Ahead," *State Government* 58 (1990).

13. State Higher Education Executive Officers, *State Higher Education Appropriations 1991–1992* (Denver: State Higher Education Executive Officers, 1992).

14. Atwell, "Financial Prospects for Higher Education."

15. State Higher Education Executive Officers, *State Higher Education Appropriations 1991–92.*

16. Edward R. Hines, Illinois State University, preliminary data on appropriations of state tax funds for operating expenses of higher education, fiscal years 1983–84, 1991–92, 1992–93, and 1993–94, with percentages of gain over one, two, and ten years, October 12, 1993.

17. National Association of State Scholarship and Grant Programs, *NASSGP 24th Annual Survey (1992–93 Academic Year), State Funded Scholarshin/Grant Programs for Students to Attend Postsecondary Educational Institutions* (Harrisburg: Pennsylvania Higher Education Assistance Agency, March 1993), pp. 1–20.

18. Elaine El-Khawas, *Camrus Trends 1993,* Higher Education Panel Report, No. 16 (Washington, D.C.: American Council on Education, 1993), p. 16.

19. For greater analysis of these developments in the 1980s see Frank Newman, *Choosing Quality;* Robert O. Berdahl and Barbara Holland, eds. *Developing State Fiscal Incentives to Improve Higher Education: Proceedings from a National Invitational Conference* (College Park: National Center for Postsecondary Governance and Finance, University of Maryland, College Park, 1990); Peter Ewell and Dennis Jones, *Assessing and Reporting Student Progress: A Response to the "New Accountability"* (Denver: State Higher Education Executive Officers, 1991); and James R. Mingle, *State Policy and Productivity in Higher Education* (Denver: State Higher Education Executive Officers, 1992).

20. This section on coordination and governance draws heavily on Aims C. McGuinness, Jr., *State Postsecondary Education Structures Handbook, 1993* (Denver: Education Commission of the States, in process).

21. See John Folger and Robert O. Berdahl, *Patterns in Evaluating Higher Education Systems: Making a Virtue Out of Necessity* (College Park: National Center for Postsecondary Governance and Finance, 1988) for an analysis and case studies of state approaches to evaluating their higher education boards and systems.

22. Clark Kerr and Marian Gade, *The Guardians: Boards of Trustees of American Colleges and Universities: What They Do and How Well They Do It* (Washington, D.C.: Association of Governing Boards of Universities and Colleges, 1989), pp. 116, 128–29.

23. For further reading on the subject of multi-campus systems, see Marian L. Gade, *Four Multicampus Systems: Some Policies and Practices That Work.* AGB Special Report (Washington, D.C.: Association of Governing Boards of Universities and Colleges, 1993); Edgar B. Schick, Richard J. Novak, James A. Norton, and Houston G. Elam, *Shared Visions of Public Higher Education Governance: Structures and Leadership Styles That Work* (Washington, D.C.: American Association of State Colleges and Universities, 1992); and Aims C. McGuinness, Jr., "Perspectives on the Current Status of and Emerging Policy Issues for Public Multicampus Higher Education Systems," AGB Occasional Paper No. 3 (Washington, D.C.: Association of Governing Boards

of Universities and Colleges, 1991).

24. Kerr and Gade, *The Guardians,* pp. 115–18.

25. For historical perspectives on statewide coordination see Ernest Boyer, *Control of the Campus* (Princeton: Carnegie Foundation for the Advancement of Teaching, 1982); Robert O. Berdahl, *Statewide Coordination of Higher Education* (Washington, D.C.: American Council on Education, 1971); Carnegie Commission on Higher Education, *The Capitol and the Campus: State Responsibility for Postsecondary Education* (New York: McGraw-Hill Book Company, 1971); Carnegie Foundation for the Advancement of Teaching, *States and Higher Education: A Proud Past and a Vital Future* (San Francisco: Jossey-Bass, 1976); Education Commission of the States, *Challenge: Coordination and Governance in the 1980s* (Denver: ECS, 1980); Lyman A. Glenny, *Autonomy of Public Colleges* (New York: McGraw-Hill Book Company, 1959; Glenny and others, *Coordinating Higher Education for the '70s* (Berkeley: Center for Research and Development in Higher Education, University of California, 1971); John D. Millet, *Conflict in Higher Education: State Government versus Institutional Independence* (San Francisco: Jossey-Bass, 1982).

26. For more recent commentaries on statewide coordination see Patrick M. Callan, *Perspectives on the Current Status and Emerging Issues for State Coordinating Boards.* AGB Occasional Paper (Washington, D.C.: Association of Governing Boards of Universities and Colleges, 1991); Lyman A. Glenny, *State Coordination of Higher Education: The Modern Concert* (Denver: State Higher Education Executive Officers, 1985); James R. Mingle, "Effective Coordination of Higher Education. What Is It? Why Is It So Difficult To Achieve?" *Issues in Higher Education* (Southern Regional Higher Education Board, Atlanta) 23 (1988); and State Higher Education Executive Officers, *New Issues—New Roles: A Conversation with State Higher Education Executive Officers* (Denver: SHEEO, January 1989).

27. See Don A. Carpenter, *Role and Mission Development: A Comparison of Different Approaches;* J. Kent Carruthers, *Mission Maintenance: Tools for Change and the Consultative Process;* and Ellen Earle Chaffee, *System Strategy and Effectiveness* (Denver: State Higher Education Executive Officers, 1987).

28. The Productivity, Quality and Performance (PQP) initiative of the Illinois Board of Higher Education is perhaps the best example of a comprehensive, aggressive coordinating board initiative that links program review with restructuring of institutions to meet the economic realities of the next decade.

29. For further information on basic program review processes see Robert J. Barak and Barbara E. Breier, *Successful Program Review* (San Francisco: Jossey-Bass Publishers, 1990); and Barak, *Program Review in Higher Education* (Boulder: National Center for Higher Education Management Systems, 1982).

30. See Dennis P. Jones, *Higher Education Budgeting at the State Level: Concepts and Principles* (Boulder: National Center for Higher Education Management Systems, 1984); and John K. Folger and Dennis P. Jones, *The Use of Financing Policy to Achieve State Objectives* (Denver: Education Commission of the States, 1993).

31. See Peter T. Ewell, Assessment and the "New Accountability": Challenge for Higher Education's Leadership (Denver: Education Commission of the States, 1990), publication PA-90-3; and Ewell, *State Policy on Assessment: The Linkage to Learning* (Denver: ECS, 1990), publication PA-90-4.

32. For different approaches to classification see Berdahl, *State Coordination,* pp.

18–19; Millet, *Conflict,* and Kerr and Gade, *The Guardians,* pp. 117, 128–29.

33. See Millet, *Conflict,* pp. 102–107, for discussion of differences, advantages, and disadvantages of different kinds of state boards.

34. Berdahl, *State Coordination,* p. 15.

35. See McGuinness, "Perspectives on Current Issues . . . for Public Multi-campus University Systems," for discussion of origins of systems.

36. Kerr and Gade, *The Guardians,* pp. 118–19.

37. See Gade, *Four Multicampus Systems: Some Policies and Practices That Work;* Schick et al., *Shared Visions;* and D. Bruce Johnstone, *Central Administrations of Public Multi-Campus University Systems.* Studies in Public Higher Education, No. 1 (Albany: State University of New York, 1992).

38. Alene Bycer Russell, *Faculty Workload: State and System Perspectives.* State Policy and College Learning Project. (Denver: State Higher Education Executives and Education Commission of the States, 1992). The survey respondents included 27 coordinating boards, 36 governing boards, and 8 community college boards, for a total of 71.

39. Portions of this section are drawn from Aims C. McGuinness, Jr., "Lessons from European Integration for U.S. Higher Education."

40. James R. Mingle, "Funding Higher Education in the 1990s: The Choices We Face," Remarks to the Quality Reinvestment Conference of the University of Wisconsin, Madison, Wisconsin, April 3, 1992.

41. Ray Marshall and Marc Tucker, *Thinking for a Living* (New York: Basic Books, 1992).

42. National Center for Education and the Economy, *America's Choice: High Skills or Low Wages!* Report of the Commission on the Skills of the American Workforce (Rochester: National Center for Education and the Economy, 1990).

43. See D. Bruce Johnstone, *Learning Productivity: A New Imperative for American Higher Education.* Studies in Public Higher Education, No. 3. (Albany: State University of New York, April 1993).

44. National Education Goals Panel, *Report of the Task Force on Assessing the National Goal Relating to Postsecondary Education* (Washington, D.C.: National Education Goals Panel, 1992).

45. See Pew Higher Education Research Program, "The End of Sanctuary," *Policy Perspectives* (1991) 3, 4A, and other issues of *Policy Perspectives.*

46. Relevant publications from the State Policy and College Learning Project funded by the Pew Charitable Trusts, include Peter Ewell and Dennis Jones, *The Effect of State Policy on Undergraduate Education.* Publication No. PS 92-5 (Denver: ECS and NCHEMS, 1993); Richard B. Heydinger and Hassan Simsek, *An Agenda for Reshaping Faculty Productivity.* Publication No. PS 92-3 (Denver: ECS and SHEEO, 1993); Dennis Jones and John Folger, *Use of Fiscal Policy to Achieve States' Educational Goals* (Denver: ECS and NCHEMS, 1993); Stephen M. Jordon and Daniel T. Layzell. *A Case of Faculty Workload Issues in Arizona: Implications for State Higher Education Policy.* Publication No. PS 92-2 (Denver: ECS and SHEEO, 1993); Aims C. McGuinness, Jr., *Redesigning the State's Higher Education System for the 21st Century.* Mock legislation for debate (Denver: ECS,1992); Richard C. Richardson, Jr., *Creating Effective Learning Environments.* Publication No.92-4 (Denver: ECS, 1993). Publications to be available in late 1993 from ECS include: Richard Heydinger and Peter Hutchinson,

"Redesigned Governance Structures to Improve Accountability"; James R. Mingle and Arthur Hauptman, "Reassessing the Federal/State/Private Role in Postsecondary Education and Training"; and Aims C. McGuinness, "State Policy and Systemic Change in Higher Education: Guidance for State Policy-Makers," a review of the lessons from the State Policy and College Learning Project (available in January 1994).

47. Alice M. Rivlin, *Reviving the American Dream: The Economy, the States and the Federal Government* (Washington, D.C.: The Brookings Institution, 1992).

48. Clark Kerr, "The Internationalization of Learning and the Nationalization of the Purposes of Higher Education: Two 'Laws in Motion' in Conflict?" *European Journal of Education* 25 (1989): 5–22.

49. El-Khawas, *Campus Trends.*

8

The Courts
Walter C. Hobbs

It has been fashionable among academics for the past two-and-a-half decades to decry the alleged increased involvement of the courts in higher education's affairs. The traditional deference, it is said, long paid by courts to decisions made by academic experts, has been replaced by a judicial activism that inhibits the autonomy of the academy. The view is widespread. But is it valid? This chapter will summarize the early complaints, review the countercriticisms, examine the doctrine of "academic abstention" (judicial deference to academic expertise), describe the functions of the courts, and discuss the impact of judge-made law on three core academic concerns. We shall conclude the chapter by arguing that to the very slight extent judicial deference to academe has indeed been eroded, the consequence has been a modest limitation on institutional autonomy in favor of a major reinforcement of the legal bases of academic freedom. In that outcome, higher education—not to be confused with colleges and universities, let alone with academic administrators only—has the better end of the bargain. Both individuals within the academic enterprise and the enterprise per se have been and are today the beneficiaries of a strong judicial bias toward academic liberty, a bias that operates generally to limit incursions by others, including the courts, on the autonomy of the academics, but that refuses even to academics the liberty to infringe academic liberty.

Complaint: The Courts Were Intruding Too Much

In an eloquent and lengthy passage we only excerpt here, Fishbein spoke for many an academic who was persuaded the courts had hobbled academic administration by heaping inappropriate and dysfunctional procedural requirements on the everyday activity of college and university personnel:

[T]he due process requirements that the courts have imposed upon public universities have had an unfortunate consequence, namely, that today students and faculty alike appear to have a legal cause of action no matter how minor the dispute. Almost every [administrative decision] is thus escalated to the level of a constitutional issue, and there is commonly a race to the door of the federal courthouse by every dissatisfied party. . . . In other words, everything becomes a federal case. As a result, . . . relationships between students and administrators, between students and faculty and between faculty and administrators become increasingly adversarial. . . . This is an appalling development. . . . It is regrettable that so many aspects of life at public universities have been remolded in a legalistic, highly procedural fashion. It means, of course, that the administrator in the public university must undertake his or her daily tasks in the company of a lawyer.[1]

Six years earlier, O'Neil reviewed challenges posed to campus autonomy by various elements of government including the courts and offered the following comment concerning the costs incurred by colleges and universities by reason of court activity:

Judicial intervention . . . poses a significant threat, as witness the suits . . . brought against campus administrators and governing boards as a result of campus disorder. All but one of the cases [O'Neil had described] were ultimately dismissed—but not without considerable costs in legal fees, time and energy, and a virtually certain chilling effect upon future administrative behavior.[2]

The Sloan Commission on Government and Higher Education worried about not only the inhibition of effective academic management born of caution in the face of the likelihood of litigation, but also the changes that litigation itself produces in interpersonal relations:

The Commission views the reliance on litigation as counterproductive since it reinforces adversary relations. . . . The adversarial cast of the trial process fosters tensions that may continue for years, tensions inimical to [academic productivity].[3]

In sum, said the complainants, the willingness of the courts to review and, at times, to reform the decisions made within academe inflicted on colleges and universities costs both direct and indirect. Resources of time and money that would ordinarily go to support teaching, scholarship, and the ancillary services on which these central activities depend were diverted instead to lawyers' and court stenographers' fees and the various other expenses incurred when defending against a lawsuit. Institutional personnel, moreover, were becoming skittish about exercising their creative judgment, preferring to "play it safe" rather than to run the risk of legal challenge to themselves and to their institution. Most seriously of all, the collegiality that is the warp and woof of the academic fabric was being brought to the tearing point by the adversarial character of the litigation encouraged by the judicial willingness to be involved in academic disputes.

On the face of things, the complaints were at least plausible. Lawsuits are indeed expensive; anyone who has been involved in litigation will do or refrain from doing almost anything to avoid getting to court again, and the character of the dispute process before the bench forever changes relationships among former friends.

Response: The Complaints Were Overdrawn

Edwards sharply disagreed both with the particulars of the complaints and with the thread of the argument.[4] He addressed each element of the complaint, and he appended a countercomplaint of his own:

a. *Monetary costs:* Quoting the U.S. Supreme Court in *Cannon* v. *Chicago* (441 U.S. 677 [1979]) and implicitly generalizing to all of academe, Edwards recited *Cannon:*

> Although victims of discrimination on the basis of race, religion or national origin have had private Title VI [of the Civil Rights Act of 1964] remedies available at least since 1965, . . . [the university has] not come forward with any demonstration that Title VI litigation has been so costly or voluminous that either the academic community or the courts have been unduly burdened.[5]

The Court's observation was consistent also with the Sloan Commission's findings concerning the cost to academe of the regulatory process: in a study prepared expressly for the commission, Kershaw found that (in Edward's words) "many of the institutions surveyed viewed the monetary costs of dealing with the Federal Government as a bargain."[6] From other reports as well, Edwards concluded "that the financial benefit derived from governmental assistance outweigh[ed] the financial costs of regulation."[7]

b. *Nonmonetary costs:* The fear that academic administrators and/or faculty would be coerced by judge-made law (not to be confused with legislation) to reach and implement decisions that dilute academic quality plainly irritated Edwards. Statutory law might have produced such effects, for

> There is nothing in national policy to support the exemption of [college and university] employees—primarily teachers—from [coverage by the Civil Rights Acts]. Discrimination against minorities and women in the field of education is as perverse as discrimination in any other area of employment. (House of Representatives Rep. No. 238, 92d Congress, 2d Sess. [1971].[8]

But the courts did not see fit to give force to that congressional intent. As the U.S. Circuit Court of Appeals for the Second Circuit put it (*Powell* v. *Syracuse University*, 580 F.2d 1150 [1978]):

[M]any courts have accepted the broad proposition that courts should exercise minimal scrutiny of college and university employment practices. This anti-interventionist policy has rendered universities virtually immune to charges of employment bias, at least when that bias is not expressed overtly.[9]

If there is yet any substance to the oft-heard claim that the judicial presence hangs like Damocles' sword over the wary decision-maker in academe, that person need only peek up to see that the sword swings for, not against, the institution and its administrators. It is the plaintiff, usually female or minority, not the defendant college, who stands to learn from the litigation: "faculty status is not won in the courtroom."[10]

c. *The death of collegiality:* The short answer here is that neither litigation nor the courts themselves ever kill collegiality; they only constitute the evidence of a death already transpired. One can not prevent conflict by choking off its channels,[11] for conflict will find a path to follow or, like lava, create its own. Nevertheless, whatever academics may do to one another in their internecine warfare, Edwards noted that the courts— unfairly the putative culprits here— abstemiously avoid to the extent possible playing any role in wrecking collegiality. As a matter of law, indeed, spoken by the U.S. Supreme Court, "traditions of collegiality [demand] that principles developed for use [elsewhere] cannot be 'imposed blindly on the academic world.' "[12]

d. *A countercomplaint:* Edwards appreciated the frustration that academics feel who have long perceived themselves as immune to judicial prescription and proscription and then begin to experience the reality of judicial power. But not only did he contend that that power is sparsely used and its effects greatly exaggerated when scrutinized against hard data, he went on as well to suggest that in given matters the courts ought to do more than they do— not more expansively, certainly not more harshly, but simply more pointedly in response to appeals for redress of academe's injustices. Public institutions, for example, can dismiss an untenured faculty member for false and damaging reasons without affording him/her opportunity of rebuttal, simply by not making public the basis of dismissal. But what will the person do when asked by the next employer why he/she left the college? Similarly, a person who believes that he/she has been discriminated against for promotion by reason of race or gender must show that the institution's stated reasons for nonpromotion (e.g., poor teaching performance, inadequate research) are pretext, rather than being able to throw on the institution the burden of demonstrating they used legally permissible grounds. The imbalance of advantage in such instances, where the individual must make the entire case while the institution may simply stand pat, says little to Edwards on behalf of the judicial system's sensitivity to fairness in the resolution of academic dispute.

Judicial Deference: The Doctrine of "Academic Abstention"

Fundamental to the foregoing debate was, and still is, the question whether the courts should, can, and/or do refrain in given circumstances from exercising their considerable powers, yielding to others who enjoy expertise in the matter at hand the final substantive determination of the issue. Courts do refuse, for example, to reach a judgment whether a surgical procedure used by a physician was the best approach that might have been taken to a plaintiff/patient's malady. Neither will courts decide questions of scholarly competence, such as whether a given researcher's experiment was well designed or a given teacher's syllabus was sound.

The vocabulary of law refers to the principle of judicial deference to academic expertise as "the doctrine of academic abstention." It is not a novelty in the law, for courts traditionally have in fact deferred to expertise in all esoteric areas: such deference is the bedrock, for example, on which rests the judicial review of administrative agency actions such as the promulgation of pure food standards.[13] But it is important to distinguish judicial deference to the expertise of others from the exercise of judicial power in matters well within the courts' undoubted competence, e.g., the question whether an institution has complied with standards duly promulgated by a government agency. Whether the standards should have been imposed on academe was a question for the legislative branch to decide; whether the standards are substantively valid is a question for the agency (and ultimately the legislature) to decide, so long as no arbitrariness can be shown in their actions; but whether the college or university has in fact complied with the standards is a question no court need avoid.

The simple reality that a court will not substitute its own judgment in an esoteric matter for the judgment of a trained professional such as a physician or an educator, or for the judgment of an agency established by a legislature, does not mean there is nothing else for courts to decide. Courts are especially sensitive to the *procedural* care that experts show to those they affect. The student whose grade was a disappointment will seek in vain for a court to raise it, but if arbitrariness can be shown in the evaluation process that led to the grade, the student will find in the court a champion quick to require the academic professionals to behave fairly. Judicial deference, in other words, does not mean complete judicial abstinence.

Neither does deference rest on a legal doctrine of institutional autonomy. There is no such doctrine. Judicial deference to any party at all, academic or other, is a function of the court's self-acknowledged incapacity to address esoteric concerns, not of some imagined legal monopoly of the experts in that area. Where a court is precluded by law from addressing a matter, e.g., "has the Rev. Dr. Smith, theologian of a given denomination, embraced a heresy?" there the court is not exhibiting deference: it is legally powerless to act (in this illustrative instance by the First Amendment's "wall" between church and state). But courts *can* constitutionally evaluate a student's work and order that his/her grade be changed. They simply don't—not because colleges and universities are legally autonomous, but because courts understand the wisdom of leaving professional judgments to professionals.

Judicial deference is most commonly confused with the court's jurisdiction of a case. In the federal jurisprudence of the United States (and in the vast majority of the states), courts sit to decide cases and controversies. They are not at liberty to refuse to decide cases properly brought before them, nor are they empowered to solicit or compel parties to seek redress from them. To the extent there was a detectable period in history when little or no academic dispute was decided by the courts, it is not because courts were refusing to decide such cases in deference to academic expertise; it is rather because academics were not bringing their quarrels before the bar. Likewise, any increase in the incidence of academic litigation tells us little about judicial activism; chiefly it tells us that academics are becoming more litigious.

The incidence of academic litigation has clearly increased since the mid-1960s. But as is elaborated in the last section of this chapter, with one instructive exception there has been no perceptible decline of judicial deference to academic expertise, the conventional wisdom in many quarters to the contrary notwithstanding. Courts have made clear that public universities, under the requirements of the U.S. Constitution's Fourteenth Amendment, which covers all public entities, must provide procedural safeguards to students about to be suspended or expelled for misconduct, and to tenured faculty about to be discharged. But the courts have maintained deferential silence concerning the criteria on which such dismissals are decided, inquiring only into the character of the procedures by which a person may be deprived of a significant interest—which hardly bespeaks an unsophisticated meddler intruding on the domain of the academic professionals.

The sole exception to the general practice of judicial deference to academic expertise, the archetypal instance in which the courts have unhesitantly substituted their own judgment for the positions taken by colleges and universities, has arisen when in the name of institutional autonomy constitutionally impermissible limits have been placed on the liberty of expression by faculty and students. In such cases, the doctrine of "academic abstention" has been ignored, judicial deference has been eschewed, and the courts have landed foursquare on the side of free expression— "academic freedom"—against institutional autonomy.

The Functions of Courts

Government in the United States finds its theoretical underpinnings in the twin principles that (1) sovereignty lies in the people, not in a monarch or other ruling body, and (2) an effective system of "checks and balances" protects the people against abuse of power by the government that they create. As to the latter principle, government comprises three branches—the legislature, the executive, and the judiciary—each of which enjoys primacy within its own sphere of responsibility, but the exercise of the power of each is limited by the counterpart powers of the other branches. Legislatures declare social policy and enact statutes to implement it; the executive, however, may veto the enactments or may implement them less vigorously than the legislature contemplated. The courts may invalidate the legislation either for its unconstitutional character or for its impermissible application in given instances. Legislatures may override vetoes, and they typically have opportunity to review prospective judicial appointees nominated by the executive, preventing the coming to the bench of those they deem unfit.

All these safeguards and more are rooted in the constitutions of the federal government and of the several states. The federal government is one of limited jurisdiction: only such matters as are enumerated in its constitution fall within its power, all others being retained by the states or the sovereign people. But within that limited scope, the constitution and laws of the United States are "the supreme law of the land," binding on all judges in every state regardless of state law (Article VI, Constitution of the United States). By contrast, the governments of the several states are governments of general jurisdiction and, save for matters included in the federal power and therefore covered by the aforementioned "supremacy clause," state governments may authoritatively address any topic of interest.

When in 1787 the Continental Congress submitted the proposed federal constitution to the states for ratification, it was understood that several matters too controversial for initial inclusion would be taken up immediately upon formation of the new government. The Congress of the United States was convened in March 1789, and by December 1791 the first ten amendments to the Constitution, often called the Bill of Rights,[14] had been adopted. But in the first test of the amendments' power to protect a citizen against the action of state government, the U.S. Supreme Court held they were not applicable at the state level.[15]

Following the War Between the States, the Thirteenth Amendment was adopted rendering slavery unconstitutional, together with the Fourteenth Amendment requiring evenhandedness in the treatment of all persons within the reach of state power: "No state shall deprive any person of life, liberty or property without due process of law; nor deny to any person within its jurisdiction equal protection of the law."

The Fourteenth Amendment's provisions, fashioned in the aftermath of emancipation, were designed to secure to former slaves legal rights long enjoyed only by free persons, and initially the U.S. Supreme Court insisted upon maintaining that focus.[16] In later years, however, the doctrines of due process and equal protection were interpreted literally to include "any person" regardless of race or former condition of servitude, regardless even whether he/she were a citizen of the United States. Moreover, beginning in the 1930s and continuing through the 1960s, the Court incorporated— piecemeal and never completely, but substantially nonetheless—many of the protections of the Bill of Rights against abuse of power by state government as well as by the federal, by interpreting the term "liberty" (in "No state shall deprive any person of liberty . . . without due process of law") to include many of the liberties guaranteed by the first ten amendments.

Two fundamental implications for academic law derive from the foregoing review. One concerns the respective boundaries of federal vis-a-vis state jurisdiction in academic matters, and the other concerns the relative limits imposed by the federal Constitution on governmental vis-a-vis independent (on "public" as distinguished from "private") higher education. Education is nowhere mentioned in the federal Constitution. By reason, therefore, of the principle (made explicit in the Tenth Amendment) that all matters not enumerated in the federal Constitution are reserved to the states and/or to the people, the federal government is without power to address educational matters per se. To reach education—which, of course, it does—the government must address itself to aspects of education constitutionally within its power, e.g., by funding various programs within education under the provision of the preamble to the Constitution that government is to "promote the general welfare"; or by prohibiting school authorities from infringing a person's First Amendment right of free expression; or by requiring educational management to engage in collective bargaining with employees in order that labor disputes not impede commerce among the states (Article 1, Section 8, Constitution of the United States).

The jurisdictions of the two court systems—federal and state—mirror the enumerated constitutional powers, but with important qualifications. As courts of general jurisdiction, state courts enjoy wide latitude in what issues they are legally authorized to decide, whereas federal courts are limited to hearing disputes involving some federal issue. A zoning dispute, for example, over the legality of operating a college pub on a given street corner may go only to a state court, but a dispute over whether a person has been discriminatorily refused employment in that pub in violation of the equal protection clause may go to either a state or a federal court. State courts, that is, may hear disputes grounded in federal claims; but they may not decide those disputes on the basis of state law if it is inconsistent with the federal. The federal courts, on the other hand, may not entertain any suits between residents of the same state quarreling over a matter devoid of any element of federal law, e.g., again, a zoning ordinance.

Most litigants prefer to take federally based claims to a federal court for disposition, especially when the federal law runs counter to the mores of the locality. Consequently, as the momentum of the civil rights movements of the 1950s and 1960s built to a crescendo in the late 1960s and early 1970s, the pattern of primarily state court activity in academic litigation gave way to chiefly federal activity instead, leading many an observer to conclude the federal courts were activist. As indicated above, however, courts sit to hear cases, and hear them they must. Activity, therefore, i.e., the relative incidence of cases that come before a bench, is a function primarily of social forces over which the courts exercise negligible control. Activism, on the other hand, i.e., the forsaking of the traditional judicial deference to academic expertise in favor of the courts' own judgments, has yet to be demonstrated. We shall return to the question more fully below.

The second implication for higher education of the "separation of powers" principle in American government concerns the legal distinctions drawn between the public and private sectors of academe when they come before the courts. The celebrated *Dartmouth College* case initiated a new genre of academic organization in American higher education. The divorce of *control* by the state of colleges and universities from their *creation* by the state gave rise almost immediately to institutions controlled instead by independent boards of private citizens. Later, public institutions governed by boards of state officials re-emerged under authority either of statute or of a state's constitution. And the difference in the control of "private" vis-a-vis "public" institutions became crucial in litigation.

Private institutions cannot be reached by the Bill of Rights or the due process or equal protection clauses, because such institutions are neither part of the federal government nor part of a state's, the only entities addressed by those constitutional provisions. If one wishes to draw a private college or university within the prescriptions and proscriptions of those constitutional demands, the task must be accomplished by building bridges from the state to the institution by means of the doctrine of "state action." One of two tests will suffice: if a state has so pervasively insinuated itself into the activities of the institution that, for all practical purposes, the state and the college are interdependent partners, then the college—though formally private by reason of its charter and the composition of its governing board—will be deemed a public institution for purposes of constitutional analysis; the University of Pittsburgh is a case in point.[17] Or if an institution acts on behalf of the state to secure the latter's interests, then in whatever matter it so serves it too will be deemed for constitutional purposes a public institution; the colleges under contract to New York State, such as Cornell University's College of Agriculture and Life Sciences, and Alfred University's College of Ceramics, are cases in point: these institutions are "public," though sister colleges within these universities are not.

Absent evidence of "state action," however, the private institution is free of constitutional constraints. But that is not to say it is at liberty to be a law unto itself. It means only that the legal grounds of any challenge to the college's actions must be found elsewhere than in the Bill of Rights or in due process or equal protection. The two most common grounds are the law of contract and the statutes, rules, and regulations enforced by government administrative agencies. Together they comprise the basic arsenal of the litigant who seeks to vindicate his/her rights as a "consumer" of higher education.[18]

Separately they constitute the primary legal wherewithal of the litigant who seeks redress for losses sustained when an institution fails, say, to honor the terms of his/her employment contract, or when the institution discriminatorily refuses to promote the person on grounds of gender. However, if the success rate of such suits is indicative of the power of these weapons, the legal arsenal is full of BB guns and noisemakers.[19]

The Impact of the Courts on Academe

To this point in the discussion, we have persistently gainsaid the prevalent view that judicial activism has placed institutional autonomy in check, both directly by the substitution of the judgment of the court for academic expertise, and indirectly by the chilling effect it has had on the exercise of administrative discretion. It is time for demonstration instead of assertion. Three core interests of academe have been brought before the bench sufficiently to provide a clear statement of where and why, if at all, courts are willing to second-guess academics: the admission and retention of students; the appointment, promotion, and dismissal of faculty; and the freedom of faculty and students to inquire into and advance whatever points of view they wish.

STUDENTS

Cases now speak the law of (a) standards of admission; (b) discipline for misconduct; and (c) bases of academic dismissal. None of them impinges upon the power of institutions to establish effective criteria in any of the three areas of student affairs.

a. In private institutions, "a State through its courts does not have the authority to interfere with the power of [the] school to make rules concerning the admission of students."[20] In public colleges and universities, no particular admissions standards have ever been judicially required, and only two—race and physical condition—have ever been considered. As to race, it is a permissible but not mandatory criterion,[21] and as to physical ability or disability, "[n]othing in the language or history of [the Rehabilitation Act of 1973] reflects an intention to limit the freedom of an educational institution to require reasonable physical qualifications for admission."[22]

b. Students in public institutions may not be suspended or expelled for misconduct without opportunity to hear the charges placed against them, to defend themselves against those charges before an impartial tribunal, and to purchase a written record of the proceedings.[23] No substantive standards of the validity of such charges beyond "reasonableness" have been required. Nor is such "due process" required when lesser penalties are inflicted. No student in any private institution is afforded any such protection except the requirement of reasonableness, unless the institution chooses to extend it.

It is commonly presumed in academic circles that the doctrine of *in loco parentis,* i.e., the institution stands "in the place of the parent" with respect to the student, is dead. As a practical matter, the presumption is probably sound; *in loco parentis* is dead at many, if not most, colleges and universities. But it was the institutions, not the courts, that sounded its death knell (indeed, in the wake of increased violence and physical danger on many campuses, some courts are "revisiting" the concept and suggesting a contemporary application to institutional responsibility).[24] Nor is it implicitly overruled by the requirement of minimal due process in cases of suspension or expulsion for misconduct any more than a true parent's legal power over a child is dissolved simply because in most jurisdictions parents are no longer immune to suit by their children for conduct that visits a legal injury on the minor.

c. If the procedural requirements in disciplinary action are minimal, they are virtually nil in cases of academic termination. In *Horowitz,*[25] the landmark case in the matter, the U.S. Supreme Court held that "the significant difference between the failure of a student to meet academic standards and the violation by a student of valid rules of conduct . . . calls for *far less* stringent procedural requirements in the case of academic dismissal" (emphasis added). "Far less" stringency than is required in disciplinary actions is tantamount to astringency. In addition, and more important to the issue of institutional autonomy, the Court continued:

> [W]e decline to ignore the historic judgment of educators [and] to further enlarge the judicial presence in the academic community. . . . We recognize . . . that a hearing may be "useless or even harmful in finding out the truth as to scholarship."
>
> "Judicial interposition in the operation of the public school system of the Nation raises problems requiring care and restraint." . . . Courts are particularly ill-equipped to evaluate academic performance. The factors discussed [earlier] with respect to procedural due process . . . warn against any such judicial intrusion into academic decision-making.

In short, the challenges brought in the last several decades to institutional policy and practice toward students may have made for greater activity in the courts, but the courts themselves have not used the opportunity thus provided them to become more activist in their treatment of academic issues. Their sole imposition was procedural only, limited narrowly to instances of disciplinary suspension or expulsion, and avoiding admissions and academic evaluations questions virtually completely. Nor were they any more rigorous procedurally than to require that a charged party who could be suspended or expelled have the opportunity to know and rebut if he/she can the charges on which the discipline is laid, and to secure at the individual's own expense a written record of the proceedings. Institutional autonomy is hardly threatened by such judicial involvement in academic dispute. A reasonable person might even think it strengthened.

FACULTY

The power of courts to impose criteria alien to the academic profession on the faculty appointment/retention function is probably more unsettling to academe than the counterpart judicial power in student admission/retention. But academics have no more reason to date to fear intrusion by the judiciary at this level than has been experienced in student affairs. No court has ever required any institution to hire a given candidate for a faculty position. Moreover, (a) nonrenewal of term contracts by an institution can be decided with impunity, for no reasons whatever need be provided; (b) in any controversy whether unlawful discrimination prevented one's promotion, the burden of proof rests with the plaintiff faculty member, not with the defendant institution; and (c) faculty in private institutions who participate extensively in university governance are precluded from compelling the administration to negotiate a collective bargaining agreement with their union.

a. The law of faculty termination in public institutions (contract law controls the issue in private colleges and universities) was enunciated by the U.S. Supreme Court in two companion cases handed down in 1972, *Roth*[26] and *Sindermann*.[27] No untenured faculty member need be provided a hearing at which to contest his/her nonrenewal of contract unless (i) there are grounds on which to believe the nonrenewal may be in impermissible reprisal for his/her exercise of a constitutionally protected right such as public criticism of the university administration; or (ii) the reasons for nonrenewal are defamatory or would otherwise injure his/her reputation such that employment elsewhere is prevented. Defamation and/or the staining of one's reputation, however, must be public to trigger a hearing. If the institution refrains from publicizing such grounds of the nonrenewal, no opportunity to rebut the reasons need be provided.[28]

As to impermissible reprisals for the exercise of constitutionally protected freedoms such as expression or association, institutional administrators responsible for such unconstitutional behavior who knew or should have known the unlawful character of their action can be held personally liable in money damages to the plaintiff.[29] It is here that some critics contend that judicial awards of such damages have a chilling effect on other administrators' willingness to exercise their judgment in whether to renew an incompetent but outspoken faculty member's contract. The argument is not compelling. The penalty is for behavior that not even the most rabid advocate of absolute institutional autonomy can justify, namely, the deliberate or exceedingly careless infringement of another person's right of expression. The penalty does not apply when the actual grounds of renewal are the candidate's professional performance, but only when the administrator has infringed the individual's rights. That will never trouble the truthful decision-maker.

When the faculty member about to be dismissed is tenured, then in the public university he/she must be provided a hearing, if requested, "where he could be informed of the grounds for his nonretention and challenge their sufficiency."[30] But the Court imposes no definition of "sufficiency" on the university; the standards to be met for retention still are formulated by academics to whom the Court pays judicial deference. And when the grounds for dismissal of the tenured faculty member are not his/her professional performance or other personal characteristic but rather the financial exigency of the institution, no procedural protection is afforded: it is "peculiarly within the province of the [college] administration to determine which teachers should be released, and which should be retained. . . . [I]t is not the province of the court to interfere and substitute its judgment for that of the administrative body."[31]

b. Much of the concern over judicial intrusion into the faculty employment process focuses on the courts' interpretations of the "affirmative action" requirements of the Civil Rights Acts of 1866, 1871, and 1964, as enforced by the regulatory process. *Sweeney*[32] suggests the concern is probably misplaced (from candidate to institution) and at least unnecessary. There the U.S. Supreme Court held the aggrieved candidate must first establish a plausible showing that he/she was denied promotion on grounds of gender or race, following which the institution need only "articulate some legitimate, nondiscriminatory reason for the employee's rejection" (hardly an insuperable barrier to overcome). That done, the burden returns to the plaintiff to show that the institution's alleged reasons are sham, a mere pretext to disguise the true and discriminatory reasons—which is an almost impossible task. The institution, of course, has control of the essential information in the matter: minutes of committee meetings, memoranda, personnel who participated in the decision process, resources with which to store and retrieve the data. Nonetheless, the Court has seen fit to allocate the significant burden in the case to the individual. It is left to the plaintiff to secure whatever he/she can of the information necessary to his/her argument through pretrial "discovery" (inquiries posed by litigants to one another in preparing the arguments they will present at trial).

c. The faculty of Yeshiva University in New York City formed a union and sought through the regulatory process of the National Labor Relations Board to compel a reticent Board of Trustees to negotiate a labor agreement with the union. The trustees insisted that Yeshiva faculty were "managerial employees" excluded from the coverage of the National Labor Relations Act, and the U.S. Supreme Court concurred (see n.12). Of greater general importance to higher education than the Court's interpretation of what actually took place at Yeshiva University is their stated view (quoted earlier in this chapter) that "traditions of collegiality [between faculty and administrators] continue to play a significant role at many universities [and therefore] principles developed for use [elsewhere] *cannot be 'imposed blindly on the academic world'* " (emphasis added). Courts, that is, may not treat academe as but one more enterprise; instead, says the Supreme Court, they must accommodate higher education's distinctive traditions of collegiality in their resolution of academic disputes.

On point of faculty, then, we see no greater evidence of judicial activism than was exhibited in respect of students. Tenured faculty in public institutions are owed a hearing, if requested, at which to challenge the sufficiency of the grounds on which their appointment is about to be terminated (other than financial exigency; no protections are afforded in such cases). The Court does not, however, delimit the character of permissible grounds. That substantive determination is left to academe. And where it is plausible that the basis of one's nonrenewal/nonpromotion is impermissible by reason of statute, e.g., discrimination on grounds of gender, the burden rests nonetheless with the challenger to make the case, not with the institution to show they have acted lawfully. As to collegiality, the tradition so evident in the historic faculty role in institutional governance may not be sacrificed to principles of labor relations developed in other sectors of the economy. In such data as these, one finds no showing of judicial impairment of institutional autonomy.

ACADEMIC FREEDOM

At last the critics hit pay dirt. The courts do quite blatantly intrude on autonomy in the matter of academic freedom. The difficulty, however, is of course that they do so in defense of the value that academe professes to cherish above all others. Several cases make the point, but two will suffice here. The constitutional foundation of academic freedom is in the First Amendment's Provisions that Congress (and now the states) "shall make no law . . . abridging the freedom of speech or of the press; or the right of the people peaceably to assemble." In a loyalty oath case that reached the U.S. Supreme Court in 1967, the Court held:

> Our Nation is deeply committed to safeguarding academic freedom, which is of transcendent value to all of us and not merely to the teachers concerned. That freedom is therefore a *special* concern of the First Amendment, which does not tolerate laws that cast a pall of orthodoxy over the classroom (emphasis added).[33]

Quoting from an earlier case,[34] the Court continued:

> The essentiality of freedom in the community of American universities is almost self-evident. . . . Scholarship cannot flourish in an atmosphere of suspicion and distrust. Teachers and students must always remain free to inquire, to study and to evaluate, to gain new maturity and understanding; otherwise, our civilization will stagnate and die.

One can hardly conceive a more potent, more authoritative affirmation of the legal vitality of academe's *raison d'être*. But in nourishing academic freedom thus, the Court knowingly and deliberately intruded upon the autonomy of the governing authorities in a state university who had required a loyalty oath of the faculty.

Later the Court similarly intruded upon the autonomy of another institution, this time to safeguard the academic freedom of a group of students.[35] The students had been denied official recognition by a state college as a local chapter of Students for a Democratic Society (SDS) on grounds that their professed independence from the politically radical and often disruptive national organization was doubtful and that SDS philosophy was antithetical to college policy. Consistent with established case law, the Court held that even if the group were not independent of the national SDS, their association with an unpopular organization would not be a legally valid basis on which their First Amendment rights of expression and association may be denied. Only action or specific intent to engage in or to further unlawful action—not the advocacy of ideas, no matter how repugnant, may be proscribed. And the burden falls upon the college to demonstrate a legal basis of any refusal to extend official recognition, not upon the student group to show they are entitled to enjoy their First Amendment freedoms.

Three quotations from the several opinions in the case provide glimpses into the justices' views of institutional autonomy and the role of the judiciary. From the majority opinion:

> [W]here state-operated educational institutions are involved, this Court has long recognized "the need for affirming the comprehensive authority of the States and of school officials, consistent with fundamental constitutional safeguards, to prescribe and control conduct in the schools." . . . Yet, the precedents of this Court leave no room for the view that because of the acknowledged need for order, First Amendment freedoms should apply with less force on college campuses than in the community at large.

From the concurring opinion of a justice who had also joined the majority opinion:

> It is within . . . the academic community that problems such as these should be resolved. The courts, state or federal, should be a last resort. . . . [But] in spite of the wisdom of the [trial] court in sending [this] case back to the college, the issue was . . . not adequately addressed in the [college's] hearing.

And from the concurrence of another such justice who had also joined the majority opinion:

> [T]he fact that [this case] had to come here for ultimate resolution indicates the sickness of our academic world, measured by First Amendment standards.

Strong stuff! The U.S. Supreme Court's preference is that higher education on its own initiative conform its behavior to the fundamental constitutional principles that sustain its claim to academic freedom. But if academe elects not to do so, the Court will unabashedly exercise its considerable power to require conformance, no matter what unfettered authority a given party might otherwise enjoy.

Conclusion

There is no evidence that courts today are more activist than were their counterparts of an earlier day. To be sure, they are undeniably more active in the adjudication of academic dispute. But that is not because courts are exercising an invalid "roving commission" to go about setting wrongs right. They are hearing more cases today because more are being brought to them. Especially are plaintiffs appealing to the federal judiciary for relief from various alleged harms as the statutory and regulatory fallout, including backlash, of the civil rights movement continues to stimulate litigation in academic matters as well as elsewhere.

Activity, however, is not to be confused with activism. Today's courts, though busier in academic concerns than were their predecessors, are no more likely than were their forebears to substitute their own judgments for judgments reached by experts within academe. To the contrary, despite the anguished cries of a few academics, deference to institutional determinations is still the rule. The doctrine of "academic abstention" is as robust as ever. Where the courts might plausibly be considered "activist" (especially if one has a high tolerance for hyperbole) is in the vindication of the constitutional rights, especially the First Amendment freedoms of expression and association, of academic plaintiffs. But to the very minor extent that the activism has infringed upon institutional autonomy, the loss is heavily outweighed by the strength it has brought to the legal bases of academic freedom.

We recognize that one might reasonably contend the legislatures and regulatory agencies of government have gone "too far" in their invasion by statute and promulgated rule of institutional self-determination. That is not, however, an issue discussed in this chapter, nor is it one on which we here take a position. Courts, in any event, are not to be lumped willy-nilly together with the other branches of government. For better or for worse they have become increasingly involved in academic dispute, but consistently they have maintained a very sensitive deference to academic judgment.

Notes

1. Estelle A. Fishbein, "The Academic Industry—A Dangerous Premise," in *Government Regulation of Higher Education,* ed. Walter C. Hobbs (Cambridge, Mass.: Ballinger, 1978), pp. 57–58.

2. Robert M. O'Neil, *The Courts, Government and Higher Education* (New York Committee for Economic Development, 1972), p. 10.

3. The Sloan Commission on Government and Higher Education, *A Program for Renewed Partnership* (Cambridge, Mass.: Ballinger, 1980), pp. 10, 55.

4. Harry T. Edwards, *Higher Education and the Unholy Crusade Against Governmental Regulation* (Cambridge, Mass.: Harvard University Institute for Edu-

cational Management, 1980).

    5. Ibid., p. 39.

    6. Ibid., p. 17.

    7. Ibid., p. 20. Perhaps, retorts the critic. But when I must raise $10,000 to render reports that none of my $100,000 categorical grant may be used to prepare, or to improve physical facilities for which I receive no grant, then it's costing me money I don't have and which I must generate to comply with government regulation.

    8. Ibid., p. 20.

    9. Ibid., p. 29.

    10. Sloan Report, *Program for Renewed Partnership,* p. 61.

    11. Walter C. Hobbs, "The 'Defective Pressure-Cooker' Syndrome: Dispute Process in the University," *Journal of Higher Education* 45 (November 1974).

    12. *National Labor Relations Board* v. *Yeshiva University,* 444 U.S. 672 (1980).

    13. Walter C. Hobbs, "The Theory of Government Regulation," in *Government Regulation,* pp. 4–5.

    14. The rights are actually enumerated in the first eight amendments.

    15. *Barron* v. *Mayor and City Council of Baltimore,* 8 L. Ed. 672 (1833).

    16. The Slaughterhouse Cases, 16 Wall. 36 (1873).

    17. *Braden* v. *University of Pittsburgh,* 552 F.2d 948 (1977).

    18. Joan S. Stark, ed., *Promoting Consumer Protection for Students* (San Francisco: Jossey-Bass, 1976).

    19. Edwards, *Higher Education and the Unholy Crusade,* p. 19.

    20. *Steinberg* v. *Chicago Medical School,* 354 N.E.2d 586 (1976).

    21. *Regents of the University of California* v. *Bakke,* 438 U.S. 265 (1978).

    22. *Southeastern Community College* v. *Davis,* 442 U.S. 397 (1979).

    23. *Dixon* v. *Alabama State Board of Education,* 294 F.2d 150 (1961); *Esteban* v. *Central Missouri State College,* 277 F.Supp. 649 (1967), afmd., 415 F.2d 1077 (1969).

    24. *Eiseman* v. *State of New York,* 489 N.Y.S.2d 957 (1985), rvsd. 511 N.E.2d 1128.

    25. *Board of Curators of the University of Missouri* v. *Horowitz,* 435 U.S. 78 (1978).

    26. *Board of Regents* v. *Roth,* 408 U.S. 564 (1972).

    27. *Perry* v. *Sindermann,* 408 U.S. 593 (1972).

    28. *Bishop* v. *Woods,* 426 U.S. 341 (1976).

    29. *Wood* v. *Strickland,* 420 U.S. 308 (1975).

    30. *Sindermann* case.

    31. *Levitt* v. *Board of Trustees of Nebraska State Colleges,* 376 F. Supp. 945 (1974).

    32. *Board of Trustees of Keene State College* v. *Sweeney,* 439 U.S. 24 (1978).

    33. *Keyishian* v. *Board of Regents of the University of the State of New York,* 385 U.S. 589 (1967).

    34. *Sweezy* v. *New Hampshire,* 354 U.S. 234 (1957).

    35. *Healy* v. *James,* 408 U.S. 169 (1972).

9

Other External Constituencies and Their Impact on Higher Education
Fred F. Harcleroad

Postsecondary institutions have opened and endured in the United States for over three and one-half centuries. All except those established very recently have been modified over the years and changed greatly in response to pressures from external forces. Particularly in the last century and a half, literally thousands of diverse institutions have opened their doors, only to close when they were no longer needed by (1) sufficient students, or (2) the public and private constituencies that originally founded and supported them. Those in existence today are the survivors, the institutions that adapted to the needs of their constituencies.

Both of the oldest institutions in the country, Harvard (established in 1636) and the College of William and Mary (established in 1693), closed for different reasons, but opened up again when changes were made. Harvard closed for what would have been its second year (in 1639-40) after Nathaniel Eaton, its first head, was dismissed for cruelty to students and stealing much of the college funds. After being closed for the year government officials determined that the Massachusetts Bay Colony still needed a college to train ministers and advance learning. A new president, Henry Dunster, reopened the college in 1640, and by changing regularly, and sometimes dramatically, it has remained in operation ever since. Two small examples illustrate this impact. As Massachusetts grew and secularized, ministerial training at Harvard was only one function, so it was placed in a separate divinity school. Also, by the late 1700s required instruction in Hebrew was replaced by student choice, a beginning of our current elective system. William and Mary was the richest of the colonial colleges, with good support from the Commonwealth of Virginia, including the income from taxes on tobacco, skins, and hides. Nevertheless, it made many adaptations in order to remain politically supported. For example, after the Revolution, in 1779, it dropped its chair of Divinity and established the nation's first professorship of Law and Police. The College closed during the 1861–1865 period of civil war, re-opened briefly but closed again in 1881. It eventually reopened in 1888 when the state agreed to make it a state-supported institution if it would become Virginia's main teacher education college, with a first charge to prepare teachers. Thus it changed from being essentially a private college operated by the Episcopal Church, an excellent example of a government taking over a private institution to meet the developing needs in the society as a whole. Interaction of this type between government and private constituencies is a singular characteristic of the democratic republic established in the United States, and important to consider in studying the relationships of colleges and universities to their external environment.

The varied set of external forces affecting postsecondary education in the United States has grown out of our unique three-sector system of providing goods and services for both "collective consumption" and "private" use. First, the *voluntary enterprise sector,* composed of over six million independent nonprofit organizations, often has initiated efforts to provide such things as schools, hospitals, bridges, libraries, environmental controls, and public parks. They are protected by constitutional rights to peaceful assembly, free speech, and petition for redress of grievances. These formidable protections plus their record of useful service led to their being nontaxable, with contributions to them being tax free. Second, the *public enterprise group,* composed of all local, state, and federal governments, administers the laws that hold our society together. Third, the *private enterprise sector,* composed of profit-seeking business and commerce, provides much of the excess wealth needed to support the other two sectors. This pluralistic and diverse set of organizations implements very well the basic ideas behind our federated republic.

Our constitution provides for detailed separation of powers at the federal level between the presidency, the Congress, and the judiciary. The Tenth Amendment establishes the states as governments with "general" powers and delegates "limited" powers to the federal government. Education is not a delegated power and therefore is reserved to the states, where their constitutions often treated it almost as a fourth branch of government. In addition, the Tenth Amendment reserves "general" powers to citizens who operate through their own voluntary organizations, their state governments, or state-authorized private enterprise. Consequently, only a few higher education institutions are creations of the federal government (mostly military institutions, to provide for the common defense), but over 99 percent are creations of states, voluntary organizations, or profit-seeking business.

External groups, associations, and agencies from all three sectors impact on the many varied types of institutions of postsecondary education. This very diverse group of organizations includes everything from athletic conferences and alumni associations to employer associations and unions (or organized faculty groups that function as unions). Of course, the corporate boards that administer all of the private colleges, universities, and institutes authorized to operate in the respective states belong in this group. Their power to determine institutional policies is clear and well known. However, many other voluntary associations can and do have significant effects on specific institutions or units of the institutions. To illustrate their potential, these five selected types of organizations will be described in some detail to indicate their backgrounds, development, and possible areas of impact on institutional autonomy and academic freedom. They are:

1. Private foundations;

2. Institutionally based associations;

3. Voluntary accrediting associations;

4. Voluntary consortia;

5. Regional compacts.

Private Foundations[1]

The first beginnings of private foundations in the U.S. took place over two centuries ago. As a precursor, Benjamin Franklin led in the establishment in Philadelphia of a number of voluntary sector organizations, including the American Philosophical Society in 1743, an association with many foundation characteristics. In 1800 the Magdalen Society of Philadelphia, possibly the first private foundation in the United States, was established as a perpetual trust to assist "unhappy females who had been seduced from the paths of virtue." In the 1890s and early 1900s the Carnegie foundations, followed shortly by the Rockefeller foundations, set a pattern that continues to this day. These foundations established a high standard of operations and valuable service. Few academics realize that their current TIAA pensions were developed and are presently administered by a foundation resulting from Andrew Carnegie's feeling of public service responsibility. Decades before it became legal to tax incomes and before such "contributions" became tax deductible, he gave several million dollars to set up the first pension fund for college teachers.

Today, private foundations vary greatly in form, purpose, size, function, and constituency. Some are corporate in nature, many are trusts, and some are only associations. Many of them can affect postsecondary institutions through their choice of areas to support. They can be classified into five types as follows: (1) community foundations, often city-wide or regional, which make a variety of bequests or gifts (local postsecondary institutions often can count on some limited support from such foundations for locally related projects); (2) family or personal foundations, often with very limited purposes; (3) special purpose foundations (including such varied examples as the Harvard Glee Club, and a fund set up to provide every girl at Bryn Mawr with one baked potato at each meal); (4) company foundations established to channel corporate giving through one main source; and (5) national, independent foundations (including many of the large, well-known foundations such as Ford, Kellogg, Johnson, Lilly, and Carnegie, plus recent additions such as Murdock, MacArthur, and Hewlett). Over 90 percent of private foundation grant funds to higher education come from these national foundations. They usually are interested in making grants with national or international implications, often within carefully determined target areas of interest.

The total number of grant making foundations is huge, with estimates varying from 24,000 to 32,401 in 1992. Every state has a number of foundations, with New York the most at 5,736. Their assets total over 142 billion dollars, and their 1992 grants totaled close to 9 billion dollars. A special report of the Foundation Center in 1991 reported that 228 of the larger foundations made grants totaling over 980 million dollars in thirty-eight varied primary fields of interest such as adult education, environment, history, medical education, public health, rural development, theater, dance, and vocational education.

Foundations, especially the national, independent category, provide significant help to higher education institutions, and by their choice of the areas they will finance they entice supposedly autonomous colleges to do things they might not do otherwise. Institutional change continues to be a prime goal of foundations, as it has been for most of the past century. Thus, although their grants provide a relatively small proportion of the total financing of institutions, they have had significant effects on program development and even on operations. Important support has been provided for such critical activities as the upgrading of medical education, the development of honors programs, and the international exchange of students. Grants from foundations have been instrumental in the establishment of new academic fields such as microbiology and anthropology and the redirection of the fields of business and the education of teachers. Significant support has been provided particularly for the increasing opportunities for minority students' attendance at both undergraduate and graduate levels, and especially in professional fields. Complaints that the private foundations limit their significant funding efforts to "establishment" activities fail to recognize the many critical social changes in which private foundations have led the way. Often, foundation funds have encouraged colleges and universities to take forefront positions in some social causes.

It is important to stress, however, that private foundations affect institutional freedom only if the institutions voluntarily accept the funds for the purposes prescribed by the foundation. Redirection of programs, and even private institutional goals, is possible and has occurred on occasion. Nevertheless, the private foundation model has been so successful that government has adopted it in forming and funding such agencies as the National Science Foundation, the Fund for the Improvement of Postsecondary Education, and the National Endowments for the Arts and for the Humanities. Clearly, private foundations have been and undoubtedly will continue to be important external forces affecting postsecondary education.

Institutionally Based Associations[2]

Voluntary membership organizations of this type are almost infinite in possible numbers. Although formed by officials from institutions for their own purposes, the associations often end up having either indirect or direct effects on the institutions themselves. Several large and quite powerful associations represent many of the institutions. The American Council on Education, probably the major policy advocate for postsecondary education at the national level, plays a critical coordinative role as an umbrella-type organization composed of a wide spectrum of institutions. Seven other major national institutional organizations include (1) the Association of American Colleges, (2) the American Association of Community Colleges, (3) the American Association of State Colleges and Universities, (4) the Association of American Universities, (5) the Council of Independent Colleges, (6) the National Association of Independent Colleges and Universities, and (7) the National Association of State Universities and Land-Grant Colleges. These organizations represent most of the public and private nonprofit postsecondary institutions of the United States, with some institutions belonging to two or three of them. All are based in Washington, D.C., and are important in representing differing interests of the varied groups of institutions. Also, especially when they work together as a united front, they can influence congressional committees and government agencies on key issues affecting higher education. A larger group of thirty-five associations works together under the umbrella of the American Council on Education, as the Washington Higher Education Secretariat. It meets monthly to exchange information and to discuss ongoing or projected activities, many of them dealing with national policy issues.

The strength of these national associations will continue to grow along with taxes, the federal budget, and federal purchase of selected services from their member institutions. Even though most of the postsecondary institutions are state chartered and many basically are state funded, the increasing power of the federal tax system will make such national associations even more necessary.

Many specialized voluntary membership associations contribute in diverse ways to the development and operations of functional areas within institutions. For example, both the American College Testing Program and the College Entrance Examination Board (its service bureau, the Educational Testing Service, is not a membership organization) provide extensive information resources to their member institutions and program areas. These data are vital for counseling and guidance purposes, admissions of students, student financial aid programs, and related activities. In addition, different administrative functions (such as graduate schools, registrars, institutional research units, and business offices) have their own extremely useful representative associations. Likewise, most different academic fields and their constantly increasing subdivisions or spin-offs have set up specialized groups. Prime examples are engineering and the allied health professions, both with dozens of separate associations. Many of these academic organizations affect institutions and their program planning in very direct ways. In particular, the associations that set up extensive detailed criteria for membership in the association often influence very directly the allocation of resources. Of the several thousand membership organizations in this category, sixty to seventy of them, from architecture to veterinary medicine, probably exert the greatest influence, since those programs or academic units admitted to membership are considered "accredited." The following section will provide more detail on this group.

A small sampling of these varied types of organizations will illustrate their services, emphasize their significance, and show in a limited way their potential impact.

1. *The American Council on Education* includes separate institutions and other associations, with approximately 1600 members of this type, representing over 70 percent of all college and university enrollments in the United States. Close to 200 non-institutional members make the total association membership over 1800. Since its establishment in 1916 the work of the Council has changed from emphasis on "consensus building," a first charge for the first 50 years, to initiating action to improve higher education. Its special offices and centers indicate its thrusts: Office of Women in Higher Education; Center for Adult Learning and Educational Credentials; Office of Minorities in Higher Education; Business-Higher Education Forum; Center for Leadership Development; International Initiatives; Division of Policy Analysis and Research; Division of Governmental Relations; the Washington Higher Education Secretariat; and numerous other special programs. The extensive publication program provides major documents of the field of higher education, such as the annual editions of *American Universities and Colleges.* It also prepares and distributes such important guidebooks as the *Guide to the Evaluation of Educational Experiences in the Armed Services.* This guide is updated periodically and serves as a "bible" for most registrars' offices. Another comparable ACE publication is *The National Guide to Credit Recommendations for Non-Collegiate Courses.* The extensive overall service and publications program includes reports from the policy analysis service and many special studies on current critical issues in higher education.

2. *The National Association of College and University Business Officers* plays a critical role in all institutional administrative areas. From its origins in 1912 it has grown to a membership of over 2700. It represents college and university management and financial interests nationally and regionally. It has a Center for Financial Management, a Department of Professional Development

(which offers many seminars throughout the nation), and a department for Public Policy and Management Programs. An extensive publication program includes the Business Officer magazine, and the regular updates of *College and University Business Administration* (which provides the national standards for public accounting in higher education). NACUBO leads in analysis of many other related areas. A critical instance was its central role in establishing the agreement for royalty payments to be paid by colleges and universities for their use of copyrighted music.

3. *The Council of Independent Colleges* began in 1956, as the Council For the Advancement of Small Colleges. In the middle 1990s it had grown to membership of 400, including over 320 college and university members, about 50 sponsoring members, and the remainder affiliate members including state associations of private colleges, regional consortia, and educational offices of religious denominations. The Council, from its beginnings, has had a significant, comprehensive program of services to its members. In its earlier years some of its member institutions had operated without planned budgets or accreditation and with only limited accounting records. Many CIC institutions took advantage of its workshops, seminars, handbooks, and consultants and earned regional accreditation. CIC has secured many millions of dollars to operate programs for its constituency. Many of its special services are supported by useful publications such as its *Academic Workplace Audit* and *Future Focusing: An Alternative to Long Range Planning.* Two other examples of its innovative services are: its six year project on the integration of technology and the liberal arts into "the new liberal learning," and an extensive program "enhancing black college leadership" (85 percent of the private historically black colleges and universities are association members).

4. *The Association of Governing Boards of Universities and Colleges* is a nonprofit association serving over 32,000 varied trustees and officials of close to 1,700 colleges and universities, and/or their foundations, from all types of boards—private, public, two year, four year, governing, coordinating, and advisory. Its mission is best described as "to strengthen the practice of voluntary trusteeship as the best alternative to direct government and political control of higher education." In addition to membership fees it is strongly supported by several dozen national, personal, private, and corporate foundations. Its extensive program of publications, videotapes, conferences, and seminars is designed to provide trustees and institutional leaders with timely and useful resources in this specialized area. One package of materials deals with the *Fundamentals of Trusteeship,* especially for orientation of new trustees. Another specialized service is its Presidential Search Consultation Service, which often serves several dozen institutions a year. Various projects include a major study of multicampus system operation, a compendium of *Strategic Indicators For Higher Education* (a selection of 150 financial and non-financial indicators

from over 700 colleges and universities) and a Trustee Information Center which provides answers to queries on all aspects of lay trusteeship and governance of higher education institutions (from 1,500 to 2,000 a year) based on the "most comprehensive governance library in existence."

5. *The American Association of State Colleges and Universities* represents nearly four hundred comprehensive, public colleges and universities, over 90 percent of the total, plus thirty-three coordinating or governing boards for these institutions. Since its beginnings in 1961, the association has been a leading stimulator of all facets of international education. Its many presidential missions to such countries as Egypt, Israel, Greece, Poland, The People's Republic of China, Cuba, Argentina, Taiwan, Malaysia, and Mexico have fostered continuing educational exchange and on-campus programs. It has taken national leadership in developing cooperative interassociation and interinstitutional programs and networks such as the Servicemembers Opportunity Colleges (with many AASCU institutions involved) and the Urban College and University Network. Its Office of Federal Programs monitors current funding programs and priorities and has been instrumental in increasing AASCU institutions' participation in this ever-increasing source of funds. Its Office of Governmental Relations and Policy Analysis analyzes pending legislation, prepares testimony on major national issues, monitors state issues affecting public higher education, conducts surveys, studies trends, and keeps institutional officials informed. The Academic Affairs Resource Center and Academic Leadership Academy serve the chief academic officers of the institutions, emphasizing future planning, faculty development, opportunities for minorities and women to attain senior administrative positions, leadership training, financial management, legal matters, and innovative educational ideas for new clientele. An extensive seminar, conference, and publication program supports this extensive alignment of institutional services. Overall, the association has had a profound effect on these institutions and their graduates, over one-fourth of those earning baccalaureate degrees and one-third of those earning masters degrees in the United States.

These vignettes from a few associations illustrate the significance and impact of this type of voluntary association. Each of them contributes in varied ways to the diverse needs of their member institutions, or to the program units within them. However, since these organizations continue to be the creatures of their founding members, their efforts do not seem to have noticeable effects on institutional autonomy or academic freedom. Quite the contrary, they seem to be buffering agencies that assist in this regard.

Voluntary Accrediting Associations[3]

The voluntary membership organizations in this important group barely existed a century ago. However, the end of the nineteenth century was a confused and uneasy time in higher education and major changes were underway. Five key factors contributed to the turbulent state of affairs in the period from 1870 to 1910: (1) the final breakdown of the fixed, classical curriculum and broad expansion of the elective system; (2) new academic fields were being developed and legitimized (such as psychology, education, sociology, and American literature); (3) new, diverse types of institutions were being organized to meet developing social needs (such as teachers colleges, junior colleges, land-grant colleges, research universities, and specialized professional schools); (4) both secondary and postsecondary education were expanding and overlapping, leading to a basic question, "What is a college?"; and (5) there was a lack of commonly accepted standards for admission to college and for completing a college degree.

To work on some of these problems the University of Michigan as early as 1871 sent out faculty members to inspect high schools and admitted graduates of the acceptable and approved high schools on the basis of their diploma. Shortly thereafter pressures developed for regional approaches to these problems in order to facilitate uniform college entrance requirements.

In keeping with accepted American practice and custom, groups of educators banded together in various regions to organize private, voluntary membership groups for this purpose. In New England, for example, it was a group of secondary schoolmasters who took the initiative. In the southern states it was Chancellor Kirkland and the faculty of Vanderbilt University. Six regional associations have developed throughout the United States starting with the New England Association of Schools and Colleges in 1885. It was followed in 1887 by the Middle States Association of Colleges and Schools, in 1895 by the Southern Association of Colleges and Schools and the North Central Association of Colleges and Schools, in 1917 by the Northwest Association of Schools and Colleges, and in 1923 by the Western Association of Schools and Colleges. Criteria and requirements for institutional membership (which now serve as the basis for institutions being considered "accredited") were formally established by these six associations at different times: in 1910 by North Central, with the first list of accredited colleges in 1913; in 1919 by Southern; in 1921 by Northwest and Middle States; in 1949 by Western; and in 1954 by New England. Thus, at the same time that the federal government instituted regulatory commissions to control similar problems (the Interstate Commerce Commission in 1887, the Federal Trade Commission in 1914, and the Federal Power Commission in 1920), these nongovernmental, voluntary membership groups sprang up to provide yardsticks for student achievement and institutional operations.

Regional groups dealt in the main with colleges rather than with specialized professional schools or programs. The North Central Association finally determined to admit normal schools and teachers colleges, but on a separate list of acceptable institutions. Practitioners and faculty in professional associations gradually set up their own membership associations. These groups established criteria for approving schools and based on these criteria made lists of "accredited" schools and program units. In some cases, only individuals with degrees from an "approved" school could join the professional association. Later, some membership groups made the approved program unit or school a basis for association membership. In any case the specialized academic program and its operational unit had to meet exacting criteria, externally imposed, to acquire and retain standing in the field.

The first of the specialized or programmatic discipline-oriented associations was the American Medical Association in 1847. However, approving processes for medical schools did not start until the early 1900s. From 1905 to 1907 the Council on Medical Education of the AMA led a movement for rating of medical schools. The first ratings in 1905 were a list based on the percentages of failures on licensing examinations by students from each school. This was followed in 1906–1907 by a more sophisticated system based on ten specific areas to be examined and inspections of each school. Of 160 schools inspected, classified, and listed, 32 were in Class C, "unapproved," 46 were in Class B, on "probation," and 82 were in Class A, "approved." The Council on Medical Education was attacked vigorously for this listing and approving activity. The recently established Carnegie Foundation for the Advancement of Teaching (1905) provided funds for Abraham Flexner and N. P. Colwell to make their famous study (1908–1910) of the 155 schools still in existence. Obviously, five already had closed. By 1915, only 95 medical schools remained, a 40 percent reduction, and they were again classified by the AMA Council on Medical Education, with 66 approved, 17 on probation, and 12 still listed as unapproved. This voluntary effort led to the ultimate in accountability, the merger and closing of 65 existing medical schools. In the process medical education was changed drastically, and the remaining schools completely revised and changed their curricula, a process still continuing to this day. This provides an excellent example of the work of an external voluntary professional association, with financial support from a private foundation, that took the initiative and acted on its own to protect the public interest. Thus, in some cases intrusions into "autonomy" can have beneficial results.

The success of the AMA did not go unnoticed. The National Home Study Council started in 1926 to do for correspondence education what the AMA after seventy years had done for medical education. Between 1914–1935 many other professional disciplinary and service associations were started in the fields of business, dentistry, law, library science, music, engineering, forestry, and dietetics, plus the medically related fields of podiatry, pharmacy, veterinary medicine, optometry, and nurse anesthesia. From 1935 to 1948 new associations starting up included architecture, art, Bible schools, chemistry, journalism, and theology, plus four more medically related fields, medical technology, medical records, occupational therapy, and physical therapy. Between 1948 and 1975 the number of specialized associations continued to expand rapidly, for programs from social service to graduate psychology and from construction education to funeral direction. Medical care subspecialties also proliferated, particularly in the allied health field, which included over twenty-five separate groups. After 1975 the expansion slowed greatly, and only a few new specialized associations developed during the following two decades. A few began in developing allied health areas, for non-traditional types of institutions which could not obtain "listing" by recognized national associations, or to expand accreditation opportunities in fields where existing associations were unduly restrictive. For example, the new Association of Collegiate Business Schools and Programs (established in 1988 and recognized by the U.S. Department of Education in 1992) met a need for improved articulation and recognition of business programs in community colleges and teaching-oriented four year/graduate colleges and universities. By 1993 it had five hundred members about equally divided between the two types of institutions, and an established, on-going program of accreditation and service to its members.

All of these external professional associations affect institutional operations very directly, including curricular patterns, faculty, degrees offered, teaching methods, support staff patterns, and capital outlay decisions. In many cases priorities in internal judgments result from the outside pressures. Local resource allocations often are heavily influenced by accreditation reports. For example, the law library, a chemistry or engineering laboratory, and teaching loads in business or social work may have been judged substandard by these external private constituents. If teaching loads in English or history also are heavy or physics laboratories are inadequate, will they get the same attention and treatment as specialized program areas with outside pressures? In such cases these association memberships are not really "voluntary" if the institution is placed on probation or no longer an "accredited" member and sanctions are actually applied. Often students will withdraw from or not consider attending a professional school or college that is not accredited. States often limit professional licenses to practice in a field to graduates of accredited schools. Federal agencies may not allow students from unaccredited institutions to obtain scholarships, loans, or work-study funds. The leverage of a voluntary association in such cases becomes tremendous, and the pressure for accredited status can be extremely powerful.

Presidents of some of the larger institutions, starting in 1924, have attempted to limit the effects of accrediting associations and the number of these independent organizations with which they would work. Through some of the institutionally based associations described in the previous section, they established limited sanctions and attempted to restrict the number of accrediting associations to which they would pay dues and allow on-campus site visits. These efforts to limit association membership and accreditation failed repeatedly to stem the tide. Shortly after World War II, in 1949, a group of university presidents finally organized the National Commission on Accrediting, a separate voluntary membership association of their own. It was designed to cut down the demands and influence of existing external associations and to delay or stop the development of new ones. The number of new ones dropped for a few years but pressures of new, developing disciplines on campus led to the many new organizations of this type since the 1950s.

In 1949, the regional associations also felt the need for a new cooperative association and set up what became the Federation of Regional Accrediting Commissions. In 1975 the two organizations, FRACHE and NCA, agreed to merge and they became major factors in the founding of the new Council on Postsecondary Accreditation. COPA also included four national groups accrediting specialized institutions, plus seven major, institutionally based associations. They in turn endorsed COPA as the central, leading voluntary association for the establishment of policies and procedures in postsecondary accreditation. After a few years the large representative board became unwieldy and was made much smaller. Also, the presidents, through their various associations, pushed vigorously for more representation. As a result the Council on Postsecondary Accreditation reorganized further, into three assemblies, Assembly of Institutional Accrediting Bodies (6 national and 8 regional), Assembly of Specialized Accrediting Bodies (42 associations), and the Presidents Policy Assembly on Accreditation (7 national associations of presidents from differing types of institutions). This three-sided group lasted about a decade, and in 1993 voted to disband on December 31, 1993. The different groups had very different concerns and interests. The regional associations decided to withdraw and set up their own group. COPA's funding system required the member associations to collect dues to support COPA from their own association members. Without these funds, COPA would have had difficulty operating. One of COPA's major functions was the "recognition" and listing of approved voluntary accrediting associations. A new, less expensive and streamlined "Commission" on Postsecondary Accreditation (also called COPA) has been developed to continue this key function and maintain a limited presence in the nation's capital.

The relationship of voluntary accrediting associations to the state and federal governments also is a major factor in current considerations of academic freedom, institutional autonomy, and institutional accountability. Of course, the states charter most of the institutions, and by so doing establish their missions, general purposes, and degree levels offered. However, the states also license individuals to practice most vocations and professions. In many fields the licensing of individuals is based on graduation from "accredited" programs. Thus a form of sanctions has developed and membership in the involved, specialized professional associations, supposedly voluntary, becomes almost obligatory. In the federal area, "listing" of institutions by federal government agencies had little or no effect prior to World War II. However, the entrance of the federal government into the funding of higher education on a massive basis since World War II has drastically changed the overall uses of accreditation. Reported abuses of the Servicemen's Readjustment Act of 1944 (G.I. Bill) led to a series of congressional · hearings, which led in turn to major additions related to accreditation in Public Law 550, the Veterans Readjustment Act of 1952. Section 253 of that law empowered the Commissioner of Education to publish a list of accrediting agencies and associations that could be relied upon to assess the quality of training offered by educational institutions. State approving agencies then used the resulting actions of such accrediting associations or agencies as a basis for approval of the courses specifically accredited. The enormous increase in federal assistance to students attending postsecondary education since 1972 made this federal listing process extremely important. Federal efforts to exert control over institutional processes have been constant for the past quarter century, with institutional membership in a "listed" accrediting association almost obligatory. Default rates on student loans have been blamed on the institutions and the accrediting associations, and laws passed which make the institutions serve to enforce the police power of the government. In 1992 Sub-part 2, Section 496 of the Higher Education Amendments moved even farther toward federal control of institutions' inner operations. National attention to this effort, totally contrary to the intent of the Tenth Amendment, is badly needed.

Extensive legal arguments about the resulting powers of the Department of Education still continue. However, greater institutional dependence on "eligibility" for funding is now based on membership in much less voluntary accrediting associations. The courts normally have ruled that accreditation by accrediting associations is not quasi-governmental action. Nevertheless, there has grown up an important new concept called the "triad." The triad involves delicate relationships between the federal government and eligibility for funding, the state government and its responsibilities for establishing or chartering institutions and credentialing through certification or licensure, and voluntary membership associations that require accreditation for membership.

Thus these voluntary associations have come to represent a major form of private constituency with direct impact on internal institution activities. The possible multiple sanctions from state licensing of graduates, loss of eligibility for funds from federal agencies, and problems caused by peer approval or disapproval enhance the importance of these sometimes overlooked educational organizations.

Voluntary Consortia[4]

Formal arrangements for voluntary consortia based on interinstitutional cooperation among and between postsecondary institutions have been in operation for many decades. The Claremont Colleges (California) started in

1925 with Pomona College and the Claremont University Center and were joined by Scripps College in 1926. The Atlanta University Center (Georgia), sometimes called the "Affiliation," started shortly thereafter in 1929, including Morehouse College, Spelman College, and Atlanta University. Over the decades both of these groups have added additional institutions to their cooperative arrangements and proven that voluntary consortia can be valuable for long periods of time. Some early examples from 1927–1929 illustrate the reality of the cooperation between Morehouse and Spelman. In those years several faculty were jointly appointed to both faculties. Upper division students could cross-register and take courses offered by the other college. Also, they operated a joint summer school with Atlanta University. In 1932, a new library was built and the three libraries consolidated into a joint library serving all of the institutions. Thus, although they remained separate institutions, they sacrificed some autonomy to extend the academic offerings and services available to their students.

In the years since these early beginnings, hundreds of institutions have developed informal and increasingly formal arrangements for interinstitutional cooperation. In 1966, a national survey conducted by the United States Office of Education determined that there were 1017 consortiums operating in the United States and that the evidence indicated that a number of consortiums were not reported. The list included all types of consortia, from simple bilateral arrangements dealing with a single area of service to large complex consortia performing many services and contributing in many areas of education. In 1967, the staff of the Kansas City Regional Council For Higher Education, a leading consortium, published the first directory of consortia, with a list of 31 having these exacting criteria: (1) it is a voluntary formal organization, (2) it has three or more member institutions, (3) it has multi-academic programs, (4) it is administered by at least one full-time professional, and (5) it has a required annual contribution or other tangible membership support. A voluntary national organization grew up, the Council For Interinstitutional Leadership, composed of many of the consortia. It has published an updated directory regularly for over two decades. The 1991 Consortium Directory (the 13th edition) listed over 1400 colleges and universities which were members of a very diverse group of 122 consortia. Thus today consortia represent a major development in American higher education and a significant factor in current planning and development of institutions.

The big push for the development of consortia in the 1950s, 1960s, and 1970s was based on the need to maximize the use of resources to meet the challenge of increasing enrollments, expanding research efforts, and increasing demands on the higher education community for additional services. The needs of current decades appear to be precisely the opposite. The demands for efficiency in the use of the plant, facilities, and faculty again require interinstitutional arrangements. For both state-supported colleges and universities and private independent institutions, there appears to be a continuing need for more cooperation among various types of educational institutions, including shared use of facilities and joint programs.

The importance of voluntary consortia to concerns regarding institutional autonomy becomes evident with the enumeration of their varied activities. The recent Directory of the Council For Interinstitutional Leadership listed 60 different topics which were carried on cooperatively by, and among, the participant institutions. They can be grouped into seven major areas: (1) administrative and business services, (2) enrollment and admissions, (3) academic programs, including continuing education, (4) libraries, information services, and computer services, (5) student services, (6) faculty, and (7) community services, including economic development. In each of these areas several (in some cases, many) consortia carry on significant cooperative efforts. Also, there is widespread geographic distribution of each of the categories of activities and the participating institutions.

The advantages for many institutions, both private and public, have become so great that they have been willing to give up total autonomy and institutional separatism. These arrangements may be formal, consortia-type agreements involving several institutions, or they may be much more simple agreements for cooperative endeavors between two institutions. An example of this latter type is the 1993-94 agreement of Arizona State University (public) and Thunderbird Graduate School of International Management (private) to offer a joint degree in "international management of technology." It was created to make use of the distinctive specialties of the two institutions, with 24 units at ASU's School of Engineering and 30 units at Thunderbird. Thus it combines a graduate year of engineering and a second year of international business, leading to graduates with understanding of different cultures and prepared to work in a global setting. Such a graduate degree program would have been extremely expensive and difficult for either of the institutions to offer separately, but very possible (and mutually desirable) when offered together. Many other examples of such agreements exist and follow these same principles. The consortia system, however, goes beyond these types of agreements and institutionalizes much wider and more extensive operations.

The latest Consortium Directory, published by the Council on Interinstitutional Leadership, emphasizes the wide variety of services provided by consortia to their members. Of the sixty different areas of service a few stand out as most common: cross registration (41), library (37), joint conferences, workshops and seminars (33), professional development (34), and business-industry relations (24). Rather surprisingly, joint purchasing was listed by only 18 consortia, although those using it were exceedingly successful in achieving considerable economies of scale. A small selected sample of current operating consortia clearly demonstrates their geographic spread and diversity of services.

Virginia Tidewater Consortium for Higher Education is one of six regional consortia covering all of Virginia. They were established in 1973 by state law to coordinate the offering of off-campus continuing education courses. The

Tidewater consortium is a good example of growth patterns which can take place when the leadership of the institutions works cooperatively. It now offers a wide variety of service activities, including cross-registration of students, faculty exchanges, interlibrary courier services, some cooperative degree programs, and faculty and administrative development programs. In addition, it operates the consortium's higher education cable channel, off-campus centers and continuing education programs in them, an Equal Opportunity Center, the Beginning Teacher Assistance program for the State Department of Education, and the promotion of college courses by television.

The Northern Rockies Consortium for Higher Education (started in 1977) includes 22 institutions in Montana, Utah, Idaho and Wyoming. With the original funding by the Fund for Improvement of Postsecondary Education it demonstrated its usefulness to both two-year and four-year institutions, and is supported by funds from the members. Its major projects are the sharing of resources between members (i.e., libraries) and support of faculty instructional activities and of institutional development.

The National University Teleconference Network, which originally had 63 members in 1982 (plus the Smithsonian Institution), had 263 members in 1993-94. A precursor of the North American Free Trade Agreement, it serves members in Canada, Mexico and the United States. Located at Oklahoma State University, its unique purpose is to provide for the teleconferencing needs of higher education in North America, including the educational needs of their various constituencies, including business and industry.

The Kansas City Regional Council For Higher Education, started in 1962, has been a major participant and leader in this movement. In 1993-94 this organization shared facilities and worked together with the Council of Interinstitutional Leadership to develop publications and information about this important movement. In 1967, Lewis Patterson, at that time its director, established it as the information center regarding consortia, the core of several national meetings of consortia directors, and acted as archivist and editor. He started *The Acquainter: an International Newsletter for Academic Consortia* and the annual directory listing existing consortia. The information/archivist function moved to Washington, D.C. for a few years but returned to KCRCHE. In addition to this activity, KCRCHE continues to be one of the outstanding innovative consortia of the country with thrusts into many academic and service areas. It has sixteen member colleges and universities in Kansas and Missouri, plus additional cooperating institutions and a number of corporate participants. In 1993 it reported three types of services: professional/development, information, and purchasing. In the first area it conducts annual College Days for high school students on behalf of its member institutions and for two decades has conducted the Undergraduate Student Art Show featuring the one hundred selected winning works of the region's best art students. Working with the local Metropolitan Community Colleges it provides professional development services to four hundred fifty two-year colleges in the nineteen North Central states. Other such services include a library network, the local interinstitutional television network serving local business and industry, workshops for faculty development and for administrators studying total quality management, and support for regional efforts to improve health and mathematics curricula articulation and transfer. Its Community Connections program stressed the development of volunteer community service projects which could be combined with academic learning internships. In the information area KCRCHE publishes many items, including the annual "Guide" with complete information about the regional colleges and their programs, a special International Visitor's Guide for institutions to use with their own international student recruitment and service, and a special biennial report on the Economic Impact of Higher Education within the region. In the area of purchasing services, its Cooperative Purchasing Service has expanded to other local public and private organizations, including small businesses, and has a potential buying power of over a billion dollars. It conducts bidding for over seventy different products in five main categories (general office supplies, office furniture and machinery, physical plant goods and services, professional services (i.e., rental cars), and insurance/healthcare) with savings from 32 percent to 68 percent off list prices. In limited areas these savings were made available to individual employees also, through a special ID card. Locally, KCRCHE was recognized as a major factor in helping small business in the region as a result of expanding the purchasing program for them. This listing of their total services is not complete but gives a good idea of the extent to which a higher education consortium can provide service to its region.

Hudson-Mohawk Association of Colleges and Universities is another of the very successful, older consortia, with sixteen members (private, public, two-year and four-year) in the Capital region of New York State. One major program is its Commission on Minority Awareness, a considerable success. Many workshops and conferences have been sponsored on a continuing basis by this Commission, including Career Awareness camp, educational leadership corps, a corporate internship program, and diverse workshops. It publishes the groups' Guide to Part-Time Study, the monthly Newsletter of campus events, sponsors the College Information Day for several thousand high school students and parents, and coordinates the multi-university Safety Training program and many varied workshops in the student affairs area. It has had an outstanding cooperative purchasing program with documented savings of over a million dollars per year for its member institutions.

Christian College Consortium and its offshoot the *Christian College Coalition* has as its mission to establish a national, cooperative system of accredited liberal arts colleges and universities with a Christian emphasis. The consortium, founded in 1971 with nine charter members, established the coalition with 78 members in 1976. In 1982 the consortium moved to St. Paul, with thirteen members, and the Coalition stayed in Washington, D.C. The consortium coordinates a number of professional development programs for faculty and students at the thirteen member colleges; a teacher exchange program, a student visitor program (similar to cross-registration), an interdisciplinary faculty project stressing values, minority faculty recruitment and multi-cultural teaching, a rotating distinguished lecturer program, and regular Faith-Learning-Living Institutes for faculty, held at one of the member colleges.

The example above from Virginia is one of many that indicate the move of consortia from being primarily private institutions to extensive development by all three types of sectors. Although started essentially by the voluntary enterprise sector, the public enterprise sector has moved in, and several consortia now include the profit seeking sector. A number of states passed laws to facilitate their start-up, such as Illinois. The Illinois Higher Education Cooperative Act of 1972 provided some state support for voluntary combinations of private and public institutions, including some from out of state, that applied for funds on a competitive basis. The Quad-Cities Graduate Center in Rock Island, Illinois, administered by Augustana College, combined the offerings of ten public and private colleges and universities in Iowa and Illinois to provide graduate degree programs to several thousand graduate students. Funding is provided by both states and the result is a major, free-standing graduate school drawing strength from its ten members. Several other states such as California, Connecticut, Massachusetts, Minnesota, Ohio, Pennsylvania, Virginia, and Texas have used the consortium approach for specific, sometimes limited purposes. This trend toward public financing of consortia thus becomes another key factor to consider in future institutional planning, along with limited efforts to promote regional, intrastate planning.

In the past, consortia have been developed to provide for interinstitutional needs both in times of growth and in times of decline. They are uniquely capable of handling mutual problems of public and private institutions, and thus provide a powerful deterrent to further governmental incursions into private and sometimes public institutional operation. At various levels of formality, consortia currently are being used by significant numbers of institutions of all types to adjust to changing curricular and funding necessities. As governmental controls continue to increase and to affect institutional autonomy and academic freedom, voluntary consortia provide another way to plan independently for future operations and program development.

Regional Compacts

Regional compacts, although they are nonprofit, private organizations, are quasi-governmental. Groups of states create them, provide their basic funding, and contract for services through them. They operate much like private organizations and receive considerable funding from other sources, including private foundations. Some of their studies, seminars, workshops, and policy studies affect very directly the institutions in their regions.

Soon after World War II three regional interstate compacts developed to meet postsecondary education needs that crossed state lines. Originally they concentrated on student exchange programs for the medical education field; however, in the past twenty-five to thirty years their areas of service and influence have expanded considerably. Although established, funded, and supported basically by state governors and legislatures, their indirect effects on institutional programs and operations can be very significant. Listed in order of establishment, they are:

1. Southern Regional Education Board (1948)

2. Western Interstate Commission for Higher Education (1953)

3. New England Board of Higher Education (1955)

4. Midwestern Higher Education Commission (1991)

The Southern Regional Education Board includes key governors, legislators, and other key figures, some from higher education, from fourteen states, Alabama, Arkansas, Florida, Georgia, Kentucky, Louisiana, Maryland, Mississippi, North Carolina, South Carolina, Tennessee, Texas, Virginia, and West Virginia.

The SREB was formed by the political leaders of its member states, and they have retained leadership in the organization. At the time it was started the "separate but equal" doctrine determined by the U.S. Supreme Court, in *Plessy* v. *Ferguson,* was in effect. To meet its requirements in the education of medical doctors these states sent students to Meharry Medical School in Nashville, Tennessee. Its funding was poor in the post-World War II era and it was seriously considering closing. Through SREB and a new funding principle, black students from each of the states could be sent there, with states paying the costs of attendance, and keeping the medical school open. Since that time, the Southern Regional Education Board has become one of the finest research and development offices in the country. It has played a major part in the development of such important areas as equal opportunity for all students in higher education and expanded graduate and professional education. Its research and information program has been vital in state and institutional planning. Its regular legislative work conferences, planned by its Legislative Advisory Council, have been very influential in setting policy and funding directions in the region.

The Western Interstate Compact for Higher Education now has members from thirteen states: Alaska, Arizona, California, Colorado, Hawaii, Idaho, Montana, Nevada, New Mexico, Oregon, Utah, Washington, and Wyoming. In addition it has two affiliate states, North Dakota and South Dakota, which participate in some of its programs. Minnesota did for a few years, but it became part of the new Midwestern Commission when that group formed.

WICHE was planned originally to pool educational resources, to help the states plan jointly for the preparation of specialized skilled manpower, and to avoid, where feasible, the duplication of expensive facilities. The student exchange program in the fields of medicine, dentistry, veterinary medicine, and later in dental hygiene, nursing, mental health, and other specialized fields, has been a major effort. Regional conferences on critical topics, annual legislative workshops, and extensive research studies and publications also are regularly carried on by WICHE. One of its developments, the program in higher education management and information systems, created so much demand for participation in the other thirty-seven states that it was "spun-off" to become the National Center for Higher Education Management Systems. The original professional student exchange program has been expanded and WICHE now coordinates an undergraduate exchange program to take advantage of under-used capacity. In 1993–94 there were 92 colleges and universities (in 12 states) participating. Almost 5,000 students were in these programs, paying 50 percent more than the states' standard state resident tuition. Also, a Regional Graduate Program was providing non-resident student tuition waivers at 40 institutions in 142 graduate degree programs.

WICHE also contributes by sponsoring currently needed special projects. In the 1950s it began and operated an extensive program to encourage the education of nurses for decades. In the 1990s special projects included an extensive program to recruit minority college students, potential college teachers and support for minority students in doctoral programs. Programs to support international education, particularly in Mexico and Canada, were underway, and publications included a directory of international expertise in the western states. Another extensive project in educational telecommunications facilitates academic programs delivered by satellite and expedites such component parts as on-line listings of planning documents for such networks and analyses of state laws affecting educational uses of telecommunications networks.

The New England Board of Higher Education serves six states: Connecticut, Maine, Massachusetts, New Hampshire, Rhode Island, and Vermont. It administers such programs as the regional student exchange program, the New England Council on Higher Education for Nursing, a library information network, and an academic science information center. It also conducts studies regarding current needs in higher education that cross state lines. It conducted extensive studies in the field of veterinary medicine to see if any agreements could be reached many years ago, but the political disputes were so great that the program was not developed.

The Midwestern Higher Education Commission developed many years after the other three were established. Originally, a consortium of the Big Ten universities plus the University of Chicago was developed, at least partially to forestall establishment of such a state-originated commission (the Committee on Institutional Cooperation, founded in 1958). However, plans went ahead and between 1978 and 1980 the Minnesota, South Dakota, North Dakota, and Ohio legislatures approved its establishment. In order to begin operations, six states had to adopt the plan. If established, it would have provided for interstate student exchanges at in-state tuition rates, cooperative programs in vocational and higher education, and an area-wide approach to gathering and reporting information needed for educational planning. Finally, in 1991, six state legislatures approved the Midwestern Regional Education Compact (Illinois, Kansas, Michigan, Missouri, Nebraska and Ohio). Three other states (Indiana, Wisconsin, and Iowa) were giving serious legislative consideration to joining the Compact in 1993-94, and North Dakota and South Dakota might consider it in the future.

By 1993, MHEC had developed four major service programs, a student exchange program where various states list institutions and programs (undergraduate, graduate and professional) in which students from other states can be enrolled at a specified savings from the regular tuition charge, a tele-communications program (a Virtual Private Network System) at an enormous savings but with two-way interactive video programming and distance learning, a comprehensive umbrella master property insurance policy which can save millions of dollars for the participating institutions, and a region-wide program of minority faculty development, designed to expand tenure track opportunities in under-represented disciplines and to improve their retention. Several areas for possible future development were additional purchasing initiatives, providing a regional data base system, cooperative economic development activities, and related activities.

The current four interstate compacts cover all but a very few of the states of the entire country. Their diversified programs change as the needs of their regions change. The basic costs of their operations are funded by state legislatures from tax revenues, but foundation grants plus federal projects pay for much of the new thrusts of the regional commissions. This provides another excellent example of the flexible way that the mixed society of the United States operates to adapt to changing needs and emphases.

Conclusion

During the first two centuries of American higher education's existence religious tenets and basic social agreements resulted in a relatively fixed, classically oriented program of studies. However, as the society began to open up, to industrialize and expand, it demanded change in its colleges. When this was slow to occur, new institutions met these needs and many existing ones closed. Normal schools, engineering schools, military academies, and universities were copied from Europe and adapted to American needs between 1830 and 1900. However, even these were not sufficient to meet democracy's needs. New types of institutions were developed, unique or almost unique to America. The land-grant colleges of 1862 and 1890, the junior colleges of the early 1900s, the comprehensive state colleges of the 1930s to 1960s, and the post-world war community colleges all represent essentially new types of institutions. Private constituency groups often pressured state or local governments to establish them. In some cases private constituency groups pressured Congress into funding some of them, including both the 1862 land-grant colleges, and particularly the 1890 land-grant colleges. The critical point, again, is that in the United States new institutions replace existing ones that do not change.

Private constituencies such as the five types detailed here can and do have significant impact on institutional autonomy and academic freedom. Much of this impact is positive, supportive, and welcome. However, those that provide funds can affect institutional trends and direction by determining what types of academic program or research efforts to support. As federal and state funds tighten up even more in the years ahead, funds from alternate sources will become even more attractive. Acceptance of grants moves institutions in the direction dictated by fund sources, and faculties are well advised to consider this possibility as the "crunch" of the 1990s becomes greater in more and more institutions.

Finally, the very real benefits provided to institutions by private organizations have been stressed previously. Many membership organizations have been created to provide such anticipated benefits. In some cases these benefits have been greater than anyone could have foreseen. Probably the most dramatic examples have come from private accrediting associations in relation to state political efforts to limit seriously the autonomy and academic freedom of their own public institutions. In 1938 the North Central Association dropped North Dakota Agricultural College from membership because of undue political interference. The U.S. Court of Appeals upheld the action of NCA and the state government basically backed away from its prior method of political interference in internal institutional affairs. In the post-World War II period, sanctions of the Southern Association basically stopped on-campus speaker-ban legislation in North Carolina and, after 1954, contributed strongly to the development of open campuses in other states in its region. As the nation has worked diligently to expand higher education opportunities for minorities in the 1990s almost every type of association has participated. And as the society has demanded that higher education become more cost effective, many of these associations and commissions have adopted systems which have saved very large amounts of money, so that the academic programs may still be offered to the students they were established to serve.

Private organizations related in some way to postsecondary education clearly continue the great tradition of direct action by voluntary citizen associations. Increasingly, they stand in the middle between control-oriented federal and state agencies and both private and public institutions. Governments, literally, have abandoned the "self-denying ordinance" that in recent decades kept the "state" at a distance from the essence of many of its institutions. The nurturance of supportive and helpful private constituencies therefore becomes even more critical as higher education enters the twenty-first century.

Notes

1. For detailed information about foundations the best overall source is The Foundation Center, 79 Fifth Avenue, New York, NY 10003. They have twelve regular publications which constitute their core collection, with answers to almost any conceivable question. They have offices in San Francisco, California, Washington, D.C., and Cleveland, Ohio, and cooperating collection centers in numerous libraries in each state. Two main references are the annual *Foundation Directory and The National Data Book of Foundations.*

2. Two major references with extensive information about institutionally based associations are the *Encyclopedia of Associations,* published annually by Gale Research, Inc., 835 Penobscot, Detroit, Michigan 48226, and the regular editions of *American Universities and Colleges,* produced by the American Council on Education in cooperation with Walter de Gruyter, Inc.

3. Two key sources of information regarding voluntary institutional accreditation are Kenneth E. Young, Charles Chambers, H. R. Kells, and Associates, *Understanding Accreditation* (San Francisco: Jossey-Bass Publishers,1983) and Fred F. Harcleroad, *Accreditation: History, Process, and Problems* (Washington, D.C.: ERIC Clearinghouse on Higher Education, 1980). Annual updated listings of recognized accrediting associations were published for many years through the Council on Postsecondary Accreditation until 1993, when the Council stopped its operation. A somewhat different list of accrediting associations, by the United States Department of Education, has been available since it was required in the Veterans Readjustment Assistance Act of 1952. Inclusion on this list is one of several ways that institutions can participate in a number of federal funding programs.

4. The best source of current information on consortia is the biennial *Consortium Directory* compiled and made available by the Council For Interinstitutional Leadership and the Kansas City Council for Higher Education, both at Suite 205, 8016 State Line Road, Leawood, Kansas 66208.

PART THREE

THE ACADEMIC COMMUNITY

10

Problems and Possibilities: The American Academic Profession

Philip G. Altbach

Introduction

American higher education is in a period of unprecedented decline. Financial cutbacks, enrollment uncertainties, economic recession, pressures for account-ability, and confusion about academic goals are among the challenges facing American colleges and universities at the end of the twentieth century. The situation is in many ways quite paradoxical. The American academic model is the most successful in the world—it is admired internationally because it has permitted wide access to higher education while maintaining some of the best universities in the world. Yet, higher education has come under widespread criticism. Some have argued that the academic system is wasteful and inefficient and that the professoriate is at the heart of the problem.[1] Others have urged that higher education reconsider its priorities and place more emphasis on teaching; arguing that the core function of the university has been underemphasized as the professoriate has focused on research.[2] Again, the professoriate is central to this criticism.

A combination of economic recession, the restructuring of the American economy, and a popular revolt against paying for public services, including education, have contributed to the pervasive fiscal problems that colleges and universities face. While the economic recession should ease, most observers believe that higher education will not fully recover financially in the foreseeable future. It has been argued that higher education's "golden age"—the period of strong enrollment growth, increasing research budgets, and general public support—is over.[3] This will mean that the academic profession, as well as higher education in general, must adjust to new circumstances. This adjustment, which has already begun, is difficult under any circumstances, but it is all the more

225

troubling to the professoriate because it comes directly following the greatest period of growth and prosperity in the history of American higher education.

The American professoriate has been profoundly influenced by the social, political, and economic context of higher education. While academe has relatively strong internal autonomy and, with some exceptions, a considerable degree of academic freedom, societal trends and public policy have played a major role in shaping institutions of higher education as well as national and state policies concerning academe. There are many examples. The Land Grant Acts in the 1860s stimulated the expansion of public higher education and an emphasis on both service and research, while the G.I. Bill following World War II stimulated the greatest and most sustained period of growth in the history of American higher education. Court decisions regarding the role of government in private higher education, race relations, affirmative action, the scope of unions on campus, and other issues have had an impact on higher education policy. Because education is a basic responsibility of the states, the actions of the various state governments have been primary, ranging from governmental support for the Wisconsin Idea in the nineteenth century in that state to the promulgation of the California Master Plan in the 1960s. In New York, Massachusetts, and elsewhere, state policies in the postwar period had a profound influence on the shape of postsecondary education and on the professoriate.[4] A recurring theme in this essay is the tension between the autonomy and "internal life" of the academic profession, on one hand, and the many external forces for accountability that have shaped the direction of American higher education, on the other.

Precisely because the university is one of the central institutions of postmodern society, the professoriate finds itself subject to pressures from many directions. Increasingly complicated accounting procedures attempt to measure professorial "productivity"—part of the effort to increase accountability. But there is so far no way to measure accurately the educational outcomes of teaching. Calls for the professoriate to provide "social relevance" in the 1960s were replaced in the 1980s by student demands for vocationally oriented courses. A deteriorating academic job market raised the standards for the award of tenure and increased the emphasis on research and publication. At the same time, there were demands to devote more time and attention to teaching.

A constant tension exists between the traditional autonomy of the academic profession and external pressures. The processes of academic promotion and hiring remain in professorial hands, but with significant changes—affirmative action requirements, tenure quotas in some institutions, and the occasional intrusion of the courts into promotion and tenure decisions. The curriculum is still largely a responsibility of the faculty, but the debates over multicultural courses, for more or fewer vocational courses, for example, affect curricular decisions. Governmental agencies influence the curriculum through grants and awards. The states engage in program reviews and approvals and through these procedures have gained some power in areas traditionally in the hands of the faculty.

The academic profession has been largely ineffective in explaining its centrality to society and in making the case for traditional academic values. Entrenched power, a complicated governance structure, and the weight of tradition have helped to protect academic perquisites in a difficult period. But the professoriate itself has not articulated its own ethos.[5] The rise of academic unions helped to increase salaries during the 1970s, but has contributed to an increasingly adversarial relationship between the faculty and administrators in some universities.[6]

The unions, with the partial exception of the American Association of University Professors, have not defended or articulated the traditional professorial role. Few have effectively argued that the traditional autonomy of the faculty and of faculty control over many key aspects of academic governance should be maintained. We are in a period of profound change in American higher education, and it is likely that these changes will result in further weakening of the power and autonomy of the professoriate. This essay focuses on the interplay of forces that have influenced the changing role of the American academic profession.

A Diverse Profession

The American professoriate is large and highly differentiated, making generalizations difficult. There are more than 370,000 full-time faculty members in America's 3,535 institutions of postsecondary education. Almost 1,400 of these institutions grant baccalaureate or higher degrees and 213 give the doctoral degree. More than a quarter of the total number of institutions are community colleges. A growing number of faculty are part-time academic staff, numbering at least 200,000 nationwide. They have little or no job security and only tenuous ties with their employing institutions. The proportion of part-time staff has been growing in recent years, reflecting fiscal constraints. Faculty are further divided by discipline and department. While it is possible to speak broadly of the American professoriate, the working life and culture of most academics is encapsulated in a disciplinary and institutional framework. Variations among the different sectors within the academic system—research universities, community colleges, liberal arts institutions, and others—also shape the academic profession.[7] The differences in working styles, outlooks, remuneration, and responsibilities of a senior professor at Harvard and a beginning assistant professor in a community college are enormous. Further distinctions reflect field and disciplinethe outlooks of medical school professors, on the one hand, and scholars of medieval philosophy, on the other, are quite dissimilar.

A half-century ago, the academic profession was largely white, male and Protestant. It has grown increasingly diverse. In recent years, the proportion of women in academe has grown steadily and is now 29 percent of the total, although women tend to be concentrated at lower academic ranks and suffer some salary discrimination.[8] Yet, it is a fact that the proportion of women in the academic profession has increased only a few percent since the 1930s, despite the existence of affirmative action programs. Racial and ethnic minority participation has also grown, and while Asian Americans are well represented in the academic profession, African Americans and Hispanics remain proportionately few. African Americans constitute only around three percent of the total professoriate, and they are concentrated in the historically black colleges and universities.[9] Racial minorities number about 9 percent of the total academic profession. The substantial discrimination that once existed against Catholics and Jews has been largely overcome, and there has been a modest decline in the middle and upper middle class domination of the academic profession.[10] Despite these demographic changes and expansion in higher education, the academic profession retains considerable continuity in terms of its overall composition.

Without question, any consideration of the role of the professoriate must take into account the demographic, cultural, disciplinary, and other variations in the academic profession. If there ever was a sense of community among professors in the United States, it has long since disappeared. Some elements are common to the academic profession, but these grow weaker as numbers increase and the profession becomes more diverse.

The Historical Context

The academic profession is conditioned by a complex historical development. Universities have a long historical tradition, dating to medieval Europe, and the professoriate is the most visible repository of this tradition.[11] It should be noted that while national academic systems differ, all stem from common roots in Europe. The vision of professorial power that characterized the medieval University of Paris, the power of the dons at Oxford and Cambridge, and the centrality of the "chairs" in the nineteenth century German universities are all part of the history of American higher education. The medieval origins were instrumental for the recognition of the self-governing nature of the professorial community and the idea that universities are "communities of scholars." Much later, the reforms in German higher education in the nineteenth century greatly increased the power and prestige of the professoriate, while at the same time linking both the universities and the academic profession to the state.[12] Professors were civil servants and the universities were expected to contribute to the development of Germany as a modern industrial nation. For the first time, research became a key responsibility for universities. The role and status of the academic profession at Oxford and Cambridge in England also had an impact on the American professoriate, since the early American colleges were patterned on the British model and the United States, for many years, was greatly influenced by intellectual trends from Britain.[13]

These models, plus academic realities in the United States, helped to shape the American academic profession. To understand the contemporary academic profession, the most crucial period of development begins with the rise of land-grant colleges following the Civil War and the establishment of the innovative, research-oriented private universities in the last decade of the nineteenth century.[14] Several aspects of the development of the modern American university are critical to the growth of the academic profession. The commitment of the university to public service and to "relevance" meant that many academics became involved with societal issues, with applied aspects of scholarship, and with training for the emerging professions and for skilled occupations involving technology. The contribution of the land-grant colleges to American agriculture was the first and best known example. Following the German lead, the new innovative private universities (Johns Hopkins, Chicago, Stanford, and Cornell), followed a little later by such public universities as Michigan, Wisconsin, and California, emphasized research and graduate training. The doctorate soon became a requirement for entry into at least the upper reaches of the academic profession—earlier, top American professors obtained their doctorates in Germany. The prestige of elite universities gradually came to dominate the academic system, and the ethos of research, graduate training, and profes-sionalism spread throughout much of American academe. As these norms and values gradually permeated the American academic enterprise, they came to form the base of professional values in the late twentieth century.

The hallmark of the post–World War II period has been massive growth in all sectors of American higher education. The profession tripled in numbers, and student numbers expanded equally rapidly. The number of institutions also grew, and many universities added graduate programs. Expansion char-acterized every sector from the community colleges to the research universities. Expansion was especially rapid in the decade of the 1960s, a fact that has special relevance for the 1990s, for many academics hired at that time will soon be retiring, creating an unprecedented generational shift in the academic profession. Expansion became the norm, and departments, academic institutions, and individuals based their plans on continued expansion.

But expansion ended in the early 1970s, and a combination of circumstances, including broader population shifts, inflation, and government fiscal deficits, all brought the expansion to an end. Part of the problem in adjusting to the current period of diminished resources is the very fact that the previous period was one of unusual expansion—a temporary condition. Indeed, it can be argued that the period of postwar growth was an aberration and that the *current* situation is more "normal."[15] The legacy of the period of expansion is quite significant for understanding contemporary realities.

Expansion shaped the vision of the academic profession for several decades, just as prolonged stagnation now affects perceptions. Postwar growth introduced other changes—factors that came to be seen as permanent, when in fact they were not. The academic job market became a "sellers market" in which individual professors were able to sell their services at a premium. Almost every field had a shortage of teachers and researchers.[16] Average academic salaries improved significantly and the American professor moved from a state of semipenury into the increasingly affluent middle class.[17] The image of Mr. Chips was replaced by the jet-set professor. University budgets increased and research-oriented institutions at the top of the academic hierarchy had unprecedented access to research funds. The space program, the cold war, rapid advances in technology, and a fear in 1958 (after Sputnik) that the United States was "falling behind" in education contributed to greater spending by the federal government for higher education. Expanding enrollments meant that the states also invested more in higher education and that private institutions also prospered.

The academic profession benefited substantially. Those obtaining their doctorates found ready employment. Rapid career advancement could be expected, and interinstitutional mobility was fairly easy. This contributed to diminished institutional loyalty and commitment. In order to retain faculty, colleges and universities lowered teaching loads. The average time spent in the classroom declined during the 1960s. Salaries and fringe benefits increased. Access to research funds from external sources increased substantially, not only in the sciences but also to a lesser extent in the social sciences and humanities. The availability of external research funds made academics with such access less dependent on their institutions. Those few professors able to obtain significant funds were able to build institutes, centers, and in general to develop "empires" within their institutions.

Rapid expansion also meant unprecedented growth in the profession itself, and this has had lasting implications. An abnormally large cohort of young academics entered professorial ranks in the 1960s. This extraordinarily large academic generation is now causing a variety of problems relating to its size, training, and experiences. With the end of expansion, this large group has, in effect, limited entry to new scholars and has created a "bulge" of tenured faculty members who will retire in massive numbers in the 1990s. Many in this cohort participated in the campus turmoil of the 1960s and were affected by it. Some graduated from universities of lower prestige which began to offer doctoral degrees during this period and may not have been fully socialized into the traditional academic values and norms. But this generation expected a continuing improvement in the working conditions of higher education. When these expectations were dashed with the changing circumstances of the 1970s, morale plummeted and adjustment has been difficult.

A final influence of the recent past is the turmoil of the 1960s. A number of factors converged in the turbulent sixties that contributed to emerging problems for higher education. The very success of the universities in moving to the center of society meant that they were taken more seriously. In the heady days of expansion, many in the academic community thought that higher education could solve the nation's social problems, from providing mobility to minorities to suggesting solutions to urban blight and deteriorating standards in the public schools. It is not surprising, in this context, that the colleges and universities became involved in the most traumatic social crises of the period—the civil rights struggle and the Vietnam War. The antiwar movement emerged from the campuses and was most powerful there.[18] Student activism came to be seen by many, including government officials, as a social problem for which the universities were to be blamed. Many saw the professors as contributing to student militancy.

The campus crisis of the 1960s went deeper than the antiwar movement. A new and much larger generation of students, from more diverse backgrounds, seemed less committed to traditional academic values. The faculty turned its attention from undergraduate education, abandoned *in loco parentis,* and allowed the undergraduate curriculum to fall into disarray. Overcrowded facilities were common. The overwhelming malaise caused by the Vietnam War, racial unrest, and related social problems produced a powerful combination of discontent. Many faculty, unable to deal constructively with the crisis and feeling under attack from students, the public, and government authority, quickly became demoralized. Faculty governance structures proved unable to bring the diverse interests of the academic community together. This period was one of considerable debate and intellectual liveliness on campus, with faculty taking part in teach-ins, and a small number becoming involved in the antiwar movement. However, the lasting legacy of the 1960s for the professoriate was largely one of divisiveness, and the politicization of the campus.

The Sociological and Organizational Context

Academics are at the same time both professionals and employees of large bureaucratic organizations. Their self-image as independent scholars with considerable control over their working environment is increasingly at odds with the realities of the modern American university.[19] Indeed, the conflict between the traditional autonomy of the scholar and demands for accountability to a variety of internal and external constituencies is one of the central issues of contemporary American higher education. The rules of academic institutions, from stipulations concerning teaching loads to policies concerning the granting of tenure, govern the working lives of the professoriate. Despite the existence in most institutions of the infrastructures of collegial self-government, academics feel themselves increasingly alienated from their institutions and somewhat demoralized. For example, two-thirds in a recent poll described faculty morale as fair or poor, and 60 percent had negative feelings about the "sense of community" at their institution.[20]

Academics continue to exercise considerable autonomy over their basic working conditions, although even here pressures are evident. The classroom remains virtually sacrosanct and beyond bureaucratic controls. Professors have considerable say over the use of their time outside of the classroom. They choose their own research topics and largely determine what and how much they publish, although research in some fields and on some topics requires substantial funding and therefore depends on external support. There are considerable variations based on institutional type, with faculty at community colleges and at unselective teaching-oriented institutions subject to more restraints on autonomy than professors at prestigious research universities.

As colleges and universities have become increasingly bureaucratized and as demands for "accountability" have extended to professors, this sense of autonomy has come under attack. The trend toward decreased teaching loads for academics during the 1960s has been reversed, and now more emphasis is placed on teaching and, to some extent, on the quality of teaching. Without question, there is now considerable tension between the norm (some would say the myth) of professional autonomy and the pressures for accountability. There is little doubt that the academic profession will be subjected to increased controls as academic institutions seek to survive in an environment of financial difficulties. Professorial myths of collegial decision making, individual autonomy, and of the disinterested pursuit of knowledge have come into conflict with the realities of complex organizational structures and bureaucracies. Important academic decisions are reviewed by a bewildering assortment of committees and administrators. These levels of authority have become more powerful as arbiters of academic decision making.

The American academic system is enmeshed in a series of complex hierarchies. These hierarchies, framed by discipline, institution, rank, and specialty, help to determine working conditions, prestige, and, in many ways, one's orientation to the profession. As David Riesman pointed out three decades ago, American higher education is a "meandering procession" dominated by the prestigious graduate schools and ebbing downward through other universities, four-year colleges, and finally to the community college system.[21] Most of the profession attempts to follow the norms, and the fads, of the prestigious research-oriented universities. Notable exceptions are the community colleges, which employ one-fourth of American academics, and some of the nonselective four-year schools. Generally, prestige is defined by how close an institution, or an individual professor's working life, comes to the norm of publication and research, of participation in the "cosmopolitan" orientation to the discipline and the national profession, rather than to "local" teaching and institutionally focused norms.[22] Even in periods of fiscal constraint, the hold of the traditional academic models remains very strong indeed. Current efforts to emphasize teaching and to ensure greater "productivity" from the faculty face considerable challenges from the traditional academic hierarchy.

Within institutions, academics are also part of a hierarchical system, with the distinctions between tenured and untenured staff a key to this hierarchy. The dramatic growth of part-time teachers has added another layer at the bottom of the institutional hierarchy.[23] Disciplines and departments are also ranked into hierarchies, with the traditional academic specialties in the arts and sciences along with medicine and, to some extent, law at the top. The "hard" sciences tend to have more prestige than the social sciences or humanities. Other applied fields, such as education and agriculture, are considerably lower on the scale. These hierarchies are very much part of the realities and perceptions of the academic profession.

Just as the realities of postwar expansion shaped academic organizations and affected salaries, prestige, and working conditions, and gave more power to the professoriate over the governance of colleges and universities, current diminished circumstances also bring change. While it is unlikely that the basic structural or organizational realities of American higher education will profoundly change, there has been an increase in the authority of administrators and increased bureaucratic control over working conditions on campus. In general, the professors have lost a significant part of their bargaining power—power that was rooted in moral authority. As academic institutions adjust to a period of declining resources, there will be ongoing subtle organizational shifts that will inevitably work against the perquisites, and the authority, of the academic profession. Universities, as organizations, adjust to changing realities, and these adjustments will work against the professoriate.

Legislation, Regulations, Guidelines, and the Courts

In a number of areas the academic profession has been directly affected by the decisions of external authorities. American higher education has always been subject to external decisions, from the Dartmouth College case in the period immediately following the American Revolution to the Land Grant Act in the mid-nineteenth century. The actions by the courts or by legislative authority have profoundly affected higher education and the professoriate. In the contemporary period, governmental decisions continue to have an impact on American higher education and the academic profession. It is not possible in this context to discuss all of the government policies that have shaped the profession. It is my intention to indicate how decisions create a context for academic life. The fiscal crisis of higher education has already been discussed. However, academe's problems stem not only from a downturn in the American economy, but also from quite deliberate policies by government at both the federal and state levels to deemphasize higher education and research. Other pressing social needs combined with public reluctance to pay higher taxes worked to restrict higher education budget allocations, which especially affected public colleges and universities. Cuts in research funding have been felt by both public and private institutions and by faculty.

Specific governmental policies have also had an impact on the profession. One area of considerable controversy has been affirmative action, the effort to ensure that college and university faculties include larger numbers of women and members of underrepresented minorities to reflect the national population.[24] A variety of specific regulations have been mandated by federal and state governments relating to hiring, promotion, and other aspects of faculty life to ensure that women and minorities have opportunities in the academic profession. Many professors have opposed these regulations, viewing them as an unwarranted intrusion on academic autonomy. These policies have nonetheless had an impact on academic life. Special admissions and remedial programs for underrepresented students have also aroused considerable controversy on campus and have also been opposed by many faculty—they too have been implemented by governmental intervention.

The legal system has had a profound influence on the academic profession in the past several decades. The courts have ruled on university hiring and promotion policies, as well as on specific personnel cases. While the courts are generally reluctant to interfere in the internal workings of academic institutions, they have reviewed cases of gender or other discrimination, sometimes reversing academic decisions. Recently, the U.S. Supreme Court ruled that compulsory retirement regulations were unconstitutional. This ruling is having a profound impact on the academic profession and on institutions since mandatory retirement is no longer legal.

These examples illustrate the significance and pervasiveness of governmental policies on the academic profession. Legislation concerning faculty workloads as well as policies on affirmative action affect the profession. Shifts in public opinion are often reflected in governmental policies concerning higher education and the professoriate.[25] The courts, through the cases they are called on to decide, also play a role. The cumulative impact of governmental policies, laws, and decisions of all kinds have profoundly influenced the professoriate.[25] In the post–World War II era, as higher education has become more central to the society, government has involved itself to a greater extent with higher education and this trend is likely to continue.

The Realities at the End of the Century

The academic profession faces an uncertain future in the decade of the 1990s. The past decade has been, without question, one of the low points in the postwar history of the American professoriate. The immediate coming period does not offer the promise of any significant improvement. However, demographic changes and the possibility that the profession itself will be able to successfully adjust to new circumstances may provide a somewhat more optimistic future. The basic configuration of American higher education is unlikely to change dramatically. There has been deterioration but all within the context of the established system. This section examines some of the realities of the decade of the 1990s, with a particular stress on the relationship of the academic profession to the structure of the higher education system and the impact of society on the profession.

TEACHING, RESEARCH, AND SERVICE

One of the main debates of the decade concerns the appropriate balance between teaching and research in academe—a debate that goes to the role of the university as an institution and is critical for the academic profession. Many outside academe, and quite a few within the universities, have argued that there should be more emphasis on teaching in the American higher education system. It is agreed that research is overvalued and that, especially considering fiscal constraints and demands for accountability, professors should be more "productive."[26] The reward system in academe has produced this imbalance. Critics charge that, outside the one hundred or so major research universities, the quality and relevance of much academic research is questionable. Some have gone further to say that much academic research is a "scam."[27]

The issue of faculty productivity has produced action in several states and on a few campuses. Massachusetts, Nevada, New York, Arizona, and Wisconsin are among the states that have been involved in workload studies. The California State University has compared teaching loads of its faculty members with professors in other institutions. A few states require annual reports on workloads, and some have mandated minimum teaching loadsHawaii and Florida, for example, require twelve hours of classroom instruction or the equivalent for faculty in four-year institutions.[28] Academic institutions are also studying workloads.

American professors seem to be working longer, not shorter hours, and classroom hours have not declined in recent years. In 1992, according to a study by the Carnegie Foundation for the Advancement of Teaching, American professors spent a median 18.7 hours in activities relating to teaching (including preparation, student advisement, etc.).[29] On average, professors spend 13.1 hours per week in direct instructional activity, with those in research universities spending 11.4 hours and those in other four-year institutions teaching 13.8 per week.[30] Not surprisingly, professors in research universities produce more publications than their colleagues in other institutions. For example, 61 percent of faculty in research universities report publishing six or more journal articles in the past three years as compared to 31 percent of faculty working elsewhere.[31]

With the pressure for the professoriate to focus more on teaching and to spend more time in the classroom, there is likely to be more differentiation among sectors within the academic system, so that academics at the top research universities will teach significantly less than their compeers in comprehensive colleges and universities. Greater stratification between the academic sectors and perhaps less mobility among them are probable outcomes. A shift in thinking has taken place about research and its role. External funding for research has declined and competition for resources is in most fields intense. There is also an orientation toward more applied research, closer links between industry and the universities, and more service to the private sector. These changes will affect the kind of research that is conducted. There may well be less basic research and more small-scale research linked to products.

So far, the professoriate has not fully responded to these externally induced debates and changes. The profession has sought to adapt to changing patterns in funding and to the more competitive research climate. In the long run, however, these structural changes will transform the research culture and the organization of research. In some ways, academics have moved closer to their clientele through the emphasis on service to external constituencies. The debate about Total Quality Management (TQM) in higher education is, in part, an effort to convince academic institutions, and the professoriate, to think more directly about student needs, using a model designed to focus attention on the "customer."[32]

DEMOGRAPHIC CHANGES AND THE DECLINE OF COMMUNITY

The "age bulge" discussed earlier means that the large cohort of academics who entered the profession in the 1960s and 1970s take up a disproportionate share of jobs, especially when openings are restricted. Part-time faculty make up an increasing segment of the profession, further altering the nature and orientation of the profession.[33] It is much harder for a mid-career academic to find another position if he or she becomes dissatisfied or desires a change in location. The "safety valve" of job mobility no longer functions as well. While the number of retirements is rising rapidly and many institutions have used early retirement incentives to meet mandated budget cuts, this has not produced significant numbers of full-time academic jobs. This is still a time of diminished expectations.

Prospects for new entrants into the profession also declined. Few young Ph.D.s were hired and, as it became clear that the academic job market had dried up, enrollments in many fields at the graduate level fell, especially in the traditional arts and sciences disciplines. Bright undergraduates gravitated to law school or management studies. Perhaps the greatest long-term implication is a "missing generation" of younger scholars. The combination of the enlarged academic cohort of the 1960s and the decline of new positions in the 1970s and 1980s meant that very few younger scholars were being hired, with reverberations on the age structure of the profession. Further, a generation of fresh ideas has been lost. According to some demographic projections, there will be another shortage of trained doctorates around the turn of the century, causing different but nonetheless serious strains on the profession and on the universities.[34]

The size and increased diversity of the academic profession have made a sense of community more difficult.[35] As institutions have grown to include well over one thousand academic staff, with elected senates and other, more bureaucratic governance arrangements in place of the traditional general faculty meeting, a sense of shared academic purpose has become more elusive. Even academic departments in larger American universities can number up to fifty.

Committees have become ubiquitous and the sense of participation in a common academic enterprise has declined. Increasing specialization in the disciplines contributed to this trend. Two-thirds of the American professoriate in the Carnegie study judged morale to be fair or poor on campus and 60 percent felt similarly about the "sense of community" at their institution.[36]

TENURE, RETRENCHMENT, AND UNIONS

The profession has seen its economic status eroded after a decade of significant gains in "real income" during the 1960s. Academic salaries began to decline in terms of actual purchasing power in the 1970s, and the slide has continued unabated. Indeed, many faculty members in such states as Massachusetts and California have faced actual salary cuts while many states, including New York and Maryland, froze salaries, sometimes for more than one year. Professional prerogatives seemed less secure, and autonomy was threatened.

Perhaps most significantly, the tenure system came under attack in the 1970s. Some argued that the permanent appointments offered to professors once they had been evaluated and promoted from assistant to associate professor bred sloth among those with tenurealthough there was little evidence to back up this claim.[37] Tenure was also criticized because it interfered with the institution's ability to respond to fiscal problems or changes in program needs. Professors could not easily be replaced or fired. Originally intended to protect academic freedom, the tenure system grew into a means of evaluating assistant professors as well as offering lifetime appointments. As fiscal problems grew and the job market deteriorated, it became somewhat harder for young assistant professors to be promoted. Tenure quotas were imposed at some institutions, and many simply raised the standards for awarding tenure. These measures added to the pressures felt by junior staff. The system that was put into place to protect professors was increasingly seen as a problem.

It is significant that the intense debate about the tenure system that characterized the 1970s has, for the most part, ended. Tenure remains one of the keystones of American higher education and, as a concept, is not now under threat. The professoriate sees tenure as one its most important perquisites and has defended it vigorously. Administrators and policymakers have recognized the centrality of tenure to the self-concept of the profession.

Retrenchment—the firing of academic staff without regard to tenure—has always been one of the major fears of the professoriate.[38] During the first wave of fiscal crises in the 1970s, a number of universities attempted to solve their financial problems by firing professors, including some with tenure, following programmatic reviews and analyses of enrollment trends. The American Association of University Professors (AAUP), several academic unions, and a number of individual professors sued the universities in the courts, claiming that such retrenchment was against the implied lifetime employment arrangement offered through the tenure system. The courts consistently ruled against the professors, arguing that tenure protects academic freedom but does not prevent firings due to fiscal crisis. Universities that were especially hard hit, such as the City University of New York and the State University of New York, declared fiscal emergencies and fired academic staff—including some tenured professors—and closed departments and programs. Many institutions found that the legal challenges, decline in morale, and bad national publicity were not worth the financial savings, and in later crises fewer tenured faculty were terminated. The fact is that tenure in American higher education does not fully protect lifetime employment, although in general commitments are honored by colleges and universities.[39] The retrenchments and discussions and debates about retrenchment have left a significant imprint on the thinking of the academic profession, contributing to low morale and feelings of alienation.

The growth of academic unions in the 1970s was a direct reaction to the difficulties faced by the professoriate in this period. Most professors turned to unions with some reluctance, and despite accelerating difficulties in the universities, the union movement has not become dominant. Indeed, the growth of unions slowed and even stopped in the late 1980s. In 1980, 682 campuses were represented by academic unions. Of this number, 254 were four-year institutions—unions are most entrenched in the community college sector. Very few research universities are unionized—only one of the members of the prestigious Association of American Universities, for example. Unions are concentrated in the community college sector and in the public lower and middle tiers of the system.[40] Relatively few private colleges and universities are unionized, in part because the U.S. Supreme Court, in the *Yeshiva* case, made unionization in private institutions quite difficult. The Court ruled that faculty members in private institutions were by definition part of "management" and could not be seen as "workers" in the traditional sense.

The growth of academic unions has essentially stopped in the past decade. Legal challenges such as the *Yeshiva* decision and a perception that academic unions were not able to solve the basic problems of higher education have been contributing factors. In addition, while unions brought significant increases in salaries in the first years of contractual arrangements, this advantage ended in later contract periods. In normal periods, many faculty see unions as somehow opposed to the traditional values, such as meritocratic evaluation, of academe—often, unions are voted in following severe campus conflict between faculty and administration. Further, unions have been unable to save faculty from retrenchment or a deterioration in working conditions. Both public university systems in New York are unionized, and both have been hard hit by fiscal problems. Faculty unions have not shielded staff from retrenchment, salary freezes and the like. Neither the rhetoric of the AAUP nor the trade union tactics of the American Federation of Teachers has kept academic institutions, and sometimes state legislatures, from cutting budgets, increasing workloads, or, in some cases, firing professors. Unions, however, were part of an effort to stop the erosion of faculty advantages in the 1970s. Unions were also an expression of the attempt on the part of professors in institutions with only limited autonomy and weak faculty governance structures to assert faculty power. In both of these areas, unions had only limited success.

ACCOUNTABILITY AND AUTONOMY

The academic profession has traditionally enjoyed a high degree of autonomy, particularly in the classroom and in research. While most academics are only dimly aware of it, the thrust toward accountability has begun to affect their professional lives. This trend will intensify not only due to fiscal constraints but because all public institutions have come under greater scrutiny. Institutions, often impelled (in the case of public universities) by state budget offices, require an increasingly large amount of data concerning faculty work, research productivity, the expenditure of funds for ancillary support, and other aspects of academic life. What is more, criteria for student-faculty ratios and levels of financial support for different kinds of postsecondary education and for productivity of academic staff have been established. The new sources of data permit fiscal authorities to monitor closely how institutions meet established criteria so that adjustments in budgets can be quickly implemented. While most of these measures of accountability are only indirectly perceived by most academics, they nonetheless have a considerable impact on the operation of universities and colleges, since resources are allocated on the basis of formulas that are more closely measured. It is worth noting that the basic "outputs" of academic institutions—the quality of teaching and the quality and impact of research—cannot be calculated through these efforts at accountability. Indeed, even the definitions of teaching quality and research productivity remain elusive.

If autonomy is the opposite side of the accountability coin, then one would expect academic autonomy to have significantly declined. But, at least on the surface, this has not yet occurred. Basic decisions concerning the curriculum, course and degree requirements, the process of teaching and learning, and indeed all of the matters traditionally the domain of the faculty have remained in the hands of departments and other parts of the faculty governance structure. Most academics retain the sense of autonomy that has characterized higher education for a century. This is especially the case in the top-tier institutions. There have been few efforts to dismantle the basic structure of academic work in ways that would destroy the traditional arrangements.

Yet, there is change taking place at the margins that will continue to shift the balance increasingly from autonomy to accountability and erode the base of faculty power. Decisions concerning class size, the future of low-enrollment fields, the overall academic direction of the institution, and other issues have been shifted from the faculty to the administration or even to systemwide agencies. Academic planning, traditionally far removed from the individual professor and seldom impinging on the academic career, has become more of a reality

240 PART THREE: THE ACADEMIC COMMUNITY

as institutions seek to streamline their operations and worry more about external measures of productivity.

ACADEMIC FREEDOM

American professors at present enjoy a fairly high degree of academic freedom, although only half of the professoriate agrees that there are "no political or ideological restrictions on what a scholar may publish."[41] There are few public pressures aimed at ensuring political or intellectual conformity from professors and the concept of academic freedom seems well entrenched. The AAUP noted very few cases in which institutions have sought to violate the academic freedom of their staff. There has been virtually no governmental pressure to limit academic freedom. The tensions of the McCarthy era seem far removed from the current period. The fact that the past decade or more has been without the major ideological and political unrest and activism that characterized some earlier periods, such as the Vietnam War era, certainly contributed to the calm on campus; however, even during the Vietnam period, academic freedom remained relatively secure. That record was, however, not entirely spotless. A number of junior faculty were denied tenure during this period because of their political views.[42]

However, academic freedom remains a contentious issue. Perhaps the most visible academic debate of the current period relates to "political correctness"— an unfortunate shorthand term for a variety of disputes concerning the nature and organization of the undergraduate curriculum, the interpretation of American culture, and the perspectives of some disciplines in the humanities and social sciences, and what some conservatives have claimed is the infusion of ideology into academe. Dinesh D'Souza, a conservative writer, argued in his 1991 book, *Illiberal Education,* that American higher education was being taken over by left-wing ideologists seeking to transform the curriculum through the infusion of multicultural approaches and the destruction of the traditional focus on Western values and civilization.[43] Conservative critics, including then Secretary of Education William Bennett, took up the call and a major national discussion ensued.[44] Some conservatives claim that the academic freedom of some conservative faculty is being violated, although there is no evidence that this is the case. The debate, however, has made an impression on thinking about the curriculum and the role of multiculturalism on campus. While it has not affected academic freedom directly, the politics of race, gender, and ethnicity have had a significant effect on academic life.[45] These social issues have entered into discussions of the curriculum and some faculty have claimed that they have inappropriately influenced decision making. There have also been incidents of racial or gender-based intolerance on some campuses.

Most would say that academic freedom is quite free from structural restraints and that external authorities, including both government and college and university trustees, have been overwhelmingly supportive of academic freedom during the past several decades. Contemporary concerns come from public debate about "political correctness" and from the resulting campus acrimony. Recently outlawed restrictions on student expression may also have added to professorial concern.

STUDENTS

The two basic elements of academia are students and faculty. These two central groups within the college and university are not often linked in analyses of higher education. Students have profoundly affected the academic profession throughout the history of American higher education. Prior to the rise of the research university at the end of the nineteenth century, American higher education was student-oriented and the interaction between faculty and students was substantial. Even in the postwar period, most colleges remained oriented to teaching, although with the decline of *in loco parentis* in the 1960s, faculty became less centrally involved in the lives of students.[46] Students affect faculty in many ways. Increases in student numbers had the result of expanding the professoriate and changes in patterns of enrollments also affected the academic profession. Student demands for "relevance" in the 1960s had implications for the faculty, as did the later vocationalism of student interests. American higher education has traditionally responded to changing student curricular interests by expanding fields and departments—or by cutting offerings in unpopular areas. Student "consumerism" is a central part of the ethos of American higher education.[47]

Student interests have also had a limited impact on academic policy and governance. In the 1960s, students demanded participation in academic governance, and many colleges and universities opened committees and other structures to them. The lasting impact of these changes was minimal, but the student demands aroused considerable debate and tension on campus.[48] Recently, students have shown little interest in participating in governance and have been only minimally involved in any political activism, on campus or off, although there has been a recent increase in student voluntarism for social causes. Student interests and attitudes affect the classroom and enrollments in different fields of study. Students are themselves influenced by societal trends, government policies concerning the financial aspects of higher education, perceptions of the employment market, and many other factors. These impressions are brought to the campus and are translated into attitudes, choices and orientations to higher education. Student opinions of the faculty and of the academic enterprise have a significant influence on institutional culture and morale.[49]

Conclusion

The analysis presented in this essay is not terribly optimistic. The academic profession has been under considerable pressure, and the basic conditions of academic work in America have deteriorated. Some, but by no means all, of the gains made during the period of postwar expansion have been lost. The "golden age" of the American university is probably over, but it is likely that the medium term future will be somewhat more favorable than the immediate past because of changing demographic realities, although even here the imposition of larger classes and the increased use of instructional technology as well as the continued use of part-time faculty has meant that conditions will not dramatically improve. The basic fact is, however, that the essential structure of American higher education remains unaltered and it is unlikely to fundamentally change. There will, thus, be a considerable degree of continuity amidst change.

The professoriate stands at the center of any academic institution and is, in a way, buffered from direct interaction with many of higher education's external constituencies. Academics do not generally deal with trustees, legislators, or parents. Their concerns are with their own teaching and research, and with their direct academic surroundings, such as the department. Yet, external constituencies and realities increasingly affect academic life.

It is possible to summarize some of the basic trends that have been discussed in this analysisrealities that are likely to continue to affect the academic profession in the coming period.

- Reallocations and increased competition for federal research funds made research funds in most fields more difficult to obtain.[50] Governmental commitment to basic research declined as well, and funds for the social sciences and humanities have declined. With the end of the cold war, the emphasis on military research has diminished, but there are few signs of other fields benefiting from the "peace dividend."

- Financial difficulties for scholarly publishers and cutbacks in budgets for academic libraries reduced opportunities for publishing scholarly work, thereby placing added stress on younger scholars, in particular, and on the entire knowledge system in academe. Library cutbacks also place restrictions on access to knowledge.

- Changes in student curricular choices have been significant in the past two decades from the social sciences in the 1960s to business, engineering, and law in the 1980s and currently back, to a limited extent, to the social sciences. Declines in enrollments in the traditional arts and sciences at the graduate level were also notable.

- Demands for budgetary and programmatic accountability from government have affected higher education at every level.

- In this climate of increased accountability, academic administrators have gained power over their institutions and, inevitably, over the lives of the professoriate.

- Economic problems in society have caused major financial problems for higher education, affecting the faculty directly in terms of salaries, perquisites, and sometimes higher teaching loads. The financial future of higher education, regardless of broader economic trends, is not favorable in the medium term.

- A decline in public esteem and support for higher education, triggered first by the unrest of the 1960s and enhanced by widespread questioning of the academic benefits of a college degree, has caused additional stress for the professoriate. There is a tendency to see an academic degree as a "private good" rather than a "public good," meaning that individuals and families rather than the state should pay for higher education.

- The shrinking academic employment market has meant that few younger scholars have been able to enter the profession, and has limited the mobility of those currently in the profession. The increased use of part-time faculty has further restricted growth.

Given these factors, it is surprising that the basic working conditions of the American professoriate have remained relatively stable. The structure of postsecondary education remains essentially unchanged, but there have been important qualitative changes, generally in a negative direction from the perspective of the professoriate. Academic freedom and the tenure system remain largely intact, but there have been increased demands for accountability. Academics retain basic control over the curriculum, and most institutions continue to be based on the department, which remains strongly influenced by the professoriate. Institutional governance, although increasingly influenced by administrators, remains unchanged.

The period of expansion and professorial power of the middle years of the century will not return. How, then, can academics face the challenges of the coming period? At one level, the academic profession needs to represent itself effectively to external constituencies. If academic unions could more effectively assimilate traditional academic norms, they might have the potential of representing the academic profession. The traditional academic governance structures are the most logical agency to take responsibility for presenting the case for the academic profession to a wider audience, both to the public and to political leaders, probably in cooperation with university administrators.

The professoriate reacted to the challenges of the postwar period. It was glad to accept more responsibilities, move into research, and seek funding from external agencies. It relinquished much of its responsibility to students (at least in the research-oriented universities) as research became the dominating academic value. The curriculum lost its coherence in the rush toward specialization. Now it is necessary to reestablish a sense of academic mission that emphasizes teaching and the curriculum. To an extent, this has been done on many campuses with the rebuilding of the undergraduate general education curriculum and the reestablishment of liberal education as a key curricular goal. The current emphasis on teaching is another important trend that may restore the credibility of the profession.

It is always more difficult to induce changes as a result of conscious planning and concern than it is to react to external circumstances. For much of this century the professoriate has reacted. Now there are signs that the crisis has stimulated the academic profession to implement positive solutions to difficult problems.

Notes

I am indebted to Lionel S. Lewis, Patricia Gumport, Robert Berdahl, and Edith S. Hoshino for comments on this essay.

1. See Allan Bloom, *The Closing of the American Mind: How Higher Education has Failed Democracy and Impoverished the Souls of Today's Students* (New York: Simon and Schuster, 1987); Charles J. Sykes, *Profscam: Professors and the Demise of Higher Education* (Washington, D.C.: Regenery, 1988); and Martin Anderson, *Imposters in the Temple* (New York: Simon and Schuster, 1992).

2. Ernest L. Boyer, *Scholarship Reconsidered: Priorities of the Professoriate* (Princeton, N.J.: Carnegie Foundation for the Advancement of Teaching, 1990).

3. Harold T. Shapiro, "The Functions and Resources of the American University of the Twenty-First Century," *Minerva* 30 (Summer,1992): 16–74.

4. Richard M. Freeland, *Academia's Golden Age: Universities in Massachusetts, 1945–1970* (New York: Oxford University Press, 1992).

5. Edward Shils, "The Academic Ethos under Strain," *Minerva* 13 (Spring 1975): 1–37. See also Henry Rosovsky, *The University: An Owner's Manual* (New York: Norton, 1990).

6. Robert Birnbaum, "Unionization and Faculty Compensation, Part II," *Educational Record* 57 (Spring 1976): 116–18.

7. Kenneth P. Ruscio, "Many Sectors, Many Professions," in *The Academic Profession: National, Disciplinary and Institutional Settings,* ed. Burton R. Clark (Berkeley: University of California Press, 1987), pp. 331–68.

8. Mary M. Dwyer, Arlene A. Flynn, and Patricia S. Inman, "Differential Progress of Women Faculty: 1980–1990," *Status in Higher Education: Handbook of Theory and Research, Volume 7,* ed. John Smart (New York: Agathon, 1991), pp. 173–222.

9. Martin J. Finkelstein, *The American Academic Profession* (Columbus: Ohio State University Press, 1984), pp. 187–89.

10. Jake Ryan and Charles Sackrey, *Strangers in Paradise: Academics from the*

Working Class (Boston, Mass.: South End Press, 1984).

11. Charles Homer Haskins, *The Rise of Universities* (Ithaca, N.Y.: Cornell University Press, 1965).

12. Joseph Ben-David and Awraham Zloczower, "Universities and Academic Systems in Modern Societies," *European Journal of Sociology* 3, no. 1 (1962): 45–84.

13. Frederick Rudolph, *The American College and University: A History* (New York: Vintage, 1965).

14. Laurence Veysey, *The Emergence of the American University* (Chicago: University of Chicago Press, 1965).

15. This theme is developed at greater length in David Henry, *Challenges Past, Challenges Present* (San Francisco: Jossey-Bass, 1975).

16. The academic job market of this period is captured well in Theodore Caplow and Reece J. McGee, *The Academic Marketplace* (New York: Basic Books, 1958). Current realities are reflected in Dolores L. Burke, *A New Academic Marketplace* (Westport, Conn.: Greenwood, 1988), a replication of the earlier Caplow and McGee study.

17. See Logan Wilson, *American Academics: Then and Now* (New York: Oxford University Press, 1979).

18. Seymour Martin Lipset, *Rebellion in the University* (New Brunswick, N.J.: Transaction, 1993).

19. Burton R. Clark, *The Academic Life* (Princeton, N.J.: Carnegie Foundation for the Advancement of Teaching, 1987). For a structural discussion of American higher education, see Talcott Parsons and Gerald Plan, *The American University* (Cambridge: Harvard University Press, 1973).

20. These figures come from a survey of the views of the American academic profession undertaken by the Carnegie Foundation for the Advancement of Teaching in 1992. See Eugene Haas, "International Survey of the Academic Profession: Draft Report on U.S. Faculty" (unpublished report, 1993).

21. David Riesman, "The Academic Procession," in *Constraint and Variety in American Education* (Garden City, N.Y.: Doubleday, 1958), pp. 25–65.

22. Alvin Gouldner, "Cosmopolitans and Locals: Toward an Analysis of Latent Social Roles, 1 and 2," *Administrative Science Quarterly* 2 (December 1957 and March 1958): 281–303 and 445–67.

23. Judith M. Gappa and David W. Leslie, *The Invisible Faculty: Improving the Status of Part-timers in Higher Education* (San Francisco: Jossey-Bass, 1993).

24. See, for example, Valora Washington and William Harvey, *Affirmative Rhetoric, Negative Action: African-American and Hispanic Faculty at Predominantly White Institutions* (Washington, D.C.: School of Education, George Washington University, 1989).

25. Edward R. Hines and L. S. Hartmark, *The Politics of Higher Education* (Washington, D.C.: American Association for Higher Education, 1980).

26. The most influential consideration of this topic is Boyer, *Scholarship Reconsidered.* See also William F. Massy and Robert Zemsky, *Faculty Discretionary Time: Departments and the Academic Ratchet* (Philadelphia, Pa.: Pew Higher Education Research Program, 1992), and "The Lattice and the Ratchet," *Policy Perspectives* 2, no. 4 (1990).

27. Sykes, *Profscam*. See also Page Smith, *Killing the Spirit: Higher Education in America* (New York: Viking, 1990). Both of these volumes received widespread attention in the popular media and sold well.

28. Arthur Levine and Jana Nidiffer, "Faculty Productivity: A Re-examination of Current Attitudes and Actions" (unpublished paper, Institute of Educational Management, Harvard Graduate School of Education, 1993).

29. 1992 Carnegie Survey of the International Academic Profession. It is worth noting that academics in other countries report that they teach similar amounts—Germany, 16.4 hours per week; Japan, 19.4; Sweden, 15.9; England, 21.3.

30. Haas, 11.

31. Haas, 20.

32. D. Seymour, "TQM: Focus on Performance, Not Resources," *Educational Record* 74 (Spring 1993): 614.

33. Elaine El-Khawas, *Campus Trends, 1991* (Washington, D.C.: American Council on Education, 1991), p. 7.

34. William G. Bowen and Julie Ann Sosa, *Prospects for Faculty in the Arts and Sciences* (Princeton, N.J.: Princeton University Press, 1989). Demographic projections, however, must be evaluated carefully, because they have frequently been wrong.

35. Carnegie Foundation for the Advancement of Teaching, *Campus Life: In Search of Community* (Princeton, N.J.: Carnegie Foundation for the Advancement of Teaching, 1990). See also Irving J. Spitzberg, Jr., and Virginia V. Thorndike, *Creating Community on College Campuses* (Albany: State University of New York Press, 1992).

36. Haas, 5.

37. Bardwell Smith, et al., eds., *The Tenure Debate* (San Francisco: Jossey-Bass, 1973). For a more recent attack on tenure, see Anderson, *Imposters in the Temple*.

38. See Marjorie C. Mix, *Tenure and Termination in Financial Exigency* (Washington, D.C.: American Association for Higher Education, 1978).

39. Sheila Slaughter, "Retrenchment in the 1980s: The Politics of Prestige and Gender," *Journal of Higher Education* 64 (May/June 1993): 250–82. See also Patricia Gumport, "The Contested Terrain of Academic Program Reduction," *Journal of Higher Educaticn* 64 (May/June 1993): 283–311.

40. For example, in the sixty-four campus State University of New York system, which is unionized, there is a bifurcation between the four research-oriented university centers, which have been reluctant to unionize, and the fourteen four-year colleges, which favor the union. Since the four-year college faculty are in the majority, the union has prevailed.

41. 1992 Carnegie Survey of the Academic Profession. It may be worth noting that the United States falls at the lower end on this question, with scholars in Russia, Sweden, Mexico, Germany, Japan and other countries feeling more positive about the freedom to publish.

42. Joseph Fashing and Stephen F. Deutsch, *Academics in Retreat* (Albuquerque, N.M.: University of New Mexico Press, 1971).

43. Dinesh D'Souza, *Illiberal Education: The Politics of Race and Sex on Campus* (New York: Free Press, 1991).

44. Among the numerous books on the topic, see Paul Berman, ed., *Debating P.C.: The Controversy over Political Correctness on College Campuses* (New York:

Dell, 1992); Patricia Aufderheide, ed. *Beyond PC: Towards a Politics of Understanding* (Saint Paul, Minn.: Graywolf Press, 1992); and Francis J. Beckwith and Michael E. Bauman, eds., *Are You Politically Correct?: Debating America's Cultural Standards* (Buffalo, N.Y.: Prometheus Books, 1993).

45. Phihp G. Altbach and Kofi Lomotey, eds., *The Racial Crisis in American Higher Education* (Albany: State University of New York Press, 1991).

46. Helen Leflowitz Horowitz, *Campus Life: Undergraduate Cultures from the End of the Eighteenth Century to the Present* (Chicago: University of Chicago Press, 1987).

47. Arthur Levine, *When Dreams and Heroes Died: A Portrait of Today's College Student* (San Francisco: Jossey-Bass, 1980).

4B. Alexander W. Astin, et al., *The Power of Protest* (San Francisco: Jossey-Bass, 1975).

4g. Alexander W. Astin, *What Matters in College: Four Critical Years Revisited* (San Francisco: Jossey-Bass, 1993).

50. See Roger L. Geiger, *Research and Relevant Knowledge: American Research Universities Since World War II* (New York: Oxford University Press, 1993).

11

College Students in Changing Contexts
Eric L. Dey and Sylvia Hurtado

The relationship between higher education and society is one in which students play an unrecognized, yet influential role. Students bring values and attitudes associated with larger social forces into academe, thereby creating change within the higher education system. At the same time, students transmit to the wider society ideas, interests, and attitudes cultivated within colleges and universities, thereby helping to bring about change in other social, cultural, and political institutions. In short, the continuing relationship between students and higher education is reciprocal and dynamic, and is informed by and shapes American society.

One reason that the complexity of the student role is sometimes obscured is that we tend to view undergraduates from one of several perspectives. As practitioners and researchers, we usually see students in terms of the ways in which their background characteristics (e.g., prior academic preparation, gender, race, etc.) contribute to particular institutional cultures. This predominant perspective views students simply as inputs into the higher education system. More recently, we have started to think of the student as the recipient of collegiate influences that produce certain psychological, social, and economic outcomes for individuals and the larger society. This perspective, popularized by the assessment movement and scholarly interest in questions of college impact, views students as outputs from higher education.[1] In addition to these two main perspectives, it is also important to consider the ways in which students influence colleges and universities. This view, which acknowledges students as sources of institutional change, has received much less attention in the research literature.[2]

Each of these three views is useful in helping us understand different aspects of the role of students within higher education and American society. Taken separately, however, they can also serve to restrict the ways in which we see students. A more complete view is one in which the relationship between students and the college environment is seen as being both reciprocal and dynamic. This ecological perspective encompasses the many and varied roles of college students by portraying students as actively shaping their collegiate and social environments, with these environments simultaneously providing the potential for transforming the individual.[3] Thus, rather than simply looking at the ways in which students are affected by external forces or how students create institutional and social change, we need to adopt a deeper perspective that acknowledges the simultaneous occurrence of both dynamics.

In order to explore the dynamic relationship between students and institutions, we will discuss three important, interrelated social and educational trends that have shaped American higher education over the past three decades: (1) Changes in the demography of higher education; (2) the sociopolitical culture of students; and (3) educational plans and preferences of entering college students. We will also consider the changes in the experiences of undergraduates *during college* as a fourth group of data-based observations. In examining these four aspects of the college student experience, it becomes clear that larger social forces are constantly transforming the dynamic relationship between students and colleges. This is reflected in the changing nature of students, institutional characteristics, and the reciprocal influences of students and higher education institutions.

The Changing Demography of Higher Education

Who is the American college student? How would you describe today's typical undergraduate? Despite the many changes that have occurred in higher education access and attendance over the past several decades, the traditional image of the American college student is surprisingly common and somewhat mistaken. One reason that traditional images are so persistent is that we tend to think of specific generations of college students when trying to describe their attributes. Unfortunately, truth and fiction are intertwined in stereotypes that become attached to each generation. At the same time, it is important to note that some of these generational stereotypes do come close to describing groups of students at particular institutions. To be sure, some institutions continue to seek students that fit the "traditional" college student image, while others have taken on more diverse clienteles in order to better serve changing state and local populations. This, then, suggests that there have been changes not only in the type of student now attending college, but also in institutional mission and policy that help differentiate institutions across the higher education system. The enrollment patterns associated with the changing demography of higher education have, in short, transformed the nature of our institutions.

Spurred on by the great social movements of the 1960s, higher education enrollments have grown considerably and continue to expand. Despite predictions of a declining number of college-age students during the 1980s, we have witnessed a 13.3 percent increase in the last decade, with a record enrollment of 13.7 million students in 1990. Much of the growth over the last three decades has been due to increased access of non-traditional students. Adults over the age of 25 have been the fastest growing group, representing over 40 percent of all students in higher education today. There has been a shift toward part-time enrollment in higher education since 1965, with part-time students now representing 43 percent of all students. Women have entered higher education in record numbers, constituting a large proportion of the growth in part-time, adult, and minority enrollment increases over the last three decades.

In addition to the changes wrought by the large numbers of "nontraditional" students, striking changes in the composition of college entrants have also redefined our conception of the "traditional" college student. Table 1 shows the changing demographics of first-time, full-time students entering four-year colleges.[4] The typical college student in the 1990s is likely to be female: Women constituted 53 percent of first year students pursuing a baccalaureate degree in 1991, compared to 44 percent in 1961. As a result of society's changing views of women's roles, coupled with institutional initiatives to enroll more women and an overall increase in the level of educational attainment, today's college student is also more likely to have a mother who has completed a college degree. The proportion of older students attending college for the first time has also steadily increased over time. These changes in the traditional college-going population indicate that child care services, re-entry services, women's centers, women's studies, and incorporating gender-related issues in the classroom will continue to be salient for increasing proportions of campus communities.

Improved access for students of diverse socioeconomic backgrounds is one of the most significant trends of the last three decades and warrants monitoring in the future. The median family income of traditional students attending college in the 1960s was almost twice as high as the national median income. This gap was dramatically reduced by federal financial aid policies that enabled students of diverse economic backgrounds to pursue a college education. Although national family incomes steadily increased, the trend toward closing the gap between national family income and the families of fouryear college students stagnated during the 1980s. This lack of progress toward economic equity may be largely attributable to changes in federal student aid programs during the Reagan-Bush administrations, rapidly rising college tuition rates, as well as the country's recent economic problems.[5] The combined effect of these factors during the 1980s suggests that four-year colleges will face the challenge of recruiting and retaining students of diverse economic backgrounds in the years to come.

Table 1 also shows that the proportion of white students has steadily declined, while the representation of all other ethnic groups has increased among firsttime entrants to four-year colleges. Increased access over the years, coupled with

Table 1
Demographic Characteristics of New Students Entering Four-Year Colleges, 1961–1991

	1961	1971	1981	1991
Percent women	44	46	51	53
Percentage of students with mothers who held a college degree	21	22	30	39
Age distribution				
18 or younger	—	78	76	69
19 or older	—	23	25	31
Socioeconomic background				
Median freshman family income	45,922	41,770	40,289	43,600
National median family income	24,864	33,238	33,346	35,353
Ratio of national to freshman income	.54	.80	.83	.81
Racial/ethnic background				
White/Caucasian	97	91	87	78
African-American/Black	2	7	9	12
American Indian	Z	1	1	2
Asian-American/Oriental	1	1	1	4
Mexican-American/Chicano	—	Z	1	2
Puerto Rican	—	Z	1	1
Other	Z	1	2	2

NOTES: Racial/ethnic labels vary between survey years. Racial ethnic percentages may total more than 100 after 1971 due to multiple responses of students. Family income estimates given in 1990 dollars. Due to differences in response options for mother's education, postsecondary certificate holders are included with high school graduates; those with some graduate school are included with college graduates. Z indicates less than 0.5 percent; — indicates data not available.

SOURCE: 1961 data are from Astin and Panos, 1968; 1971 and 1981 data are from Dey, Astin, and Korn, 1991; 1991 data are from Dey, Astin, Korn, and Riggs, 1992. National median family income estimates are from the Statistical Abstract of the United States, 1992, Table 703, and Current Population Reports (Series P-60), No. 80.

the growing representation of minorities within college-age cohorts, have changed the ethnic composition of many campuses. As a result, campuses will need to continue the restructuring process of becoming multicultural environments. What is not evident from this table, however, is that while all racial and ethnic groups have recorded enrollment gains, some ethnic groups continue to face considerable inequities in access to college. For example, although Hispanics posted gains in higher education, they have experienced an actual decline in their college participation rate.[6] Both Native Americans (52 percent) and Hispanics (55 percent) are also more likely to be represented in two-year colleges than either African American or white students (42 and 37 percent respectively).[7]

These changing characteristics of America's college students are a direct result of a combination of demographic growth, changing social views, government policies, and institutional initiatives to recruit students from all potential college populations. Some institutions, for example, have altered their missions and strengthened their commitment to serving special populations. Such changes would have been impossible without the equity reform movements that brought about changes in the nation's collective consciousness as well as tangible federal assistance in the form of financial aid policies. We have witnessed the development of tribal colleges, the strengthened position of many historically black and women's colleges, and now an increasing number of Hispanic-serving institutions.[8] In each of these specific cases, student characteristics have helped give further definition to the institution's mission. Aside from these special types of institutions, we are also witnessing a gradual transformation of "traditional" institutions as they respond to the new student populations by creating new services[9] and incorporating new perspectives in the curriculum and in extracurricular programming.[10]

While these changes may appear to have occurred rapidly, change continues to come about slowly for those who confront institutional resistance. A college's historical legacy of exclusion of specific groups may, for example, continue to influence seemingly "neutral" institutional policies.[11] Generating a commitment to institutional transformation among administrators and faculty who refuse to examine their own attitudes and practices that affect students remains one of the greatest challenges.[12] Thus ideologies at the institutional and individual level continue to present barriers to recognizing and meeting the needs of the new American college student. These ideologies find reinforcement and resistance depending on the tenor of the social context. This is especially true when examining student political views.

Students' Political Preferences

Along with the changing demographics of higher education, there has been a shift in the values and ideologies of students as compared to those held by students in the recent past. One area where this has occurred most visibly is in the area of student politics. Following on the heels of the volatile, activist 1960s, there is the perception that recent generations of students are more conservative, apathetic, and politically inactive. As we will discuss, this perception is true only if we continue to think about student political preferences in traditional ways.

From an institutional perspective, the sociopolitical character of students is important for several reasons. To begin, there is an accumulation of research evidence concerning the influence that student peers have upon one another.[13] Thus, when the attitudes and values within college peer environments change, this alters the impact of college *regardless of institutional intentions.* In addition, it is important to recognize that the educational process requires some common ground between students and faculty. If students and faculty find few points of agreement on political issues, these ideological differences increase the potential for divisive conflicts between students and faculty.

How have the political preferences of students changed? As we can see in the data from entering college students shown in Table 2, there has been an interesting pattern of changes in the way that students characterize themselves politically. For example, the percentage of students who classified themselves as liberal declined by nearly one-half between the early 1970s and the early 1980s. While the decline in the number of self-declared liberals was sharp, it is interesting to note that this decline stabilized and actually rebounded somewhat during the 1980s, a time period in which we might have expected to see the strongest conservative influences, given events within the national political scene.

Another interesting trend is that the declining number of student liberals seems to have been accompanied mainly by increases in the number of political moderates. Indeed, the number of students who said they were in the "middle-of-the-road" jumped by about onequarter in the 1970s, while the number of self-proclaimed conservatives increased a scant two percentage points. This may suggest that the issues associated with the 1960s political and social movements are now seen as relatively mainstream issues, and no longer "liberal" causes. It also seems to reflect political trends within the larger society, with politicos of nearly all political persuasions concertedly trying to appear moderate, while simultaneously painting all others as being outside of the political mainstream.

Taken together, these trends reveal that there has been a tremendous shift in the balance of liberals and conservatives on campus: whereas there were two liberals for every conservative during the early 1970s, by the early 1980s the numbers of liberals and conservatives were roughly equal. Although this ratio has shifted somewhat back to favor the politically liberal, the ratio of liberals to conservatives is much closer to 1-to-1 than it was two decades ago. This may help explain the relatively increased effectiveness of conservative political agendas on college campuses, and may portend a continuation of the polarized campus politics which have become evident in recent years.

Another way to look at the political preferences of students is to consider the changing patterns of attitudes that entering students have toward a variety of different political and social values. The results in the bottom panel of Table 2 show a complex set of trends among attitudes that would traditionally be classified as both conservative and liberal. For example, there has been a

Table 2
Political Self-Characterization and Attitudes of Entering College Students

	Average values between		
	1970–72	1980–82	1990–92
Political Self-Characterization			
Liberal	37%	21%	26%
Middle of the road	47	60	54
Conservative	17	19	21
Number of Conservatives per 100 Liberals	46	94	80
Political and Social Attitudes			
Federal government is not doing enough to control environmental pollution	90%	79%	87%
Increase Federal military spending	—	39	24
Busing is OK if it helps to achieve racial balance in the schools	—	45	55
Wealthy people should pay a larger share of taxes than they do now	73	71	72
A national health care plan is needed to cover everybody's medical costs	—	57	76
Abortion should be legal	—	54	64
The activities of married women are best confined to the home and family	42	26	26
Marijuana should be legalized	41	34	21
Capital punishment should be abolished	57	31	21
There is too much concern in the courts for the rights of criminals	50	68	66

NOTES: Political self-characterization originally measured on a five-point scale, with "far left" and "liberal" responses being collapsed in Liberal and "far right" and "conservative" responses making up the Conservative category. The figures shown for the selected political and social attitudes indicate the percentages of students who "agree" or "strongly agree."

SOURCE: Cooperative Institutional Research Program, Higher Education Research Institute, UCLA.

movement toward the liberal position in areas such as military spending, school busing, national health care, abortion rights, and women's rights, with entering students maintaining a relatively liberal stance toward the environment and taxation. At the same time, students have clearly become more conservative on issues related to crime and drugs: the number of students who believed capital punishment should be abolished dropped by nearly twothirds since the early 1970s, while the percentage of students who supported the legalization of marijuana dropped by one-half over the same period.

While these attitudes seem to reflect changing political views on the national political landscape, it is important to remember that they also affect the issues that students choose to pursue within the campus political environment. But will today's student choose to pursue these and other issues, or are they politically apathetic as common wisdom has it? The data from entering college students are complex in this area as well. For example, the number of students who worked in political campaigns declined by about twofifths between the late 1960s and late 1970s, while the number who reported having frequent discussions about politics declined by about onethird between the late 1960s and late 1980s. These figures clearly suggest that students are not politically active *in traditional ways,* while other information suggests that students may simply be disillusioned with and alienated from traditional politics. For example, among entering college students: (a) the number of students who participated in organized demonstrations has more than doubled since the late 1960s (about 2 in 5 college entrants reported being involved in demonstrations in 1991); (b) students increasingly expect to be involved in future protests; and (c) students are becoming more interested in influencing social and political values.[14]

These trends suggest that there is a rapidly expanding number of American college students who are dissatisfied with the status quo, and with traditional political methods of bringing about social change. If this trend continues, we are likely to see a growing interest among college students in promoting social and institutional change. This interest may take on forms other than protests or participation in political campaigns. For example, the increased interest in community service and organizations like the National Teacher Corps reflects ways that students are trying to make a positive difference in today's society.[15]

Educational Plans and Preferences

In addition to the composition and the sociopolitical culture of students, there have been changes in student plans and preferences for college. Some of these patterns appear to be clearly related to economic forces, while others seem more closely related to social forces like changing views about the role of women in American society. Let us first consider the changing patterns of preferences that students have for various undergraduate majors when they enter college (Table 3). This is an important consideration, since a college's ability to maintain its curricular focus beyond all of the educational philosophy that goes into designing a curriculum, is necessarily dependent upon its ability to enroll students in the courses it offers.

From a traditional liberal-arts perspective, the past 25 years have not been

Table 3
Undergraduate Major Preferences Among Entering College Students

	Percentage of Entering College Students Expressing an Interest in Various Majors in					
	1967	1972	1977	1982	1987	1992
Biological sciences	4	4	5	4	4	5
Business	16	16	22	24	27	16
Education	11	7	9	6	9	10
Engineering	10	7	9	13	9	9
English	4	2	1	.8	1	1
Health professions (nursing, pre-med, etc.)	5	11	10	9	7	16
History or political science	7	4	3	2	3	3
Humanities	5	4	2	2	3	2
Fine arts (applied and performing)	9	9	6	4	5	5
Mathematics or statistics	4	2	.8	.6	.6	.6
Physical sciences	3	2	2	2	2	2
Social sciences	—	8	5	4	6	6
Undecided	2	5	5	5	7	7

NOTE: indicates comparable data not available.

SOURCE: Cooperative Institutional Research Program Trends File, Higher Education Research Institute, UCLA.

good ones with regard to interest in liberal arts fields among entering students: interest in majoring in the humanities, the fine and performing arts, and the social sciences has been declining consistently. Interest in majoring in English, for example, dropped by nearly three-quarters between 1967 and 1992. Interest in majoring in biological or physical sciences has remained somewhat stable since the 1960s, while interest in mathematics and statistics has experienced a large decline, dropping from 4 percent in 1967 to 0.6 percent in 1992. Although the relatively new and developing field of computer science may have captured some of the students who otherwise might have majored in mathematics or statistics, the 85 percent decline in the number of students who enter college with an interest in math and statistics is quite alarming. Interest in the engineering fields has been relatively stable over the past several years after peaking in the early 1980s.

Table 3 also shows that the greatest changes in the popularity of different fields is associated with the field of business. After a period of relative stability, the percentage of students interested in business majors increased sharply during the late 1970s and 1980s. During the past few years, however, interest in business has stopped its climb and is currently in steep decline, with student interest now equal to that registered in 1967. The cause for this turnaround is not clear: it may be that competition for jobs has increased in the recent economic slowdown, or that many students are simply disillusioned with the field of business because of scandals such as insider trading, stock fraud, and the savings and loan debacle of the 1980s. While the explanation for these trends may not be clear, one thing is: institutions which rapidly expanded their business programs to take advantage of this growth in student interest may soon have to contend with the new problem of having too many highly-paid faculty in the field of business relative to student demand. This problem may be especially troublesome for the many small liberal arts colleges which avoided closure during the 1980s by moving away from a traditional liberal arts program to incorporate business education into the curriculum.[16]

While interest in business is now in steep decline after recordsetting increases, interest in majoring in the health professions has been increasing rapidly and is now at an all-time high. This surge of interest may well reflect the students of today, who seem to be searching for majors that will lead to profitable and stable careers since business has apparently lost its attraction. It will be more difficult for colleges and universities to respond to this increased interest since education for the health professions, which is largely based in the sciences, is inherently more expensive than that associated with the field of business. Moreover, it is impossible to predict how long this trend will last.

Given the pronounced changes in the major field choices of students entering college, it is not surprising to find that the educational preferences of women have also changed quite dramatically. Table 4, for example, shows trends in aspirations for various postgraduate degrees and interest in different undergraduate majors over the past two decades. This table shows the number of women students interested in certain degrees and fields of study for every 100 men interested in the same option. If men and women were equally likely to aspire to a certain degree we would, for example, see 100 women per 100 men expressing an interest.

These changes clearly show the effectiveness of the women's movement in changing the way that women (and to a lesser extent men) think about certain degrees and careers. For example, with respect to postgraduate degree aspirations upon entry into college, Table 4 shows that women have essentially reached a point of parity. Indeed, aspiration for law and medical degrees among women now slightly exceeds that of men. It is important to note, however, that this pattern changes after four years in college: The number of women per 100 men aspiring to law, medical, and doctoral degrees is 91, 51, and 92, respectively.[17] The marked drop in aspirations for medical degrees for women relative to that of men underscores the possibility that the undergraduate environment is relatively unsupportive for women aspiring to become physicians.

The bottom panel of Table 4 shows how women's preferences for different

Table 4
Academic Plans of New College Students by Gender

	Number of Women per 100 Men Aspiring to Selected Degrees and Undergraduate Majors in		
	1972	1982	1992
Postgraduate degree aspiration			
Law	32	81	106
Medical	44	90	103
Doctoral	64	86	99
Undergraduate major field preferences			
Biological sciences	64	103	102
Business	80	115	91
Education	329	375	286
Engineering	3	16	16
English	278	167	167
Health professions (nursing, pre-med, etc.)	550	331	239
History or political science	54	69	83
Humanities	204	163	121
Fine arts (applied and performing)	124	102	60
Mathematics or statistics	100	117	71
Physical sciences	27	38	54
Social sciences	227	275	247

SOURCE: Cooperative Institutional Research Program, Higher Education Research Institute, UCLA.

fields of study have been changing, and reveals a mixture of trends. For example, in the fields where women were most underrepresented in 1972—engineering, history/political science, biological sciences, and physical sciences—we see a pattern of progress toward parity that varies by field. Engineering, for example, had the smallest representation of women in 1972, and this fact remains true two decades later. Despite a five-fold jump in interest in this field between 1972 and 1982, there has been no real change since that time. There may still be strong institutional barriers, such as heavy mathematical course requirements without a realistic possibility of remediation, and a male–dominated climate that is unwelcoming for women, that are preventing interest levels from moving beyond this plateau. The other science fields with an early underrepresentation of women have fared differently: women's interest in the biological sciences moved quickly to a position of parity, while the physical sciences still have a long way to go despite the doubling of interest that occurred. History/ political science has also made progress in attracting the interest of women, but still remains far below a point of parity.

Other fields have also shown gender differences in patterns of student interest. Education, for example, shows a declining rate of interest among women despite the fact that it remains strongly dominated by women. The health professions, which in addition to medicine include the large, female dominated field of nursing, now attract the interest of fewer women relative to men than in the past. In the fields of English, the humanities, and the fine arts, we have also seen a lessening of interest among women, with the decline in interest so sharp in the fine arts that women are now underrepresented. Women are now also underrepresented in the field of business, after reaching and exceeding a position of parity in the 1980s.

All of these changes will continue to have an impact on institutions as they attempt to balance their traditional educational missions with the changing interests of students. This is especially true of the changing patterns of interest among women and members of other underrepresented groups as such trends bring with them pressure to remove inequities and achievement barriers for these groups. In addition to influencing institutional policy and practice, these shifts in student interest are also linked to larger social and economic forces (such as the projected job market), and have direct implications for the nation's talent pool. The continued advancement of all fields of practice or inquiry is determined by the pool of student talent in each particular field.

Experiences during College

As one might expect given the many changes we have described, there have been changes in the nature of the college student experience. Table 5 shows changes in student academic performance, activities, and student satisfaction during college from the late 1960s to the beginning of this decade. Perhaps one of the most striking changes has been the shift toward earning high grades in college and a related drop in the proportion of students who earn less than a B minus since the late 1960s. This indicates that performance and academic success in college has been redefined, creating a certain amount of grade inflation relative to earlier eras. This may reflect the fact that students have become more grade conscious over the years and may be more likely to contest their grades. However, it may that this trend is fueled by external pressure because maintaining good college grades has become more closely linked to such economic considerations as the receipt of financial aid, auto insurance discounts, and access to graduate schools and jobs after college. At the same time that there are more students making high grades, it appears to be more difficult for students to graduate with honors.

Despite the changing political views of students and the persistent (and

Table 5
Trends in Student Experiences during College, 1966–70 and 1987–91

	1966–70	1987–91	Percentage Difference
Undergraduate grade point average			
A+ or A	1	6	5
A– or B+	5	27	22
B	21	36	15
B– or C+	35	24	–11
C	26	7	–19
C– or less	13	2	–11
Activities since entering college			
Joined a fraternity or sorority	20	21	1
Graduated with honors	14	12	–2
Frequent activities during student's last year of college			
Drank wine or liquor	12	22	10
Drank beer	30	38	8
Stayed up all night	8	14	6
Participated in an organized demonstration/ protest*	19	18	–1
Attended a religious service	33	25	–8
Smoked cigarettes	27	12	–15
Percent of students who were satisfied with:			
Overall quality of instruction	92	90	–2
Opportunity to discuss coursework with profes- sors outside of class	84	88	4
Lab facilities	90	88	–2
Library	83	83	0
Overall satisfaction	74	87	13

NOTE: Percentage includes those students marking "frequently" or "occasionally."

SOURCE: Unpublished tabulations, Higher Education Research Institute, UCLA.

somewhat contradictory) images of the typical college student as an activist or a member of a fraternity/sorority, we find very little change in the proportion of students who actually participated in either of these activities since the 1960s. This suggests that these two activities are relatively generation free in the sense that a roughly stable proportion of students participates. Despite the apparent constancy in the proportion of students involved in these activities, different generations of students become closely associated with these images due to larger social and political contexts. For example, although a minority of students participated in demonstrations in the late 1960s, the tenor of the historical era captured a tremendous amount of media attention because of linkages with issues of national concern.

In terms of health and social behavior, students today are less likely to report frequent smoking due in part to increased health awareness and related restrictions on smoking in school, work, and places of entertainment. However, a higher proportion of students in college reported that they drank wine, liquor or beer in college than in the late 1960s. While most of the students surveyed here would meet drinking-age requirements by their fourth year of college, it is difficult to restrict their associations with other students who are under the age limit. This shift in student behavior makes it extremely problematic for colleges to monitor and comply with legislation that raised the drinking-age in the last decade. Colleges continue to provide opportunities for alcohol-free activities, but providing alternatives for healthy social lives will remain one of the continuing challenges for student affairs staffs on campus.

Student satisfaction and retention are aspects of student experience that are closely related to college impact and institutional accountability. The data show that student satisfaction with the college experience has remained generally high over time, with only small changes in specific areas of satisfaction. Although students are somewhat less satisfied with lab facilities and the quality of instruction on campus, in the early 1990s they were more satisfied with opportunities to discuss course work with professors outside of class. Overall satisfaction with college has increased from 74 percent in the late 1960s to approximately 87 percent of college students at the beginning of this decade.

It is interesting to note that overall satisfaction remains high, even though student retention has changed over the years. Table 6 shows the proportion of three undergraduate student cohorts who were retained at the college they originally entered using two different retention rates. These data clearly show a decreasing proportion of each cohort that have obtained a degree in four years. At the same time, a higher proportion of each cohort persists through four years, indicating that students are simply taking longer to graduate than earlier cohorts. There is perhaps no single explanation for why students are taking longer to graduate. Students are now faced with additional financial pressures—financial aid has shifted from grants to loans, and to avoid excessive debt, more students are working and attending college part-time.[18] In addition, the anecdotal evidence suggests that some students are finding it hard to enroll in required courses at many large institutions, while others may be delaying their completion by taking advantage of study abroad programs or other opportunities that broaden their experiences but that lengthen the amount of time it takes to earn a degree.

Student retention will remain an important area of institutional accountability, and we can expect that more institutions will begin to follow closely

Table 6

Trends in Undergraduate Retention Rates

Undergraduate Cohort	Obtained a Bachelor's degree	Obtained a Bachelor's degree or completed four years
1966–1970	47	59
1978–1982	43	56
1987–1991	40	56

SOURCE: 1966–70 data are from Astin, 1971; 1978–82 data are from Green, Astin, Korn, and McNamara, 1983; 1987–91 data are based on unpublished tabulations, Higher Education Research Institute, UCLA.

the progress of students and make efforts to improve their college experiences. It is clear that trends in student graduation rates have redefined persistence in such a way that we must monitor persistence from year to year and examine degree attainment rates over a longer time span. Six years has become the new guideline established by NCAA Division I institutions that many agree is more accurate that the four-year retention rate. Even so, only 53 percent of 1984 first-time, full-time students graduated in six years from their college.[19] Administrators, legislators, and the general public are becoming increasingly concerned about institutional retention rates while new federal regulations require that institutions report these rates.

The Complexity of the Student Role

Changes in the composition of the undergraduate student body in American higher education force us to reconceptualize our notions of typical college students, as well as their potential influence on institutions and society at large. Our examination of the trends across generations of college students has allowed us to adopt a more complex view of the role of students in American higher education. When we think of students and change, we naturally think of the ways institutions influence students: students are supposed to be influenced by the educational programs in which they participate. However, the reverse is also true: many institutions undergo significant change in their recruitment strategies, services, and curricula as the constituencies they serve change. The relationship between students and the college environment is a dynamic one that is also influenced by larger social forces in our society. The value of adopting an ecological perspective is reflected in the changing demography of higher education, trends in student political preferences and academic interests, and significant changes in aspects of the college experience we have reviewed.

Changes in the composition of students in higher education requires that we reconceptualize our notions of typical college students, and the influence they have on institutions. Service to special populations has become a central mission of some colleges, while changes in the type of the students attending traditional four-year institutions reflect new needs and create new demands for institutional change. It is important to note that not all student-originated change is a direct result of student protests and other forms of political action. In fact, a tremendous amount of student-originated change arises as a result of natural institutional responses to student needs. Although many of these changes represent institutional responses to recognized problems and come about with pressures from external constituencies (e.g., parents, alumni, taxpayers, legislators, peer institutions), they represent an attempt on the part of institutions to improve aspects of the educational process for students. Concern about student retention offers a prime example. Institutional efforts to improve re-tention rates have led to the creation of remedial programs in response to shifts in student preparation, the establishment of co-curricular programming to make the social environment more conducive for all students, and the im-provement of academic counseling and opportunities for student-faculty contact.

Active attempts by students to change institutions through protest, and other forms of direct action, tend to receive the most attention. Relatively recent examples of activism include student efforts to institutionalize ethnic studies and multicultural centers, prevent tuition increases, and urge institutions to develop proactive responses to racist/sexist situations on campus.[20] Such issues are especially important to the increased numbers of minorities, women, and students of diverse economic backgrounds on college campuses. In many cases, student protest has served as the impetus for institutional self-examination and the adoption of new institutional policy. Given the increasing amount of disaffection with traditional political methods among college students, and the numbers of entering students who report participating in demonstrations, we can expect to see continued protest activity when institutions are slow to respond to student needs or refuse to assume a leadership role in addressing matters of social concern.

Students can also actively resist attempts to change institutions, and ad-ministrators may find it particularly difficult to change student social habits at institutions with strong student cultures. The trends in college student ex-periences show that drinking has increased, even though new national policies designed to decrease alcohol use have been implemented. Institutional efforts designed to eliminate hazing and racist or sexist games in fraternities have also met with varied success. While the roots of this resistance may be based both in politics and in popular youth culture, it is clear that institutional rules and regulations cannot guarantee success in changing student behavior regardless of the amount of input students have in developing such rules and regulations.

Finally, there are many areas that constitute problems for institutions simply because students have their own ideas and preferences. Perhaps the most troubling information we presented has to do with the future talent pool of students in specific fields. How can institutions influence students to pursue careers that will be vital for our nation in the future? At some level students are attuned to job market opportunities, but their goals may not be synchronized with the nation's changing economic future: by the time that students graduate from college with specific training, the availability of jobs in certain fields may have disappeared. The increasing rapidity with which the economy has been changing suggests that the extended length of an undergraduate education will plague students seeking employment in a variety of fields where there is an unstable pattern of job growth.

Although we have a tendency to think of students in one of several unidimensional ways, a more complete view is one in which the relationship between students and the college environment is seen as both reciprocal and dynamic. Adopting this ecological perspective requires that we rethink the nature of students' role in relation to institutions and the wider society. Students have proactively and subtly induced institutional and social change throughout history and will continue to do so in the future. These changes, in turn, have altered the nature of the student experience and the impact college has on students. We hope that those interested in the relationship between higher education and American society will begin to recognize these interconnections and begin to view the role of college students in different and more complex ways.

Notes

1. T. Dary Erwin, *Assessing Student Learning and Development: A Guide to the Principles, Goals, and Methods of Determining Outcomes* (San Francisco: Jossey-Bass, 1991); Ernest T. Pascarella and Patrick T. Terenzini, *How College Affects Students* (San Francisco: Jossey-Bass, 1991).

2. Philip G. Altbach, "Students: Interests, Culture, and Activism," in *Higher Learning in America, 1980–2000*, ed. Arthur Levine (Baltimore: Johns Hopkins University Press, 1993).

3. Duane F. Alwin, Ronald L. Cohen, and Theodore M. Newcomb, *Political Attitudes Over the Life Span: The Bennington Women after Fifty Years* (Madison: Univewrsity of Wisconsin Press, 1991), p. 252; Urie Bronfenbrenner, *The Ecology of Human Development: Experiments by Nature and Design* (Cambridge: Harvard University Press, 1979).

4. These and other tabular data on entering college students come primarily from the Cooperative Institutional Research Program (CIRP) coordinated by the Higher Education Research Institue at UCLA. The CIRP data are based on responses from an annual survey of some 250,000 students entering about 600 colleges and universities nationwide. Since the CIRP focuses primarily on the what might be considered "traditional" students, the patterns discussed are probably conservative estimates of the larger trends within American higher education.

5. College Board, *Trends in Student Aid: 1980 to 1989* (New York: College Board, 1989).

6. Deborah Carter and Reginald Wilson, *Minorities in Higher Education: Tenth Annual Status Report* (Washington, D.C.: American Council on Education, Office of Minority Concerns: 1992).

7. Statistics based on calculations of college enrollment by racial and ethnic group for 1990 from *The Chronicle of Higher Education Almanac* (August 26, 1992).

8. Over the past two decades, twenty-six tribal colleges have been established and have steadily increased their enrollments (see Eileen M. O'Brien, *American Indians in Higher Education*, ACE Research Brief Series, Washington, D.C.: American Council on Education, 1992). Women's colleges and historically black institutions have strengthened their position in terms of attaining a relatively stable and increasing student enrollment in the last ten years (Carter & Wilson, 1992; see also Judith Touchton & Lynne Davis, *Factbook on Women in Higher Education*, New York: ACE/Macmillan, 1991). Hispanic-serving institutions are defined by the Hispanic Association of Colleges and Universities (HACU) as institutions that meet a Hispanic enrollment minimum of 25 percent. An increasing number of institutions are expected to become Hispanic-serving toward the end of this decade (Hispanic Association of Colleges and Universities, *Annual Report*. San Antonio, TX: HACU, 1990).

9. For an overview of institutional responses and problems related to diverse student populations see Daryl Smith, *The Challenge of Diversity Involvement or Alienation in the Academy* [ASHE-ERIC Higher Education Report no. 5] (Washington, D.C.: George Washington University, 1989), and Carol Pearson, Donna L. Shavlik, and Judith G. Touchton, eds., *Educating the Majority: Women Challenge Tradition in Higher Education* (New York: ACE/Macmillan, 1989).

10. Margaret L. Anderson, "Changing the Curriculum in Higher Education," in *Reconstructing the Academy: Women's Education and Women's Studies*, ed. Elizabeth Minnich, Jean O'Barr, and Rachel Rosenfled (Chicago: University of Chicago, 1988).

11. Sylvia Hurtado, "The Institutional Climate for Talented Latino Students," *Research in Higher Education* 35, no. 4 (1994, in press).

12. Susan Hardy Aiken, Karen Anderson, Myra Dinnerstein, Judy Lensink, and Patricia MacCorquodale, "Trying Transformations: Curriculum Integration and the Problem of Resistance," in *Reconstructing the Academy: Women's Education and Women's Studies*.

13. See for example Alexander W. Astin, *What Matters in College: Four Critical Years Revisited* (San Francisco: Jossey-Bass, 1993).

14. Eric L. Dey, Alexander W. Astin, and William S. Korn, *The American Freshman: Twenty-Five-Year Trends* (Los Angeles: Higher Education Research Institute, UCLA, 1991).

15. Surveys of entering college students reveal a steady increase in the percentage of students who report that they participated in some sort of volunteer work before college and are interested in continuing this activity during college; see Eric L. Dey, Alexander W. Astin, William S. Korn, and Ellyne R. Riggs, *The American Freshman: National Norms for Fall 1992* (Los Angeles: Higher Education Research Institute, UCLA, 1992).

16. David W. Breneman, "Liberal Arts Colleges: What Price Survival?," in *Higher Learning in America, 1980–2000*.

17. Higher Education Research Institute, *The American College Student: National Norms for 1987 and 1989 College Freshmen* (Los Angeles: Higher Education Research Institute, UCLA, 1992).

18. College Board, *Trends in Student Aid: 1980 to 1980* (New York: College Board, 1989); Alexander W. Astin, Eric L. Dey, William S. Korn, and Ellyne R. Riggs, *The American Freshman: National Norms for Fall 1991* (Los Angeles: Higher Education Research Institute, UCLA, 1991).

19. *The Chronicle of Higher Education* (July 15, 1992).

20. Tony Vellela, *New Voices: Student Activism in the '80s and '90s* (Boston: South End Press, 1988).

12

Comparative Reflections on Leadership in Higher Education*
Martin Trow

I

In this chapter I want, first, to explore in somewhat general terms what we mean by "leadership" in universities, what its major dimensions may be; second, to contrast the American university presidency with its counterparts in other European countries; and third, to sketch the historical sources of the unique role of the university president that we have developed in America.

Finally, I will try to identify some of the structures and institutional mechanisms through which the American university president does in fact take initiatives, deploy resources, and exercise leadership. (The male pronoun will here be used conventionally to refer to both sexes.) One caveat: many of these observations about the presidency of American universities also apply to four-year colleges, and particularly to the best of them. But this chapter will focus on the role of the presidency as it can be seen in the great American research universities, perhaps thirty or so in all. Moreover, when I refer to university "presidents," I will be speaking mainly about chief campus officers, though in some multi-campus universities—for example, those in Illinois and California—the chief campus officer is called "Chancellor." The special problems of the heads of multi-campus systems deserve a lecture, or a library, of their own.[1]

Leadership in higher education in large part is the taking of effective action to shape the character and direction of a college or university, presumably for the better. That leadership shows itself chiefly along symbolic, political, managerial, and academic dimensions. *Symbolic* leadership is the ability

---

*This chapter is a revision of the Ninth David D. Henry Lecture, University of Illinois at Urbana-Champaign, October 1984.

to express, to project, indeed to seem to embody, the character of the institu-tion, its central goals and values, in a powerful way. Internally, leadership of that kind serves to explain and justify the institution and its decisions to participants by linking its organization and processes to the larger purposes of teaching and learning in ways that strengthen their motivation and morale. Externally, a leader's ability to articulate the nature and purposes of the institution effectively helps to shape its image, affecting its capacity to gain support from its environment and to recruit able staff and students.[2] *Political* leadership refers to an ability to resolve the conflicting demands and pressures of many con-stituencies, internal and external, and in gaining their support for the institution's goals and purposes, as they are defined. *Managerial* leadership is the familiar capacity to direct and coordinate the various support activities of the institution; this includes good judgment in the selection of staff, the ability to develop and manage a budget, to plan for the future, and to build and maintain a plant. *Academic* leadership shows itself, among other ways, as the ability to recognize excellence in teaching, learning, and research; in knowing where and how to intervene to strengthen academic structures; in the choice of able academic administrators; and in support for the latter in their efforts to recruit and advance talented teachers and scholars.

Any particular university president need not excel personally in all these dimensions of his office; leaders vary in how their talents and energies are distributed among these facets of academic life. Some are largely "external presidents," presenting the image of the institution to its external constituen-cies and seeking their support, while giving to a provost or dean the main responsibility for academic affairs and to a vice-president for administration the chief responsibility for internal management. Other presidents spend more of their time and attention on internal matters.

But however a leader fills the several dimensions of the role—in the definition of its character and purpose, in its quest for resources, in the management of its organization, or in the pursuit of ever higher levels of academic excellence—effective action in all areas requires that the president have the legal authority and resources to act, to choose among alternatives, even to create alternatives, in short, to exercise discretion. Without that discretion and the authority and resources behind it, a president or chancellor cannot exercise leadership, whatever his personal qualities.

So a discussion of leadership in American higher education must involve, first, a comparison of the potential for leadership—the power and opportunities for discretionary decisions and action—of American college and university presidents as compared with their counterparts abroad; second, some suggestions as to why those differences exist—an historical reference that allows us to see more clearly how and why our institutions and their presidents are as they are; and third, a somewhat closer examination of how American college and university presidents exercise power, and a look at some of the institutional characteristics and mechanisms that allow them to take initiatives.

II

The American university presidency in recent years has received bad press. Some of the most influential theorists about the organization and governance of higher education argue that colleges and universities are really ungovernable, and that leadership in them is impossible. James March in his various writings, alone and with collaborators, has stressed the sheer chaos and unmanageability of organizations within higher education, institutions characterized by "garbage-can decision processes," in which problems are more often evaded than solved. Colleges and universities, in his view, are prototypical "organized anarchies," characterized by ambiguous goals, unclear technology, and fluid participation.[3] Since their goals are ambiguous, nobody is sure where the organization is going or how it will get there. Decisions are often by-products of activity that is unintended and unplanned. They are not so much "made" as they "happen"—they are events in which problems, choices and decision-makers happen to coalesce to form temporary solutions. From this point of view, "an organization is a collection of choices looking for problems, issues and feelings looking for decision situations in which they might be aired, solutions looking for issues to which they might be the answer, and decision-makers looking for work."[4] Such inept, leaderless organizations must be unable to initiate anything or to innovate. As Cohen and March put it somewhat epigrammatically, "anything that requires the coordinated effort of the organization to start is unlikely to be started. Anything that requires a coordinated effort of the organization in order to be stopped is unlikely to be stopped."[5] And if the university cannot be led or moved, then consistently enough in their view,

> the presidency is an illusion. Important aspects of the role seem to disappear on close examination. In particular, decision making in the university seems to result extensively from a process that decouples problems and choices and makes the president's role more commonly sporadic and symbolic than significant.[6]

Similarly, George Keller cites Cohen, et al., approvingly when he says that "Universities love to explore process and methodology but hate to make decisions. . . . Decisions in a university often get made randomly—by deans, legislators, a financial officer, the president."[7]

But oddly enough, all of Keller's illustrative cases show just the contrary, whether he is talking about planning for cuts at the University of California; the survival of a private college in Maryland; responses to cuts at the University of Minnesota; Carnegie-Mellon; or Teachers College, Columbia. These institutions are not exceptions. While each of course is unique, with its own configuration of problems and leaders, the capacity of American colleges and universities to adapt to new circumstances, whether a demographic crisis, budget cuts, cultural and religious change, or technological explosions, is on the whole astonishing; and most of the gloomiest prophecies in recent decades have not been fulfilled. To take only one example: for at least a decade we have been told that starting in 1979 enrollments in American colleges and universities would begin to decline, impelled inexorably by a decline in the size of the college-age cohorts, a decline nationally of some 23 percent between 1979 and 1992 when these cohorts would be at their lowest levels. And according to these forecasts, the population of college-age youth would not start to grow again until perhaps 1995. It is true that the number of high school graduates peaked in 1979 as predicted; by 1984 the size of the graduating class had already fallen some 13 percent below the 1979 peak. But to almost everyone's surprise, enrollments in colleges and universities nationally did not fall; on the contrary, they actually grew by 6 percent between 1979 and 1984 overall during this time of shrinking college-age cohorts.[8]

Of course there are variations by region and by type of institution. But nevertheless, American colleges and universities have shown a remarkable capacity to respond both to recession and to declining age cohorts, and have continued to attract growing numbers. I would suggest that much of this capacity to respond creatively and successfully to difficult, and in some cases to life-threatening, circumstances must be attributed to the ability of institutional leaders to innovate, to motivate, and above all to lead. Our task is to learn more about the nature of that effective and creative leadership and how it works, rather than to assert in the face of much contrary evidence that it is impossible.

The thoughtful 1984 report of the Commission on Strengthening Presidential Leadership,[9] is also rather gloomy about the state of the college and university presidency. In the course of giving sound advice to institutions, presidents, and governing boards, the report identifies and discusses some recent and current developments that the commission believes have made the college and university presidency less attractive now to able people than it was formerly. Its authors are especially concerned with the growing constraints on the presidency ("more barbed wire around smaller corrals," as one of their informants put it). Oddly enough, though they reach the somber conclusion that "the American college and university presidency is in trouble," they note that "about one-fourth of all presidents [whom they interviewed] are quite satisfied with their situations (some are even euphoric); about one-half are clearly more satisfied than dissatisfied most of the time; and about one-fourth are dissatisfied—some even in despair."[10] But upon reading this report one is struck by the fact that many of the problems that university presidents face, including some of those that have grown in difficulty recently, arise out of the very strength and centrality of the role, a role that has no real counterpart outside the United States.

III

However constrained American college and university presidents may seem to observers, however weak and ineffective they may appear to students of university organization, they look very strong by contrast with the power and influence of their "counterparts" abroad. The question may be raised as to whether they *have* any true counterparts abroad. Certainly in any genuine sense they do not. The weakness of the "chief campus officer" (the rectors, vice-chancellors, or presidents) of European institutions of higher education, arises out of the history and development of those universities. They arose, as we know, initially as guilds of masters, in some places with important initiatives from students. European universities retained their character as corporate bodies of academics that in modern times came to be regulated, funded, and in varying degrees governed by agencies of the state. The basic power relationship in European higher education has been between the guild of academics and its chairman (the rector) on one side and the relevant church authorities or governmental ministries on the other. Their discussions have centered on the issues of autonomy and support. The leading university academic officer, whether he is called rector, vice-chancellor or president, was and still is largely a chairman of the corporate body, and on the continent and in the British ancient universities was until recently elected by the guild from among its own members. On the continent, he is still elected, though now from a wider and more politicized electorate.

Since the Second World War there has been much talk in European academic circles about the desirability of strenghtening the hand of the chief officer, making him more like his American counterparts, and indeed sometimes an effort has been made to do so merely by changing his name from "rector" to "president." But I do not think that European countries or institutions have actually gone very far in that direction, beyond the change of name. The broad reforms of higher education introduced since 1968 in almost all Euroopean countries have had the effect less of strengthening the president or rector than of weakening the professoriate, "democratizing" governance internally by giving more power and influence to the nonprofessional staff and to students; and externally, by increasing the influence of politicians, civil servants, and organized economic interest groups on institutional and regional governing boards. The literature on these reforms and reorganizations is not about more powerful institutional leadership, but about more and mroe complex internal group politics, with central government trying to retain and extend its influence on the nature and direction of the institutions in the face of their claims to traditional autonomies and their newly expanded participatory democracy.[11]

The comparative perspective on American higher education and its leadership is one of American exceptionalism, of a sharp contrast between the role of institutional leadership here as compared with that in almost every other modern society, as well as one of quite astonishing success. We can understand better the highly particularized character of the American college and university presidency if we look at it in historical perspective. The strength of the university presidency in this country, as compared with its overseas counterparts, arose out of the weakness of the academic profession in America throughout most of our history in conjunction with the tradition of noninvolvement by the federal government in education generally, and in higher education particularly.

These two factors—the weak academic guild and weak central government—are also related to the strength of lay boards as the chief governing bodies of colleges and universities. The lay board originated at Harvard, the first American university. The founders of Harvard, community leaders most of whom had studied at the University of Cambridge, had intended to carry on the English tradition of resident faculty control. The senior academic members of the Oxford and Cambridge colleges, the "dons," comprised then, as now, a corporate body that governed each of the constituent colleges comprising those ancient universities. But in the colonial United States there simply were no scholars already in residence. Harvard had to be founded and not just developed. Without a body of scholars to be brought together who could govern themselves, the laymen who created the institution had to find someone to take responsibility for the operation of the infant university, and that person was the president. He was in fact the only professor to begin with, and he both governed and carried a major part of instruction himself, with some younger men to help him. And this pattern lasted for quite a long time in each new institution—long enough to set governing patterns throughout our history. Harvard was established for more than eighty-five years, Yale for some fifty, before either had another professor to stand alongside its president. For a very long time, both before and after the American Revolution, many colleges and universities relied wholly on the college president and a few tutors who would serve for a few years and then go on to another career.[12]

To this set of historical facts we may attribute the singular role of the college and university president in American higher education. He combined in himself the academic role with the administration of the institution. The members of the lay governing boards from the very beginning have had other things to do, and have delegated very large powers to the president whom they appointed, a president who did not until this century have to deal with a large or powerful body of academic peers. The American college and university president still holds his office wholly at the pleasure of the external board that appoints him. Most of the rest of the academic staff have tenure in their jobs. But the president of a college or university never has tenure, at least not as president (though he may return to a professorship if he has such an appointment in the institution). That lack of tenure in office partly accounts for the broad power the board delegates to him; they can always take it back, and often do.

For a long time in American history there were very few who made academic life a career; as long as that was true there was no real challenge to the authority of the president so long as he had the support of the lay board that governed the institution. This of course is quite unlike arrangements in most other countries. European universities, as we know, arose out of guilds, the corporations of doctors and masters and other learned men in Paris, Bologna, and elsewhere. And where they arose differently, as in the modern universities, the academics in their faculties claimed the same powers as their counterparts in the ancient universities. In America, by contrast, colleges and universities were created by a lay board and a president. This has had an enormous impact on the development of our institutions.

The near absolute authority of the American college president has been lost in most of our universities over time, especially with the rise of the research university and the emergence of a genuine academic profession in the last decade of the nineteenth century. In this century, and especially in the stronger universities, a great deal of autonomy over academic affairs has been delegated to the faculty and its senates. But the American college or university president remains far more powerful than his counterparts in European institutions, whose formal authority is shared with the professoriate, the junior staff, government ministries, advisory boards, student organizations, and trade unions. The European rector or vice-chancellor really is a political man, a power broker, a negotiator, a seeker for compromise without much power or authority of his own.

IV

The role of the faculty in the governance of the leading colleges and universities in the United States is substantial and important, but it is as much a source of presidential power as a limitation on it. The two generations of presidential giants—White at Cornell, Eliot at Harvard, Angell at Michigan, Gilman at Hopkins, Harper at Chicago, Van Hise at Wisconsin, Jordan at Stanford, Wheeler at California, among others—the men who governed the great American universities between the Civil War and the First World War, essentially created the American academic profession, a development that coincided with the emergence and growth of the great research universities. Those creative presidents flourished, however, before their universities had large numbers of specialized scholars and scientists with high prestige in American society as well as national and international reputations in their disciplines. Those presidents recruited distinguished scholars and scientists, paid them decent salaries, rewarded their scholarship and research, and thus created the faculty of the modern research university, a body of men and women who could meet them, collectively at least, as equals. The American academic profession and its instruments—the senates on campus and the American Association of University Professors (AAUP) and various disciplinary associations nationally—were the institutionalized expression or reflection of those scholars and scientists brought together in the new research universities by this generation of great university presidents. It was the growth of that body of academics, increasingly aware of their collective importance to the university and to its supporters and constituents outside the university, that gave rise to the modern university faculty, determined to be treated as members and not merely as employees of the university. They thus came to be included in the governance of the universities, in a role that stressed their right to be consulted on matters of importance to them.

In the leading universities, both public and private—though matters are quite different in the second- and third-tier universities—what has evolved is a system of shared governance, marked by a degree of cooperation and mutual trust that has survived the political stresses of the 1960s, the demands for greater accountability from state governments of the 1970s, the growth of federal law and regulation, the consequent elabortion and formalization of procedures, record-keeping and reporting, and the explosion of litigation against the university over the past two decades. Despite all of these forces and the internal stresses they have engendered, academic senates and committees in the leading universities still gain the willing and largely unrewarded participation of active and leading scholars and scientists in the process of governance by consultation. The nature of this shared governance by consultation is extremely complicated and subtle, never adequately captured in the description of the formal arrangements that differ on every campus. Moreover, the power of the faculty varies sharply depending on the status of the university and of its faculty.

It is sometimes suggested that a strong academic senate reduces the power of the president or chancellor. I believe, on the contrary, that a strong senate enhances that power. An academic senate is, above all, an instrument for the defense of academic and scholarly standards in the face of all the other pressures and demands on the university and on its president. Senates function on the whole through committees; committees are, or can be, excellent bodies for articulating and applying academic values to a variety of conditions and issues that arise. Though committees are splendid at saying no, they are poor instruments for taking initiatives or implementing them. By being consulted routinely on a wide variety of initiatives emanating from the office of the president, the senate may in fact give wise and useful advice. But above all, it makes itself and faculty sentiments felt by giving or withholding its approval and legitimacy to presidential initiatives. Without that consultation and support, the relation of president and faculty would be largely adversarial—which is what we often see where the senate has been replaced by a faculty union, or where the faculty and president are deeply at odds. And there the power of the president is certainly diminished.

Of course, there are frictions between senate and president; the relationship at its best is marked, in Jacques Barzun's words, by "the good steady friction that shows the wheels are gripping." In such a happy relationship, faculty members recognize that just as the effectiveness of the president depends in large part on a strong senate, so also does the strength of the senate depend on a strong president. It is *not* a zero sum game. For much of the senate's power is exercised through its advice to and influence on the president: where *he* has little power, *they* have little power. Effective power then lies outside the institution altogether, in the hands of politicians or ministries, as in European nations or some American states.

V

I have suggested that on historical and comparative grounds that the president of a leading American college or university can exercise leadership: symbolic, political, intellectual, and administrative. But what are his resources for the exercise of leadership, especially when looked at in a comparative perspective? What I will say here is familiar to all, and yet is often dismissed or discounted by commentators except when they are actually describing specific leaders and policies.

First, a president has substantial control over the budget of his institution and its allocation, even though his discretion is constrained by the very large fraction of the budget that is committed to tenured faculty salaries and to support services that must be funded if the institution is to continue functioning. In a public university, he usually works with a block grant; thus he can view the budget as a whole and make internal adjustments subject to the above constraints. By contrast, most European institutions are funded by central state authorities on what is closer to a line item budget—sums are earmarked for particular chairpersons and the support staff around them, and to particular services, such as a library. The rector or president ordinarily has little power over these internal allocations of funds. Moreover, in the United States it is now widespread practice, if not quite universal, that faculty vacancies resulting from death or retirement revert to the president's office and are not the property of the departments where the vacancy occurred. This reversion of resources permits the president and his associates over time to modify the internal distribution of faculty places in response to changing student demand or market demand, to developments in the disciplines themselves, or to his own ideas about the right mix of fields and subjects.

Academic autonomy is related, if not perfectly, to the multiplicity of funding sources.[13] Here again, by contrast with their European counterparts, American universities are funded in a variety of ways, which in itself gives presidents a certain power to bargain from strength in the face of demands from one or another funding source. Even such public universities as the University of California are not state-supported so much as "state-aided." The University of California gets about 40 percent of its current operating budget from state sources; about 15 percent from federal grants and contracts; about 13 percent from fees, tuition, gifts and endowment; and about 30 percent from various enterprises such as teaching hospitals, educational extension, and sales of educational services.[14]

But in addition to the sheer multiplicity of sources, some of them are more discretionary than others. The use of unearmarked private contributions, research overhead funds, some of the return on the endowment, is largely at the discretion of the president or chancellor, though over time, of course, those discretionary funds become encumbered by expectations if not by formal programmatic commitments. Programs and people supported by such discretionary funds come to expect that they will continue to be supported. But presidents and their staffs can vary the levels of those commitments, especially if they do so incrementally, and thus maintain a genuine degree of discretionary power over their allocations.

Even where discretion is not total, it may be large within a category. For example, "student services" is a very broad rubric indeed, and gives a president equally broad discretion for shaping the mix of such services as between a learning center, medical services, counseling services, intramural athletics, recruitment and admissions, and various forms of remedial education and outreach to the secondary school system, among others. The very size of student support services in American universities, as compared with those overseas, increases the power of presidents; where academic staff is largely tenured, and their programs and departments difficult to modify except slowly and incrementally, the president has far greater (though never total) freedom to restructure support services whose staff members are not tenured (though increasingly unionized). These large support staffs report to someone directly in the president's office, and they constitute a substantial body of resources and people whom the president can draw on in support of his own priorities, again within certain political, legal, and normative constraints. A large staff provides the resources to put behind the president's own ideas about a stronger development office, or larger affirmative action programs, or whatever it is he may think important.

But the discretionary resources built into student services are only part of the staff resources available to American university presidents. In the United States, the great authority of lay governing boards, much of it delegated to the president, together with the relatively smaller role of central government, ensured that as the public universities grew and needed larger administrative staffs, those staffs would be extensions of the president's office rather than civil servants responsible to a faculty body or to state authorities. As a result, the strong president, supported by his own large administrative staff, has been able to preserve much autonomy and power inside the university. Having his own internal staff allows the college or university president to deal with state authorities with equal skill and expertise, rather than as a scholarly amateur against a body of professional planners and managers. Several points need to be made about this large internal staff:

Many staff people (and most of those at the upper levels) owe their appointments to the president they serve, and hold those appointments at his discretion. In some institutions there are "untouchables" on the staff, who have independent ties to the board or powerful alumni; these sometimes constitute a problem for new presidents.[15] But on the whole, few members of the administrative staff have any formal or informal security of employment, and even they owe their advancement, and sometimes their jobs in periods of contraction, to the sitting president. They are for the most part his employees, in a part of the university that much more closely resembles the hierarchical structures of bureaucracies than the collegial structures of departments and research centers. Presidential leadership is often found in programs that rest largely on this administrative staff rather than on the reshaping of the academic programs directly; and that, I think, is because that is where so many of his discretionary resources lie.

These support staffs under the president's direction and leadership can also develop programs that further increase his discretion. For example, strengthening a development office, increasing the effectiveness of market research and student recruitment, writing better proposals for government or foundation grants, all increase the discretion of top administrators. These activities and funds can provide the staff support for new academic programs, new links to secondary schools, remedial courses, creative connections with local industry, and other colleges and universities. They give the president the needed resources to create priorities, to be an entrepreneur and to take advantage of opportunities as they arise.

In the United States the president of a college or university is the link between "the administration" and its support services on the one hand, and the faculty and its programs of teaching, learning, and research on the other. And here again the American college and university differs fundamentally from its overseas counterparts. Almost everywhere else, alongside the rector or president stands a registrar, a "curator," an administrative officer who is not appointed by the president, and who is not really responsible to him but is appointed by the lay governing council or by a government ministry. In the United Kingdom, a vice-chancellor plays a large part in the appointment of the registrar, but the appointment is rather like a senior civil service post, and ordinarily continues beyond the term of any sitting vice-chancellor. And that sharp separation of the academic (and symbolic) leadership from the day-to-day management and administration of the institution enormously reduces the authority and discretion of the chief campus officer of European universities, as compared with his American counterparts.

In addition to the support staff I have spoken of, the American college or university president also appoints the chief academic officers; the vice-president for academic affairs, the provost, the deans, and through them the department chairmen, who are both heads of their departments and administrative officers. The president appoints them, and he can replace them. Of course he cannot do so frivolously or too often without loss of respect and credibility. Nevertheless, the fact that the president appoints the senior academic administrators, unlike his counterparts overseas (and the British case is intermediate in this regard), gives him a degree of leverage over changes in the academic program: for example, the opportunity to influence the balance of subjects, the sub-disciplines represented, and above all the quality and character of new appointments.

Another consequence of the fact that the president appoints his senior administrative colleagues, his cabinet so to speak, is that he largely defines their areas of authority and responsibility; they are not inherent in the job or office, or in fixed regulations of the institution or ministry. University presidents in the United States (unlike their European counterparts) can and indeed often do change the administrative structures under them in the service of their own purposes and conceptions of the interests of the institution. And that restructuring—ordinarily at the beginning or early in the tenure of a president—may be one of his most creative acts. Moreover, presidents can modify the charge and scope of responsibility of any given academic administrator in response to the interests, talents, and capacities of the individual whom they appoint to a post, as well as to new problems and opportunities that develop around it. In addition, leaders can create decision-making structures *ad hoc,* in response to different issues that arise.

If we ask what is the decision-making process at a college or university, we have to answer, "it depends on the issue." Different people and interests are brought together to solve or address different problems. But who is brought together to address what problems is determined chiefly by the president, and that indeed is an important area for the exercise of his discretion and the demonstration of his capacity for leadership. Should a senior academic officer be brought into a discussion of changes in admission procedures, which often conceal changes in academic standards? Should faculty members or academic senate committees be involved in decisions about the athletic program? Should a university financial officer be involved in discussions about a change in the requirements for graduation? What interests, what expertise, what individuals and perspectives should be brought together to deal with a particular problem; at what point will a greater diversity of perspectives not improve and inform a decision, but paralyze it? Those are among the most consequential judgments and decisions that a college or university president makes.

There is another mechanism of presidential power and initiative, one that lies directly at the heart of the academic enterprise, but which I think has not been adequately studied or discussed by students of American college and university life, and that is the power of a president to take a department or program "into receivership." Various observers have emphasized that colleges and universities are organizationally "bottom-heavy," in that expertise, both with respect to teaching and research, is located among the faculty members and in the departments. This is certainly true, and under ordinary conditions college and university presidents are wise not to interfere in the private life of departments, in what and how they teach, what they study, who they appoint, and who they promote. The autonomy of departments, rooted in their expertise, is an important constraint on the power of administrators, including presidents.

But in American colleges and universities, that autonomy can be overridden and set aside when something goes wrong: when, for example, factional fights within a department make it ungovernable, or prevent new appointments from being made, or block all promotions; or other tendencies and events lead to a decline in the unit's standing in the periodic national ranking of departments, or a fall-off in its external research support, or a degree of politicization that affects the quality of instruction, or a loss in the department's ability to attract able students or junior staff. These are among the reasons that lead presidents to take departments into receivership. When they do, they take the government and management of the unit out of the hands of the department members themselves, and of their chairman, and put it in the hands of others, with a clear understanding on how to proceed and what to do. The caretaker may be a person from another related department, or from the same discipline in another university, or even a committee of leading scientists and scholars from within the same institution. In my own university, this has happened to five or six departments over the past decade, including most recently to all of the biological sciences in some twenty-five departments and schools.[16]

The surprising thing is that when a department is "put into receivership," there is remarkably little resistance or opposition within the faculty—probably because it happens rarely enough and in extreme cases, so that there is a general consensus that something really has gone wrong. That is to say, it can be treated as an exceptional case, and the treatment of that case is not going to be an attack on the ordinary processes of academic governance in which the faculty plays a major role. Something has gone wrong, and the president or his senior advisers intervene to help put it right, so that the action is in the service of the fundamental values of the faculty anyway. It does not happen very often, but it is extremely important that it can, and there are times when departments know "we can't let things go on like this or they will come and take us over." Like all drastic sanctions, the power to put departments into receivership is a powerful threat as well as an act, and affects behavior even when it is not employed.

Control over the budget and especially over the discretionary resources in "student services"; the relatively large staff appointed by and responsible to the president; his power to set the institution's priorities, define problems, and specify who is to solve them; his power to take departments into receivership—these are some of the organizational resources and mechanisms for intervention and change by which presidential leadership can be exercised in American research universities.

VI

To sum up, this chapter is an effort to get beyond the descriptions of universities as "organized anarchies" engaged in "garbage-can processes of decision making." I believe those conceptions of the university stand in the way of a clearer description and understanding of what leadership in higher education consists of and how it functions. But if they are not true, if indeed the presidency of great research universities is as strong and effective as I claim, why has it had such bad press in recent years; why is it seen as weak, ineffective, and unattractive? Some speculations, if not explanations, may be helpful here.

First, much of the gloomiest writing about university leadership addresses the situation of weaker second- and third-rank institutions. In the American system, marked by a very high level of competitiveness among institutions for students, for faculty, for resources, for prestige and rank, the power of the leading universities as models, both as organizations and as normative communities, is very great. All universities judge themselves by the standards and criteria of the leading universities, and share their high expectations regarding research, graduate work, and institutional autonomy. But those second- and third-ranking institutions do not command the resources of the leading ones: their financial support, both public and private, their libraries and laboratories, their eminent faculties, all the traditions of autonomy that the leading institutions have gained over the years. It may be that the difficulties of university presidents in most institutions commonly arise out of the tension between their high aspirations and inadequate resources, and their resulting sense of relative failure when they compare themselves to Harvard, Stanford, Berkeley, Michigan, or Illinois.

In addition to the costs of this kind of "relative deprivation" are the often frustrating experiences of university presidents even in the leading institutions. The corral does sometimes seem smaller, the barbed wire higher than it was, or at least as it is remembered.[17] It may be that the presidency of a research university is a more effective than attractive position. In one of the most poignant commentaries on the role, the report of the Commission on Presidential Leadership quotes one president as follows:

> On any issue I will enjoy an incredibly high 90 to 95 percent of faculty support. Even so, five percent are dissatisfied with my decision, and they remember. On the next issue, I'll again enjoy the same 90 to 95 percent support, but the five to ten percent of dissenters will be a different group, and they, too, will remember. Eventually one manages to make at least one decision against the convictions of virtually every member of the faculty. By recognizing and providing an outlet for such accumulated discontent, the formal evaluation process merely increases the speed by which courageous decision makers are turned over. This does nothing for attracting the best people into the jobs.[18]

This "accumulation of discontent" threatens to make the aggregate of many small successes into one big failure. And the inexorable erosion of support that this process describes casts its pall over both the role and the office.

Moreover, university presidents are most likely to underplay their power and effectiveness, and exaggerate the importance of the process of "shared governance" of which they are a part, than they are to claim undue credit for their achievements. In this democratic, indeed populist, age, the towering figures of the heroic age of the university presidency would surely find themselves under attack as authoritarian, power-driven, and without a sensitive concern for the interests of their varied constituencies in the university.

One example: Clark Kerr was, as we all know, a very strong chancellor of the University of California, Berkeley, from 1952 to 1958 and an equally strong chancellor of the University of California system from 1958 to 1967. In both roles he had an enormous impact on the institutions that he led— for example, he shaped the quite distinct characteristics of the new campuses of the university that were established during his tenure as president. And yet, in his seminal book, *The Uses of the University,* erhaps the most illuminating essay on the modern research university (and after some nostalgic references to the giants of the past), Kerr observes that in his own time a university president is likely to be "the Captain of the Bureaucracy who is sometimes a galley slave on his own ship."[19] And he quotes Allan Nevins's observations that the type of president required by the new university, the "multiversity" as Kerr called it, "will be a coordinator rather than a creative leader . . . an expert executive, a tactful moderator. . . ." In Kerr's own words, "he is mostly a mediator."[20]

This, I suggest, is at odds with the realities of university leadership both as Clark Kerr employed it and as it now exists. Of course, leadership may be more visible and dramatic during periods of growth and expansion, and not all presidents carry to the role the talents that Kerr did. Of course, coordination and mediation were important parts of the job, both then and now. But boldness, the undertaking of initiatives, the acting by a president on and through the institution in the service of his own conception of its nature and future— in my view, all of that does not have the weight and emphasis in Kerr's analysis of university leadership that it did in his own exercise of leadership. Kerr's analysis reflects his concern (reflected again in the report of the Commission on Strengthening Presidential Leadership that he chaired) regarding the decline of institutional leadership as a result of the growth of countervailing forces and complex power centers within and around the university. I believe his analysis also reflects his sense that modern university leaders, if they are to be effective, must keep a low profile, must appear to be finding "a sense of the meeting," rather than imposing themselves on the institution and taking important initiatives within it. If we compare the modern university president to those of the heroic age, we find today more problems, more restraints, even more resources, more of everything except authority. The exercise of authority is today often "authoritarian," and successful presidents have learned the trick of exercising authority without appearing to do so: to lead while appearing to follow, facilitate, mediate, or coordinate.

Of course the interplay among the characteristics of the person who occupies the office, the role, and the university's institutional environment is tremendously complex, and successful leadership today requires high skills and careful attention to the process of governance. And finally, even when the presidency is successful, expectations rise, troubles multiply and opposition accumulates: it is perhaps inevitably a case of "doing better and feeling worse."

This may be why presidents tend to underplay their own effectiveness. But why do observers and analysts do likewise? I have already set forth some of the reasons, but there is one other, and that is the apparent anarchy of intertwined purposeful policies in universities. I suspect that observers have been looking at the university president's role as if it were a cross-section of a thick cable, made up of many-colored strands or wires, each strand representing another program or activity, and all together in cross-section representing a heterogeneous collection of issues, solutions, and problems, showing little coherence or purpose. But in the research university this model is misleading. For if this rope is cut along the dimension of time, we see that each strand extends backwards and forwards, moving along in its own coherent, purposeful, even rational way, each marked by its own set of purposes that are largely insulated from other strands even as they intertwine.[21] So what appears as a random or haphazard collection of events, problems, evasions, and solutions when viewed in cross section at a given moment, looks more like a set of purposeful programs each being pursued in relative isolation within the boundaries of the same institution when viewed along the dimension of time. And the variety of these programs in their purposes and participants will be greater the more comprehensive and varied the role of the university in society at large.

It is this multiplicity of activities, governed by different norms and purposes in different ways, that defines the comprehensive university. And it is of some interest to consider how these activities, apparently governed by different and even incompatible values, can be pursued on the same campus, under the general authority of the same president. The key lies in the institutional insulations of activities governed by different values, and the ways in which these activities are brought together in the office of the president. One common situation finds presidents serving what appear to be the mutually incompatible values of academic excellence and social equity, the latter taking the form of increased access to the institution of underrepresented groups. In Berkeley currently, the commitment to excellence is represented by a major reform of the biological sciences very much keyed to strengthening modern currents in biology, both in research and teaching. This involved a major intervention by the chancellor with the advice and support of leading biologists on campus, an intervention that required the creation of new institutional forms and the temporary but substantial reduction of the power and autonomy of the existing biological departments to control their own faculty recruitment, graduate training, and the like. At the same time, other units of the chancellor's office were engaged in major efforts to upgrade the secondary education of minority groups in the cities surrounding Berkeley, from which many of its undergraduates are drawn. These activities come together in the office of the chancellor, and only there, although they are carried on quite separately and in many ways are highly insulated from one another. It is doubtful if any of the distinguished biologists involved in the renewal of their discipline at Berkeley know very much about the outreach programs into the Oakland secondary schools, or the outreach staff know anything about developments in the biological sciences on campus. In the particular circumstances of Berkeley at the moment—and I suspect this is true much more widely—it is necessary for the university to serve the values of both excellence and equity, and to be seen doing so. How that is done depends very much on the sensitivity of a university leader both to his external political environment and to the internal groups and values with whom he must work, most notably the faculty.

There is of course an apparent contradiction in the values that govern these two kinds of programs. But these two strands of policy, differently colored and serving different ends and values, are not competitive but supportive, closely intertwined as they move along the dimension of time. It is, I suggest, the task of university leadership to tend both of these strands of university policy, and to weave them together. And if that is done effectively, it may not be visible to observers of the office of the president or chancellor, observers who may be more impressed by the illogic or inconsistency of the values served than by the skills and initiative that enter into their accommodation within the same institution. Of course, incoherence and the loss of institutional integrity always threaten the American research university, which says yes to almost all claims on its energies, resources, and attention. But it is precisely the nature of leadership in American universities, the broad conceptions of power and the resources at its disposal, that enable the president or chancellor to give coherence, character, and direction to an institution so large in size and aspiration, so various in its functions and constituencies, so deeply implicated in the life of learning and of action, with links to so many parts of the surrounding society. These great research universities are among the most successful institutions in the world. They could not be if their presidents were unable to give them direction as well as the capacity for responding to what is almost always an unanticipated future. It is in the office of the president that the necessary resources and opportunities lie.

VII

Problems with which we have the resources to cope can also be seen as opportunities. The great research universities currently face a series of such problems (or opportunities) that are uniquely the responsibility of their presidents, however useful their aides and staff members may be. Each of us will have his or her own short list of grave problems that face university presidents, and these lists will change over time, but my own list would include at least the following, though not necessarily in this order of importance:

(i) There is the problem each president faces of accommodating to or reconciling demands for broadened access by students from historically underrepresented groups with the maintenance of the highest standards in teaching and research. This is the familiar tension in education between equity and excellence, both served in different ways within the same institution, and to differing degrees by different institutions.

(ii) There is the problem of the evolving relations between research universities and industry. The question presents itself as how to serve industry while using its funds, research facilities, and know-how for the university's own purposes, at the same time maintaining the unique qualities— the very integrity—of the university as a place committed to the pursuit of truth in an atmosphere of open inquiry and free communication.

(iii) There are the problems created for the university by the very rapid growth of scientific knowledge, and the impact of that growth on the organization of the schools and departments of science and technology, and on the physical facilities in which science is done within the university.

(iv) Closely linked to the third is the problem of maintaining a flow of new scientists and scholars into departments and research labs, without institutional growth and with a largely tenured and aging faculty that is not retiring in large numbers until the 1990s or later.

(v) On the other side of the campus, there is the problem of sustaining the humanities and the performing arts—that is, of maintaining the crucial balance of subjects within the university—in the face of the expansion of scientific and technological knowledge, and the growing attractiveness of professional training, especially at the undergraduate level.

(vi) Finally, there is the problem upon which perhaps all others depend: the defense of freedom of speech and of academic freedom on campus in the face of intense pressure from vocal minorities of students and faculty who, unlike the rest of us, do not have to pursue the truth since they already possess it, and who are loathe to permit others with whom they disagree to express and propagate what they view to be error and pernicious doctrines. (The theological language here is intentional.)

What a list! Yet we expect presidents to cope with large problems, as no other national university system does, because in fact our society gives them the authority and the resources to cope. There are never enough resources, in their view, yet by and large they do cope. It is still in part a mystery how they cope so successfully when so much of the theory of organizational leadership tells us they cannot and should not be able to do so.

But I think that the office of the university president has not been properly appreciated; it has been the object more of compassion and criticism than of understanding. The university presidency deserves understanding, though I suspect that incumbents will continue to speak of it deprecatingly and, with good reason, as fraught with difficulties and constraints. And meanwhile, under their leadership in that extraordinary office, our research universities go on from strength to strength.

Notes

1. On multi-campus systems, see Eugene Lee and Frank Bowen, *The Multi-campus University: A Study of Academic Governance* (New York: McGraw-Hill, 1971).

2. On the distinction between organizations and institutions, and the role of leadership in defining purpose and mission, see Philip Selznick, *Leadership in Administration* (Evanston, Ill.: Row, Peterson, 1957), esp. 5–28.

3. M. Cohen and J. G. March, *Leadership and Ambiguity* (New York: McGraw-Hill, 1974), 3.

4. Ibid., 81.

5. Ibid., 206.

6. Ibid., 2.

7. George Keller, *Academic Strategy* (Baltimore: Johns Hopkins, 1983), 86.

8. Martin Trow, "American Higher Education: Past, Present and Future," in *Social Welfare and the Social Service: USA/USSR,* ed. G. W. Lapidus and G. E. Swanson (Berkeley, 1986).

9. The Commission on Strengthening Presidential Leadership, *Presidents Make a Difference* (Washington, D.C.: The Association of Governing Boards, 1984).

10. Ibid., xix and xviii.

11. See Guy Neave, "Strategic Planning, Reform and Governance in French Higher Education," *Studies in Higher Education,* 10, no. 1 (1985); and Alain Bienayme, "The New Reforms in French Higher Education," *European Journal of Education* 19, no. 2 (1984). See for example, Maurice Kogan, "Implementing Expenditure Cuts in British Higher Education," in *Higher Education Organization,* ed. Rune Premfors (Stockholm: Almqvist and Wiksell, 1984).

12. See Frederick Rudolph, *The American College and University* (New York: Alfred A. Knopf, 1962), pp. 161–166.

13. See Martin Trow, "Defining the Issues in University-Government Relations,"

Studies in Higher Education 8, no. 2 (1983).

14. Private communication, University of California Budget Office.

15. Clark Kerr and Marian L. Gade, *The Many Lives of Academic Presidents: Time, Place & Character* (Washington, D.C.: Association of Governing Boards of Universities and Colleges, 1986), p. 27.

16. See Martin Trow, "Leadership and Organization: The Case of Biology at Berkeley," in *Higher Education Organization,* ed. Rune Premfors (Stockholm: Almqvist and Wiksell, 1984).

17. The phrase is drawn from the Commission on Strengthening Presidential Leadership, *Presidents Make a Difference.*

18. Ibid., p. 54.

19. Clark Kerr, *The Uses of the University* (Cambridge, Mass. Harvard University Press, 1963), p. 33.

20. Ibid., p. 36.

21. This image, and the next few paragraphs, are drawn from my essay "Leadership and Organization: The Case of Biology at Berkeley," in *Higher Education Organization,* ed. Rune Premfors, pp. 166–167.

13

It's Academic:
The Politics of the Curriculum
Irving J. Spitzberg, Jr.

Rarely have so many faculty and off-campus kibitzers said so much to achieve so little. This is likely to be the judgment history will render about curriculum reform in American higher education in the 1980s. The judgment about the 1990s may well be that never has the silence of so many faculty and administrators been so deafening, while a handful of students and faculty screamed so loudly to persuade so few colleagues and off-campus constituencies.

To understand these judgments about campus curriculum politics, one will need to appreciate the structure of American higher education, the nature of academic decision making, and the larger social and technological environment in which academic change takes place. This chapter will provide an analysis of the politics of the curriculum. It will focus on the campus-based political system as it affects curriculum decisions, and on the complex interrelationship between the campus and its national political context in the 1980s and the early years of the 1990s. It will comment on both the explicit curricular debate and the hidden curriculum of faculty and student behavior that provides powerful forms of learning.

The Historical Context

Since history regularly repeats itself, with minor variations on the themes, a thumbnail sketch of the twentieth-century history of the university and college curriculum will provide the foundation of my subsequent analysis.[1] In the late nineteenth century a group of small colleges and rudimentary land grant universities began the process of professionalization: they separated the professional and the practical from the arts and sciences. At the same time, the arts and sciences themselves were becoming professionalized through the development of graduate faculties at a few institutions. On the eve of the twentieth century, the scholars plowed the fields of the disciplines and planted the seeds that would produce the husks of disciplinary dominance. As often happens with Harvard's role in the history of American higher education, it directed professionalization in the construction of the elective undergraduate curriculum.

After the world fell apart during the First World War, there was a temporary reaction to the fragmentation and destruction as the world searched for an understanding of the cataclysm that had occurred. This search led to the reconstruction of a core in the undergraduate curriculum, e.g., the Contemporary Civilization sequence at Columbia University and the Hutchins era at the University of Chicago.[2] It provided anew interest in the relationship among the arts, sciences, and social studies at the graduate level. Throughout American higher education, Western Civilization courses tempered electives and various Chinese menus of distribution requirements. Just after the Second World War, the Harvard "Redbook" provided a justification for the distribution requirements that would characterize American higher education through the mid-1960s. The Chinese menu would build its Great Wall around the curricular process, and the twentieth-century enlightenment of the 1950s, with its faith in and fear of technology, would define undergraduate education as a sequence of exposures very much like the achievement of the perfect sun tan.

In the context of the turmoil brought on by the civil rights movement of the 1960s and the war protests of the 1970s, the campus student revolutions occurred. The appeal of the authority of the curriculum eroded with all other features of authority. This third moment of societal disruption and campus change differed from the earlier ones in that it destroyed the existing structure of the curriculum and left only a market basket full of products. The most anti-market social and political movement of the twentieth century, the 1960s student movement, had left the American curriculum at the direct mercy of the academic market. The faculty producers of the products essentially threw up their hands and said, "Let them eat cake." They then were quite surprised when the consumers only wanted cake, even while the faculty producers were still producing the same pork and beans that had been their staple for years. The American undergraduate curriculum had become a supermarket where each department offered its wares and the institution was only a sum of its parts. As in most economic markets where the structure is really oligopolistic, the big and elite departmental winners got bigger and at the same time more selective, and the small departments that accepted all comers and were not presently in demand lost on a large scale. The irony was that many of those departments most active in the revolution were the biggest losers, e.g., sociology and philosophy.

The student political agenda of active participation in decision making succeeded in only one part of college life—in decisions about the curriculum— where the decision-making process, in theory governed by faculty, essentially was abdicated to a market of student consumers without adequate advising and information. The faculty, in their corporate and collegial guises, viewed the risks of campus political system judgments about value priorities as too great for the parts. The reward of leaving the decisions to the individual students turned out to be great for some and nonexistent for others.

By the end of the 1970s the impact of laissez faire on the undergraduate curriculum was clear in the redistribution of enrollments to professional and preprofessional courses from the arts and sciences. The change was not only in selection of majors, where everyone either became preprofessional or a business major; it was also in choices of supposedly general education electives that served similar vocational ends. These changes had serious implications for many faculty and for the graduate schools. The surplus of Ph.D.s in many arts and sciences disciplines in the 1970s in response to high expectations of increasing student enrollments and university budgets but in spite of larger market forces illustrates the impact of these changes. The subsequent real declines in faculty salaries and general social support for higher education in the 1970s and 1980s were equally traumatic legacies of the abdication of curricular responsibility in higher education. Faculty could tolerate market decision making when it did not risk the very existence of parts of the campus. When the market put at risk the core disciplines of the university and their respective faculties, then the need to reassert campus judgment about the curriculum became clear.

This account of the late twentieth-century history of the curriculum suggests that major changes have correlated with, though not necessarily followed from, important social changes, often political disruptions, in the larger society. Even when there was a clear and landmark event or sequence of events, such as a war or the civil rights movement, the campus changes always emerged from campus politics, never directly from external intervention. The changes of the 1980s, to which we now turn our attention, have flowed even more from within the university than from the larger society.

The National Politics of the Curriculum in the 1980s

When one looks at the politics of curriculum on campus in the 1980s with the benefit of modest historical perspective in the decade of the 1990s, the experience of much talk and little action is confirmed. The invocation of great books in the national reports of the 1980s led to a benediction of Chinese menus on most campuses.

The 1980s version of the politics of the curriculum actually began in the mid-1970s with the appointment of Henry Rosovsky as Dean of Faculty at Harvard University. He and Harvard President Derek Bok, along with a cadre of senior faculty, decided to begin a long process of reconsideration of the Harvard curriculum that culminated in 1979 when the faculty reintroduced a narrowed set of distribution requirements built around the skills they wished students to have at graduation. The jury is still out on the impact of that change on students; its impact on the larger universe of American higher education is clear.

In the early 1980s, while the Federal government, the states, and individual households were cutting budgets and coping with inflation by downsizing, American higher education had already begun its own reconstruction by downsizing the freedom of choice of students. It resurrected distribution requirements on many campuses as a way of regulating the free market that had concentrated enrollments in management, engineering, and computer science. Campuses also restored a faculty role in decision making, although that had eroded so that only the curriculum offered an arena where the faculty could exercise authority. Serious financial pressures imposed by Federal budget cutting and weak state budgets severely constrained this decision-making process. (In addition, it is important to record that this fiscal constraint occurred during a period of time when student tuition was rising far faster than inflation. This trend created a student consumer psychology of demand for attention given the high price of the product they were buying.) Curriculum discussions in this context of scarcity exacerbated even more the territorial imperative of the departmental structure of the university, since faculty control reigned preeminent.

In this historical context, Secretary of Education Terrell Bell appointed a distinguished panel of citizens to assess the state of elementary and secondary education. The panel reported in 1983 in the now famous document *A Nation at Risk*.[3] Its report characterized the public school system as so weak as to threaten the security of the United States. The report's hyperbole generated a national reconsideration of quality in public education, in part because of its clever and catchy conclusionary statements, and in part because President Reagan decided that it offered an agenda he could adopt that would not cost the Federal government money. *A Nation at Risk* became the bible for educational reform at the local and state level. A number of governors sponsored substantial educational reform focusing on quality as the major political issue in their states. They also became interested in the quality of university education and made improvement of universities part of their overall educational plans. In Arkansas, South Carolina, and Tennessee, as well as many other states, the reform of teacher education became a state political issue. Florida and Georgia initiated testing programs for students mid-way in their college careers as well as for teachers. It is important to understand that these higher education initiatives flowed from *A Nation at Risk* and not from any higher education reports.

A Nation at Risk had a threefold impact on campus: first, in a few states, it led to the imposition from outside of testing programs—Florida and Georgia generally, and in many other states for students in teacher education. In many states the increases in funding for public schools also occasioned increases in state funding for higher education. Finally, the report seemed to spawn a number of subsequent reports focusing specifically on higher education, although many of these efforts were already in process. This national report was of such importance because it concentrated American attention on educational questions for the first time in two decades, and because the interest that it mobilized focused on an agenda that also included universities and colleges through the impact of the subsequent reports. It is to these latter reports that we now turn.

Three general reports targeting undergraduate education followed within months after *A Nation at Risk*. First, then National Endowment for the Humanities Chairman William Bennett and a study group of advisors looked at the teaching of the humanities. Bennett wrote his report, *To Reclaim a Legacy,* to assert the importance of revitalizing the humanities by strengthening the understanding of Western Civilization.[4] Bennett asked that institutions agree on a core of texts that every student should read. He had his own list that became the touchstone for his report and the center of controversy in selection.

Bennett's "great books of Western civilization" became the catch phrase that characterized his arguments in campus discussions about the undergraduate curriculum. The high visibility of the Bennett report helped catapult its author into the position of Secretary of Education when Terrell Bell resigned under pressure from the religious right for being too liberal.

After *A Nation at Risk,* Secretary Bell had appointed a small group to review higher education and the implications of the earlier report. This group, chaired by Dr. Kenneth Mortimer, then of Pennsylvania State University, published *Involvement in Learning,*[5] which considered not only the curriculum but also the pedagogy and priority (or lack thereof) of teaching, as well as the co-curricular environment for teaching in universities and colleges. This report came to be known as the report that prescribed greater student engagement with the learning process. It called for more writing, speaking, and creativity and fewer large lectures and impersonal learning settings. The higher education community identified Mortimer's group report with pedagogical method more than recommendations for curricular structure, an identification that marginalized the report, because pedagogy is marginal in the American higher educational enterprise. The third report following *A Nation at Risk* was from the Association of American Colleges (AAC). Professor Frederick Rudolph, the distinguished historian of the undergraduate curriculum, drafted Integrity in the *Undergraduate Curriculum*[6] which listed six skill areas that set the standards for high-quality undergraduate education and found that faculty had not given priority to these necessary skills in the structure of the undergraduate curriculum. The AAC report abjured text-centered recommendations or the use of Chinese menus. It emphasized the importance of a planned course sequence in undergraduate education as a tactic to offer greater coherence to the market-driven reality in colleges across the country.

These three reports provided the framework for the debate about the undergraduate curriculum as it evolved in the mid-1980s. Their impact was twofold: first, together they created momentum for campus discussion of the undergraduate curriculum at a level of visibility unseen since the late 1950s;

second, they provided the footnotes for the particular discussions on individual campuses, although they did not—either one or all—dominate the reconstruction of the undergraduate curriculum that continues to proceed, though much more slowly, into the 1990s. Since all three were conclusionary and rhetorical rather than based upon substantial research and analysis about current campus reality, the actual debates focused on parochial realities of given campuses. The three reports together framed the poles of the debates and offered appropriate justifications for nearly any argument mounted on behalf of new curricular structure, although they all ruled out the recent approach of institutional abdication of judgment. Their rhetoric was their strength in that there was an aphorism for all seasons; it was also their weakness.

Martin Trow concluded that these reports did more harm than good "because these reports, by substituting prescription for analysis, misled our supporters and the general public into believing that these difficult problems are simpler than they are. . . ."[7] An important distinction between the impact of these reports and *A Nation at Risk* was that no consensus about the details of reform emerged in higher education. The substance and potential resource implications of this debate meant that on most campuses at the end of the 1980s the systemic inertia limited change to the reintroduction of the Chinese menu as it emerged on most campuses after the Second World War. The campus-based politics of the curriculum has always been characterized by negotiations among departments about the hours devoted to general education and hours devoted to the major. These deliberations have resulted in a balance of power not unlike the treaties negotiated by Metternich or Kissinger.

The debate about the curriculum in higher education in the 1980s focused on the undergraduate curriculum, in part because the policy debate had ignored it and in part because the political economy and the disciplinary sociology had created a campus structure that had made it difficult to look at the undergraduate curriculum as a whole since the Harvard Red Book. It took a national, off-campus political debate to force each institution to confront the institution-wide issues, although the confrontation itself necessarily took place on each campus. Even though the debate was enriched off campus, it is essential to see that the higher education system itself provided the brainpower for the enterprise. The panels that fueled discussion included faculty and administrators from higher education to a much greater degree than those commissions reporting on the schools had involved teachers and principals. The culture of campus autonomy was not breached insofar as campus insiders actually wrote the outisde reports.[8]

The substantive focus on undergraduate education was part of a cycle of discussion about education that arose from the campus but took place in national forums and then returned to campus. All of these national reports and the national politics of the curriculum at most provided the environment within which the college and university citizens made the real decisions on campus. The politics of curriculum at the national level did not generate detailed debate in Congress or the Executive Branch, or even in the halls of many state legislatures, although it did, occasionally provide the focus of comments. The national political discussion occurred on the campuses with the occasional interest of politicians. The legislatures, governors, and Federal officials are most often interested in budgets but only rarely in curriculum; their curricular interest is usually flagged by reports written by campus citizens. Because currcicular decisions emerge in a culture that emphasizes campus autonomy, we must consider in greater detail the paradigm of curricular politics as campuses played the game in the 19480s and continue to play in the 1990s.

The Politics of Change: Making Curriculum Decisions on University Standard Time

To clarify the reality of curriculum decision making for the whole institution, I offer a synthetic case of change drawn from a number of examples. This model uses the case study database of the Carnegie Foundation study that led to Ernest Boyer's conclusions in *College*, and from my own impressions gathered from over two hundred college visits.[9] It also draws on the insights of eighteen research teams that visited campuses in 1989 in preparation for the Carnegie Report—*Campus Life*, and Virginia Thorndike's and my *Creating Community on College Campuses*.[10] It is enough to offer only one example, because the paradigm I will describe is unusually typical across institutional types ranging from community colleges through elite private universities.

In order to appreciate the texture of this case, one must always keep in mind the fact that, even in the intricate world of American politics, campus politics is especially Byzantine. Woodrow Wilson could say that he went to Washington from Princeton University to find a less complicated system, and that political conflict on campuses is so petty and mean because so little is at stake. Wilson was right about campus political pettiness, but wrong about little being at stake. Since substantive academic decisions are the heart of the university, much is at stake in these decisions: principle, status, and resources.

The very fact that so much is at stake, and that the culture of the university prizes consultation, makes decisions about curriculum especially laborious and time consuming. In many areas of university life and across the spectrum of institutions, the faculty no longer has an extensive and meaningful role in decision-making. Yet it is in the arena of curriculum that the faculty role is still primary and certainly meets the standard set by the American Association of University Professors (AAUP) in its "1966 Statement on University and College Government."[11] This reality means that even considering incremental decisions about the nature of departmental curriculum takes a long time to talk through. When an institution reviews its whole educational program for assessment and possible reform, one measures the consultative process in years, not months. This leads universities to be very conservative institutions.

Clark Kerr has observed that most of the changes in American higher education have come from creating new institutions, not from dramatically changing old ones.[12] And the model of departmental dominance of research institutions has not changed significantly since the Second World War. Changes occur within institutions at the margin, seldom at the core. And they generally evolve over long periods of time. Even revolutions and coups d'etat on campuses take a couple of years. This fact that everything in universities takes so long to decide leads to what I call "university standard time." This reality correlates with another irony: the knowledge produced and disseminated in colleges and universities is on the cutting edge. Most new understanding becomes immediately available to the research community around the world, as does the latest rumor about the love life of a distant colleague. We may explain this discontinuity with the distinction between research dissemination and agreement for action.

With this framework for analysis we can examine the curricular political process at Flagship University. This campus initiated a review of the under-graduate curriculum with special attention to what is or ought to be common in the required work for all students. As usual, the initiative for such a review came from a new provost/academic vice-president, who was dismayed to find that an earlier faculty curriculum review process had gone on for a decade and ended with a divided implementation committee. Once the provost initiated the review, it became the property of the faculty or university senate. The president appointed the committee with the consent of the faculty. It included senior faculty carefully balanced by discipline and by educational ideology—particularly selected not to have too many innovators—with a sprinkling of senior administrators and one or two figurehead students. The senior adminis-trator(s) and the faculty charged the committee to review the undergraduate curriculum and the existing requirements or lack thereof, and then to report to the faculty senate for first review no later than "next term."

During the first few months of deliberation, the committee had a debate within itself that invoked all of the national reports of the 1980s, the Harvard Red Book, Columbia, and the University of Chicago. It generated as many as a dozen opposing plans for dramatic reform of the undergraduate curriculum. Impatience quickly reduced twelve options to three, which invariably included modest change in an existing "Chinese menu," restoration of Western Civilization and a "Great Books" core with a new diverse cultures course, abolition of all requirements, and/or a distinctive approach unique to the particular campus usually in the form of courses with "subject and . . ." titles, such as international affairs and physics, or the environment and economics. "Next term" came much too quickly, so the committee reported it had only begun its deliberation and would report next year. An enlightened subcommittee initiated empirical studies of experiences of similarly situated institutions based on telephone surveys, and also examined the actual longitudinal course patterns of students based upon samples of transcripts. A chemist on the committee designed the survey, which was implemented by a part-time institutional researcher who spent most of her time doing budget and enrollment projections.

Two years later than originally promised, the select committee finally reported to the faculty senate a plan, which was heralded as a major change in the requirements for all undergraduates. The reform actually took the existing Chinese menu and reduced the choices in each column, and established another committee to evaluate proposed courses for inclusion in the general education program. There were three minority reports—one from the quarter of the committee that wanted a true restructuring with lots of required courses; one from the two students, who wanted a required American cultures course; and a final one from a lone faculty member who wished to do away with requirements altogether. The first minority report referred to Columbia, Chicago, and William Bennett; the second cited campus reports at Berkeley and UCLA; and the last invoked that "hot" university, Brown. The majority report was replete with references to Harvard, Derek Bok, and Ernest Boyer, selecting from each the most radical statements that then were used to justify only the most modest change.

At its final meeting the faculty senate approved the revised recommendations for a Chinese menu on a 55/45 vote, endorsing implementation during the next academic year.

Significant variations on this campus political process theme are relatively rare. In many community colleges, the academic dean—the equivalent of the provost—may take a much more active role and the faculty a more reactive role. In a historically Black college the campus president and its Title III Coordinator may be the only serious actors. An elite private university will have a council of elders composed of the most visible and senior professors and the dean of the undergraduate college as the main actors on stage with subsequent decision making a *fait accompli.*

This case documents the institutional conservatism of universities and colleges. Even when there is political radicalism on the spectrum of national political views and dynamic discovery of new knowledge, the political process for deciding about the curriculum seems to guarantee an institutional entropy that tolerates little change. The power of departments that is central to the organization of knowledge by disciplines creates a number of decentralized power centers that seem to exercise veto more than contribute to shifting coalitions. Undoubtedly some are more equal than others in the university or college setting. Those who are most equal are the faculty with the most research, the most students, and the most to get out of the status quo.

Finally, it is important to understand that the quality of the educational venture begins in the classroom but also depends upon the whole campus environment. Ernest Boyer in *College,* following the precedent of *Involvement in Learning,* correctly included in his review and suggestions a critical assessment of co-curricular life, the role of libraries, and the admissions process. Yet the campus curricular review process seldom gives this complexity its due, because the professionals engaged in the correlative work are second-class citizens in the campus political community. The reality is that curricular politics has been parochial, and as such has not had extensive impact on student learning.

Ending the Century: Some Second Thoughts on Parochial Campus Politics and the Hidden Curriculum in the 1990s

It is premature to write about the academic politics of the 1990s. However, it is essential to see that the 1990s are still playing the scores of the 1980s, but with some important variations. The brass of the 1980s reports has given way to the rhythms of slow faculty percussion. And new silence rests even when broken by off-key atonality of students seeking to rewrite a number of passages in the score. In this reflection on the first third of the decade of the 1990s, I see the emergence of old themes with new sounds.

The debates about distribution requirements and core curriculum continued into the early 1990s. However, there were no new national reports to spark further debate. Most of the changes in the 1990s have actually been implementation of policy decisions made in the 1980s. The occasional dispute that has emerged has often been over one course or requirement focusing on multiculturalism. Should all students be required to study about other American cultures, or should they be asked to study about world cultures? On most campuses, the result of the debate has been a requirement of a course or two chosen from a long list. The Chinese menu continues to structure solutions, if not debates. The 1990s have seen further restriction of the number of dishes from which students choose, but there is still no curriculum equivalent to a shared egg roll that everyone tastes.

There is an element of irony in the fact that it was a national conservative political movement that initiated the debates of the 1980s, when in the 1990s the debate has now become a conversation about syllabi, and whether or not a particular course has enough content diversity. Students in particular attempt to micromanage the curriculum. The reemergence of campus-wide discussion of academic issues in the 1980s created an expectation that there would be university-wide discussion of curriculum issues and campus implementation of curriculum-committee rhetoric in particular courses. From campuses as different as the George Mason University Law School to Harvard, the focus has moved from general curriculum issues to particular course content. At George Mason, a law professor illustrating a point about control of hate speech was condemned by students for using derogatory language that was required to make a hypothetical statement accurate. At Harvard a political science faculty member no longer teaches a course that students said included sexist readings. This is micro-managing curriculum by special interest.

A legacy of the 1980s debate about curriculum is a public discussion of political correctness—PC. This discussion is wholly centered on the humanities and the social sciences, the very academic areas that had the greatest erosion of student enrollment in the 1980s, although there seems to be some modest recovery in these disciplines in the 1990s. Highly visible English and Women's Studies Departments, where deconstruction, a literary criticism movement that says that one must "deconstruct" the language of the text to understand it, was a 1980s fashion, have become the media targets of the debate. The public issue seems to be whether left-wing professors create a political orthodoxy in their classrooms that subverts academic values and student learning. Although the academic debates about these matters have been visible on the campuses of a few research universities, there has been little systematic evidence of substantial problems in the classroom. The issue is not faculty telling students what to believe; rather it is students limiting faculty in what they can pursue, and colleagues' silence in the face of these challenges.

Once again, irony seems to abound. Concern about faculty left-wing brain washing in the 1990s emerged just as the former Soviet Union imploded and Eastern Europe dissolved into nationalism, so socialism as a movement was disappearing as a world force. Even more importantly, the very fact that so few students major in the humanities and social sciences means that even if there were a problem, very few would be affected by it. There has been no suggestion of left-wing bias in American business, health-related professions, and engineering faculties. So the PC tempest has been much larger than its teapot, although it continues to rage. The alarmist position taken by some conservative critics, though correct in regard to particular anecdotes on specific campuses, is not justified by more general evidence from many campuses.[13] But the issues posed are real and important.

The most serious curriculum issues of the 1990s would not even be considered to be curriculum issues on most campuses—the role model for learning provided by faculty to students, and both faculty and student indulgence of threats to the fundamental values of free enquiry. The invisibility of these issues leads to the suggestion that they are a hidden curriculum that structures student learning. Of course, these issues are not new. The failure of the high curriculum aspirations of the 1990s makes attention to these issues even more important as campuses seek to improve educational quality.

In *Creating Community on College Campuses*, Virginia Thorndike and I found that there are three critical features of the faculty role model that create the vision of what it is to engage in scholarly analysis and critical thinking: first, academic scholarship is often pursued alone, although there is variation among disciplines, from little or no cooperation in humanities and social sciences to significant organizational teamwork in the sciences and engineering; second, volume of publication, not quality, is the measure of success; third, there is an obvious devaluation of what goes on in the classroom. The professor is not rewarded for teaching. Students are a necessary distraction. Together these features create a learning environment where individuals pursue scholarly self-interest and devalue engagement in the classroom. Success is publication of articles by faculty, whether cited or not. Achievement for students is good grades on multiple choice examinations that are machine read, whether or not answering the questions requires critical thought. This "hidden" curriculum is in fact quite obvious to the students, though seldom the focus of faculty meetings. The hidden curriculum encourages students to marginalize academic accomplishment and critical thought, since the faculty often ignore them and the reward of good grades is accessible without hard academic work.[14]

Indulgence of threats to free enquiry is a matter of campus and national debates, although it is not seen as a curriculum issue. In the 1980s, campuses passed speech codes that Courts found did not pass constitutional muster, although they were systematically approved by faculty senates. In the 1990s, students wishing to control speech on campus are taking matters into their own hands. For example, when a group of Black students stole a whole publication run of the student newspaper at the University of Pennsylvania because the students did not like the content of an opinion column, the campus president responded with a vacillating statement about competing values of free press and diversity. And later the campus did not punish the students, because it thought they had learned enough just from the debate.

At the University of Michigan Law School, St. Mary's College in Indiana, the University of Alabama at Birmingham, and Colgate University, students have forced artists to remove art because the art offended feminist sensibilities or religious beliefs.[15] In all of these cases, the response of official faculty bodies and administrators has been silence. There are many other campus examples where the institutional voices, including faculty senates, were silent in response to serious breaches of academic freedom that originated from student action. This behavior of silence is a powerful curriculum element when actions that threaten the very essence of the university are not clearly condemned.

With the emergence in the 1990s of a society and a university community preoccupied with threats to fiscal integrity and no clear social movement directing the future of the university, the historical parochialism of campus politics of the curriculum leaves to each campus its autonomy to proceed on its path and an accompanying narrowing of view affected by the demands of campus based interest groups. The recession of the early 1990s and the continuing impact of federal deficit, state resistance to tax increases, and parental and student unwillingness to absorb high tuition increases, have created a political psychology on campus that parallels the psychology in Washington—"It is the campus economy, stupid!" This very real sense of precariousness and need to address pressing practical problems has reinforced the hidden curriculum of silence. The great risk of this silence is continuing erosion of support from the larger society because of the unwillingness to teach by condemning actions that subvert intellectual freedom.

In the mid-1990s, the formal curriculum is now on the back-burner, and the grand talk of the 1980s is only yesterday's stale rhetoric. The issues of change continue to be real because of the fast pace of change in the environment and the endorsement of change that American society clearly communicated in the Presidential election in 1992, when two-thirds of the American electorate voted to reject the dominant conservative ideology of the 1980s. The challenge now is to speak up against the threats to the basic values of the university and to embrace the leadership of change in a fast changing environment.

Improving Quality and Reforming Curriculum

The realities of change on the cusp of the twenty-first century require that we explore how to deal with change in an institutional setting that changes slowly and cyclically, if at all. How do we improve quality by reforming curriculum?

This account of the politics of the curriculum in higher education may discourage those interested in improving the quality of teaching and learning. Two caveats are in order: brevity has required an emphasis on one part of the curriculum-the undergraduate experience taken as a whole—not graduate and professional education or the departmental curricula with the major as a significant part; second, earlier I quoted Clark Kerr making the point that substantively new opportunities were provided in American higher education by the creation of new institutions, not by the substantial reform of the old. Both of these caveats should moderate the message of most of this chapter: that the politics of the curriculum, with its faculty conservatism and institutional silence, often precludes dramatic change. In particular programs on every campus, quality is effectively monitored and the substantive nature of the programs often changes surprisingly quickly through the individual actions of faculty at the lead in their disciplines and groups of faculty in departments committed to their students. For example, biological sciences programs on many campuses have restructured themselves dramatically in the last decade to reflect the multidisciplinarity of the new scientific methods of the field. Also, as new organizational needs have surfaced at the systems level, new institutions have emerged. The creation of a national system of community colleges and the transformation of teachers colleges into comprehensive universities in the 1970s testify to higher education's flexibility.[16] However, it is essential to note that the system displayed no such innovation in the 1980s.

It is easier to be flexible in a period of expanding rather than steady or contracting resources. The percentage of family income invested in higher education in the 1970s and 1980s did not change significantly; inflation was about equal to increases in federal aid. Federal budget deficits and sluggish economic growth make it unlikely that significant new resources will be available in the 1990s as we move into the twenty-first century. Therefore, we must think creatively about dealing with the lethargy of existing campuses. Yet we do have a silver lining to the current grey: the retirement of faculty between 1995 and 2010. New blood may—but only may—bring new curricular ideas.

The focus of the spate of reports and the efforts at curricular reform of the 1980s was revision of requirements and reallocation of current faculty efforts in teaching and learning as well as the elevation of teaching and learning on the priority agenda of campuses. This focus was eminently reasonable for the 1980s. But the time has now come to be more ambitious in our aspirations for curricular innovation and new campus political compacts about the curriculum of the twenty-first century. We must articulate our aspirations and put in place new governance processes now, because we can expect a fifteen-year window for new appointments, an opportunity unprecedented since the 1960s.[17] Decisions in the 1990s as to who will be appointed to faculty positions will set the course of higher education for the first half of the next century.

One lesson of the 1980s was that members of the university community, both on particular campuses and nationally, are willing to enter into a serious discussion about the nature of teaching and learning and debate quite vigorously the curriculum in a specific college or university. The problem has been that the deliberative institutions have been creaky in part because of lack of exercise. Many sectors of the campus community have never been effectively heard. Neither the middle-level administrators who deal with student life nor the alumni who as a constituency are prepared to take a more active role in the current life of the campus are considered important participants in the contemporary campus political system. Presidents, provosts, and boards of trustees need to create deliberative bodies for all segments of the college community, delegating authority and power where appropriate, and then resolving conflicts through small, representative cabinets who advise the whole institution and whose word decides most issues.

Faculty in particular have felt quite strongly that the campus has excluded them from university-wide decision making. The work on the curriculum may go some distance to correct this view, but it will not change until faculty believe they are consulted on issues of overall direction and the allocation of resources. This observation leads me to the most important lesson of the politics of curriculum during the 1980s for the 1990s and beyond. The best American institutions in the eyes of both faculty and students, according to the Carnegie Foundation surveys, are the selective liberal arts colleges.[18] In these institutions all members of the collegium believe they are important contributors to a community where they are respected and where the quality of life is high. The only other component of American higher education where the image and probable reality are similar is the Ivy League and elite private research institutions such as Stanford and Chicago. Insofar as a governance structure that seriously considers curricular reform and the campus environment for student learning can contribute to the quality of American higher education, such a strategy is far more likely to improve the quality of American higher education than assessment, testing, and management by objectives.

Regardless of what campuses do self-consciously, significant changes loom on the horizon of learning. In addition to the turnover of personnel with the turn of the century, we are already in the midst of the infiltration of new technologies that students and faculty will bring to the curriculum in a manner that could occasion profound change. Networks of microcomputers make possible patterns of study, interaction, and research that can greatly improve learning. University standard time may become quite compressed insofar as networks of knowledge deliver participants from the need to resolve schedule conflicts, and as they make available original data and research on a real time basis.

The social revolution driven by technological forces will not occur by majority vote; it will occur by mass connection. The information highway will have everyone on campus driving at high speed. Political action will likely confirm these changes, but they will have already become a reality. The knowledge revolution—the access of individuals directly to networks of knowledge—is the revolution of the inexpensive microcomputer, networks, and inexpensive storage media that will change the power relationships of the players of the academic games. Brilliant lecturers will lose to superb seminar leaders and insightful computer conferencing chairs. Research librarians and microcomputer hackers will be teaching traditional faculty. The faculty norm will continue to be "publish or perish," but publication may mean being stored on a prestigious computer bulletin-board, or being listed as a central participant in a select computer conference.

No matter how extensively networked we all become, electronic connections will never guarantee either community or quality of learning by students and faculty, though they can contribute to both. All curriculum change depends upon academic politics, which is unlikely to change, unless there is as much campus political action as there is educational talk. All academic change both begins and ends with writing and talking—what John Austin called "performative utterances," words that actually change things. In some ways the reality of the 1990s on campus is "performative silence," an unwillingness to consider issues such as challenges to academic freedom, because of a combination of concern about the campus economy, and basic faculty sympathy with students who play a public critical role in regard to issues of social justice. There is an attitude in regard to both the public and hidden curriculum that if we will just have patience all of the debate will pass, just as it always has.

Our task as citizens both of the campus and of the larger society is to understand the realities of academic politics—its inherent conservatism and its demand for consent by all affected interest groups—in an institution that is engaged in technological evolution on a new scale through market forces. No campus political systems seem to have created the capacity to make judgments in the interest of the long-term instead of yesterday and today. Few if any seem willing to challenge the culture of silence that enables challenges to the basic integrity of the academic political system. The consultative system seems to have degenerated into a practical reality of mutual vetoes and little agreement. This reality must change but will change only slowly and with leadership.

The talk and reports, such as those of the 1980s, were about academics, and appear to have become "academic" and not real. But the talk of the 1980s was better than the silence of the 1990s. Silence in the face of challenge of the 1990s is the greatest negative force facing the campus. Actions must be talked about in a consultative political system, whether national or local. And talking requires doing in order to channel change. However difficult it may be to break a culture of silence about actions that threaten academic integrity, it is equally difficult to make the choices that allow action in response to fast-paced change.

Change, particularly technological change, is reality. Constructive response is not. And if the campuses do not respond constructively, society in the person of legislators, students paying tuition, and donors will direct change through the power of the purse. The larger society has shown that it is willing to consider change through deficit reduction, health care reform, and creation of new national service programs such as Americorp. The question enroute to the next century is whether campuses will navigate or be pushed aground by the rapids of technology and national and state politics. The answer will be found in whether campus leadership meets the challenge in the politics of curriculum change as we turn to the twenty-first century. The jury of history is still out.

Notes

1. The following commentary on the modern history of the college curriculum has been informed by but should not be blamed on Frederick Rudolph, *Curriculum* (San Francisco: Jossey-Bass, 1977) and Clifton Conrad, ed., *ASHE Reader on Academic Programs in Colleges and Universities* (Lexington, Mass.: Ginn Press, 1985).

2. See Daniel Bell, *Reforming General Education* (New York: Columbia University Press, 1964).

3. *A Nation At Risk* (Washington, D.C.: U.S. Government Printing Office, 1983).

4. William Bennett, *To Reclaim a Legacy* (Washington: National Endowment for the Humanities, 1984).

5. Study Group on the Conditions of Excellence in American Higher Education, *Involvement in Learning* (Washington, D.C.: National Institute of Education, 1984).

6. Frederick Rudolph, *Integrity of the Undergraduate Curriculum* (Washington, D.C.: Association of American Colleges, 1985).

7. Martin Trow, paper presented to the faculty seminar on "Ideas of the University," Southern Methodist University, Dallas, Texas, March 12, 1986, p. 19.

8. For a comparison with other reports, see Janet R. Johnson and Laurence R. Marcus, *Blue Ribbon Commissions and Higher Education. Changing Academics* (Washington, D.C.: ASHE-ERIC, 1986).

9. As a consultant to the Carnegie Foundation, I reviewed all of the survey data and also all of the twenty-nine case studies prepared as background for the book. These data reinforced one another and proved the power of research that combines quantitative survey data with case studies, in this instance written by journalists who

spent at least two weeks on the campuses about which they reported. My review of these data has persuaded me of the general wisdom of the analysis and recommendations by Ernest Boyer in *College* (New York: Harper and Row, 1987) but my impression of the case study data suggests that the general quality of undergraduate education for the majority of students inAmerican colleges is worse than one might conclude from Boyer's evenhanded reporting, since about twenty-five of the twenty-nine reports described harassed and/or disinterested faculty teaching passive and unprepared students. Yet the best institutions rank with the most excellent in the world. Later research for Carnegie by Virginia Thorndike and I and eighteen research teams visiting campuses reinforced my conclusions based on the analysis of the earlier Carnegie data.

10. Irving Spitzberg and Virginia Thorndike, *Creating Community on College Campuses* (Albany, N.Y.: SUNY Press, 1992).

11. *AAUP Policy, Documents* (The Redbook) (Washington, D.C.: American Association of University Professors, 1984).

12. Clark Kerr, *The Uses of the University* (New York: Harvard University Press, 1980), Postscript–1982, pp. 151–56.

13. Dinesh D'Souza, *Illiberal Education* (New York: Vintage, 1992).

14. Spitzberg and Thorndike, *Creating Community on College Campuses.*

15. *Chronicle of Higher Education,* September 20, 1993, and Liza Mundy, "The New Critics," *Linguafranca* (September/October, 1993): 26–33.

16. Kerr, *The Uses of the University.*

17. Howard Bowen and Jack Shuster, *American Professors* (New York: Oxford University Press, 1986).

18. Boyer, in my review of both case and survey data.

14

Graduate Education: Changing Conduct in Changing Contexts

Patricia J. Gumport

Signs of strain are evident on the contemporary scene in American graduate education. Some of these have been reflected in events captured by *The Chronicle of Higher Education* in 1993: graduate students on strike at Berkeley to gain bargaining status as employees; the Internal Revenue Service subpoenas students' financial records for failure to pay tax on scholarship income; a violent demonstration erupts as UCLA students hunger-strike to gain departmental status for Chicano studies; a doctoral candidate at Washington State is imprisoned after refusing to disclose confidential information about animal rights activities from his research subjects; a former University of South Florida student is imprisoned for "stealing his own intellectual property."[1]

How are we to interpret this dizzying array of events? Although perhaps local aberrations, the events are not to be dismissed for their lack of representativeness. Rather, they may prompt us to consider some signs of strain in the structural and normative foundations of graduate education. Specific dimensions of strain are evident: problematic mechanisms for the finance of graduate education, the differential valuing across academic fields of study, variable expectations for the conduct of research, and the instrumental valuing of research products. Moreover, when viewed historically, these events can be seen as evidence that wider social, political and economic contexts have prominent manifestations in the content and conduct of graduate programs. A range of contextual influences generates "external" demands: state governing boards, government financial aid policies, research funding sources, and broad social movements—to name a few that are evident in the aforementioned news items.

Such contextual influences on graduate education have potentially far-reaching implications that warrant careful examination. As a step in that direction, the purpose of this chapter is to show some elements of this dynamic interplay between graduate education and its wider social, political and economic context.[2] The chapter begins with a historical overview and concludes with an assessment of the contemporary era. Given space limitations, it is necessary to set some parameters. Accordingly, I emphasize the intersection between doctoral education, academic research and the federal government, since these intertwined activities reveal the force of contextual influences, and since fluctuations in funding patterns serve as a suitable proxy for shifts in dominant societal values.[3]

The thesis I develop is as follows: Although the past century reflects continuity, especially in the structural foundations of graduate education programs, changes in the political-economic context of graduate education and academic research have altered the very conduct of graduate level programs; especially since the early 1970s, signs of strain in graduate education have become more evident as universities have come to act more like modern research complexes.[4] An underlying theme in the historical development of graduate education is a tension between, on the one hand, the legacy of autonomy that resides in decentralized, departmentally-based graduate programs and, on the other hand, the initiatives of campus administrative officials and outspoken external authorities who seek greater control in the conduct of academic affairs.

Historical Overview

Amidst the major transformations that have occurred in American higher education over the past century, graduate education has grown within a shifting context of societal forces. Primary among them, the federal government has been the major substantive and symbolic "external" presence in graduate education. In the evolving relationship between universities and the federal government, American graduate education expanded and became intertwined with complex organizational arrangements for academic research and research funding. The thrust of this historical overview identifies a paradox of continued structural foundations in the midst of qualitative changes in the nature of social relations.

In a fundamental sense, the historical development reflects much structural consistency in graduate programs, especially at the doctoral level. Graduate education in the United States has been neither a unified nor a standardized educational enterprise. By cross-national standards, this country has the largest, most decentralized and highly differentiated set of arrangements for advanced education, spanning over 800 campuses, enrolling over one and a half million students and granting annually about 340,000 master's degrees and 38,000 doctorates.[5]

Although the content of graduate programs varies across campuses and disciplines, the decentralized organization with faculty authority at the department level remains. In addition, the basic model for doctoral education has remained: a few years of prescribed courses, followed by examinations for advancement to candidacy, culminating in a dissertation which reflects research done by the student under guidance of a faculty committee. The ideal, dating back to Humboldt, has been for students to engage in advanced study along with research training.[6] Arrangements for research training have reflected consistent disciplinary differences: In the sciences where research is laboratory intensive, a graduate student may work under faculty supervision, with the dissertation as a piece of a faculty member's research project, while in the humanities where research is library intensive, a student may work independently, having infrequent contact with faculty supervisors and graduate student peers.

In spite of such structural consistencies, the historical development simultaneously reveals some profound changes in the nature of social and intellectual relations, especially among graduate students and faculty. As Nevitt Sanford assessed with critical concern back in 1976:

> The structure of graduate education seems to have changed hardly at all since the 1930s. . . . What has changed are the purposes for which the structure is used and the spirit with which it is managed. The motives of professors and graduate students are less purely intellectual and more professional. . . . The general climate of today is one of competitiveness among universities, between departments in a given university, and between subgroups and individuals within the same department. Students are regarded less as potential intellectual leaders and more as resources to be used in the struggle for a place in the sun.[7]

To the extent that Sanford's characterization may be correct, changes in funding patterns for graduate education and university research need to be examined as a mediating force in this transformation.[8]

Historically, the finance of graduate education has relied primarily on the sponsorship of university research, and secondarily on a variety of loan programs and some state-funded teaching assistantships. Federal support of academic research has been concentrated in the most visible one hundred research universities (less than three percent of American higher education institutions), which currently produce about 80 percent of doctorates and 50 percent of master's degrees.[9] Sponsorship of university research has its greatest effect on this sector of dependent campuses and heavily-funded sciences within them, but it also has salience for others throughout the system, even if only by denying them funds.

Federal involvement in graduate education and research can be traced back to the late 19th century, when the emergence of the modern research university entailed adapting campus organizational structures to graduate programs and scientific research. As these activities expanded in scale, and as faculty and campus administrators sought more external sponsors, the funding base for both activities became a source and a condition for further organizational changes on campuses and throughout the higher education system. Since the federal government has been a principal source of funds, it has been a pivotal influence in these and other more subtle changes in the nature of graduate education. Three changes have been most apparent: an increased specialization of faculty and administrative positions and procedures, greater system-wide stratification along with heightened within-sector competition for fiscal and human resources, and a proliferation of organizational subunits for academic research that reflect the instrumental and increasingly economic agendas of external sponsors.

NINETEENTH-CENTURY BEGINNINGS

Graduate education achieved a stable American presence during the last two decades of the nineteenth century, when awarding the Ph.D. became a laudable academic goal. The founding of Johns Hopkins University in 1876 is often thought of as marking the establishment of graduate education. Hopkins became known as the "prototype and propagator" of research as a major university function.[10] Coupled with its commitment to scientific research, Hopkins offered merit-based graduate fellowships for full-time study that included state-of-the-art research training.

Both within and immediately surrounding higher education, interest in scientific research had been burgeoning since the mid-nineteenth century. With great frequency, scientists and those seeking advanced study travelled to Germany for the requisite exposure; work in chemistry even into the 1870s required a trip to Germany. On the American front, after initial resistance to the German idea of studying science for its own sake, and after conflicts between self-identified pure and applied scientists, scientific research gradually gained more acceptance, although it took on a distinctive meaning in the American context: American science would be "a collective enterprise like those in business. Modern science needed labor, capital and management."[11] Proclamations at Hopkins reflected this change in scientific research from "a rare and peculiar opportunity for study and research, eagerly seized by men who had been hungering and thirsting for such a possibility" to an increasingly more prestigious endeavor, proclaimed by Clark University's president as "the very highest vocation of man—research."[12] Science became an increasingly specialized activity that professors could pursue autonomously, yet with the security of support, personal advancement, and even prominence, within an academic institution.

Following Hopkins' ideal of linking scientific research and graduate education, other graduate schools emerged in the 1890s as parts of larger universities whose undergraduate missions and size offered a broad and stable base of support in endowment funds and tuition. Some were established by the founding of a new university soon to offer both undergraduate and graduate instruction, as in Stanford (1891) and Chicago (1892). Others added the graduate school onto an older established private college, as in the case of Harvard and Columbia. Some existing state universities—Wisconsin, Michigan, and Illinois—evolved out of origins as land grant colleges established with government funds for agriculture and mechanical arts through the Morrill Acts of 1862 and 1890 and the funding of experimental agricultural stations through the Hatch Act of 1887. By 1900, the number of Ph.D.-granting institutions had grown to fourteen, awarding a total of three hundred doctorates.[13]

In addition to taking on scientific research commitments, Ph.D. programs came to be seen as an attractive feature for expansion and for advancing an institution's competitive position in the growing higher education system. Based on a desire to confer prestige on their institutions, an increasing number of institutions sought to hire faculty with research interests and actively sought sponsored research funds to build laboratories that would attract eminent scientists. Since faculty increasingly wanted to pursue basic research and to train selectively-chosen graduate students, institutions were propelled to provide them with opportunities for research and advanced training, and hence graduate programs across the disciplines.

THE PRINCIPLE OF DEPARTMENTAL ORGANIZATION

The widespread adoption of graduate programs within higher education institutions was enhanced by the development of departmental organization that occurred in the last quarter of the nineteenth century. Departments provided a flexible organizational structure for decentralizing and compartmentalizing graduate instruction. While Ph.D. programs were integrated organizationally as a separate level from the liberal education of undergraduate colleges, they also were made parts of departments responsible for undergraduate instruction in a discipline, a linking arrangement that has been remarkably stable and uniform over time and across campuses. The drive to conform to this structure was so strong that Hopkins expanded its organizational structures to offer undergraduate as well as graduate programs.

This organizational arrangement permitted control of undergraduate and graduate programs to reside within the same faculty.[14] Coursework as well as research training could be designed appropriate to each discipline and coordinated by each department's faculty. One functional by-product of this arrangement was that graduate programs maintained both faculty and institutional continuity: they allowed faculty to reproduce themselves by training their professional successors; and they promoted cohesion, since the responsibility for graduate students kept faculty attentive to their departments. Graduate programs kept the research and teaching activities interlocked and the institution functionally integrated—at least at the department level—in spite of increased disciplinary specialization.

Corresponding to established areas of knowledge at the time, departments were able to design different kinds of research apprenticeships that were appropriate to the specialized training in each of the disciplines. The specialization of disciplines that was mirrored by departments represented professors' vocational aspirations, which were especially apparent in the newly established natural and social science departments whose very existence was justified on the basis of specialized research. Beyond the campus level, as disciplines crystallized into national professional associations, they came to serve as visible external referent groups that would give a semblance of standardization across graduate programs: "Disciplines and departments had powerful reciprocal effects upon one another" in reinforcing the authority of departments on campus and the professional judgements of faculty nationally.[15] Thus, the emergence of associations further facilitated the growth of Ph.D. programs.

Especially during the 1890s, the size and complexity of the graduate education and research enterprise encouraged coordination and control that were reflected in the emergent bureaucratic administration on campuses. While departments served faculty interests for autonomy in research and instruction, the hierarchies of rank within departments and competition across departments served administrative interests for "productive work" as measured by research output. One observer notes, "Clearly it had become a necessity, from the administrator's point of view, to foster the prestigeful evidences of original inquiry."[16]

The dual tasks of graduate education and research were institutionalized most easily in those institutions that had greater resources, both financial and reputational. Thus at the system-wide level, those who succeeded in the competitive drive for advancement became a leading peer group of institutions. The prominence of this tier in the U.S. system was reflected in their founding of the Association of American Universities (AAU) in 1900, which marked the culmination of nineteenth-century efforts to establish graduate education and research activities. Ostensibly the AAU was founded to establish uniformity of standards, yet it simultaneously functioned as an exclusive club.[17] The establishment of the AAU signifies an implicit system-wide division of labor in the United States, where the elite institutions have differentiated themselves as a sector at the top of the hierarchy that is engaged in graduate education and research. Although institutions competed for faculty, graduate students, and philanthropic support, the persistent concentration of fiscal and status resources in this sector is a distinctive feature of the American system and an institutional version of Merton's Matthew Effect.[18]

Characterized as "a new epoch of institutional empire-building," this period of American higher education reflects the surfacing of university concerns for status in an increasingly stratified system. Such concerns were evident in dynamics of academic rivalry such as bidding for faculty and emulating academic departments. While the American system is not unique in its inclination toward stratification, the institutional drive for competitive advancement within the research university sector has reflected, according to one American scholar, "almost an obsession."[19]

Thus, the end of the nineteenth century marks the creation of the research university as a new kind of social institution devoted to scientific research as well as to graduate education. The extent of institutional ambition was so pervasive that the developing universities imitated one another in the departments, programs and faculties that they sought to develop. Across the country, homogeneity in the proliferation of graduate programs and faculty positions suggests that campuses sought to acquire not only intellectual legitimacy but a new kind of economic and political legitimacy as well.

TWENTIETH-CENTURY RISE OF SPONSORED ACADEMIC RESEARCH

The expansion of graduate education in the modern university developed hand in hand with the expansion of a national system of sponsored research. Initially, external resources for academic science were amassed principally from philanthropic foundations, while industry played a minimal role. Not until after World War II were foundations and industry eclipsed by a surge of federal government involvement.

The earliest sources of research sponsorship were wealthy benefactors and their philanthropic foundations. In the 1870s, philanthropic contributions to higher education averaged six million dollars per year, mainly to individual scientists. By 1890, philanthropic support reflected a more widespread and instrumental orientation, directing funds to the emerging universities for their potential contributions to industrial growth, employment and commercial endeavors. Philanthropic funds supported a wide array of institutional activities, especially in the applied sciences, including funds for equipment, overall plant expansion, and new professional schools. In some cases, the support provided large sums of money, like John D. Rockefeller's thirty-five-million-dollar endowment to the University of Chicago. On a national scale, John D. Rockefeller and Andrew Carnegie established the two largest foundations involved in research: the Rockefeller Foundation, established in 1913 with one hundred eighty-two million dollars, and the Carnegie Corporation, created in 1911 with one hundred twenty-five million dollars. In the early 1920s these foundations favored donations to separate research institutes, such as the Rockefeller Institute of Medicine and the Carnegie Institute of Washington.[20]

By the 1930s, universities found themselves uncertain of whether foundations would be stable external sponsors for academic science: foundations reoriented their giving to become an integral funding base for university research by allocating project grants and postdoctoral fellowships (by the Guggenheim Foundation), especially in medical research, the natural sciences and somewhat less so the social sciences. For example, in 1934 the Rockefeller Foundation constituted 35 percent of foundation giving, 64 percent of that in the social sciences and 72 percent of that in the natural sciences.[21]

Such voluntary contributions enabled universities to have essential resources required to institutionalize graduate education and scientific research. Universities and their faculties built their own rationales and adapted organizational structures to expand the scope of their research activities while training the next generation of knowledge producers. Upholding university autonomy and academic freedom became not only institutional concerns but also issues for individual faculty. Faculty claimed expert authority in order to establish some distance from the agendas of campus governing boards and the increasingly prominent philanthropists. Professionalization efforts of faculty in this era were, in part, due to the presence of external mandates for research, and not merely an outgrowth of knowledge explosion as is commonly cited.[22]

Private industry made an entrance on the academic scene as an unpredictable supplement.[23] As industry expenditures for research and development (R & D) rose in the 1920s, corporations conducted both applied and basic research in their own industrial laboratories in the technological areas of communications and chemicals research. The success of industrial sponsorship for university research in this era was exemplified by two prestigious research universities: Massachusetts Institute of Technology and the California Institute of Technology. Overall, however, corporate R & D funds stayed in their industrial laboratories through the 1930s and thereby remained an unpredictable presence for academic science.

By the late 1930s, university research was genuinely flourishing, although it did so primarily in the nation's most visible universities. Evidence for this concentration of research activity points to a similar concentration of research training activity: in 1937 sixteen universities accounted for half the expenditures on university research and granted 58 percent of the doctorates.[24] This consolidation of research resources with doctoral-granting activity was a pattern that would persist even after this era of university research as a privately financed operation.

THE SURGE OF FEDERAL INVOLVEMENT

The national government's sponsorship of research and research training came incrementally rather than through a coordinating policy on science or on graduate education. Beginning with federal and state governments playing a role in land grant campuses through agricultural research, universities increasingly were seen as a national resource for basic research and training that could assist in its priorities of economic growth, national security, and health care. Over time, including two world wars, the government came to be the major sponsor of scientific research and higher education.

Federal involvement in academic science began with organizational efforts to designate advisory boards for scientific research. Signifying both the value of modern science and a perceived need to oversee the country's research intentions, the first national organization was the National Academy of Sciences (NAS), founded in 1863.[25] In 1919 the National Research Council (NRC) was established by the NAS essentially to carry out the earlier Congressional mandate.

As the principal operating agency of both the NAS and (after 1964) the National Academy of Engineering, the NRC was intended to serve as a bridge between the federal government, the public, and the community of scientists and engineers. Over time, the NRC has become a principal organizational base for overseeing national research efforts and for monitoring how federal funds are channelled into university research.

Rather than actually advising the government, however, the NRC, along with the American Council of Learned Societies (founded in 1919) and the Social Sciences Research Council (founded in 1923), depended upon the resources of philanthropic foundations to assume a prominent role in the promotion of university research. As channels for foundation funds, these organizations provided interested sponsors with access to scientists and scholars, as well as administrative assistance in selecting recipients of small research grants and postdoctoral fellowships in the areas of mathematics, physics and chemistry. By the 1920s American science was mobilized under "the guidance of the private elites" who "came together for the purpose of furthering science." The memberships of the National Research Council and the National Academy of Sciences were constituted by "the same group of individuals [who] encountered one another, in slightly different combinations."[26]

The national government's expansion of a large-scale, multi-agency funding system to support academic science developed incrementally during and after each World War. In the late 1930s, annual federal expenditures for American science were estimated at $100 million; most of these funds went to applied research in federal bureaus, especially agriculture, meteorology, geology and conservation. The shift to university-based research occurred when the expertise of academic researchers became valuable for national defense efforts.[27] In World War I, for example, the federal government financed psychologists to construct intelligence tests and encouraged scientists to follow up on diagnostic physical examinations of close to four million people who were drafted. For such work, universities granted leaves to full-time life and physical scientists as well as to social scientists and historians. The government also allocated funds for researchers to work on their campuses. By World War II, government support was more extensive: in 1940, federal funds for university research totaled thirty-one million dollars. During the 1940s, the Office of Naval Research contracted with over two hundred universities to do about 1,200 research projects involving some 3,000 scientists and 2,500 graduate students. Between 1941 and 1945, the United States spent three billion dollars on total research and development, of which one-third was for university-based research aimed at winning the war and devising "new instruments of destruction and defense."[28]

The expansion of sponsored research in universities was coupled with the expansion of doctoral training. Between World War I and World War II the number of institutions awarding doctoral degrees went from fifty in 1920 to one hundred in 1940; and the number of doctorates awarded saw a fivefold increase in those two decades from 620 in 1920 to 3,300 in 1940.[29] In addition to such growth, a qualitative shift occurred, enhancing the caliber of doctoral students, whereas in the 1920s the majority of graduate students had been "undistinguished," reflecting "uneven preparation, uncertain motivation and unproven ability."[30]

By the end of World War II, the federal government came to look at research universities as a precious public resource for research and research training that was worthy of a partnership, even during peacetime. The establishment of the National Science Foundation (NSF) reflected a clear federal agenda that science would indeed offer "an endless frontier," and that universities could be ideal settings for such research, as Vannevar Bush stated in his 1945 report to President Roosevelt. In the 1950s, the federal research budget grew steadily and the academic research enterprise expanded in the top tier of institutions. In 1953–54, the top twenty spent 66 percent of federal research funds for academic science and awarded 52 percent of the doctorates, the bulk of them in life sciences, physical sciences and engineering, the same fields that received most of the federal research funds.[31]

POSTWAR EXPANSION OF FUNDS FOR
UNIVERSITY RESEARCH AND DOCTORAL EDUCATION

Spurred by the launching of Sputnik in 1957, the government provided even more funds for basic research. Federal sponsorship of research increased every year from 1958 to 1968. In that decade alone, annual federal contributions to academic research increased fivefold. As the federal investment increased, so did universities' share of total basic research, from one third to one half in that decade.[32] Thus, the post-World War II period clearly established that research was a separate function and operation largely paid for by the federal government, and that universities could perform a large share of the nation's research effort.

While higher education was perceived as having an increasingly legitimate research role, total enrollments rose from three million to seven million students and doubled within doctoral granting universities, up from 1.24 million to 2.5 million for undergraduate and graduate levels combined. Annual Ph.D. production in science and engineering grew dramatically from 5,800 in 1958 to 14,300 in 1968.[33]

The allocation of federal research funds followed two basic imperatives that have been consistent since the outset: multi-agency support and competition among individual proposals. Federal sponsorship entailed a clear Presidential directive (Executive Order #10521 in 1954) for multi-agency support, that no single agency within the government was to be given sole responsibility to distribute research funds. Rather, each agency should sponsor research related to its mission, such as health, defense, and energy. In 1959, 96 percent of federal sponsorship came from five agencies: Department of Defense, Department of Health Education and Welfare (largely the National Institutes of Health

[NIH]), Atomic Energy Commission, National Science Foundation, and Department of Agriculture; in that year over 96 percent of the 1.4 billion dollars was for research in the life sciences, physical sciences and engineering, leaving the social sciences and particularly the humanities neglected.[34]

Lacking a unified policy with specific purposes, funding arrangements were coordinated through a mechanism of peer review by researchers in the scientific community that extended beyond the federal government. A competitive system for reviewing research proposals and awarding research grants was the primary vehicle through which the national government thought it would insure that the best research would be performed. For the most part, the federal agencies' priorities were to nurture excellence, although there was some effort to disperse resources across geographic locations and smaller institutions. The resulting pattern of funding university research has reinforced the leading tier of research universities and the science fields, with life sciences and physical sciences accounting for over half of the basic research budget.

Similar to the expansion of federal basic research funding, the federal support for doctoral education intensified, mostly to train science and engineering personnel. Aside from its short-term interests to advance science and technology, the national government was mindful of improving its research capacity and developing a longer-term pipeline of trained scientists and engineers. A variety of mechanisms were employed to attract and keep talented students in the pipeline: direct student aid (as fellowships), student aid channelled through institutions (traineeships), and individual project grants to individual faculty, which included salaries for graduate student research assistants. The precedent was set for this explicit twofold agenda in the 1937 National Cancer Act, which set up grants-in-aid to non-government scientists and direct student aid in the form of fellowships. By the 1950s, the National Science Foundation offered over five hundred prestigious portable fellowships to students.

The National Defense Education Act of 1958 conveyed a commitment to rebuild the nation's research capability through "manpower training," and specifically to support science education through a host of fellowship and traineeship programs to be launched by a variety of federal agencies (NIH, NSF, NASA). Another program was the National Research Service awards, administered through three federal agencies in the 1960s. These training programs were deliberate efforts to attract talented students with stipends for predoctoral and postdoctoral support, as well as to improve the training on campuses with institutional allowances. In the decade between 1961 and 1972, these particular programs assisted over thirty thousand graduate students and twenty-seven thousand postdoctoral scholars, according to one estimate.[35]

While direct support of doctoral education (fellowships and traineeships) was done on a competitive basis, the talent and support ended up being concentrated at leading research universities, where the federally sponsored research was occurring. This resulted in a consolidation of resources for both research and doctoral education, giving these institutions a double competitive edge in attracting high quality students and faculty.[36]

Post-World War II federal initiatives were even more instrumental in cementing the legitimacy of this interdependence: sponsored university research had short-term R & D value, and sponsored graduate education promoted "manpower training." Between the end of World War II and 1972, the federal government cumulatively had spent two hundred billion dollars on R & D. Academic institutions' share of total R & D expenditures went from 5 percent to 10 percent, while their share of basic research expenditures went from one-quarter in 1953 to one-half in the early 1970s. By the end of this era, the surge of federal sponsorship resulted in a persistent pattern: about half of the country's basic research was done in universities, about two-thirds of university research expenditures came from the federal government, and about half the federal funds for basic academic research went to the top 25 research universities.

POSTWAR EXPANSION OF GRADUATE EDUCATION

Within the context of expanded sponsored research opportunities and a shifting funding base, the graduate education system continued to grow at a constant rate each decade.[37] The end of World War II marked a turning point, where more doctorates were granted in the decade of the 1950s than in all the years prior, and an increase from six thousand doctorates granted in 1950 to tend thousand in 1960. The 1960s entailed even more dramatic expansion: a threefold increase in one decade alone, from ten thousand to nearly thirty thousand. The expansion of master's degrees followed a similar pattern: annual production grew from about twenty-five thousand granted in 1940, and then genuinely flourished in the decades since World War II, where annual production of master's degrees dramatically increased to about sixty thousand in 1950, seventy-five thousand in 1960, and close to three hundred thousand two decades later.

Doctoral degrees and master's degrees both reflect an overall growth in all fields of study, especially in the sciences and professional fields. For doctoral degrees, physical sciences, life sciences and engineering accounted for close to half the doctorates in 1965; two decades later they still dominated, although life sciences Ph.D.s edged out the other two fields, while social science/psychology remained fairly constant at about 20 percent, humanities dropped from 20 percent to 10 percent, and education increased from about 15 percent to 25 percent, thus reflecting an increased professional orientation of graduate study. The overall diversification of doctoral fields is marked—over 550 fields in 1960 compared to 149 in 1916–1918. Moreover, beyond field of concentration, there are now forty-seven types of doctoral degrees besides the Ph.D., including doctor of education, doctor of social work, doctor of business administration, doctor of theology, and doctor of arts. A similar orientation to the demands of the marketplace is evident in the growth of master's degrees since 1965, especially in practitioner-oriented fields, leaving only 16 percent of master's in research-oriented M.A. programs by 1982–1983: business was up from 7 to 23 percent, engineering accounted for 10 percent, and the health professions about 6 percent; education still held the largest share while dropping from 40 to 30 percent.[38]

Since World War II, graduate education at master's and doctoral levels has grown to be a vast enterprise, in which the leading tier of research universities became the model for aspiring institutions to emulate. Since the less elite institutions had less of a resource base in facilities, departmental funds, and critical masses of faculty and students, they invested their resources in selected fields. Not until the 1970s did asserting a distinctive institutional mission become a strategy for gaining a competitive edge in specialized areas. At the leading institutions the dynamic was different: able to cover all fields, their strategy was to undertake more sponsored research and to expand Ph.D. production. This is the modern research imperative, the vehicle whereby universities protect if not advance their institutional mobility, for "the institution which is not steadily advancing is certainly falling behind."[39]

Until the contemporary period, graduate education and research in the leading modern universities were guided by opportunities from major changes at the national level: the use of scientific research for national defense and economic priorities, the rise in the research budget of the federal government, in terms both of overall R & D allocations and of basic research funds, the plurality of funding agencies to help stabilize university autonomy and a system of peer review ideally to insure distribution of resources for the best science. Universities became the main performers of basic research, having an abundance of funds unconnected to their instructional budgets, and the federal government became the dominant external source for funds. However, at the dawn of the contemporary era, shifts in organization and sponsorship suggest a context of greater uncertainty, as funding sources and amounts reflect changing perceptions of the nature of university research and research training.

The Contemporary Era: Signs of Strain

While the patterns that crystallized in the post-World War II period have remained prominent, university-government relations show signs of strain. The early 1970s brought an economic crisis that threatened even the strong research-training link of the sciences and even the solid resource base of the most prominent research universities. An era of retrenchment, roughly between 1969–1975, began with a tightening academic labor market and inflation in the wider economy. This era signified that the government could be an unstable base of economic and political support for university research and graduate education.

The national government reduced funds to support the research infrastructure that it had dramatically expanded in the post-World War II period. Between 1968 and 1971, the basic research budget fell over 10 percent in real terms.[40] Academic research expenditures that were contributed annually by the federal government declined from five billion dollars in 1968 to four billion seven million dollars in 1974. The government's attention turned to short-term research that would make scientific knowledge technologically relevant. As a result, physical resources, such as equipment and campus buildings, were neglected. In addition to the decline in funds for academic science, support for graduate students declined, thus both research and research training became "victims of federal benign neglect."[41] The government abruptly withdrew the bulk of its direct fellowship support to graduate students, especially some of the larger programs funded by the National Institutes of Health. By one count, the 57,000 federal fellowships and traineeships of 1968 fell to 41,000 in 1970; another estimate is that federal fellowships fell from 51,000 in 1968 to 6,000 by 1981. As graduate fellowships were "cut back too fast and too far," a series of national reports were conducted on the finance of graduate education, citing the destabilizing effects of "stop-and-go" federal funds and disadvantages of smaller scale fellowships, reduced to four thousand new merit-based awards for gifted students each year.

In place of the wider base of support, the government left the bulk of doctoral students to seek direct support from loans. In compensating for the reduction in fellowship support, loans increased substantially in one decade alone, from 15 to 44 percent of the total students enrolled in graduate programs from 1974 to 1984. In that year over 600,000 students working on graduate degrees borrowed two billion dollars from the federal government in Guaranteed Student Loans, now known as Stafford Loans.

In the 1980s the federal government continued its indirect support of doctoral education through the mechanism of assistantships that were embedded in thirteen billion dollars of federal academic R & D. However, along with the reduction in fellowships and traineeships in the early 1970s, stipends from assistantships were reconceptualized as taxable pay for work rather than tax-exempt subsidies for education. The 1986 Tax Reform Act marks a recent government initiative to reduce the federal deficit by taxing stipends associated with research assistantships and state-funded teaching assistantships; these were previously excluded from income tax. Although universities and their national representatives acted on behalf of themselves and their graduate students to have this legislation amended, they were able to exclude only fellowship and tuition awards from taxation. Assistantship stipends, a large part of federal support for graduate students, still became taxable income. In addition to requiring technical changes in the administration of graduate student financial assistance, the policy change can be interpreted as a sign that graduate students are instrumentally valued, rather than seen as inherently worthy of direct support.

In spite of the contemporary changes in finance of graduate education, universities continue to perform half of the country's basic research, which is proportionally a small but significant part of the overall national R & D effort. Of the total one hundred thirty billion dollars 1986 national R & D effort, fifty-five billion dollars was provided by the federal government and sixty billion dollars by industry.[42] Most R & D funds go to development.

Of the federal funds, $14.5 billion were for basic research, making the federal government the largest sponsor (at about two-thirds) of basic research. Industry was the second largest sponsor of basic research at about three billion dollars. Higher education institutions themselves were third at $1.5 billion.

The distribution of basic research funds among academic institutions reflects the persistent concentration of research activity and sponsored research resources. The top one hundred institutions account for over 80 percent of all academic R & D expenditures, the top fifty for over 60 percent, the top ten for over 20 percent. In addition, the institutions constituting the top tier in receiving four-fifths of all federal obligations (in which R & D funds are embedded) have remained remarkably stable; 81 of the top 100 in 1967 remain in that category.[43] The distribution of academic R & D across fields has been essentially the same over the past two decades: over 80 percent of federal funds go to life sciences (56 percent), engineering (14 percent) and physical sciences (11 percent). The behavioral and social sciences have seen a decline from $1 billion in 1972 to $.78 billion in 1987. Between 1976 and 1985 alone the NSF funding in this area fell by 24 percent and shortened the average grant interval to 1.2 years.

Institutions have responded to this contemporary funding base with their own initiatives, for example, by setting up their own teaching assistantships and research assistantships by drawing on institutional funds from endowments, tuition, or (for public institutions) from state revenues. Institutions have also used their own funds to support research activities, including facilities and equipment improvement, and have stepped up efforts to collaborate with industry, which causes concern among some observers and participants over a potential blurring of boundaries, if not purposes, between academic researchers and external sponsors.

In addition to seeking a broader base of funding support, universities have also elaborated their organizational structures in the form of extra-departmental research units in order to meet increasingly specialized areas of interdisciplinary and applied research. The organization of research in university settings has historically been anchored in the departmental structure, where departmental faculty work as both individual investigators and mentors to their advanced graduate students in the department's degree programs. The major exception to this mode of organization in the contemporary period is the organized research unit (ORU), academic units outside departments and lacking degree-granting status. Prior to the 20th century, ORUs were primarily observatories and museums, but in the post World War II expansion of academic research, ORUs proliferated to meet new societal demands for research that did not correspond to instructional areas outlined by departments, or that was disproportionate to departments in magnitude and expense. Funded by the national government, state governments, industry, and foundations, ORUs have extended university research into interdisciplinary, applied and capital-intensive endeavors. By the end of the 1980s, there were over 2,000 of them on American campuses; they continue to emerge in new fields of biotechnology, microelectronics, material sciences, and artificial intelligence.[44]

While the presence of external funds from a sponsor is often the impetus for a proposed ORU, other criteria have included the presence of a critical mass of faculty and the availability of administrative support. Some ORUs even have explicit commitments to graduate education, such as graduate fellowships offered by the Stanford Humanities Center. ORUs have offered important advantages for graduate education. Intellectually, they mediate between the world of disciplinary training and "real world needs and problems."[45] Practically, they provide dissertation support and stipends for graduate students. Often they make available better research equipment. Finally, as an indirect benefit, they employ specialists (postdoctoral or non-faculty researchers) in a temporary home, akin to the departmental home, in which graduate students can participate.

The administration of research and training in ORUs evokes a new set of challenges as it may be increasingly incompatible with departmental organization. Full-time non-faculty research personnel may supervise graduate student research assistants but do not have faculty status.[46] Generally, students and younger faculty want the opportunity to work in that setting, with trained researchers and up-to-date equipment. It is possible that these centers draw intellectual, organizational, and economic vitality away from department-based graduate programs and thereby jeopardize the continued viability of various departments. Not only may faculty loyalties become divided between organizational units, but budgets for research are overseen by different managers than departmental instructional budgets. Thus, a significant component of research training may end up being staffed and financed by complex administrative arrangements in which faculty allocations and budget allocations are no longer fully congruent with the actual practice of department-based graduate education. In short, increased research training of graduate education may become organizationally less visible, as it falls between the lines of departmental organization.

In recent years, ORUs have become a highly visible and controversial receptacle for forthcoming industrial funds, especially as federal initiatives have been launched to encourage industrial contributions for campus-based, larger-scale operations. Beginning with the mid-1970s, the NSF established the Industry-University Cooperative Research Projects; again in the late 1980s, NSF promoted proposals for university-based Engineering Research Centers as well as Science and Technology Centers. These programs were to be funded initially by Congressional appropriations and to be gradually weaned from NSF funds through industrial contributions. Generating controversy across these programs was an explicit orientation for universities to aid in the nation's economic competitiveness.

Graduate education and research are affected in mixed ways by these kinds of initiatives that combine or seek to replace federal support with industrial sponsorship. Not only do resources become more concentrated, but they become less flexible; for once a center is established it has to be fed. Moreover, industrial sponsorship, whether arranged formally in these kinds of ORUs or as informal collaboration, carries some potential constraints in terms of the research process (e.g., secrecy) and the product (e.g., agreements on patents). However, in favoring new interdisciplinary and applied sciences and in bringing to campus research personnel to staff those facilities, industrial sponsors provide graduate students with exposure to timely problems, state of the art research and techniques, internships which are job placement opportunities in industry, and provide faculty with supplemental income.

Attracting some university administrators and researchers to industrial collaboration or sponsorship is the recognition of a formidable problem: how will universities sustain the material conditions required for first-class, capital-intensive science? Direct appeals by universities to the federal government have brought limited results. With much lobbying on the part of university representatives, the federal government has reluctantly agreed to sponsor some of the rebuilding and replacement of campus research facilities and equipment that was neglected throughout the 1970s, and that proved insufficient as science became more capital-intensive in the 1980s. Both the National Institutes of Health and the National Science Foundation participated in this revitalization through regular research grants and center grants.

In addition to establishing ORUs, another strategy for universities to recover the enormous costs incurred in campus research has been to re-negotiate the indirect cost rate for overheads on research grants, although university administrators, campus-based researchers and the federal agencies have been struggling to reconcile their conflicting interests. The indirect cost rate is a mechanism for distributing among sponsors and research projects the indirect costs that the institution incurs through lighting, heat, libraries, and general maintenance of the campus. Since a university wants to recoup the maximum possible and the researcher wants as much as possible for the research process itself, administrators and researchers disagree. At the same time, the government wants more adequate justification of university expenses (Association of American Universities, 1989). Universities continue to vary in their indirect cost rates. For example, Columbia University is at 74 percent, while the University of Wisconsin and University of Minnesota are at 44 percent.[47]

Underlying discussions over indirect cost recovery is a widespread perception that instrumentation in university laboratories fares poorly when compared to government or commercial laboratories and the conviction that a decline in quality of instrumentation in research universities may cause a decline in research productivity of academic scientists as well as in the first-rate training opportunities for graduate students. The concern is whether universities will be able to provide interdisciplinary research and research training without reducing the strength of traditional, disciplinary graduate education. The fear is that if universities do not make "some realistic accommodation . . . an increasingly large portion of basic research and academic activity which is necessary to the quality of [graduate] education . . . will move outside the university structure." In spite of universities performing over half of American basic research, an increase in industry's proportional share may occur, especially as industries decide whether to collaborate with universities or to keep funds for their own laboratories. Ultimately, the concern is that academic departments would not be on the frontiers of research and that the best researchers would move away from graduate students, thereby jeopardizing a premise of the system—that "the best and the brightest" produce the best science and scientists at centers of excellence.[48]

The changing nature of federal funds for research, in addition to the 1970s decline in direct fellowships, has been most evident for Ph.D. students in the sciences, with potentially dramatic consequences especially in their research training experiences, although it also continues to impact Ph.D. students in the humanities where there has been no real federal support. Over the past fifteen years, graduate education continues to be supported in an ad hoc way, with the largest potential funding base of the federal government essentially unstable, and an increased pressure on professors to develop leaner research budgets within tighter time constraints.

Across the disciplines, doctoral students are taking longer to complete their programs, averaging 6.8 registered years, with humanities taking about eight years and engineering less than six years.[49] Students acquire more loan indebtedness the longer they defer employment, and become discouraged from the loss of momentum. In an effort to speed up the process, several programs across the country are reducing requirements for coursework so that students begin working on their dissertations earlier. The University of Chicago, for example, instituted a reduced coursework policy in 1982 in order to encourage students "to engage in their doctoral research as quickly, as clearly and as self-consciously as possible", which will lead to "a healthier emphasis on the research stage of graduate student work."[50] The need for such a change is especially apt for the humanities, where the prior tendency has always been to handle knowledge changes cumulatively with more and more material to incorporate into graduate coursework, while in the sciences (for example, physics and biological sciences) the faculty revamp the curricula every few years. Along similar lines, the expectations for the dissertation are being revised, especially in the sciences, as well as economics, where shorter publishable articles are more important than a long treatise.[51]

A less visible and potentially more profound transformation concerns the ways in which changes in federal sponsorship of research and graduate education have accompanied changes in the nature of student-faculty relationships during research training, especially for students in the sciences. While the historical ideal entailed a student working "at the bench" with a mentor, sponsored research is now the central medium for supervision and potential collaboration. There is some critical concern that faculty have become more like project managers and administrators rather than mentor-professors, and that students are being supervised in a more directive manner, treated like employees and technicians rather than as apprentices. As one observer suggests, "the roles of faculty member (mentor) and principal investigator (employer) are becoming inconsistent, straining the incumbents. Principles and practices that the mentor would prefer are inconsistent with the needs of the scientist as employer."[52]

Graduate student research assistants face the exigencies of an increasingly competitive arena of research support: time schedules of short-term project grants mean less leeway for mistakes; less available grant money means more competition and pressure to produce better results; sharing capital-intensive instrumentation means long hours of work, often in other cities; increased size of research teams entails perfecting a technique on one part of a project rather than completing an entire project from beginning to end; and time spent in research is valued over time spent in the "burden" of teaching younger graduate students or undergraduates. The arrangements emphasize efficiency and productivity which promote an organizational climate of a factory floor, or a "quasi-firm," rather than a learning arena.[53] Some evidence to support this assessment lies in organizing efforts of graduate students to gain bargaining status as employees.[54] There have also been disputes over academic authorship and ownership of intellectual property. Clearly, tensions are heightened in university-industry collaboration: While the exploitation of students for a faculty member's academic advancement is historically grounded in the university research system, it is another matter for a professor to profit financially from a student's work on a commercial venture.[55]

Conclusion

The trajectory of historical development is clear: graduate education in the United States has become so intertwined with sponsored research that graduate education-and-research has emerged as the foremost raison d'etre for universities in the top tier, as an increasingly noble aim for lower tiers to emulate, and as an implicit professional imperative for faculty devoted to the production of new knowledge and the preparation of new generations of knowledge producers. Historical scholarship reveals that obtaining research funds from the federal government and other patrons has been a requirement for university expansion and competitive advancement. As universities have aggressively competed for talented faculty and graduate students, they have sought to preserve their autonomy through stabilizing a base of support from a plurality of sources in external sponsors and internal revenues. At times by their own initiatives, they have attempted to create the organizational structures that would minimize the skewing of institutional priorities toward the economic incentives of short-term R & D sponsors.

Nonetheless, the contemporary era reveals that universities have been continually challenged by an inherently unstable federal funding base which left direct support to doctoral education concentrated in the physical and life sciences, even less in the social sciences, and virtually nonexistent in humanities. Particularly in the past two decades, the tension has become heightened as the national government has replaced a large proportion of fellowships and traineeships with loans that are incurred by individual students, leaving the bulk of support as indirect, through research assistantships on short-term R & D projects that strain the ideal mentor-apprentice relationship. Former ideals have been overshadowed by research-training activities that are elaborated into finer status distinctions for students to connect with "the right" principal investigator on a "cutting edge" and consistently-funded research project. To the extent that graduate education functions as professional socialization, the professional work now modeled for students is often dependent on productivity criteria tied to other-than-scholarly agendas, which inspires us to ask for what kind of profession graduate are students being prepared.

The tone of this analysis has not been optimistic, primarily because the future organization and sponsorship of graduate education requires more collective deliberation. A host of issues require further discussion beyond what graduate degree programs a campus should offer. These include the nature of research training, the nature of financial aid mechanisms, the increasing timespan of doctoral study, foreign student enrollments in doctoral programs, the neglect of humanities and non-science fields, the appropriateness of industrial sponsorship, and the ownership of intellectual property. The issues are not strictly about efficient means but also about desirable ends.

Admittedly, to identify graduate education as paying a price for its linkage to the university research enterprise marks a distinctive shift in scholarly attention. Usually undergraduate education is what is characterized as losing, since undergraduate education subsidizes faculty research and graduate assistantships.[56] In truth, an argument can be made that both suffer. With greater frequency, scholars are now critically examining other costs involved in academic science with vital consequences for the academic profession.[57] However, efforts to pursue these and related lines of inquiry have been hampered by incomplete and often contradictory historical data in addition to intermittent contemporary data gathered at the individual, department, and campus levels. At present, the most valuable resources are kept at the national level, but each of those data bases has substantial limitations for longitudinal analysis.[58]

Perhaps a more formidable obstacle to collective deliberation than data is a tendency to define the issues in graduate education too narrowly, as local organizational (administrative) problems, rather than as more fundamental questions about the interplay between higher education and society. Analytical leverage can be gained by viewing higher education as a social institution that produces goods and services, that determines and distributes positions and resources, and that regulates the use and access to power. This kind of conceptualization re-frames what is problematic, and what may be feasible solutions, through illuminating how the issues facing graduate education at the end of the century are intimately connected to pervasive political and economic tensions in society.

Notes

1. See *The Chronicle of Higher Education*, February 24, 1993; March 24, 1993; May 19,1993; September 1, 1993; August 4, 1993.

2. The historical record offers different interpretations of the ways in which such changes have come about and the extent to which universities have adapted to external sponsors or have maintained their autonomy and academic values. As to whether universities have retained autonomy from a plurality of sponsors, see Geiger and Noble for celebratory and critical interpretations, respectively. Roger Geiger, *To Advance Knowledge: The Growth of American Research Universities, 1900-1940* (New York: Oxford University Press, 1986); David Noble, *America by Design: Science, Technology and the Rise of Corporate Capitalism* (New York: Alfred Knopf, 1977). Although scholars have documented separately the rise of modern American science (R. Bruce, *The Launching of Modern American Science: 1846-1876* [New York: Alfred Knopf, 1987]), the emergence of the American research university (R. Geiger, *To Advance Knowledge: The Growth of American Research Universities in the Twentieth Century, 1900-1940* [New York: Oxford University Press, 1986] and L. Veysey, *The Emergence of the American University* [Chicago and London: University of Chicago Press, 1965]), the emergence of graduate education (R. Storr, *The Beginnings of Graduate Education in America* [Chicago: University of Chicago Press, 1953] and B. Berelson, *Graduate Education in the United States* [New York: McGraw-Hill, 1960]), and postwar changes in federal support of academic science (J. Wilson, *Academic Science, Higher Education and the Federal Government, 1950-1983* [Chicago: University of Chicago Press, 1983]), little scholarly work has been done at their intersection to examine the factors that account for their interrelationship (the major exception being J. Ben-David, *Centers of Learning: Britain, France, Germany, United States* [New York: McGraw-Hill, 1977]. To date, most research on graduate education has been on graduate students [G. Malaney, "Graduate education as an area of research in the field of higher education," in *Higher Education: Handbook of Theory and Research, Volume IV*, ed. J. Smart [New York: Agathon Press, 1988]), while graduate education as a changing social institution remains understudied and undertheorized in the higher education literature.

3. For a more comprehensive discussion of graduate education at the master's degree level, see C. Conrad and S. Millar, *The Silent Success* (Baltimore: Johns Hopkins, 1992). For doctoral education, see W. Bowen and N. Rudenstine, *In Pursuit of the Ph.D.* (Princeton, N.J.: Princeton University Press, 1992). For graduate education in cross-national perspective see B. Clark, ed., *The Research Foundations of Graduate Education* (Berkeley and Los Angeles: University of California Press, 1993).

4. For research drift to comprehensive universities, see F. Queval, *The Evolution Toward Research Orientation and Capability in Comprehensive Universities* (unpublished Ph.D. Diss. University of California at Los Angeles, 1990).

5. *The Chronicle of Higher Education*, August 25, 1993.

6. B. Clark, *Places of Inquiry* (Berkeley and Los Angeles: University of California Press, forthcoming).

7. N. Sanford, "Graduate Education: Then and Now," in *Scholars in the Making,* ed. J. Katz and R. Harnett (Ballinger, 1976), pp. 250–51.

8. See chapter 6 in this volume.

9. Adapted from National Science Foundation, *Science and Engineering Indicators, 1991* (Washington, D.C.: Division of Science Resource Studies, 1990).

10. The earliest signs of doctoral education in the United States were the granting of the first Ph.D. in 1861 by Yale's Sheffield Scientific School, the second Ph.D. by the University of Pennsylvania in 1871, and the third by Harvard a year later. More significant was the explicit organizational mission of graduate education in the founding of Johns Hopkins University in 1876 and Clark University in 1889. See R. Bruce, *The Launching of Modern American Science,* pp. 335–37.

11. D. Wolfle, *The Home of Science: The Role of the University* (New York: McGraw-Hill, 1972), p. 4.

12. L. Veysey, *The Emergence of the American University,* pp. 149, 168, 318–19.

13. R. Hofstadter and G. Hardy. *The Development and Scope of Higher Education in the United States* (New York: Columbia University Press, 1952), pp. 44–45; B. Berelson, *Graduate Education in the United States,* p. 33.

14. L. Mayhew, *Reform in Graduate Education. SREB Research Monograph No. 18* (Atlanta, Georgia: Southern Regional Education Board, 1972), p. 6; Ben-David, *Centers of Learning,* p. 61. See also B. Clark, *The Higher Education System* (Berkeley: University of California Press, 1983).

15. R. Geiger, *To Advance Knowledge,* p. 37. Ben-David, *Centers of Learning,* p. 61.

16. L. Veysey, *The Emergence of the American University,* p. 177.

17. R. Geiger, *To Advance Knowledge,* p. 19.

18. R. Merton, "The Matthew Effect in Science," *Science* 159 (January 1968): 56–63.

19. M. Trow, "The Analysis of Status," in *Perspectives on Higher Education: Eight Disciplinary and Comparative Views,* ed. B. Clark (Los Angeles and Berkeley: University of California Press. 1984), p. 134; L. Veysey, *The Emergence of the American University,* p. 312.

20. R. Bruce, *The Launching of Modern American Science,* pp. 329–34; F. Rudolph, *The American College and University: A History* (New York: Vintage/Random House, 1962), pp. 425–27.

21. B. Berelson, *Graduate Education in the United States;* R. Geiger, *To Advance Knowledge,* esp. p. 166.

22. Much of this adaptation to undertake applied research became incorporated into the ideal of service, especially for public universities. See Noble, *America by Design,* and G. Rhoades and S. Slaughter, "The Public Interest and Professional Labor," in *Culture and Ideology in Higher Education,* ed. W. Tierney (New York: Praeger, 1991).

23. R. Geiger, *To Advance Knowledge,* pp. 174–225.

24. Ibid, p. 262.

25. Over the next decade, the NAS became the site of severe conflicts over membership (which was limited to 50) and mission, as American scientists from different fields vied for control of the scientific community. Bruce, *The Launching of Modern American Science,* pp. 301–305, 315–17.

26. R. Geiger, *To Advance Knowledge,* pp. 13, 100, 165, 256.

27. P. Starr, *The Social Transformation of American Medicine* (New York: Basic

Books. 1982), p. 193.

28. D. Wolfle, *The Home of Science*, p. 110; D. Dickson, *The New Politics of Science* (Chicago: University of Chicago Press. 1984); A. Rivlin, *The Role of The Federal Government in Financing Higher Education* (Washington, D.C. The Brookings Institution, 1961), p. 31.

29. M. Finkelstein, *The American Academic Profession* (Columbus: Ohio State University Press, 1984), p. 24.

30. R. Geiger, *To Advance Knowledge*, p. 220.

31. A. Rivlin, *The Role of the Federal Government*, p. 47.

32. D. Dickson, *The New Politics of Science;* Government University Industry Research Roundtable, *Science and Technology in the Academic Enterprise* (Washington, D.C.: National Academy Press, 1989).

33. Government University Industry Research Roundtable, *Science and Technology;* Ben-David, *Centers of Learning*, p. 119.

34. Douglas Knight, et al., *The Federal Government and Higher Education* (Englewood Cliffs: Prentice Hall, 1960), pp. 135–37.

35. P. Coggeshall and P. Brown, *The Career Achievements of NIH Postdoctoral Trainees and Fellows. NIH Program Evaluation Report by Commission on National Needs for Biomedical and Behavioral Research Personnel & Institute of Medicine* (Washington, D.C.: National Academy Press, 1984).

36. The concentration of doctoral degree granting and sponsored research activity persists today. The top thirty universities in doctoral degree production are also among the top fifty receiving federal funds for science and engineering R & D. All but four of those thirty are also listed in the top forty-two universities in terms of R & D expenditures. Data adapted from National Science Foundation 1993 sources.

37. B. Berelson, *Graduate Education in the United States;* National Research Council, *Summary Report 1986: Doctorate Recipients from United States Universities* (Washington, D.C.: National Academy Press, 1987); Department of Education, *Digest of Education Statistics 1989* (Washington, D.C.,: National Center for Education Statistics, 1989.); Judith Glazer, *The Master's Degree: Tradition, Diversity, Innovation*, ASHE-ERIC Higher Education Report No. 6 (Washington, D.C.: Association for the Study of Higher Education, 1986).

38. National Research Council, *Summary Report 1986;* B. Berelson, *Graduate Education in the United States*, p. 35; Glazer, *The Master's Degree*.

39. F. Rudolph, *The American College and University: A History* (New York: Vintage/Random House, 1962), p. 239; see also P. Gumport. "The Research Imperative," in *Culture and Ideology in Higher Education*, ed. W. Tierney (New York: Praeger, 1991), pp. 87–106.

40. Government University Industry Research Roundtable, *Science and Technology*.

41. C. Kidd, "Graduate education: The New Debate," *Change* (May 1974): 43. See also: D. Wolfle, *The Home of Science*, p. 256; F. Balderston, "Organization, Funding, Incentives and Initiatives for University Research," in *The Economics of American Universities*, ed. S. Hoenack and E. Collins (Albany, N.Y.: SUNY Press, 1990), p. 40; A. Hauptman, *Students in Graduate and Professional Education: What We Know and Need to Know* (Washington, D.C.: Association of American Universities, 1986); S. Slaughter, "The Official Ideology of Higher Education," in Tierney, *Culture and Ideology*, pp. 59–86.

42. National Science Board, *Science and Engineering Indicators—1987* (Washington, D.C.: U.S. Government Printing Office, 1987).

43. J. Sommer, "Distributional Character and Consequences of the Public Funding of Science," in *Federal Support of Higher Education,* ed. R. Meiners and R. Amacher (New York: Paragon House, 1990), p. 175; F. Balderston, "Organization, Funding, Incentives"; National Science Foundation, *Science and Technology Data Book, 1988. No. NSF 87-317* (Washington, D.C.: National Science Foundation, Division of Science Resource Studies, 1987); D. Gerstein, D. Luce, N. Smelser, and S. Sperlich, eds., *The Behavioral and Social Sciences: Achievements* (Washington, D.C.: National Academy Press, 1988), p. 251.

44. R. Geiger, "Organized Research Units: The Role in the Development of University Research," *Journal of Higher Education* 61 (January/February 1990): 1–19.

45. Robert Friedman and Renee C. Friedman, "Organized Research Units in Academe Revisited," in *Managing High Technology: An Interdisciplinary Perspective,* ed. B. Mar, W. Newell, and B. Saxberg (North-Holland: Elsevier Science Publishers, 1985), pp. 75–91.

46. See Clark Kerr, *The Uses of the University* (New York: Harper & Row, 1963). Estimates of the number now employed in universities range from five thousand to over thirty thousand. Charles Kidd, "New Academic Positions: The Outlook in Europe and North America," in *The Research System in the 1980s: Public Policy Issues,* ed. John Logsdon (Philadelphia, Pa.: Franklin Institute Press, 1982), pp. 83–96; Carlos Kruytbosch, *The Organization of Research in the University: The Case of Research Personnel* (unpublished Ph.D. dissertation, University of California at Berkeley, 1970); Albert H. Teich, "Research Centers and Non-Faculty Researchers: A New Academic Role," in *Research in the Age of the Steady-State University,* ed. Don Phillips and Benjamin Shen (AAAS Selected Symposium Series, no. 60, 1982), pp. 91–108; Government University Industry Research Roundtable, *Science and Technology in the Academic Enterprise* (Washington, D.C.: National Academy Press, 1989); I. Feller, "University-Industry Research and Development Relationships," paper prepared for the Woodlands Center for Growth Studies, Conference on Growth Policy in the Age of High Technology: The Role of Regions and States, 1988.

47. *Research Review* 19 (May 1990). Minneapolis: University of Minnesota; F. Balderston, "Organization, Funding, Incentives," p. 47.

48. C. Frances, "1984: The Outlook for Higher Education," *AAHE Bulletin* 37, no. 6 (February 1985): 3–7; K. Hoving, "Interdisciplinary Programs, Centers and Institutes: Academic and Administrative Issues," paper presented at the annual meeting of the Council of Graduate Schools, Washington, D.C., 1987; C. Kruytbosch, "The Future Flow of Graduate Students into Scientific Research: A Federal Policy Issue?" paper presented at annual meeting of Council of Graduate Schools, Orlando, Florida, December 5–7, 1979; B. Smith, "Graduate Education in the United States," in *The State of Graduate Education,* ed. B. Smith (Washington, D.C.: The Brookings Institution, 1985).

49. National Research Council, *Summary Report 1986.*

50. University of Chicago, "Report of the Commission on Graduate Education," *University of Chicago Record* 16 (May 3, 1982): 2.

51. J. Berger, "Slowing Pace to Doctorates Spurs Worry on Filling Jobs," *New York Times* (May 3, 1989), p. A1.

52. E. Hackett, "Science as a Vocation in the 1990s," *Journal of Higher Education*

61 (May/June 1990): 267.

53. H. Etzkowitz, "Entrepreneurial Scientists & Entrepreneurial Universities in American Academic Science," *Minerva* 21 (1983): 198–233.

54. See P. Gumport and J. Jennings. "Students or Employees: The Ambiguity of Doctoral Assistantships," paper presented at the American Educational Association Annual Meeting, April 1993.

55. Martin Kenney, *Biotechnology: The University-Industrial Complex* (New Haven: Yale University Press, 1986), pp. 118–21.

56. A. Astin, "Moral messages of the University," *Educational Record* 70 (Spring 1989): 22–25.

57. Sheila Slaughter, *The Higher Learning and High Technology* (New York: SUNY Press, 1990); Hackett, "Science as a Vocation"; Etzkowitz, "Entrepreneurial Scientists."

58. See National Research Council's Survey of Earned Doctorates which accumulates as longitudinal data in the Doctorate Record File; the National Center for Education Statistics' data on enrollment; the National Science Foundation's data on Academic Science and Engineering Enrollment and Support, Federal Obligations to Colleges and Universities, and National Patterns of Science and Technology Resources. See also the Council of Graduate Schools' policy studies.

PART FOUR

CONCLUDING PERSPECTIVE

15

Current and Emerging Issues Facing Higher Education in the United States
Ami Zusman

In the 1990s and beyond, higher education in the United States will face profound changes and an uncertain environment. Societal expectations and public resources for higher education are undergoing fundamental shifts. Moreover, changes both within and outside the academy are altering the nature and make-up of higher education—its students, faculty, curriculum, and functions. As Kerr and Gade have noted, crisis and change in higher education "have been the rule, not the exception."[1] Nevertheless, in the 1990s the combination of these changes poses greater challenges to higher education—and may result in greater transformations—than have those for at least the past half century.

Reflecting the overall theme of this book, this chapter focuses on major *external* influences on U.S. higher education and, conversely, on how institutional decisions in matters such as admissions or research emphases may affect the broader society. A common thread runs throughout these issues: public challenges to the nature of colleges' and universities' "social contract." These challenges are apparent in ongoing conflicts between the ideals of equality and merit, the balance between teaching and research in the university, and the expectation that higher education serve as an engine for the nation's economic growth, among others.

1. Retrenchment and Reallocation

FUNDING CHANGES

Three funding trends are affecting colleges and universities, especially public institutions: budget cuts, budget uncertainty, and "privatization" of public institutions.

Budget cuts. Public higher education in the 1990s is undergoing a period of financial cutbacks unequaled since at least World War II. In 1992–93, for the first time since records were begun in the late 1950s, overall state appropriations were lower than they had been two years earlier, despite a five percent increase in public enrollments. When adjusted for inflation, 36 states provided less funding than they had two years earlier. Some large state systems suffered very significant cuts in their base budgets. For example, between 1988–89 and 1992–93, Massachusetts colleges and universities suffered a 28 percent drop in state appropriations, unadjusted for inflation, even though public enrollments remained relatively steady. California, Florida, New York, and Virginia, among others, saw substantial appropriations cuts amid increased public enrollments. Although many states increased their 1993–94 appropriations, these modest augmentations have not brought funding levels back to that of the mid-1980s, nor are they soon likely to do so, especially when inflation and enrollment growth are considered.[2]

Nor are private colleges unaffected. The American Council on Education found that one-third of all private institutions had reduced operating budgets in 1991–92. Budget cutbacks at these institutions resulted from several factors: rising costs, market limits on the extent to which tuition could be increased, reduction in corporate giving, and, at a number of research universities, reductions in allowable federal overhead costs. Lower state revenues have also led several states to eliminate or reduce financial aid for students in private institutions. On the other hand, continued state budget problems may benefit private institutions in some states if states decide to increase support to private institutions or even redirect students to them, as a less expensive alternative to meeting higher education demand than expanding public higher education systems.[3]

Uncertainty. Equally problematic for colleges are the uncertain and fluctuating funding levels with which they must deal. In 1992–93, 20 states made mid-year cuts in funding.[4] As Sherry Penney, Chancellor of the University of Massachusetts at Boston, has noted, "when the budget axe starts slashing in the public sector, you probably will not have any control over the size or timing of the cuts. They often occur unpredictably, well into the academic year when personnel and programs are set."[5]

Privatization. Over the past decade, public colleges and universities have also become increasingly "privatized" as funding has shifted from the state to student fees and to federal or corporate sources. For example, the percentage of the University of California's budget that comes from state funds (excluding the system's three federally funded Department of Energy laboratories) dropped from 37 percent in 1981–82 to less than 27 percent in 1992–93. Nor are these declines limited to research universities. In Virginia, the state percentage of the instructional budget for ten four-year colleges dropped from two-thirds in 1988 to under half four years later.[6] Although the declining percentage of state funding is due in part to institutions' success in obtaining extramural funding, it also is the result of diminished state support for public higher education, as indicated by the rise in tuition and fees. In 1960, tuition and fees comprised approximately 18 percent of the costs of instruction and academic support at public four-year colleges; in 1990, they comprised approximately 25 percent.[7] In California, Minnesota, and other states, state officials have proposed raising tuition levels, especially for graduate or professional students, still higher.

Future trends. Higher education will probably face continuing budgetary constraints and uncertainty for the immediate future. Although the nation's economic recession was primarily responsible for state budget cuts to higher education during the late 1980s and early 1990s, these cuts also reflected growing demands upon the state treasury from competing social programs such as the public schools, health, and prisons. In California, for example, corrections comprised the fastest growing segment of the state budget from 1983–84 to 1992–93, with percentage increases more than double those for higher education. Demands from competing programs will likely continue to grow. In addition, higher education is more vulnerable to state cuts than most other programs because it is one of the few discretionary areas in the state budget. Private institutions, too, will likely continue to face budgetary problems. Because higher education is a labor-intensive enterprise where costs have grown faster than the overall economy, private institutions may find it difficult to raise tuition charges enough to offset rising costs, especially if student financial aid does not keep pace.

Finally, some observers see a profound shift in public attitudes toward the value of higher education. Two demographic trends deserve particular note: the aging of the general population and the declining proportion of white, middle-class students in the 18- to 24-year-old population. As a result, a smaller proportion of individuals with economic and political power may see itself as having a direct stake in higher education.[8] When current public dissatisfaction with undergraduate education and decreased public trust resulting from perceived wasteful practices and highly publicized academic scandals are added to these long-term trends, the result is likely to be continued financial stress for U.S. colleges and universities.

IMPLICATIONS OF INSTITUTIONAL RETRENCHMENT AND REALLOCATION

Continuing budgetary constraints pose a major challenge to higher education institutions, both public and private. In turn, institutional responses to budgetary constraints may significantly impact the larger society. During the late 1980s and early 1990s, most institutions under financial stress responded as they had during previous periods of financial constraints, primarily by deferring maintenance and construction, freezing new hires, increasing tuition, and making across-the-board cuts. However, if budgetary constraints continue, as expected, higher education institutions will be forced to make long-term, fundamental cuts to programs and faculty and, indeed, to restructure and narrow institutional programs and priorities. Some institutions have begun to make more extensive and selective cuts and to implement new institutional policies and approaches. Their experiences and projected future actions raise a number of questions about the long-term impacts of institutional retrenchment and reallocation.

Impacts on students. Many institutions, both public and private, have responded to budget cuts by raising student tuition. How will these increases affect access to higher education? Unless sufficient financial aid is provided, low-income students and historically underrepresented ethnic groups are at risk of being excluded. Alternatively, if financial aid targets the poor, middle-class students may have more difficulty in paying for higher education. Overall enrollments in the public sector may be cut. Already, a number of public institutions have cut enrollments, including the twenty-campus California State University, despite increased enrollment demands. If budget constraints continue, other public institutions will follow. Enrollment contraction, at a time when the age group is again increasing, raises the question of whether the movement toward universal access to higher education might be slowed or even reversed.

Impacts on faculty. As of 1993, relatively few tenured faculty had been terminated. However, institutions have begun cutting faculty in other ways: reducing new hires, offering generous early retirement incentives, and terminating non-tenure-track faculty.[9] Conversely, many institutions have hired more part-time temporary faculty at lower salaries and benefits, as well as full-time faculty ineligible for tenure; about half of all college instructors are now ineligible for tenure. Thus, two contrary trends appear to be occurring: the elimination of many temporary faculty and the hiring (or re-hiring) of other temporary faculty, often on a more part-time basis. Growing use of temporary faculty presents both advantages and problems. On the one hand, it reduces institutional costs and increases institutions' ability to respond to changing student demand; this is particularly important at a time when institutions are less able to expand their permanent faculties. On the other hand, according to the American Association of University Professors, it may harm the tenure system and the quality of higher education.[10] Some observers fear that this situation may also create a two-tier academic labor force.[11] Overall, faculty cuts and reallocations may affect the proportion of tenured faculty, as well as faculty ethnic, gender, and age distribution. The challenge to higher education will be to ensure that faculty cuts do not reduce equity, the range of faculty perspectives, or institutions' ability to respond to changing fields. Colleges and universities also have a responsibility not to use a "buyers" job market to take unfair advantage of untenured faculty.

A paradox exists, however. Only a few years ago, many analysts predicted dramatic faculty shortages after 1997 (if not earlier) because of expected high levels of faculty retirements, increasing enrollment demand, and inadequate supply of new Ph.Ds.[12] Now, with the potential "downsizing" of institutions, these shortages may not materialize. At least three possibilities exist: (1) higher education institutions will seek to hire new faculty to meet rising student demand, with resulting faculty shortages; (2) institutions will raise the student-faculty ratio and perhaps hire more temporary, part-time faculty at lower salary levels; or (3) despite enrollment demand, institutions will cut both faculty and enrollments, resulting in a continued depressed academic market for new Ph.Ds.

Impacts on academic programs. To date, program impacts have been largely unplanned. In some cases, disproportionate numbers of faculty in certain fields have accepted early retirement, leaving a serious imbalance between faculty expertise and institutional needs. In terminating non-tenure-track faculty, institutions have indirectly made decisions to reduce or eliminate programs such as remedial education, beginning language courses, and teacher education, which often depend heavily upon non-tenure-track faculty. Repetitive across-the-board cuts have gradually weakened once viable programs until they become obvious candidates for termination.

A few institutions have made often difficult decisions to reduce, consolidate, or eliminate specific programs. In May 1993, for example, the Board of Regents for the eleven-campus University of Maryland System approved plans to discontinue, suspend, or consolidate thirty-eight bachelor's programs, twenty-four master's programs, and seven Ph.D. programs, and to reallocate over $10 million in monies saved to areas identified as high priority, including undergraduate education, the flagship campus at College Park, and historically black campuses. Generally, programs cut have been identified as academically weak, high cost, having low market demand, or less central to institutional mission or state need. Deciding what programs are low quality or less important, however, may be subjective. Based on faculty retrenchment cases in the 1980s, Slaughter suggests that departments serving primarily women and/or fields unable to tie themselves to market needs may be disproportionately cut.[13] On the other hand, because the costs of nonprofessional undergraduate programs do not differ greatly, few institutions are likely to eliminate core undergraduate arts and science fields.

As budget constraints force institutions to cut academic offerings, the challenge for higher education will be to make planned, strategic decisions as quickly as possible, in order to maintain quality and balance of programs, as well as to protect programs and functions crucial to state and national interests. To this end, institutions will need to revise program review processes designed during an era of growth, which typically are more effective in preventing the establishment of new programs than in consolidating or eliminating existing programs. To maintain institutional priorities, it will be especially important for institutions to reallocate scarce dollars to support important areas unlikely to be sustained by extramural dollars, such as the humanities and undergraduate teaching. Institutions will also need to find ways to continue new initiatives, to enable them to respond to changing needs and maintain institutional morale. As discussed further in Section 7, multicampus and statewide systems of higher education will have a critical role in ensuring that the system as a whole maintains an appropriate balance and range of programs and flexibility to respond to new needs.

Impacts on administration and governance. One result of budget constraints may be greater centralization of authority. Some university presidents have argued that when budget cuts must be made quickly and require the willingness of faculty and staff to cut their own programs, traditional participatory processes become difficult if not impossible. Slaughter concluded that retrenchment "generally undermined faculty participation in governance and faculty authority over the direction of the curriculum." Conversely, Donald Kennedy, former president of Stanford University, has argued that an over-reliance on consensus has resulted in the reservation of final decisions to the top-level; he has suggested that a middle ground be found between consensual and hierarchical management.[14] Without faculty and staff "buy-in," major program reductions and reallocations will likely lead to resistance, lower morale, and ultimately lower productivity. Moreover, many observers have argued that, in the twenty-first century, higher education institutions will face increasingly complex and uncertain environments that will require greater institutional decentralization.

For the immediate future, the challenge for higher education institutions will be to find ways to respond more quickly to urgent needs that require tough decisions while maintaining essential faculty consultation, for example, by setting up joint faculty-administrative committees. Budget cuts are also expected to result in larger cuts to administrative services and staff (which grew significantly faster than faculty in the 1980s), in order to protect academic programs. Still unclear is how these cuts will affect student services and other important areas.

Impacts on institutional infrastructure. Building maintenance, repair, and construction have been among the areas most hard hit by budget cutbacks. According to the Association of Physical Plant Administrators, the backlog of deferred maintenance and replacement of existing facilities in U.S. colleges and universities was approaching one hundred billion dollars as of 1991-92, up from about forty billion dollars a decade earlier. Ultimately, these repairs will cost more than if maintenance and replacement had been made on schedule. Moreover, failure to construct or renovate buildings and laboratories may harm the nation's ability to conduct cutting edge research, especially in the sciences.

Revenue-raising strategies. A number of institutions have begun pursuing new revenue-raising strategies with far-reaching implications. One such strategy is to "privatize" academic programs in public institutions, that is, to require programs, especially high-demand, high-return professional programs like law or business, to be fully funded by clients (students) or business. In California, the governor's 1993-94 budget called for a plan to privatize at least one of California's four public law schools. Law and business schools at other institutions, including the Universities of Michigan, Virginia, and North Carolina, have moved toward privatization. At some institutions, even teacher or school administrator training programs (which are not generally considered high-return) are being considered for privatization. Commercial technology transfer and other for-profit collaborations with industry are another strategy increasingly being adopted (see Section 5). Community colleges and other institutions also are expanding contract education programs with specific businesses or industries. Still another strategy is the "outsourcing" of institutional functions to private vendors or other education institutions, including operation of residential dorms, employment training, and such academic functions as remedial education and beginning language instruction.[15] These strategies raise several questions: On what basis will states or institutions determine that some programs warrant continued state support while others do not? How will such shifts affect access, diversity, and curriculum? How can institutions ensure that outsourcing, especially of academic functions, does not undermine overall institutional coherence and accountability?

Impacts on the higher education system as a whole. If tuition differences continue to narrow, higher education could see significant enrollment shifts from public to private higher education, as well as from four-year to less expensive two-year institutions. However, enrollment shifts to public two-year colleges assume both that two-year colleges will have the resources to enroll more students, and that students can afford their rising fees. Community colleges in California, for example, saw an unprecedented nine percent enrollment decline in 1993, as a result of budget constraints and fee increases. In such an enrollment squeeze, nontraditional students, including returning adults and those whose initial preparation precludes admission at other institutions, may well be shut out of traditionally open-door community colleges.

Perhaps a more subtle impact is the adoption of the language and values of business: "downsizing" (i.e., workforce reduction), growing use of temporary employees, privatization, and commercialization—changes that may threaten academic values and institutional integrity. Proponents of greater institutional acceptance of marketplace values and approaches argue, however, that institutions must do so in order to meet "fundamental changes—in the goods and services the public seeks; in the nature and needs of students; in faculty work and ambitions."[16] Finally, the gloomy picture presented by budget cuts is not without its positive side. Budget cuts are forcing many institutions to examine seriously their missions and priorities; this assessment may lead to clearer and more coherent institutional missions and a reinvigorated sense of purpose and academic community.

2. Changing Students, Changing Views of Student Entitlement

STUDENT POOL

Between 1980 and 1991, total higher education enrollments in the U.S. increased nearly 19 percent, from 12.1 million to 14.4 million, even though the numbers of 18–24-year-olds (the traditional college-age population) declined over 12 percent. The "college-age" pool, however, does not necessarily reflect future college attendance. African-American, Latino, and low-income students remain significantly underrepresented. Between 1985 and 1989, less than six percent of individuals receiving baccalaureate degrees by age 24 were from the bottom income quartile.[17] Moreover, while the numbers of Latino and African-American college students grew during this period, reflecting population growth, their college-going rate increased much less than that of white students. Many Latinos are eliminated from the college pool even before high school graduation; over one-third of 19–20-year-olds have not completed high school. A substantial number of these are immigrants who have never enrolled in U.S. schools. By contrast, the proportion of African-American students completing high school increased significantly between 1970 and 1981, with further increases between 1981 and 1991; nevertheless, fewer than half of these graduates entered college, compared to nearly two-thirds of white, non-Latino high school graduates. Contrary to popular assumptions, a lower percentage of African-American women than of men complete high school. As a result of these differential rates, the growth in college enrollments during the 1980s was due primarily to increases in the proportion of white students going to college, despite the increase in nonwhite eighteen- to twenty-four-year-olds from 23 to 30 percent of the age group. (See table.)

In addition, the definition of the college-age pool has expanded. In 1990, students aged 25 years and older comprised 44 percent of total college enrollments and 22 percent of full-time enrollments. The college participation rate of this age group has remained virtually unchanged for the past fifteen years; rather, these enrollments reflect the large numbers of 25- to 44-year-olds in the population. According to projections by the U.S. Department of Education, older students will likely remain a significant part of college enrollments for at least the next decade.

During the 1990s most states will see a modest increase in the college-age population, as the "baby boom echo" generation reaches adulthood. Some states (notably large "sunbelt" states like California and Florida) will see sharp increases in the college-age population. The decade will also see continued shifts in the racial and ethnic composition of this population. These shifts will be dramatic in some states, especially the growth of Latino populations in the Southwest, and of Asian populations in the West. In California, for example, Latino students comprised 36 percent of public K–12 enrollments in 1992, and

PARTICIPATION IN U.S. HIGHER EDUCATION, BY RACE AND ETHNICITY*

	African-American	Asian & other	Latino	White	Total
For Total Population					
Percent of 18–24-year-olds[a]					
1981	12.9	2.4	8.0	76.7	100
1991	13.7	4.2	12.2	69.9	100
Percent of college enrollments[b]					
1980	9.4	3.1	4.0	83.5	100
1991	9.6	5.4	6.2	78.8	100
By Ethnic Group					
Percent of 19-20-year-olds who completed high school[c]					
1981	71.8	N.A.	56.8	84.8	80.8
1990	77.6	N.A.	59.7	87.3	82.8
Percent of recent high school graduates enrolled in college[b]					
1981	42.9	N.A.	52.1	54.6	53.9
1991	45.6	N.A.	57.1	64.6	62.4
Percent of 18–24-year olds enrolled in college[b]					
1981	19.9	N.A.	16.6	27.7	26.2
1991	23.4	N.A.	17.8	36.8	33.3

*Latinos (persons of Hispanic origin) are excluded from figures for African-Americans and whites, except for percent of high school graduates enrolled in college. "Other" includes Native Americans and Pacific Islanders. Figures exclude foreign students.

[a]U.S. Bureau of the Census, Current Population Reports, Series P25–1095 (Washington, D.C.: U.S. Government Printing Office, 1993), Table 1.

[b]U.S. Department of Education, Digest of Education Statistics, 1992 (Washington, D.C.: U.S. Government Printing Office, 1992), Tables 170, 173, 193; and Fall 1991 data for college enrollments.

[c]U.S. Department of Education, Condition of Education 1992 (Washington, D.C.: U.S. Government Printing Office, 1993), Indicator 20.

Asian/Pacific Islander students comprised over 11 percent. Increasing numbers of these students speak English as a second language; 16 percent of California's public high school students were identified as limited-English-proficient in 1992. By the year 2004, California projects that Latino students will comprise 49 percent of public K–12 enrollments and Asian/Pacific Islander students another 12 percent. Barring radical changes in immigration patterns, substantial numbers of these students will have limited English proficiency.

These changes in the size and composition of the traditional college-age pool have important implications for higher education. First, growth in the pool will increase demand for higher education. Public institutions will face pressures to enroll more students with less funding. For private colleges, the larger pool may provide a seller's market, allowing them to become more selective, as many did in the 1960s. Second, a larger proportion of the pool will be comprised of historically underrepresented groups, especially African-Americans and Latinos. Unless higher education works with schools and communities to increase these students' college participation, U.S. society will lose the talents of a growing segment of the population. Third, as more diverse students enter college, they will help change the face of the campus, just as the U.S.'s increasingly diverse population is changing the face of U.S. society. These changes will be felt especially at two-year institutions, where non-white and Latino students have enrolled in greater proportions. Colleges will need to develop ways to respond effectively to these more diverse students, especially to low-income, first-generation African-American and Latino college students, who drop out of college at higher rates than do middle-class white students. In some cases, this may mean greater support for English as a second language and related curricula, as more non-native-English speakers seek to enter college. It will also require a college climate and curriculum that welcome students' differing backgrounds and perspectives as an opportunity to bring a wider range of voices and experiences into the discussion, and that build upon students' diverse language and cultural backgrounds in preparing them for a more interdependent global society.

CHANGING PUBLIC EXPECTATIONS

Growing demand for higher education may collide with counter-forces limiting enrollment that were noted earlier: long-term budgetary demands on state governments to meet other social needs, increased public readiness to consider higher education a private good, and consequent reduction in state funding. During the 1980s, students' share of total instructional costs (tuition and fees) increased significantly; at the same time, federal financial aid under the Reagan administration shifted from grants to loans.[18] Public views of who should be admitted to higher education are also changing. Over the past decade, high school students completed more college-preparatory and advanced courses than previous generations, as states raised graduation and college admission requirements in response to national and state reports on K–12 education.[19] Having achieved higher levels of academic preparation, however, students may find themselves shut out of public four-year colleges, as these institutions reduce enrollments and raise admission standards further.

Changing expectations and reduced support for higher education come at a time when historically underserved minorities will comprise an increasing proportion of the college-age pool. If state policy makers and higher education leaders close the doors to higher education just when this new generation of students are prepared to enter, serious questions will be raised about equity in a democratic society, as well as risks to social stability. If the "rules" change, we will have a system of exclusion and increasing frustration for minority and low-income students. Reducing access to higher education also raises concerns about meeting society's economic and civic needs at a time of increasing technological, economic, social, and, political complexity and interdependence. The potential departure from the U.S.'s historic movement toward ever greater participation in higher education is especially problematic because it is occurring largely without explicit public discussion. Rather, state and institutional decisions made on financial grounds (i.e., to cut state appropriations, raise tuition, or limit enrollments) are indirectly affecting higher education access and participation. Patrick Callan, speaking about the California situation, has described this phenomenon as changing fundamental policy on access without leaving tell-tale fingerprints.[20] Both policy makers and institutional leaders have a responsibility to address the long-term implications of their responses to budget constraints.

3. The Education Continuum: School/College Interdependence

The changing student pool, changing demands on both K–12 and higher education, and ongoing concerns about the "fit" between high school and college education have led schools and colleges to a growing recognition of their interdependence and their shared responsibility for student success. Colleges and universities have a direct stake in the quality of K–12 education because they depend on the public schools to provide the academic preparation that students entering college need to succeed. For higher education to flourish also requires effective public education for all students, because education contributes to the economic health and social stability of the larger society. Even if it were not in higher education's self-interest to do so, state policy makers are demanding that colleges and universities play a larger role in strengthening K–12 education through teacher preparation and professional development, curricular support, programs to recruit and better prepare underrepresented students, and other areas.

PREPARATION AND REFORM IN K–12 EDUCATION

Many critics argue that the schools too often do not prepare students well for college. Ten years after the publication of *A Nation at Risk,* the report that mobilized national efforts to reform K–12 education, former Secretary of Education Terrel Bell concluded that those ten years had been "a splendid misery for American education."[21] Scholastic Aptitude Test scores for college-bound high school seniors remain lower today than they were in the early 1970s, and the gap between white students' performance and that of African-American and Latino students, especially on the verbal portion, remains significant. Even the most elite institutions report spending substantial resources to provide "remedial education."

Yet the past decade has also seen some significant improvements in K–12 education and achievement. SAT mathematics scores have actually increased, and verbal scores have remained relatively stable since the mid-1970s, even though larger numbers of students in the bottom 60 percent of their classes are taking the SAT. High school graduates are also completing more mathematics, science, English, and history courses than did earlier graduates. The belief that previous generations of entering college freshmen were better prepared than current students may be more myth than fact.[22]

Serious problems still do exist in K–12 education. The tests traditionally used to measure student achievement do not adequately take into account the demands of an increasingly complex, pluralistic, and technologically oriented society. Moreover, overall improvements mask great disparities among students. Unless current trends are reversed, growing numbers of public school students will have limited proficiency in English and will live below the poverty line, conditions that correlate with low academic achievement. Over 20 percent of children in the U.S. now live in poverty, and these percentages are expected to increase, especially in large industrialized states. The disparities between rich and poor extend to school districts as well. Unless school financing is reformed, low-income students in poor school districts will continue to receive much lower quality education, by almost every measurable indicator, than that provided middle-class and upper-class students in wealthier districts—what Jonathan Kozol has characterized as "savage inequalities" in how the U.S. supports its school children.[23] Because U.S. higher education depends upon an educated society, colleges and universities have a self-interest (as well as a responsibility) in informing public debate about the implications of these trends, and in working with schools and teachers to address them. Colleges and universities also need to expand their involvement at the preschool, elementary, and middle school levels; by high school, many students have been lost to the educational system.

While colleges and universities continue to focus primarily on K–12 students' SAT scores and high school courses, they have been slower to recognize the implications of K–12 reforms now underway in curriculum, instructional methods, and assessment. California has been a leader in statewide curriculum frameworks designed to promote interdisciplinary curricula, activity-based instruction, and collaborative learning, as well as efforts to develop "authentic" assessment based in part on student performance and portfolios. Other states are now pursuing similar reforms. These reforms, developed in response to earlier criticisms of K–12 education, may conflict with higher education's traditional admissions requirements, undergraduate content, instructional approaches, and assessment practices. Most problematic is the lack of fit between integrated interdisciplinary curriculum sequences at the high school level and discipline-specific admissions requirements and faculty expectations at the college level. These developments raise several questions: How can higher education institutions work with their high school colleagues to ensure an appropriate articulation between high school and college requirements and curricula? What role should higher education faculty play in helping to develop state and national curricular content and standards? How should changes in K–12 education affect teacher preparation? Finally, what lessons do these K–12 initiatives provide for higher education's own efforts to reconceive undergraduate education in order to include more emphasis on collaborative learning, interdisciplinary curricula, and alternative approaches to student assessment?

SCHOOL/COLLEGE COLLABORATION

School/college partnerships have been one response to schools' and colleges' growing recognition of their interdependence. Over the past decade, collaborations across institutions have blossomed, in programs ranging from student achievement initiatives and faculty alliances to development of new curricula, articulation of vocational education, and schoolwide reforms. State policy makers have often played an important role in promoting collaboration through financial incentives, mandated programs, and threats to reduce funding if institutions failed to work together. Because many legislators see collaboration as a way to save money by reducing redundant programs, they may encourage further collaboration in the future.[24]

School/college partnerships have also begun to change in significant ways. First, recent collaborations are more likely to be real partnerships that recognize the needs, strengths, and shared values of both sides. The academic alliances among faculty in different disciplines are an example of this. More significantly, although most university educators still consider schools as the partner that needs to change, there is growing recognition within higher education that colleges, too, must make changes, for example, by revising admissions criteria to address reformed K–12 curricula and assessments. Second, school/college partnerships have begun to be more comprehensive. Initially, most partnerships involved programs to assist individual elementary and secondary students or teachers. While these still predominate, increasing numbers of collaborations involve multiple elements of the school system—students, teachers, curriculum, and administration—to try to effect schoolwide change. Third, a growing number of collaborations involve systemwide, statewide, and even national collaborations. The National Writing Project, for example, has created a system of over 150 project sites across the U.S. that promote sustained, peer-oriented professional development for teachers and an ongoing professional network. Such large-scale collaborations not only have the resources to encourage and facilitate change at the local level, but can help create a coherent vision of teaching and learning across the state or U.S. and across education levels. Finally, school/college partnerships have begun to include organizations and agencies outside education, such as business, social service agencies, and minority community organizations, in an effort to develop a comprehensive, integrated system for children's services. These more comprehensive partnerships recognize that only by integrating health, nutrition, and other factors that affect children, and by incorporating the resources that other organizations can provide are sustained and significant improvements in students' learning likely.

School/college partnerships present several challenges. For partnerships to succeed, sustained college and university participation and leadership are essential. Research studies have found that new initiatives need time for participants to learn how to implement change effectively, adjust to new structures and procedures, and develop commitment and trust, especially between partners from different organizations, before change can be institutionalized. Especially in the early years of a new initiative, colleges and universities can offer unique resources to help conceive, develop, and implement educational reforms. In addition, several barriers to school/college partnerships must be overcome. Chief among these are the differences in cultures, perceptions, and priorities between schools and colleges, and the lack of institutional rewards and incentives for participation in collaborations. Higher education can encourage faculty participation in K–12 activities through such means as funding for collaborative research on schooling issues, and faculty promotion criteria that better recognize faculty research and service to the schools.[25]

4. Challenges to Undergraduate Education

Higher education is in the midst of a major re-evaluation of its roles and responsibilities in undergraduate education, driven by pressures and new developments both within and outside the academy. Two issues which have drawn the sharpest external concerns and intervention pose particular challenges: undergraduate teaching and assessment of student learning.

UNDERGRADUATE TEACHING

Over the past twenty-five years, faculty involvement in undergraduate teaching has diminished, as universities and colleges have sought to strengthen their research and graduate education missions. According to several studies, faculty members teach fewer undergraduate courses than they did 25 to 30 years ago, temporary part-time instructors and graduate teaching assistants meet a larger part of the teaching load, and institutions have largely delegated advising, mentoring, and tutoring responsibilities to student services staff. These shifts have been prompted by changing incentives. Faculty tenure and promotion decisions, especially at universities but increasingly at four-year colleges as well, have come to depend much more heavily on research excellence and publications than on teaching. In science and technology fields, research universities' growing reliance on federal research dollars has led them to provide additional incentives, including reduced teaching loads, to faculty who can generate these funds. According to Massy and Wilger, faculty and institutional norms are caught in an "academic ratchet" in which research norms gradually rise while expected teaching loads decline.[26]

While state policy makers have expressed dissatisfaction for a number of years with what they see as the neglect of undergraduate teaching, current budgetary constraints have increased their readiness to intervene. At a time when many undergraduates are paying higher tuition yet having difficulty enrolling in required courses, political authorities and other stakeholders, especially tuition-paying students and parents, are pressuring institutions, including research universities, to make undergraduate education and teaching their top priority. A number of states have begun intensive re-examinations of higher education's functions and priorities, raising fundamental questions about the balance between teaching and research and between undergraduate and graduate education.

Faculty teaching workload has become a particular target of these re-examinations, prompted in part by current budget realities. As Mingle notes, because faculty salaries are the largest single expenditure in state higher education budgets, "the costs of faculty stand out as a target of opportunity" for budget cutting, and a growing number of U.S. states have mandated studies of faculty workload.[27] Although few states have yet done so, political authorities appear more willing than in the past to mandate minimum faculty course loads, an action that previously would have been considered an inappropriate political intrusion into institutional authority over core academic matters. More often, the threat of budget cuts or legislative intervention has prompted institutions to adopt revised teaching policies and practices on their own. At private institutions, higher tuition and competition for enrollments have a similar impact in encouraging many institutions to place more emphasis on undergraduate teaching and to take other steps to improve undergraduate "productivity," including such innovative ideas as a three-year baccalaureate.

The challenge to higher education institutions from these trends and the political response to them is two-fold. First, institutions will need to assess their missions and priorities, rather than allowing institutional drift to determine their priorities, and to adopt approaches to support undergraduate teaching appropriate to their missions. Most importantly, faculty reward structures will need to recognize scholarship in teaching more adequately. Boyer's call for expanding the definition of scholarship to include integration, application, and teaching, as well as discovery, has stimulated much interest and discussion. Another provocative proposal is to hold departments responsible for faculty teaching by allocating resources based on departmental teaching participation and excellence.[28] Institutions are implementing a range of policies to encourage undergraduate teaching or increase teaching productivity. These include developing departmental workload policies to ensure fair and reasonable teaching loads, eliminating low-enrollment courses and programs, and utilizing educational technology more effectively. Many institutions are also increasing faculty teaching loads.

Second, institutions will need to persuade policy makers and the public not only that they are now doing a better job of undergraduate teaching than is frequently perceived, but also that research, graduate education, and public service functions are important as well. Institutions will need to demonstrate more clearly how faculty research activities not only infuse the content of undergraduate courses, but also contribute to students' understanding about how to acquire knowledge. Finally, institutions will need to shift the focus from how much faculty teach to how well students are learning.

ASSESSMENT OF STUDENT LEARNING

State officials, as well as accrediting agencies, are in fact increasingly requiring institutions to demonstrate what and how much students are learning. By 1992, nineteen states had required public higher education institutions to establish programs to assess what students learn in college, including Florida, New Jersey, and Tennessee, and more were considering such requirements. Some states provide financial bonuses to colleges that improve student performance.

As with undergraduate teaching, state interest in student assessment reflects continuing state concerns about the quality, purposes, and cost-effectiveness of state-funded undergraduate education. It also reflects states' growing requirements for institutional accountability, as well as policy makers' readiness to apply to higher education the concept of student performance assessments that they have implemented in K–12 education. State officials and accrediting agencies are requiring institutions to assess what students know, what have they learned (i.e., the "value added" by college attendance), graduation rates, including those for historically underrepresented students, and time required to obtain a degree. While most states permit institutions to determine their own goals and how these will be measured, based on institutional missions, some like Florida set statewide minimal standards for students or institutions. Given continuing budget constraints and public dissatisfaction with undergraduate education, external pressures for assessments to demonstrate the quality and cost-effectiveness of undergraduate education will likely continue.

Externally mandated assessments raise institutional concerns that simplistic or inappropriate measures will be adopted, that assessment will actually lower educational quality by encouraging faculty to teach to the test (as has sometimes happened at the K–12 level), and that resources that could be used for direct improvement of education (such as curricular reform) will instead be diverted to demonstrate what is already known. Non-traditional students and institutions that take greater risks to enroll them may be penalized. Assessment is especially problematic when the state mandates statewide standardized testing and uses the results to make decisions on institutional funding or student advancement, as in Florida, Georgia, and Texas, among others. The president of Miami-Dade Community College, for example, has argued that Florida's standardized and time-limited test has had a "devastating" impact on the institution's large number of limited-English-proficient students and disadvantaged African-American students.[29]

Yet institutions can make assessment meet their own needs. Most importantly, assessment can provide a mechanism for colleges and universities to improve teaching and learning. Effective assessment must be related to the institution's own goals, and must both reflect and provide feedback on teaching and curriculum. Unless faculty are involved in developing the effort, assessment will either drive the curriculum or be irrelevant. Second, assessment can provide a means to support institutions' argument that they are providing high-quality undergraduate education, or to bolster their case for more funding to remedy deficiencies. State officials in one survey stated that they believed that assessment could in fact strengthen institutions' case for more funding. Third, if institutions take the initiative, assessment can provide an opportunity to set the public agenda for higher education, i.e., to determine what values, resources, and outcomes are important, rather than allowing external actors to do so. As noted earlier, evidence that students are learning can help reduce external interest in regulating intrinsically academic decisions such as faculty workload. Institutions must persuade policy makers that only if faculty and institutions see the assessments as their own are they likely to make a difference.[30]

Nevertheless, externally mandated assessments continue to present problems in at least two regards. First, states continue to use statewide standardized testing to make academic decisions in some areas, especially in teacher education, where many states require passage of statewide tests for entrance into teacher preparation programs. Second, ongoing state budgetary constraints renew concerns about the kinds and uses of assessments. Facing budget constraints, will states retreat from more authentic, but more expensive, assessment measurements? Will states provide more money to remedy deficiencies identified by assessments? Or will they simply use assessment results to justify cutting institutional allocations?

5. The Changing Nature of Science in the University

Over the past ten to twenty years, universities have witnessed, and sometimes sponsored, significant changes in the nature of scientific research within the university: the development of new fields and techniques not even imagined twenty years ago, growing university-industry collaboration in the commercial marketing of research discoveries, a further shift toward directed and applied research and development, and a movement toward "big science" projects involving hundreds of researchers and billions of dollars.

UNIVERSITY-INDUSTRY COLLABORATION

Industry sponsorship. Between 1972 and 1989, industrial sponsorship of university research and development in science and engineering more than doubled as a percentage of university research dollars; actual funds from industry nearly quadrupled. By one estimate, research for industry directly or indirectly now accounts for approximately 10 percent of university research. By contrast, federal funds declined from 68 percent to less than 60 percent during this period, and state and local funding proportions declined as well. While the growth in industrial sponsorship provides new sources of support for university research, it also presents potential problems. Industrial support may hinder the flow of research information because industrial sponsors often require researchers to delay release of potentially marketable results. It may also may alter research priorities; a 1985 Harvard study found that 30 percent of a national sample of researchers said that they chose research topics based on how marketable the results might be.[31]

Commercialization. Even more problematic is the growing involvement of university researchers, and of universities themselves, in the commercial marketing of scientific and technological discoveries. During the 1980s a number of leading research faculty established or became associated with for-profit biotechnology and other "high tech" companies based on their federally funded university research—a development that prompted Congressional intervention to enact conflict-of-interest regulations. A number of research universities are establishing or exploring commercial enterprises such as technology-transfer corporations, designed to speed the flow of scientific discoveries and products to the private sector.

Although these initiatives have sometimes run into strong faculty opposition, they are likely to continue to grow because they benefit both industry, by providing a cost-effective means for research development, and universities, by promising increased revenues, particularly during a period of cutbacks in state and federal funding. But these trends also pose potential threats to higher education, among them the possibility that they could create conflicts of interest for individuals and institutions with financial stakes in a project, restrict the flow of information, increase the university's fragmentation into entrepreneurial fiefdoms, and shift power to nonacademic personnel who typically control for-profit enterprises within the university. Perhaps most importantly, com-mercialization may further shift research priorities toward more marketable areas and distort traditional academic missions. Especially during a period of retrenchment and reallocation, commercialization may further shift resources away from resource-poor humanities and social science fields and toward those science and technology fields that can generate additional revenues.[32]

SHIFTS TOWARD DIRECTED AND APPLIED RESEARCH AND DEVELOPMENT

Directed research. Over the past decade, federal and state policy makers, private industry, and university leaders have pressed for university research to contribute more directly to the nation's economic growth and other social priorities. The public often perceives university research to be arcane and, simultaneously, believes that university research holds great promise for resolving economic and other needs. As a result, federal funding for basic scientific research (still the largest source of university research dollars) has increasingly supported directed research, i.e., research on specific projects or problems determined by the federal government, rather than investigator-driven research. Directed (as well as applied) research funding for such projects and research areas as the human genome project, AIDS research, radio telescopes, and magnet labs has gained a larger proportion of total funds allocated by the National Institutes of Health, the National Science Foundation, and the U.S. Department of Defense, the main federal agencies supporting university research. "Earmarked" funds, which bypass the peer-review system to fund projects primarily at specific universities in Congress members' districts, have also increased.

Applied research and development. Applied research and development (i.e., investigations designed to gain and use research knowledge for specific technological, biomedical, or other improvements) has received greater emphasis within universities as well. This trend reflects increased industrial sponsorship and institutional incentives for commercialization, as well as governmental pressures for greater relevance. Between 1972 and 1981, applied research and development increased from 23 percent to 33 percent of total university research and development expenditures. Although the proportion remained relatively steady during the 1980s, and although to date federal funds have primarily supported basic research (including directed research), many observers believe that federal support for applied research will increase. Despite calls by some policy makers for more attention to social needs, most applied research funding is narrowly focused on efforts designed to boost U.S. industrial competitiveness.[33]

"BIG SCIENCE"

Concurrent with shifts toward more directed and applied science research has been a trend toward "big science" projects. Over the past decade, the U.S. government has funded long-term, multi-billion-dollar projects involving hundreds and even thousands of researchers, such as the space station, the superconducting supercollider, and the human genome project. These projects have generated enormous controversy within the scientific community. Large, long-term projects offer great promise for facilitating scientific breakthroughs that individual investigators could not accomplish. They also may provide economies of scale and, some argue, provide better training for graduate students because they provide more opportunities for collaboration and interaction with other researchers in the same field.

Many observers believe, however, that "big science" grants may divert funding for individual research, resulting in greatly increased competition for grants to individual researchers. In the early 1990s, funding of approved NIH grant applications fell below 15 percent in some categories and under 25 percent in many, compared with rates of 30 percent or more in the previous two decades. If this trend continues and if fewer grants are available to individual researchers outside the small number of centers where large-scale science is being funded, the next generation of scientists could be harmed by limited opportunities for graduate training and for grants to junior faculty outside these centers. Moreover, some scientists claim that, because large-scale collaborations provide fewer opportunities for individuals within these collaborations to design their own experiments or to see an experiment through to completion, they risk alienating creative young scientists, as well as discouraging scientific experimentation that does not conform to existing paradigms.[34]

In sum, these changes in the nature of scientific research provide opportunities for universities to develop new revenue streams and to serve economic and other public needs more effectively, but they also pose potential threats to university missions, research priorities, academic integrity, and faculty control. The challenge for research universities, and for government and private funders of university research, will be to address more fully the public's legitimate needs, including social needs, while implementing policies and decisions to maintain university support and resources for core academic areas that do not generate large amounts of external funding, i.e., the humanities, social sciences, and social service professional schools. Universities will need to find ways to take advantage of revenue opportunities while developing clear accountability mechanisms to prevent conflicts of interests, withholding of research results, or acquiescence to political or private pressures. In addition, they will need ways to pursue opportunities for scientific advances through large, long-term projects while ensuring adequate opportunities and nurturing for the next generation of scientists.

6. The Cloudy Crystal Ball

A number of other emerging external issues may have major impacts on higher education in the future, but their outcomes remain highly uncertain. Among them are the following:

• How will the labor market affect higher education enrollments? Historically, institutional enrollments have been influenced by fluctuating economic returns to a college education and by employment/unemployment rates, especially in the market-sensitive community colleges, but these economic factors are unpredictable. In addition, how will labor market demands affect student choice of major? Over the past twenty-five years, the proportion of undergraduate students enrolled in vocational and professional fields has skyrocketed, while that in arts and sciences fields has declined. The number of bachelor's degrees in business and management, for example, more than doubled and now comprises over 20 percent of all bachelor's degrees. Since the mid-1980s, however, bachelor's degrees in the humanities and social sciences have increased sharply. How will higher education institutions be able to respond to fluctuating disciplinary demands? To what extent should higher education allow enrollments by major to be driven by student demand? Of particular concern is the continuing decline, in both percentage and absolute numbers, of bachelor's degrees in the life and physical sciences; this decline is occurring among both male and female students. What are the implications of these declines for the nation's needs for individuals with strong scientific skills?

• Community colleges, which now enroll nearly 45 percent of all undergraduate students, may have an especially difficult task in the future. If four-year institutions increase tuition, reduce enrollments, and raise admission standards, community colleges will be under greater pressure to absorb students diverted from four-year institutions into transfer programs. At the same time, community colleges are being asked to strengthen their job-training programs (already a strong focus). How will community colleges respond to these multiple demands? What priorities will they set?

• Independent colleges and universities, which comprise about 20 percent of higher education enrollments, provide greater diversity of college environments than can publicly funded institutions. Historically Black colleges and universities, women's colleges, and small liberal arts colleges, for example, serve clienteles that might be less well served if these institutions were to disappear. They also provide cost savings to society, because non-public funds cover a larger proportion of instructional costs. However, they may face greater tuition and cost squeezes than do public institutions. Will independent institutions retain their share of higher education enrollments and continue to thrive? How will growing federal regulatory controls affect their distinctive functions and clientele?

• What will happen to higher education's tradition of self-evaluation and self-regulation through voluntary accreditation? In 1992, federal policy makers, who mistrusted accrediting bodies' ability to exercise adequate quality control and identify institutional accountability, seriously considered transferring authority for determining institutional eligibility for student financial aid from accrediting entities to state agencies. While ultimately the federal government retained accrediting entities' role in determining initial eligibility, a 1993 law gave state agencies significant control for determining whether institutions, public and private, will remain eligible for federal student financial aid. In addition, facing widespread member dissatisfaction, the Council on Postsecondary Accreditation (an umbrella organization of accrediting agencies) dissolved itself in 1993. These events raise serious prospects not only for weakening traditional academic self-regulation but also for shifting the accrediting role from quality control to gate keeper, at least with regard to financial aid.

• What role will the courts play in higher education? Will faculty terminations as a result of budget cutbacks spur greater court involvement in determining the conditions and criteria for hiring, promotions, and terminations of academic personnel? How will the courts adjudicate between academic freedom/free speech rights on campus versus "hate speech" codes and "hate crimes" penalties? How will institutions comply with court-ordered mandates to provide equitable athletics resources for women?

• For-profit proprietary institutions, corporations, the military, labor unions, and community and other organizations have established vast and growing opportunities for advanced education and training outside the traditional higher education arena. Some even offer professional certification and degrees. By some estimates, the number of employees engaged in corporate-based education alone may equal that in all U.S. four-colleges and universities.[35] What role will these other providers of advanced education and training play in the future? Will higher education institutions compete with them for students and dollars, or collaborate with them (for example, in joint community college/ industry programs)? How will both competition and collaboration affect higher education's programs and priorities?

• How much will the evolving electronic technologies, including interactive "distance" learning arrangements, development of an electronic "information highway" linking colleges, businesses, and other organizations, and far more sophisticated computer instructional programs, affect the ways in which information is not only disseminated but developed? What impact will these changes have on university library services? Will these technologies affect definitions of faculty workload? Will profit considerations of these new technologies limit access and constrain educational uses?

7. Revisiting the Social Contract: Institutional Responsibilities, Autonomy, and Leadership

INSTITUTIONAL AUTONOMY AND ACCOUNTABILITY

All of the trends discussed above have profound implications for the relationship between higher education, the public, and governmental authorities. As state budgets have become more constrained and student tuition fees have increased, for example, governors and legislators have become more interested in controlling institutional costs, as well as such core academic matters as faculty workloads, assessment of student learning, and program areas. Where institutions have responded to budget cuts by eliminating programs, however, legislators have sometimes intervened on behalf of program advocates. Institutions may be caught in a bind where one legislative committee advocates cuts in certain institutional programs (such as teacher education or engineering) while other legislators seek to expand them. At the federal level, concerns about economic competitiveness have prompted federal authorities to direct research dollars toward areas with perceived commercial applicability. The growing power of advocacy groups and the use of the political process by higher education institutions have led to more directed research and more earmarked funds that bypass peer review. In addition, under the aegis of accountability, the federal government has begun using student financial aid dollars to regulate institutional actions in admissions and other areas.

Although the federal government continues to have a major impact on higher education, especially through research funding and student financial aid, in the 1990s state governments will continue to be the dominant players in the public sector, which contains nearly 80 percent of all college enrollments.[36] Ironically, this is so even though the proportion of public institutions' budgets that is state-funded is declining, because states continue to fund most of public colleges' basic operating costs, including faculty and staff salaries. In addition, states retain extensive regulatory authority over most public colleges and universities, ranging from institutional missions and functions to competitive bidding and purchasing regulations. At both state and federal levels, it appears certain that current demands for institutional accountability will continue and increase and that the kinds of accountability demanded are changing: not only fiscal responsibility, but also demonstration that institutions are meeting governmental priorities, achieving desired student outcomes, and displaying greater efficiency.

The threat of governmental intervention in core academic affairs may be overstated, however. To date, most states' demands for evidence of student learning, increased faculty workload, and institutional "report cards" have left much discretion to institutions to determine appropriate responses. Of course, as noted earlier, the threat of regulatory or budgetary action has prompted many institutions "voluntarily" to adopt actions desired by policy makers. In such situations, how do we determine whether or not political authorities have wielded inappropriate influence? Three points should be noted here: First, governmental regulation and centralization of decision making in higher education tend to wax and wane over time in response to budgetary crisis, salience of higher education vis-a-vis other social needs, and particular incidents or situations.[37] Some states might grant greater institutional autonomy in return for greater institutional privatization and self-sufficiency. Second, each of the fifty states will follow its own path based on its particular conditions and history. Third, institutional autonomy and public accountability need not be in conflict, if accountability is broadly and appropriately defined.[38] Given higher education's important role in U.S. society, there are legitimate public demands for institutional accountability. The challenge for higher education is a long-standing one: to respond forthrightly to public needs while establishing with political authorities appropriate expectations for institutional accountability and autonomy.

CHANGING STRUCTURES AND GOVERNANCE

The past thirty years have seen a "revolutionary transformation" in the governance of higher education, from single-campus governance to large, complex, and heterogeneous multicampus systems.[39] Nearly three-fourths of all students enrolled in U.S. public higher education institutions now attend campuses that are part of a multicampus system (i.e., two or more campuses with a single, systemwide governing board and some kind of central system administration). These students are enrolled in about 120 systems comprising over 1,000 campuses. By contrast, in 1968 barely half of public college students were enrolled in multicampus systems comprised of about 550 campuses. Although the functions and powers of these systems vary substantially, systemwide governing boards and administrations have the potential for exercising broad leverage over their campuses through budget and program review powers. They also pose threats to campus autonomy and flexibility if they attempt to impose an inappropriately standardized set of priorities or expectations. Systems increase bureaucratization and make faculty-shared governance more difficult to achieve.[40] On the other hand, system boards and administrations can bring broader perspectives than do campuses on the overall needs of the campuses and the state as a whole. System leadership may be especially important in matters that may have weak campus constituencies but that are important to the system as a whole or to the state, such as undergraduate general education, teacher education, or affirmative action. Moreover, where a system office does not exercise adequate quality control, other more political actors, such as coordinating boards or the state's executive branch, may step in to fill the vacuum.[41]

During the 1990s, systemwide leadership (boards, administrators, and faculties) will be particularly important in responding to an environment of continuing budget constraints, demands for greater institutional accountability, questions of student access, and other changing conditions. Systemwide review will be essential to reduce unnecessary duplication among costly graduate and professional programs; increasingly, this will include review of existing programs as well as of new ones. Conversely, systemwide monitoring will be needed to ensure that significant program areas do not disappear as a result of uncoordinated decisions by individual campuses, as has happened or threatened to happen in several systems in library science, speech audiology, and other areas. Systemwide decisions must determine and, when necessary, revise missions for individual campuses; during retrenchment periods, this may mean greater specialization among campuses. Given limited resources, systems will also have a more important role in fostering intercampus programs.[42] Whether systemwide leadership will be able to exercise such initiative is uncertain, however, in light of both campus concerns for autonomy and state demands for more direct control.

There are other uncertainties as well. Will there be major structural changes in statewide governance and/or coordination of higher education during the 1990s? Callan notes that during the 1980s, although a majority of states undertook extensive reviews of the structures and functions of their higher education systems, relatively little change occurred. He argues, however, that "tight state budgets, intensified competition for resources, and concern about higher education's responsiveness to societal needs" could stimulate new structural reorganizations in the 1990s.[43] Should that happen, it would disrupt established processes and relationships and create greater uncertainty, as the new players established their authority, priorities, and rules of interaction. Will statewide coordinating agencies assume a more regulatory role? Or will they be bypassed by state governors and legislators? Will there be changes in the memberships, powers, and terms of governing board members (whether for multicampus systems or individual campuses)? These matters have come under greater legislative scrutiny in recent years. Within the campus, too, there are conflicting pressures for greater centralization, as a means to make tough budget decisions, and decentralization to departments and task groups, as a means to center accountability in the units directly responsible for instruction and research. Further faculty unionization is another unknown. How will these differing pressures affect governance and structure within the campus?

LEADERSHIP

During the turbulent and difficult period that lies ahead, higher education will need greater leadership at all levels: administrative, faculty, trustee, and public. Yet the exercise of effective leadership may become more difficult. According to a study for the National Association of State Universities and Land-Grant Colleges (NASULGC), the average tenure of presidents of member universities, already shorter than that for presidents of other institutions, further declined from 4.6 years in 1980 to 3.2 years in 1992. (By comparison, a study for the

Association of Governing Boards of Colleges and Universities found that the overall average tenure for higher education presidents remained relatively stable, at about seven years, over the previous eight-year period.) William Davis, who collected the NASULGC data, speculated that the high turnover rates for NASULGC presidents, who represent many of the U.S.'s public research universities, reflected the intense public scrutiny and increasingly politicized governing boards under which they worked.[44]

Faculty leadership in regard to determining academic priorities and ensuring academic control over the conduct of research will also be greatly needed, yet it, too, may be more difficult to obtain. Clark Kerr concludes that over the past decades faculty loyalties have shifted further away from the institutions in which they work and toward their research and professional associations. He concludes that faculty members not only are teaching less but have become less willing to serve on institutional committees, less willing to protect the academic institution from political disruption, and less careful to avoid exploiting the institution's name or facilities for economic gain. This decline of "academic citizenship" has serious implications for shared governance of universities and colleges.[45] Finally, in the face of difficult budgetary decisions, public policy makers will need to exercise leadership in support of higher education, to ensure that the social and economic benefits and quality of higher education in the U.S. are not eroded.

REVISITING THE SOCIAL CONTRACT

The twenty-first century will bring new and continuing challenges to U.S. society, among them economic constraints and organizational restructuring, further demographic shifts, increasing technological complexity, potential threats to the nation's social fabric, the reconfiguration of nations, and changes in international economic and power relationships, as well as many unforeseen changes. In this environment, higher education will not be able to stand aside from demands that it help society meet these changes through developing a highly skilled workforce, mediating social mobility, and advancing research, development, and service directed toward economic and social considerations. At the same time, it will face increasing competition from other claimants for public support and will be called upon to be more accountable, and in new ways, for the funding it receives. In short, policy makers as well as students, parents, and the private sector, are demanding changes in the social contract between higher education and its constituencies. The challenge for higher education institutions will be to take the initiative in determining their priorities (including deciding what they cannot do during an era of constraints), assessing the outcomes of their goals and programs, and strengthening their contributions to larger societal needs. The challenge for policy makers will be to provide institutions sufficient support, autonomy and flexibility to accomplish critical social and economic needs, including long-range needs such as basic research and the maintenance of colleges and universities as centers of academic thought and quality.

Notes

1. Clark Kerr and Marian Gade, "Current and Emerging Issues Facing American Higher Education," in *Higher Education in American Society, Revised Edition,* ed. Philip G. Altbach and Robert O. Berdahl (Buffalo, N.Y.: Prometheus Books, 1987) pp. 129–49. The current chapter is a follow-up to Kerr and Gade's 1987 chapter. I would like to thank Clark Kerr and especially Marian Gade for reviewing and commenting on this chapter.

2. Edward R. Hines and Gwen B. Pruyne, "State Higher Education Appropriations, 1992–93," *Grapevine* (Normal, Ill: Center for Higher Education, Illinois State University, 1992); Kit Lively, "Most University Systems Are Still Playing Catch-Up Despite Some Increases in Appropriations for 1993–94," *Chronicle of Higher Education* (July 14, 1993): A20.

3. American Council on Education, *Campus Trends 1992* (Washington, D.C.: ACE, 1992); Eliot Marshall and Joseph Falea, "Cracks in the Ivory Tower," *Science* 257 (August 28, 1992): 1196–1201; Julie L. Nicklin, "Many Fortune 500 Companies Curtail Donations to Higher Education," *Chronicle of Higher Education* (May 26, 1993): A25–27.

4. Data provided primarily by the Ame. 'can Association of State Colleges and Universities and reported by Katherine McCarron, "20 States Force Public Colleges to Cut their Budgets in Mid-Year," *Chronicle of Higher Education* (April 28, 1993): A23.

5. Sherry H. Penney, "What a University Has Learned From 4 Years of Financial Stress," *Chronicle of Higher Education* (May 5, 1993): B1–3.

6. University of California, Office of the President (unpublished figures); Goldie Blumenstyk, "College Officials and Policy Experts Ponder Implications of 'Privatizing' State Colleges," *Chronicle of Higher Education* (May 13, 1992): A25–27.

7. Jacob O. Stampen and W. Lee Hansen, cited in Goldie Blumenstyk, "College Officials and Policy Experts Ponder Implications of 'Privatizing' State Colleges." According to these researchers, while student financial aid has increased over the thirty-year period, the increase has not fully offset the rise in tuition and fees; see W. Lee Hansen and Jacob O. Stampen, "Higher Education: No Better Access without Better Quality," *Higher Education Extension Service Review* 4 (Spring 1993): 1–15.

8. Mark G. Yudof, "The Burgeoning Privatization of State Universities," *Chronicle of Higher Education* (May 13, 1992): A48.

9. Carolyn J. Mooney, "Tenured Faculty Members are Spared in Latest Round of Belt Tightening," *Chronicle of Higher Education* (January 13, 1993): A17–18.

10. "The Status of Non-Tenure-Track Faculty," *Academe: Bulletin of the American Association of University Professors* 79 (July/August 1993): 39–46.

11. Sheila Slaughter, "Retrenchment in the 1980s: The Politics of Prestige and Gender," *Journal of Higher Education* 64 (May/June 1993): 250–82.

12. William G. Bowen and Julie Ann Sosa, *Prospects for Faculty in the Arts and Sciences: A Study of Factors Affecting Demand and Supply, 1987 to 2012* (Princeton:

Princeton University Press, 1987); Howard R. Bowen and Jack H. Schuster, *American Professors: A National Resource Imperiled* (New York: Oxford University Press, 1986).

13. Sheila Slaughter, "Retrenchment in the 1980s."

14. Ibid., p. 276; Catherine Gardner, Timothy R. Warner, and Rick Biedenweg, "Stanford and the Railroad: Case Studies of Cost Cutting," *Change* 22 (November/December 1990): 23–27.

15. Robert Zemsky (senior editor), "A Call to Meeting," *Pew Higher Education Research Program* 4 (February 1993): 1A–10A.

16. Robert Zemsky, "A Call to Meeting," 1A. See also Robert Zemsky and William Massy "Cost Containment: Committing to a New Economic Reality," *Change* 22 (November/December 1990): 16–22; Hoke L. Synith, "The Incredible Shrinking College: Downsizing as Positive Planning," *Educational Record* 67 (Spring/Summer 1986): 38–41.

17. Thomas P. Wallace, "Public Higher Education Finance: The Dinosaur Age Persists," *Change* 25 (July/August 1993): 56–63.

18. Ibid.; W. Lee Hansen and Jacob O, Stampen, "Higher Education: No Better Access without Better Quality."

19. David C. Berliner, "Mythology and the American System of Education," *Phi Delta Kappan* 74 (April 1993): 632–40; U.S. Department of Education, National Center for Education Statistics, *Digest of Education Statistics 1992* (Washington, D.C.: U.S. Government Printing Office, 1992).

20. See, for example, Patrick M. Callan and Joni E. Finney, "By Design or Default?" (San Jose, Calif.: California Higher Education Policy Center, June 1993): 1–8.

21. National Commission on Excellence in Education, *A Nation at Risk: The Imperative for Educational Reform* (Washington, D.C.: U.S. Department of Education, 1983); Bell, "Reflections One Decade After *A Nation at Risk*," *Phi Delta Kappan* 74 (April 1993): 592–97, p. 597.

22. David Berliner, "Mythology and the American System of Education."

23. Jonathan Kozol, *Savage Inequalities: Children in America's Schools* (New York: Crown, 1991).

24. Elizabeth M. Hawthorne and Ami Zusman, "The Role of State Departments of Education in School/College Collaborations," *Journal of Higher Education* 63 (July/August 1992): 418–40; Kenneth A. Sirotnik and John I. Goodlad, eds., *School-University Partnerships in Action: Concepts, Cases, and Concerns* (New York: Teachers College Press, 1988); Franklin P. Wilbur and Leo M. Lambert, *Linking America's Schools and Colleges: Guide to Partnerships & National Directory* (Washington, D.C.: American Association for Higher Education, 1991).

25. Elizabeth Hawthorne and Ami Zusman, "The Role of State Departments of Education in School/College Collaborations."

26. William F. Massy and Andrea K. Wilger, "Productivity in Postsecondary Education: A New Approach," *Educational Evaluation and Policy Analysis* 14 (Winter 1992): 361–76. See also Albert Hood and Catherine Arceneaux, *Key Resources on Student Services: A Guide to the Field and its Literature* (San Francisco: Jossey-Bass, 1990). According to surveys by the Carnegie Foundation for the Advancement of Teaching, however, faculty teaching loads have been relatively stable for at least the past 15 years.

27. James R. Mingle, "Faculty Work and the Costs/Quality/Access Collision,"

AAHE Bulletin 45 (March 1993): 3–6, 13, p. 4.

28. Ernest L. Boyer, *Scholarship Reconsidered: Priorities of the Professoriate* (Princeton, N.J.: Carnegie Foundation for the Advancement of Teaching, 1990); Robert Zemsky (senior editor), Pew Higher Education Research Program, "Testimony from the Belly of the Whale," *Policy Perspectives* 4 (September 1992): 1A–8A.

29. Pat Hutchings and Ted Marchese, "Watching Assessment—Questions, Stories, Prospects," *Change* 22 (September/October 1990): 12–38.

30. Russell Edgerton, "Assessment at Half Time," *Change* 22 (September/October 1990): 4–5.

31. National Science Foundation, *Selected Data on Academic Science/Engineering R&D Expenditures FY 1989* (Washington, D.C.: NSF, 1990); Roger L. Geiger, "Research Universities in a New Era: From the 1980s to the 1990s," in *Higher Learning in America, 1980–2000,* ed. Arthur Levine (Baltimore: Johns Hopkins University Press, 1993), pp. 67–85; Julie L. Nicklin, "University Deals with Drug Companies Raise Concerns Over Autonomy, Secrecy," *Chronicle of Higher Education* (March 24, 1993): A25–26.

32. Sheila Slaughter, "Retrenchment in the 1980s"; Roger L. Geiger, "Research Universities in a New Era."

33. National Science Board, *Science Indicators—1992* (Washington, D.C.: U.S. Government Printing Office, 1983); National Science Board, *Science and Engineering Indicators—1992* (Washington, D.C.: U.S. Government Printing Office, 1992); Van Doorn Ooms, "Budget Priorities of the Nation," *Science* 258 (11 December 1992): 174–47; Colleen Cordes, "Science Foundation Under Intense Pressure to Lead Movement to Transfer Academic Research to Industry," *Chronicle of Higher Education* (October 7, 1992): A24.

34. Michael Bishop, Marc Kirschner, and Harold Varmus, "Science and the New Administration," *Science* 259 (22 January 1993): 444–45; Kim A. McDonald, "Physicists in Large Collaborations Find That 'Big' Is Not Always Better," *Chronicle of Higher Education* (December 9, 1992): A7–8.

35. Nell P. Eurich, *Corporate Classrooms: The Learning Business* (Princeton: Carnegie Foundation for the Advancement of Teaching, 1985).

36. Patrick M. Callan, "Government and Higher Education," in *Higher Learning in America: 1980–2000,* ed. Arthur Levine (Baltimore: Johns Hopkins University Press, 1993), pp. 3–19.

37. Lois Fisher, "State Legislatures and the Autonomy of Colleges and Universities: A Comparative Study of Legislatures in Four States, 1900–1979," *Journal of Higher Education* 59 (March/April 1988): 133–62; Carol Everly Floyd, "Centralization and Decentralization of State Decision Making for Public Universities: Illinois 1960–1990," *History of Higher Education Annual 1992* 12 (1992): 101–118.

38. See Frank Newman, *Choosing Quality: Reducing Conflict Between the State and the University* (Denver: Education Commission of the States, 1987) for a discussion of what constitutes appropriate public policy versus inappropriate governmental intrusion.

39. Clark Kerr and Marian L. Gade, *The Guardians: Boards of Trustees of American Colleges and Universities* (Washington, D.C.: Association of Governing Boards of Universities and Colleges, 1989), p. 116.

40. Ibid.; Marian L. Gade, *Four Multicampus Systems: Some Policies and Practices That Work* (Washington, D.C.: Association of Governing Boards of Universities and Colleges, 1993); Clark Kerr, "Foreword," in Eugene C. Lee and Frank M. Bowen,

The Multicampus University: A Study of Academic Governance (New York: McGraw-Hill, 1971), pp. xviii-xix.

41. Ami Zusman, "Multicampus University Systems: How System Offices Coordinate Undergraduate and K-12 Education" (paper presented at the annual meeting of the Association for the Study of Higher Education, Minneapolis, Minnesota, October 1992); Patrick M. Callan, "Government and Higher Education."

42. Marian L. Gade, *Four Multicampus Systems*.

43. Patrick M. Callan, "Government and Higher Education," pp. 14, 17.

44. The American Council on Education found that, between 1986 and 1990, average tenure for higher education presidents actually increased slightly, from 6.3 to 6.7 years, as reported by Carolyn J. Mooney, "Presidents' Tenure Fluctuated Little Over Past 8 Years," *Chronicle of Higher Education* (December 2, 1992): A17, A19.

45. Clark Kerr, *Higher Education Cannot Escape History: Issues for the Twenty-First Century* (Albany, N.Y.: State University of New York Press, 1994).

16

The Insulated Americans: Five Lessons from Abroad

Burton R. Clark

In thinking about postsecondary education, Americans tend to remain isolated and insular. The reasons are numerous: ours is the largest national system; we know this massive complex is the system most widely acclaimed since the second quarter of this century; we are geographically separated from the other major national models; we have many unique features; and we are busy and have more pressing things to do in Montana as well as in New York than to ask how the Austrians and Swedes do it. But there is a great deal to learn about ourselves by learning about the experiences of others in this important sector of society, and it is wise that we learn in advance of the time when events force us to do so.

To use an analogy: American business could have studied the Japanese way of business organization, and the German way, and even the Swedish way a quarter of a century ago instead of waiting until virtually forced to do so in the 1970s and 1980s by worsening competitive disadvantage and deepening worker discontent. Cross-national thinking encourages the long view in which, for once, we might get in front of our problems. We might even find out what not to do while there is still time not to do it. The perspectives that I draw from comparative research indicate that we are now making changes that not only deny the grounds on which we have been successful to date but will probably lead to arrangements that will seriously hamper us in the future.

To help develop a broad analytical framework within which legislators, chief executive officers, educational officials, faculty, and others can make wiser decisions in postsecondary education, I will set forth some rudimentary ideas in the form of five lessons from abroad. The basic points are interconnected. The first three of these lessons are largely "do nots" or warnings, and they set the stage for the last two, which are affirmations of what should remain central in our minds as we think about leadership and statesmanship in postsecondary education.

Central bureaucracy cannot effectively coordinate mass higher education. Many nations have struggled for a long time to coordinate higher education by means of national administration, treating postsecondary education as a subgovernment of the national state. The effort has been to achieve order, effectiveness, and equity by having national rules applied across the system by one or more national bureaus. France has struggled with the possibilities and limitations of this approach for a century and a half, since Napoleon created a unitary and unified national system of universities. And Italy has moved in this direction for over a century, since the unification of the nation.

Many of the well-established systems of this kind, in Europe and elsewhere, have not only a nationalized system of finance, but also: (a) much nationalization of the curriculum, with common mandated courses in centrally approved fields of study; (b) a nationalized degree structure, in which degrees are awarded by the national system and not by the individual university or college; (c) a nationalized personnel system, in which all those who work for the university are members of the civil service and are hired and promoted accordingly; and (d) a nationalized system of admissions, in which federal rules determine student access as well as rights and privileges. Such features naturally obtain strongly in Communist-controlled state administration, such as in East Germany and Poland between 1945 and 1990, where the dominant political philosophy affirms strong state control, based on a hierarchy of command. In some countries, such as West Germany, heavy reliance on central bureaucracy takes place at the state or provincial level of government rather than at the federal level, but often the results are no less thorough.

Back in the days of "elite" higher education, when the number of students and teachers was small, this approach worked to some degree—and now we know why. A bargain was struck, splitting the power between the bureaucrats at the central level and the professors at each institution. There were few middlemen—no trustees, since private individuals were not to be trusted with the care of a public interest, and not enough campus administrators to constitute a separate force. Professors developed the personal and collegial forms of control that provided the underpinnings for personal and group freedom in teaching and research. They elected their own deans and rectors and kept them on a short-term basis. Hence the professors were the power on the local scene, with the state officials often remote, even entombed hundreds of miles away in a Kafkaesque administrative monument. State administration sometimes became a bureaucracy for its own sake, a set of pretenses behind which oligarchies of professors were the real rulers, nationally as well as locally. The public was always given to understand that there was single-system accountability, while inside the structure power was so fractured and scattered that feudal lords ruled sectors of the organizational countryside. In general, this was the traditional European mode of academic organization—power concentrated at the top (in a central bureaucratic staff) and at the bottom (in the hands of chaired professors), with a weak middle at the levels of the university and its major constituent parts.

But the unitary government pyramid has become increasingly deficient over the last twenty-five years as expansion has enlarged the composite of academic tasks as well as the scale of operations. As consumer demand grows, student clienteles are not only more numerous but more varied. As labor force demands proliferate, the connections to employment grow more intricate. As demands for knowledge multiply, inside and outside the academic occupations, the disciplines and fields of knowledge increase steadily in number and kind. The tasks that modern higher education is now expected to perform differ in kind from those demanded traditionally in other sectors of public administration, and the challenge is to find the structure best suited for these new roles. There is a need to cover knowledge in fields that stretch from archeology to zoology, with business, law, physics, psychology, you name it, thrown in. Across the gamut of fields, knowledge is supposed to be discovered—the research imperative—as well as transmitted and distributed—the teaching and service imperatives. On top of all this has come an accelerated rate of change which makes it all the more difficult for coordinators, who tend to be generalists, to catch up with and comprehend what the specialists are doing.

Clearly, a transition from elite to mass higher education requires dramatic changes in structured state and national systems. The success of mass higher education systems will increasingly depend on: (a) plural rather than singular reactions, or the capacity to face simultaneously in different directions with contradictory reactions to contradictory demands; (b) quicker reactions, at least by some parts of the system, to certain demands; and (c) a command structure that allows for myriad adaptations to special contexts and local conditions. A unified system coordinated by a state bureaucracy is not set up to work in these ways. The unitary system resists differentiated and flexible approaches.

In such countries as Sweden, France, and Italy, many reformers in and out of government have been aware of this, so that the name of their game at this point in history is decentralization—efforts to disperse academic administration to regions, local authorities, and campuses. But this is extremely difficult to do through planned, deliberate effort. Federal officials with firmly fixed power do not normally give it away—abroad any more than in the United States—especially if the public, the legislature, and the chief executive still hold them responsible. But at least things are changing; responsible people in many countries have become convinced that the faults of unitary coordination far outweigh the virtues, and they are looking for ways to break up central control. They are almost ready to take seriously that great admirer of American federalism, De Tocqueville, who maintained over a century ago that while countries can be successfully governed centrally, they cannot be successfully administered centrally. There is surely no realm other than higher education where this principle more aptly applies.

Meanwhile, the United States, historically blessed with decentralization and diversity within states as well as among them, is hankering after the promised virtues: economy, efficiency, elimination of overlap, less redundancy, better articulation, transferability, accountability, equity, and equality. Our dominant line of reform since World War II has been to impose on the disorder of a market system of higher education new levels of coordination that promise administered order. We continue to do this at an accelerating rate. In fact, if our current momentum toward bureaucratic centralism is maintained, first at the state level and then at the national, we may see the day when we catch up with our friends abroad or even pass them as they travel in the direction of decentralization.

Unless strong counterforces are brought into play, higher education at the state level will increasingly resemble a ministry of education. Administrative staffs will grow, and the powers of central board and staff will shift increasingly from weakly proffered advice toward a primary role in the allocation of resources and in the approval of decisions for the system as a whole. Legislators, governors, and anyone else looking for a source to berate, blame, or whatever will increasingly saddle the central board and staff with the responsibility for economy, efficiency, equity, and all the other goals. And the oldest organizational principle in the world tells us that where there is responsibility, the authority should be commensurate. The trend toward central political and bureaucratic coordination is running strong. Just how strong can be easily seen if we compare state structures of coordination between 1945 and later periods of time. Robert Berdahl, Lyman Glenny, and other experts on state coordination have noted that in the 1960s alone a remarkably rapid centralization took place, with the states shifting from structures of little or no formal coordination to coordinating boards with regulatory powers.

To see just how fast such an evolutionary trend can change matters at the national level in a democratic nation, we have only to observe Great Britain. Like us, the British were long famous for institutional autonomy. As government money increasingly became the sole source of support, they devised the ingenious University Grants Committee (UGC), which, between 1920 and 1965, became the foremost world model for how to have governmental support without governmental control. But things have changed in recent decades. UGC, which initially received its moneys directly from the treasury and doled out lump sums with few questions asked, was placed under the national education department.

The national department has supervised and sponsored a nonuniversity sector, which operated largely without a buffer commission. But increasingly during the 1970s and 1980s the department became for both sectors a more aggressive instrument of national educational policy as determined by the party in power and senior administrators in the department. As central committees multiplied and took up a stronger regulatory role, they acquired the power to ask all kinds of questions of the institutions, favor one sector at the expense of another, tell some colleges previously out of their purview to close their doors, and suggest to other universities and colleges that they ought not to attempt A, B, and C if they hope to maintain the good will of those who must approve the next budget. Britain is still some distance from having a continental ministry of education, but evolution in that direction has recently been rapid. For the best of short-run reasons, the central administrative machinery is becoming the primary locus of power.

Our own centralization is first taking place at the state level. This allows for diversity and competition among the state systems, some outlet for personnel and students when any one system declines or otherwise becomes particularly unattractive, and the chance for some states to learn from the successes and failures of others. Apparently, it can pay sometimes to be an attentive laggard. But we are certainly heading in the direction of bureaucratic coordination. Most important, our central offices at the national level have adopted a different posture beginning in the mid-1970s from one or two decades earlier. We have already bowed to the quaint notion of taking away federal moneys flowing to an institution when it fails to obey a particular federal rule. Such an approach characterizes the sternest type of relationship between government and higher education in democratic countries with national ministries of education.

Our national policy will ricochet around on such matters for some years to come, while federal officials learn to fit the punishment to the crime. But the new world of national coordination into which we have been moving was made perfectly clear as early as 1977 in a speech by the then-Secretary of Health, Education, and Welfare. In front of an audience of hundreds of university and college presidents, he pointed out that since a recent bit of legislation opposed by academics was now national law, they would have to "comply," and he would have to "enforce." From the market to the minister in a decade! Others in Washington since that time, inside and outside of government, have felt free to speak of "federal supervision of education." Where one stands depends largely upon where one sits, and those who sit in Washington, consumed by national responsibilities and limited to a view from the top, will generally stand on formal coordination, by political and bureaucratic means, of national administration.

In short, we could learn from our friends on the European continent who now know that their national and often unified administrative structures cannot cope with mass higher education. Particularly, we could take a lesson from the British, who have evolved rapidly in the last two decades toward dependence on central bodies as an answer to the immediate demands of economy and quality. But as matters now stand, it appears that we will not do so. Rather we seem determined to learn the hard way, from brute experience.

The greatest single danger in the control of higher education is a monopoly of power, for two good reasons: a monopoly expresses the concerns and perspectives of just one group, shutting out the expression of other interests;

and no one group is wise enough to solve all the problems. The history of higher education exhibits monopolies and near monopolies by various groups. Students in some medieval Italian universities, through student guilds, could hire and fire professors and hence obtain favors from them. Senior faculty in some European and English universities during the last two centuries were answerable to no one and hence could sleep for decades. Trustees in some early and not-so-early American colleges could and did fire presidents and professors for not knowing the number of angels dancing on the head of the ecclesiastical pin, or, in the last half-century, for simply smoking cigarettes and drinking martinis. Autocratic presidents in some American institutions, especially teachers colleges, ran campuses as personal possessions; and state bureaucratic staffs and political persons in Europe and America, past and present, democratic and nondemocratic, have often been heavily dominant.

A monopoly of power can be a useful instrument of change: some states in Western Europe, normally immobilized in higher education, have effected large changes only when a combination of crisis events and a strong ruler produced a temporary monopoly, e.g., France in 1968 under DeGaulle. But the monopoly does not work well for long. It soon becomes a great source of rigidity, resisting change and freezing organization around the rights of just a few.

In the increasingly complex and turbulent organizational environment of the last quarter of this century, no small group is smart enough to know the way. This holds even for the central bureaucratic and planning staffs, who are most likely to evolve into near monopolies of control. State and party officials in East European countries, when they were still under the control of Communist regimes, found out that they could not, from on high and by themselves, effect even so simple an exercise as manpower planning—allotting educational places according to labor force targets. They were forced by their errors to back off from total dominance and to allow more room for the academic judgments of professors and the choices of students. As mentioned earlier, various countries in Western Europe have been attempting to halt and reverse a long trend of centralization in order to move decision making out to the periphery, closer to participants and to the realities of local operating conditions.

All organized systems of any complexity are replete with reciprocal ignorance. The expert in one activity will not know the time of day in another. The extent of ignorance is uncommonly high in systems of higher education, given the breadth of subjects they cover. The chief state higher education officer may not be able to do long division, let along high-energy physics, while the professor of physics, until retrained and reoriented, is ignorant in everyday matters of system coordination. Here is a fundamental feature of modern organized life: while higher education has been moving toward the formation of large hierarchies traditionally associated with business firms and government agencies, those organizations have been driven to greater dependence on the judgment of authorities in different parts of the organization as work becomes more rooted in expertise. That authority flows toward expert judgment is evident in such mechanisms as peer review and committee evaluation. The organized anarchy of the university remains a useful model of how to function as those at the nominal top become more ignorant.

Another great danger in the control of higher education is domination by a single form of organization. No single form will suffice in mass higher education. Here again some of our European counterparts have been fundamentally unlucky and we can learn from their misfortune. The European university has been around for eight centuries, predating in most locales the nation states that now encompass it. Over the centuries, the assumption grew that genuine higher education meant university education, and that made it difficult to bring other forms into being or to give them prestige. Thus, some nations were swept into mass education with only the nationally supported public university legitimated as a good place to study. As a result, since 1960, this dominant form has been greatly overloaded, with large numbers of students and faculty making more and more heterogeneous demands. This has weakened the traditional function of the university—basic research. In many European countries it is now problematic whether most basic research will remain within the university, as teaching time drives out research time, and as governments sponsor and protect the science they think they need by placing it in research institutes outside the university systems. Differentiation of form has to occur, but it will happen the hard way in those countries where one form has enjoyed a traditional monopoly.

In the United States, we are in fairly good shape on this score, despite recent worry about homogenization. We have at least five or six major sectors or types of institutions, and the best efforts to classify our 3,500 institutions reveal no less than a dozen or more categories, taking into account extensive differences among the hundreds of places now called universities, the still greater number called colleges, and the 1,400 community colleges. Here no single form dominates the system. But we may have cause to worry about voluntary and mandated convergence.

Institutional differentiation is the name of the game in the coordination of mass higher education. Lesson four is the flip side of lesson three, but the point is so fundamental that it can stand restatement. It answers the most important, substantive question in high-level system coordination and governmental policy: will and should our universities and colleges become more or less alike? The pressure of the times in many countries has been heavily toward formal institutional uniformity. Yet cross-national comparison tells us that differentiation is the prime requirement for system viability.

One of the great pressures for institutional uniformity derives from the search for equality and equity. For a long time in this country the notion of what constitutes educational equality has been broadening. At first, equality of access simply meant equal chances of getting into a limited number of openings—selection without regard to race, color, or creed. This changed to a position that there should be no selection, that the door should be open to all. But while this idea was developing, a differentiated arrangement of colleges and universities was also taking shape. Everyone could get into the system, but not into all its parts: we differentiated among the roles of the community college, the state college, and the state university, made differential selection an important part of the process, and allowed private colleges and universities to do business as they pleased. This saved us from some of the deleterious effects of letting everyone in. Now the idea of equality is being carried a step further as observers and practitioners take critical note of our institutional unevenness. The effort will grow to extend the concept of educational equality to mean equal treatment for all. To make this possible, all institutions in a system should be equated.

Europeans have already had considerable experience with this idea. It has been embedded in those systems comprising a set of national universities and not much else. The French, Italians, and others have made a sustained attempt to administer equality by formally proclaiming and often treating the constituent parts of the system as equal in program, staff, and value of degree. Still, back in the days when selection was sharp at the lower levels, only 5 percent or less graduated from the upper secondary level and were thereby guaranteed a university place of their choosing. But mass elementary and now mass secondary education have virtually eliminated the earlier selection in some countries and radically reduced it in others. As a result, much larger numbers have come washing into the old undifferentiated university structure, like a veritable tide, with all entrants expecting governmentally guaranteed equality of treatment. There has been no open way of steering the traffic, or of differentiating, which is surely the grandest irony for a national system founded on rational, deliberate administrative control.

This European version of open-door access has recently generated enormous conflict within almost all the European systems. Unless some way is found to distinguish and differentiate, everyone who wants to go to medical school has the right to attend; everyone who wants to go to the University of Rome will continue to go there—when they last stopped counting, it was well above 150,000; and the French apparently had over 200,000 at the University of Paris before a deep crisis forced them to break that totality into a dozen and one parts. Ideally, more degree levels, with appropriate underpinnings, will also have to develop, since the heterogeneous clientele, with its more uneven background and varied aptitude, needs programs of different lengths and different stopping places. But to attempt to effect selection, assignment, and barriers now, precisely at the time when the doors have finally swung open, is morally outrageous to the former have-nots and to the political parties, unions, and other groups that articulate their interests. The battle rages on the national stage, with virtually all education-related ideologies and interests brought into play. In America, we have been saved from this by a combination of decentralization and differentiation.

Other strong pressures for institutional uniformity come from within higher education systems themselves. One is a voluntary movement of sectors, now referred to as academic drift, toward the part that has highest prestige and offers highest rewards. The English have had trouble resisting such convergence, since the towering prestige of Oxford and Cambridge has induced various institutions to drift toward their style. In addition, administered systems tend toward mandated convergence. Within the European unitary systems, this is expressed in the thousand and one details of equating salaries, teaching loads, laboratory spaces, and sabbatical leaves. Have-nots within the system become pressure groups to catch up with the haves (e.g., in America, state college personnel seek equality with university personnel). Then, too, impartial and fair administration demands systemwide classifications of positions and rewards, with salaries for everyone going up or down by the same percentage. From Warsaw to Tokyo there is a strong tendency in public administration generally to expand and contract in this fashion, equalizing and linking the costs, with the result that future costs become more restrictive.

Since the historical development of our institutions has presented America with the necessary differentiation, a central task is to maintain it by legitimating different institutional roles. We have been relatively successful in initiating tripartite structures within our state systems, but cannot manage to fix this division. A classic case is the unstable role of the state college. In one state after another, the state colleges will not stay where they are supposed to, according to plan, but at a blinding rate—that is, within a decade or two—take on some or all of the functions of universities, alerting their printers to the change in title that soon will be lobbied through the legislature. In contrast, the two-year colleges have accepted their distinctive role and—outside of Connecticut and a few other backward states—have prospered in it.

This has been in the face of predictions, a quarter century ago, that two-year colleges would renounce their obviously undesirable role and evolve into four-year institutions. That convergence was cut off at the pass, more by the efforts of community college people themselves than by weakly manned state offices. There came into being a community college philosophy and a commitment to it, notably in the form of a "movement." Some leaders even became zealots, true believers, glassy eyes and all. Around the commitment, they developed strong interest groups with political muscle. Today, no one's patsy, they have a turf, the willingness and ability to defend it, and the drive and skill to explore such unoccupied territory as recurrent education and lifelong learning to see how much they can annex. When did we last hear about a state college movement? If the name of the game is institutional differentiation, the name of differentiation is legitimation of institutional roles.

Planning and autonomous action are both needed as mechanisms of differentiation, coordination, and change. The difference between the acceptance of roles and the trend toward convergence, both here and abroad, suggests that we cannot leave everything to the drift of the marketplace. Unless the anchorage is there for different roles, institutions will voluntarily converge. Clearly defined roles stand the best chance of surviving. A strong state college was never far from a weak university in the first place. It took only the addition of a few more Ph.D.s to the faculty and a little more inching into graduate work in order to say: Why not us? Teachers colleges were once quite different from universities, but as the former evolved into comprehensive state colleges, their institutional role became fuzzier and harder to stabilize. In contrast, our two-year units were inherently different from universities. Perhaps the rule is: organizational species that are markedly different can live side by side in a symbiotic relation; species that are similar, with heavily overlapping functions, are likely to conflict, with accommodation then often taking the form of convergence on a single type.

Distinct bases of support and authority seem to contribute to the stability of differentiated roles. The French have a set of institutions, the *Grandes Ecoles,* that continue to be clearly separated from the universities; many of them are supported by ministries other than the ministry of education. In Britain, teachers colleges until recently were a distinctive class of institution, operating under the control of local educational authorities. But once the national department of education began to sit on them, their separate and distinct character underwent erosion. In the United States, the community colleges worked out their separate identity primarily under local control. They came into higher education from a secondary school background and, straddling that line, have often been able to play both sides of the street. This local base has afforded some protection.

So if we must plan and coordinate at higher levels, as we must to some degree, then we should be deliberately attempting to separate and anchor institutional roles. And as formal coordination takes over, multiple sources of sponsorship and supervision will be the best guarantee of institutional diversity. Multiple agencies protect multiple types and check and balance each other. A power market of competing agencies will replace the market of competing institutions.

But not all developments must be planned. A higher order of statesmanship is to recognize the contribution—past, present, and future—of autonomous action and organic growth. There are numerous reasons for pointing our thinking in this direction. One is the basis for our relative success: the strength and preeminence of American higher education is rooted in an unplanned disorderliness that has permitted different parts to perform different tasks, adapt to different needs, and move in different directions of reform. "The benefits of disorder" (See *Change,* October 1976) ought not to be inadvertently thrown away as we assemble permanent machinery for state and national coordination.

There is another reason for putting great store in emergent developments. Whether we can effectively plan diversity remains highly problematic. The arguments for planned diversity are strong: state higher education officials surely can point to some successes in recent decades, as in the case of new campuses in the New York state system that have distinguishing specialties. But we must not congratulate ourselves too soon, since our immature central staffs have not had time yet to settle down as enlarged central bureaucracies loaded with responsibilities, expectations, and interest group demands.

Our central coordinating machinery has not been in place long enough to become the gathering spot for trouble. But the news from abroad on such matters is not promising. The experience of other countries suggests that the balance of forces in and around a central office, especially in a democracy, may not permit planned differentiation to prevail over planned and unplanned uniformity. One of the finest administrators in Europe, Ralf Dahrendorf, one-time head of the London School of Economics, addressed himself to "the problems expansion left behind" in continental and British higher education, and saw as central the need to distinguish, to differentiate. He confessed that he had reluctantly come to the conclusion that deliberate differentiation is a contradiction in terms. Why? Because in the modern world the pressures to have equal access to funds, equal status for all teachers, and so on, are too strong.

People who are held responsible for getting things done are, by the nature of their roles, inclined to value and trust deliberate effort over spontaneously generated developments. But it is the better part of reality to recognize what sociologists have long seen as the imposing weight of the unplanned. As put by Dahrendorf in taking the long view in Britain and continental Europe: "The more one looks at government action, the more one understands that most things will not be done anyway, but will happen in one way or another."

Our central procedural concern ought to be the relative contribution of planned and autonomous actions, especially in regard to differentiation. Both are needed and both are operative, so we need to assess different mixtures of the two. With current combinations tilting toward controlled action, we need to add support to the organic side. We shall need to be increasingly clever about planning for unplanned change, about devising the broad frameworks that encourage the system's constituents to generate, on their own, changes that are creative and adaptive to local contexts.

In the changing relation between higher education and government, higher education is becoming more governmental. It moves inside government, becomes a constituent part of government, a bureau within public administration. On this, perspectives from abroad are invaluable, since we are the laggards who can look down the road that others have already traveled. No small point from abroad is transferable, since context is everything, but the larger portraits of relations should catch our attention, principally to stimulate our thinking about options, potentialities, and limits.

Lessons from abroad help to construct longer time frames through which to analyze the character of our institutions. For example, in considering the problem of a relatively new U.S. Department of Education, we need to ask what it may look like a quarter century, a half century hence, when it may be many times larger in personnel, greatly extended in scope, vertically elaborated in echelons, and well established as a bureaucratic arm of the state alongside Agriculture, Labor, and Commerce. Up to this point, the largest advanced democratic country to attempt to order higher education by means of a national department has been France, a country one-fourth the size of the United States, where the effort has been crowned with failure and the name of reform is decentralization. We will be the first nation to attempt to "supervise" 3,500 institutions in a country of over 230,000,000 people by means of double pyramids in which a national department is placed over the state structures, with both levels possibly exercising surveillance over private as well as public institutions. Before taking that step, we need to gain more perspective on what we are doing.

Especially under the time constraints of governmental policy making, our canons of judgment nearly always suffer from overconcentration on immediate problems and short-run solutions. Comparative vision helps to correct these defects, thus reducing the probability of unanticipated, unwanted consequences. Anyone who studies other countries intensively will have seen futures that do not work.

Note

This is a revised version of an article that originally appeared in *Change* (November 1978).

Contributors

PHILIP G. ALTBACH is professor of higher education in the School of Education, Boston College. He is North American Editor of *Higher Education* and has edited *International Education: An Encyclopedia.* Dr. Altbach is author of *Higher Education in the Third World, Comparative Education,* and other books.

ROBERT O. BERDAHL is professor of higher education and director of the Institute for Higher and Adult Education, College of Education, University of Maryland at College Park. He has been chair of the Department of Higher Education at the State University of New York at Buffalo, and has served as president of the Association for the Study of Higher Education. In 1993, he was awarded the Howard Bowen Distinguished Career Award by the ASHE.

BURTON R. CLARK is Allan Cartter professor emeritus of education and sociology at the University of California, Los Angeles. He is author of *The Higher Education System, The Academic Life,* and other books.

ERIC L. DEY is assistant professor of higher education and assistant research scientist in the Center for the Study of Higher and Postsecondary Education at the University of Michigan. He previously directed the Cooperative Institutional Research Program at the Higher Education Research Institute at the University of California, Los Angeles.

LAWRENCE E. GLADIEUX is executive director for Policy Analysis of the College Board, Washington, D.C. He has written extensively on topics related to government and education, college affordability, and access to higher education.

PATRICIA J. GUMPORT is assistant professor of higher education and deputy director of the Stanford Institute for Higher Education Research at Stanford University. Previously, she was assistant professor of higher education at the

University of California, Los Angeles. She is the 1993 winner of the Young Scholars Award of the Association for the Study of Higher Education.

W. LEE HANSEN is professor of economics at the University of Wisconsin, Madison. He has published widely in the economics of education and has supervised the AAUP's annual surveys of academic remuneration.

FRED F. HARCLEROAD is professor emeritus of higher education at the University of Arizona and founding director of the Center for the Study of Higher Education there.

ARTHUR M. HAUPTMAN is an independent consultant specializing in higher education finance issues and federal budget policies. He previously served on the staffs of the U.S. House of Representatives Budget Committee and the U.S. Senate Labor and Human Resources Committee.

WALTER C. HOBBS is associate professor of higher education, emeritus, at the State University of New York at Buffalo. He is editor of the *Journal of Higher Education Administration*.

SYLVIA HURTADO is assistant professor of higher education in the Center for the Study of Higher and Postsecondary Education at the University of Michigan. She previously served as a University of California President's Post-doctoral Scholar in sociology at UCLA.

CLARK KERR is president emeritus of the University of California. He served as chancellor of the University of California at Berkeley and as chairman of the Carnegie Council for Policy Studies in Higher Education. He is author of *The Uses of the University* and other books.

LAURA GREENE KNAPP is assistant director for Policy Analysis in the Washington Office of the College Board. An economist, she was previously research associate at the Pennsylvania Higher Education Assistance Agency and has written extensively in the area of postsecondary finance.

T. R. McCONNELL was professor of higher education at the University of California, Berkeley. He served as chancellor of the University of Buffalo and, in 1957, established the Center for the Study of Higher Education at the University of California, Berkeley.

AIMS C. McGUINNESS, JR., is on the staff of the National Center for Higher Education Management Systems, Boulder, Colorado. He was previously at the Education Commission of the States.

WALTER P. METZGER is professor of history at Columbia University. He is coauthor of *The Development of Academic Freedom in the United States.*

SHEILA SLAUGHTER is professor of higher education, College of Education, University of Arizona. She has been associate professor of higher education at the State University of New York at Buffalo and is author of *The Higher Learning and High Technology.*

IRVING J. SPITZBERG, JR., is president of The Knowledge Company, Fairfax, Virginia. He has served as dean of the Colleges at the State University of New York at Buffalo and as executive secretary of the American Association of University Professors.

JACOB O. STAMPEN is professor in the Department of Educational Administration, University of Wisconsin, Madison.

JOHN R. THELIN is professor of higher education at Indiana University at Bloomington. He has previously taught at the College of William and Mary, where he was Chancellor Professor. He has written widely on the history of higher education. His most recent book is *Games Colleges Play: Scandal and Reform in Intercollegiate Athletics.*

MARTIN TROW is professor of public policy at the University of California, Berkeley.

AMI ZUSMAN is coordinator for academic affairs, Office of the President, University of California System, where she is involved in academic planning, program review, and school/university programs.

Index

Academic freedom, 9, 31–32
    adminstration and, 38, 41, 92–95
    cases of, 73–97
    definition of, 55–57
    doctrine of, 13, 37–54, 157
    federal courts and, 186–88, 192–95
    private constituencies and, 199–220
    the professoriate and, 240–41
Accountability
    agencies of, 59–69
    nature of, 10, 21, 57–58, 160
    students and, 65, 67–69, 262–63, 350–52
    See also government relations; autonomy
Affirmative action, 233–34
American Association of State Colleges and Universities, 206, 293
American Association of University Professors (AAUP) 31, 37, 43, 73, 78–79, 238, 240, 275, 295, 312
American Council of Education, 203, 204
American Federation of Teachers, 238
American Medical Association, 208
Arizona State University, 90
Association of Collegiate Business Schools and Programs, 209
Association of Governing Boards of Universities and Colleges, 205, 360
Astin, Alexander, 22
Atherton, George, 28
Atlanta College, 212

Auburn University, 85–86
Autonomy, 9, 13, 21, 24, 33, 55–72, 156, 157, 182, 202, 210, 213–26, 243, 277, 281, 300, 357–58
    delocalization, process of, 44–52
    the doctrine of academic abstention and, 185–86
    and governance structures, 358–59
    local, attributes of, 40–53
    private constituencies, and, 199–220
    voluntary consortia and, 213

Bell, Terrell, 292–93, 346
Bennett, William, 293
Bill of Rights, 187–89
Boards
    coordinating, 57, 62–63, 162–65, 169
    governing, 57, 60–61, 161–67
Bowen, Howard, 67–69
Boyer, Ernest, 295, 297
Brown University, 24, 30, 297

California, University of, 59, 64–65, 229, 235, 269, 271, 275, 277, 282–85, 297, 307
California Master Plan, 45, 226
Cambridge, 24, 38, 42, 228, 274
Carnegie Commission on Higher Education, 12, 107, 108
Carnegie Corporation, 313
Carnegie Council on Policy Studies in Higher Education, 64

381

Carnegie Foundation for the Advancement of Teaching, 21–22, 30, 208, 295, 303
Carnegie Institution of Washington, 313
Charters, 22–26
Chicago, University of, 275, 290, 296, 297, 310, 313, 323
Christian College Consortium, 215–6
Civil Rights Act, 193
Civil rights movement, 290
College entrance examination board, 30
College of William and Mary, 23–24, 199
Colleges
  booster, 26, 27, 30, 31
  colonial, 22–24
Collegiate way, 24–5, 184
Columbia University, 37, 271, 290, 311, 323
Commission on Strengthening Presidential Leadership, 272, 282, 283
Commonwealth, notion of, 22, 25–26, 33
Community colleges, 355
Consumerism, 28–29, 33, 229, 241
Cornell University, 30, 189
Council for Interinstitutional Leadership, 212, 213
curriculum, the, 16, 26–29
  multiculturalism and, 298–99
  political correctness and, 298–99
  quality of, 301
  reform of, 27–29, 59, 152, 241–42, 289–302
  retrenchment and, 82–84, 339–40
  school collaboration and, 346–48

Dartmouth College, 25
Dartmouth College case, 189, 233
Dressel, Paul, 57, 61
Duke University, 30, 126

Economic Issues,
  cost sharing, 118–19
  expenditures 12, 69, 112–17
  federal aid, 32, 47–53, 63–64, 107–109, 112, 114, 125, 313–25
  loan financing, 133–38, 140, 309, 320
  Pell grants, 103, 107, 133–37
  philanthropy, 24, 30, 41, 114, 313
  Stafford Loans, 133–34

state aid, 112, 114, 119, 126–28, 158–60, 309
student financial aid, 116–17, 128–30, 130–44, 309, 159
tuition, 12, 112, 114, 157, 159
See also retrenchment
Educational Testing Service, 30
Edwards, Harry, 183–84
Equity, 11, 13, 101, 103, 106, 120, 135–38, 141, 152, 251–53, 284, 286, 342–45
Expansion, 31, 105–106, 110, 172, 229–30, 250–51, 318–19
See also student enrollments

Faculty, 192–93, 225–44
  accountability and, 31, 65, 231–36, 239–40
  curriculum change and, 292–302
  foreign policy and, 90–92
  part-time, 80–81
  racial minorities and, 227–28
  research and, 352–54
  retrenchment and, 338–39
  tenure, 237
  unions, 237–38
  undergraduate teaching and, 348–50
  See also gender discrimination; academic freedom
Federal courts, 47, 65, 181–96, 234, 356
Federal intervention, 63–64
Federation of Regional Accrediting Commissions, 210
Foundations, 30, 32, 200–203

Gender discrimination, 84–91
Georgia, University of, 26
G.I. Bill, 32, 103–104, 119, 126, 132, 226
Government relations
  Clinton administration, 138, 143, 147, 149, 152–53
  federal, 26, 27, 32, 33, 41, 42, 44, 47–53, 57, 63–66, 106–114, 125–54, 309–24
  Reagan administration, 82, 96, 108–109, 134, 151, 251, 292
  state, 26, 27, 33, 60–62, 66–68, 112, 114, 119, 126, 129, 155–76

Harvard University, 25, 29, 40, 199, 227, 274, 275, 290–91, 296–98, 311, 352
Higher Education Act, 105, 127, 129, 132–33, 134, 143, 151

Illinois State University, 159
In loco parentis, 231, 241

Johns Hopkins University, 37, 229, 275, 310
Judaism, University of, 86–87
Judicial intervention, 65, 181–82
See also federal courts

Kansas City Regional Council for Higher Education, 214–15
Keller, George, 271
Kerr, Clark, 48, 49, 50, 60, 61, 106–107, 158–62, 169, 283, 296, 301, 360
Kozol, Jonathan, 346

Leadership
American presidency and, 13, 26, 31, 269–87
aspects of, 269–70
centralization and, 365–69
control and, 369–71
coordination and, 371–76
faculty and, 340
Lecht Report, 106
Lindsley, Philip, 28

Massachussetts Institute of Technology, 48
McCarthyism, 11, 32, 55, 240
Metropolitan Community Colleges, 79, 80
Miami-Dade Community College, 351
Michigan State University, 50, 282
Midwestern Higher Education Commission, 217–18
Morrill Act, 28, 32, 126, 130, 226
land grant movement and, 10, 28, 132, 219–20, 229, 233, 311

Nashville, University of, 28
Nation at Risk Report, 292–93
National Academy of Engineering, 315
National Academy of Sciences, 314, 315

National Association of College and University Business Officers, 204
National Association of State Universities and Land-Grant Colleges, 359
National Commission on Research, 58, 64
National Defense Education Act, 132, 317
National Institute of Health, 64, 127, 323, 353, 354
National Research Council, 314, 315
National Science Foundation, 49, 129, 145, 316, 317, 322, 323, 353
National Writing Project, 348
New England Board of Higher Education, 218
Newman, Frank, 156
New York, City University of, 75
New York, State University of, 45, 91, 375
North Dakota Agricultural College, 220
Northwestern University, 90–91

Oxford University, 23, 24, 38, 42, 228, 274

Peer review system, 145
Pennsylvania, University of, 24, 42, 173, 300
Pennsylvania State College, 28, 293
Pittsburgh, University of, 189
Pomona College, 212
Princeton University, 24, 48, 295
Principle of departmental organization, 311–13
Private institutions
accountability of, 64, 96
autonomy of, 41
definition of, 24
and federal courts, 189–90
governance of, 162–70
rise of, 45
Program evaluation, 61–62
Program restructuring, 75–77
Public institutions
accountability of, 59–64, 96
definition of, 24
enrollments in, 158
and federal courts, 189–90, 191–93
governance of, 161–70
rise of, 28, 45

Quality, 13, 102–105, 109, 143, 172, 284, 301

Rensselaer Polytechnic Institute, 28
Research
    AIDS, 353
    changing directions of, 352–54
    DNA, 57, 64
    military, 49
    sponsorship of, 11, 32, 44, 48–49, 64, 106, 126–27, 130, 144–47, 152–53, 233, 235, 242, 309, 313–25, 352–53
Retrenchment, 75–81, 134, 233, 237–38, 242–43, 319–21, 335–37
    implications of, 337–41
Rockefeller Foundation, 313
Rockefeller General Education Board, 30
Rockefeller Institute of Medicine, 313

Sanford, Nevitt, 309
Scholastic Aptitude Test, 346
School-College collaboration, 345–48
Sloan Commission on Government and Higher Education, 182–83
Sonoma State College, 77–79
Southern Regional Education Board, 217
Stanford University, 30, 146, 151, 229, 275, 282, 302, 310
State coordination and governance, 161–64
State government intervention, 60–63
    See also government relations; accountability
State structures, 164–70
State Student Incentive Grant, 133
Stone, Lawrence, 21
Strategic planning, 78–79
Students
    academic policy and, 241
    admissions, 57, 190
    assessment, 350–51
    attitudes, 13, 29, 249, 256–63

enrollments, 27, 29, 32, 33, 59, 77, 103–104, 110–11, 158, 250–51, 272, 316, 342–45, 355–56
    minorities and, 342–45
    nontraditional, 139, 251
    politics, 46, 253–56, 264, 290–91
    retention, 262-63
    retrenchment and, 338
    services, 278, 281

Tax policies, 147–50, 151
Temple University, 78, 80
Thorndyke, Virginia, 299
Total Quality Management, 236
Trow, Martin, 294
Truman Commission on Higher Education, 104, 107
Tulane University, 30

United States Military Academy at West Point, 27
United States Naval Academy at Annapolis, 27
University Grants Commission, 368
University-industry links, 286, 314, 322, 352–54

Vassar College, 30
Virginia, University of, 26
Virginia Tidewater Consortium for Higher Education, 213–14
Voluntary accrediting associations, 41, 66, 142–43, 207–11, 355
Voluntary Consortia, 17, 211–16

War on Poverty legislation, 105
Western Interstate Commission for Higher Education, 217–18
Wheelock, Eleazar, 25

Yale University, 151
Yeshiva University, 193, 238